WE, THE NAVIGATORS

To the veteran navigator Tevake,
lost at sea off Santa Cruz, 1970

Frontispiece Tevake navigating Isbjorn

We, the Navigators

THE ANCIENT ART OF
LANDFINDING IN THE PACIFIC

David Lewis

THE UNIVERSITY PRESS OF HAWAII
HONOLULU

Foreword

The world of the Pacific islands burst upon the conscious-
ness of the Western world with the discovery of the
Marianas by Magellan in 1521. By the eighteenth century,
a whole complex of exotic and romantic conceptions had
come into being about the people of the South Seas, an
apparatus of clichés that are even now the material of
novels and musical plays and are the subject of graphic
portrayal in travel posters. One essential part of this complex, often at the core of it, is an image of the outrigger
canoe and the heroic men who compose its crew, sailing
intrepidly over uncharted seas to yet undiscovered isles.
This stereotype of the Pacific and its native inhabitants
has a basis in the very first descriptions by the European
explorers. Pigafetta, Magellan's chronicler, marvelled at
the canoes he saw in 1521. No less deeply impressed were
the later visitors to those islands: Cavendish, Dampier,
Rogers, and Anson. The flying *proa* of the Marianas, its
sailing qualities and its speed, captured the imagination
of the explorers, and they could scarcely find words
(singular, extraordinary, ingenious, among other adjec-
tives) to express their admiration.

In similar terms, almost in awe, Ledyard describes the
excellence of the canoes that in immense throngs—3000
of them, with 15,000 passengers—surrounded the *Resolution* at Kealakekua Bay in 1779. Earlier, in 1774, at
Tahiti, Cook and Forster had observed the 'magnificent
scene' of a 'grand and noble' naval review at which they
'were perfectly lost in admiration'; it contained 330
vessels with no fewer than 7760 men. Wilkes, in the Fijis
in 1840, characterises the navigators there, their daring
and skill, and the speed of their canoes in the same lyrical
manner. Indeed, to catalogue the accounts of Pacific
canoes and native voyagers written in this glowing style
is to catalogue half of the European explorers.

Hyperbole there was, of course, and we are in debt to
Andrew Sharp for a chastening re-examination of the   vii

evidence of the abilities of the South Sea native mariners. But we cannot accept all of his strictures. As David Lewis tells us in this book, much of the navigational knowledge in many places was secret; it was an arcanum limited to a select circle of society; and even information that could have been obtained remains unknown—some of it now, fortunately, revealed through Lewis's labours—simply because questioners did not know enough to ask the right questions, which often still remain unasked. Many skills vanished under the impact of the overwhelming technology of the Western world, before the questions could be asked. But in exceptional circumstances, under special conditions, they have withstood that impact. One survival, described by Lewis, is the indigenous sidereal compass of the Carolines, which has not been superseded by the magnetic compass. It has survived precisely because the two compasses are incompatible and there is no area of conflict between them.

It should be added that European influences are not the only cause of degeneration of native arts. Bougainville in 1768 named Samoa the Navigator Islands, so impressed was he by the swarms of canoes which circled his ship. The canoes were really manned only by offshore fishermen, but Bougainville assumed that they were navigators of the high seas, hence designated them as he did. But, as Hornell points out, the Samoans would indeed have deserved the name much better six or seven hundred years before Bougainville's time, before any European had visited them. In contrast, Duperrey in 1824 and Lutké in 1827, among others, enlarge upon the landlubberly qualities of the people of Kusaie. Yet without question, the Kusaians were once great mariners, ranging far to the west; every atoll in the Central Carolines has tales of Kusaian visitors, and various clans trace their origins to women from that island; while Ponape's political charter, in the Malinowski sense of that word, is rooted in a traditional military conquest by Kusaian invaders. Whatever the reasons—perhaps on some high islands nature's generosity in the course of time saps away at the economic incentive to range abroad—internal factors can also play a role in the decline of seafaring.

What has survived of the old knowledge is examined
and studied in detail in this pioneering work of David
Lewis, which stands almost alone among studies of this
kind, which he is uniquely qualified to undertake. Of the
peoples that Lewis visited, sailed with, and whose navigational methods he studied, only those of Puluwat are
personally familiar to me. To the reasons for voyaging
set forth in chapter 11 of this book, I should like to
add one given me, along with the local equivalent of a
dig in the ribs and with an unmistakable leer, by my
Puluwatese adopted brother, a man in his sixties: to get
away from a nagging wife to a place of complaisant
women. In a more serious vein he said he travelled to
Satawal to obtain the tobacco sold there by the Yap
Trading Company, rather than make the much easier trip
to Truk to get an inferior brand. We can only wonder
and speculate what charms distant places might have
held for island navigators in the days before there was
anyone to record them.

Washington, 1972   S. H. Riesenberg

Contents

NOTE: The spelling of place names has followed *Pacific Islands*, 1943-45, the Naval Intelligence Handbook, except in the few instances where there is conflict with local usage.

Illustrations

FIGURES

PLATES

MAPS

Maps and figures drawn in the Cartographic Office, Department of
Human Geography, Australian National University

Acknowledgments

The award of an Australian National University research fellowship rendered possible the whole project.

FOR ASSISTANCE IN PREPARING THIS BOOK AND CONSULTING DOCUMENTARY SOURCES

Professor J. W. Davidson, the departmental head, guided me throughout with his helpful suggestions and cogent, not to say astringent, criticisms.

Mr H. E. Maude has not only put his vast experience of the Pacific at my disposal at all times, but has made available the late Sir Arthur Grimble's unpublished notes on Gilbertese navigation. Mr Bob Langdon has been my mentor in the unfamiliar task of searching for sources, while Dr Ben Finney, with the utmost generosity, granted me the freedom of his files. Mrs Jenny Terrell corrected my deplorable syntax and spelling. All the above patiently and critically read through drafts of the manuscript. Dr F. J. West advised me about informants. Important German material was translated for me by Mrs A. M. Johnson. The heavy task of typing successive drafts was undertaken by Mrs Rita Mathews, Mrs Félicité Swan, Mrs Robyn Walker, and Mrs Rosamund Walsh.

But such lists of names as these are necessarily invidious, for I am indebted in some measure to all the members of the Department of Pacific History. They were unfailingly patient with my queries and thoughtfully called my attention to navigational matter that they came across in the course of their own researches.

People were no less helpful outside my own department. Professor J. Golson, Head of the Prehistory Department, gave up much of his limited time to detailed criticism of the draft manuscript. Dr Colin Jack-Hinton, formerly of the A.N.U., did the same. Mr Les Groube of Prehistory has been particularly helpful. Mr John Chappell of Geography advised on Siassi navigation. Then there was Dr

Ron Crocombe, at the time head of the A.N.U.'s New Guinea Research Unit, who first suggested that I should apply for the research fellowship.

I am indebted to the staff of the Menzies Library, especially Mrs M. Day, for their patient help.

The many sketches and maps in this volume I owe to the Visual Aids Department, the Map Room of the Geography Department, especially Mr Hans Gunther and Mr Keith Mitchell, and to the help of Fiona Lewis.

So many people aided the investigation or the preparation of this book that, unwittingly, some names must inevitably have been omitted. To any such I tender my apologies.

FOR ASSISTANCE WITH FIELD WORK AND
ARRANGING CONTACTS WITH NAVIGATORS

Fiji   I want to especially thank Don Aidney, Peter Van der Hyde, and Tony Jackson for rendering mobile a reluctant *Isbjorn*, and the proprietor of the Tradewinds Hotel for his hospitality.

Solomon and   Jim Tedder, District Commissioner of Guadalcanal Cen-
Santa Cruz   tral was responsible for my learning about the navigator
Islands   Tevake. Silas Sitai, District Officer, and Dr David Dawea were extremely helpful with introductions and information. My old friends Helen and Arthur Swain were my hosts.

In Santa Cruz I wish to acknowledge the hospitality of Gabriel Paikai, ex-bosun to my late cousin Charlie Cowan of the schooner *Navanora*, Thomas Tituilu, chairman of the Ulawa Council, and the Hepworths of Pigeon Island. Mr Fred Rakei gave up a good deal of his holiday to interpret for me in the Russell Islands.

The Honiara Marine Superintendent, Captain Douglas, not only helped us with our recalcitrant vessel, but wrote a most informative commentary on aspects of Gilbertese navigation for me. Mr Ken Bradshaw, who is in charge of the Marine Base, Tulagi, most generously arranged for a complete overhaul of our deplorable engine.

Ninigo   Mr Fred Archer of Rabaul gave valuable advice. Mr Andrew Tombui of Ami acted as voluntary interpreter and Mr Sonny Nolan was generous in his hospitality.

Dr Thomas Gladwin, through his unstinting advice and *Carolines* the introductions he gave me, including one to the navigator Hipour, opened up to me the whole field of Micronesian voyaging and was responsible more than any other person for such successes as this study may have achieved in the area.

The Assistant District Administrator Juan Sablon did all in his power to facilitate the project, as did the anthropologist Dr J. Nason and Mr and Mrs Russ Curtis of Truk. Peer Lykke and Mike McCoy are two among the many helpful Peace Corps Volunteers that deserve mention. Without Chief Manipe and the Puluwat Island Council my voyages with Hipour would have been impossible.

Mr R. G. Roberts, the then Assistant Resident Commis- *Gilberts* sioner, put the administration's resources at my disposal in locating the qualified navigators, arranging introductions, and making available official interpreters. The helpfulness of all members of the Marine Department was also gratefully appreciated.

Captain V. Ward not only gave introductions and advice but generously allowed me to make use of his unpublished manuscript on the Arorae navigational sighting stones. On Onotoa in the same group pastor Toaiti Mote was our host.

H.M. King Tupou IV was unfailing in his support. Mr *Tonga* A. Reid, the British consul, through whose good offices the King first heard of the project, has allowed me to quote from his manuscript on the last of the Fijian double canoes. Mrs Tupou Posesi Fanau of the Tonga Tradition Department, Miss Siulongo Tuifua, Mr Garth Rogers, and Mr Carl Reichelman, all aided us in ways too various to mention.

It is important to remember that the *Isbjorn* survey would have been impossible without the support of my son Barry, who was mate, engineer and often the entire crew. Neither, for that matter, could the earlier *Rehu Moana* experiment have been carried out save with the backing of Fiona Lewis and of Priscilla Cairns.

Finally, there were the navigators of Oceania, our instructors, who are listed separately.

FOR HELP MAINLY VIA CORRESPONDENCE

Once again selection is invidious and necessarily incomplete. The names that follow in alphabetical order are of some of my more long-suffering correspondents. They include: Mr A. K. Akerblom, Professor William Davenport, Professor Edwin Doran Jr, Professor Samuel Elbert, who translated a key passage from Hawaiian, Mr John C. Elliot, former governor of American Samoa, Professor Raymond Firth. Dr Thomas Gladwin's voluminous correspondence demands special mention here. Miss Rosemary Grimble kindly gave me free access to her father's manuscript notes on navigation. Captain A. Hops, Professor Gordon Lewthwaite, Mr Peer Lykke, Mr Tim McCoy, Dr Maud Makemson, Professor Leonard Mason, Mr Ken Mills, Fr J. Neyret, S.M., Captain G. Playden U.S.C.G., Dr V. Radhakrishnan, Dr Saul Riesenberg, Mr James Ramsay Ullman, Professor Gerard Ward, the secretaries of the Institute of Navigation (London), and of the Deutsches Hydrographisches Institut.

FIRMS THAT SUPPLIED THEIR PRODUCTS FREE OF CHARGE

Our research expedition would have been much less successful had not the following firms helped equip *Isbjorn*.

Aladdin, Avon, Beaufort, British Ropes, Clifford Snell, International Paints and International Majura Paints, Kelvin Hughes, Lee Howl, Marconi Marine, Marine Autopilots, Mobiloil.

Introduction

Realistic evaluation of the potentials of indigenous navigation in the Pacific has been hampered by an overly theoretical approach, divorced from ocean-going small craft experience, and by sparsity of data.

My own interest in the subject stems both from lessons learnt at sea and attitudes I absorbed as a small boy attending a native school in Rarotonga in the Cook Islands. The traditional voyaging sagas that were related by my elder Polynesian cousins were readily perceived to be, in the critical light of maturity, clearly poetical and allegorical. But this did not apply to their general assumption that the ocean was a homely and not unfriendly place —an attitude that persists among Polynesians and Micronesians to this day.

The tall clippers, whose splendour marked the closing days of sail, followed clearly defined sea lanes. Moreover they were large ships. Ocean-going yachtsmen, then, seeking to learn from their predecessors, are forced to search back over the centuries to vessels of similar dimensions to their own that faced equivalent conditions. Thus when sailing a 25-foot yacht alone in the late autumn of 1960 from Newfoundland to Shetland, then to Norway, and to Iceland three years later in another craft, I faced challenges more nearly akin to those of Viking longships than of so (comparatively) modern a vessel as the *Mayflower*.

Given my life-long interest in Polynesian seafaring, I possessed two advantages. One was a rather rudimentary experience of the scientific discipline of medical research and the other was some practical small boat experience. The latter included three single-handed Atlantic crossings prior to a voyage round the world in the catamaran *Rehu Moana*. While in the central Pacific it seemed an obvious step to bring academic theories about oceanic navigation down to sea level by testing in practice methods reputed to have been used by the old-time Polynesians. Such a trial was staged in 1965 in the course of the circumnavigation and is described below.

Only later did I learn that there remained Pacific Islanders who still possessed some of the old orally transmitted knowledge and even some who still practised techniques similar to, or identical with, what we believe to have been the ancient ones. Here clearly was a totally unlooked for possibility of, even at this late date, substantially supplementing the inadequate original sources. To make contact with these men was the purpose of the 1968-9 A.N.U. research fellowship sponsored voyages to gather much of the data set out in this work. The book's structure must inevitably reflect the *mélange* of early references and present day residual practices that together constitute its raw material.

How can we account for the remarkable persistence of these survivals? Much has been lost, of course, and the most sophisticated, complex, and secret techniques, that were probably always the property of exclusive circles, seem to have suffered the greatest decline. Thus even in the Carolines, where a relatively complete navigational discipline is still extant, such erstwhile concepts as the 'wind compass' (Cantova, 1728: 209, 210) or the zenith star (Sanchez, 1886: 263) seem to have been forgotten. What kind of arts have survived, then? Apparently those that were either relatively straightforward, like steering by horizon stars, or else so completely incompatible with European systems as to resist anything more than marginal modification, and so remain almost intact until their final replacement. Instances of the latter include the Carolinian 'star compass', wave orientation, the *etak* or 'moving' reference island system, the 'expanded' target concept and techniques related thereto, and the zenith star concepts. Incidentally, no navigational instruments or artifacts of any importance are recorded as ever having been used at sea in Oceania.

FIELD INVESTIGATIONS

I decided to stage an experiment in Polynesian navi- *The*
gational methods in the course of a voyage round the Rehu Moana
world in the 40-foot catamaran *Rehu Moana*.[1] The ship's *Test Voyage*
company comprised my wife, Fiona, our daughters, then *November-*
aged 3 and 4, and a friend, Priscilla Cairns, an experienced *December*
navigator. *1965*

It was proposed to retrace the approximate route of
Eastern Polynesian migration to New Zealand, which took
place something over a millennium ago, navigating entirely
without instruments, and following a traditional Maori
sun course of doubtful authenticity—but undoubted
accuracy, as experience was to demonstrate. The component sea passages were from Tahiti, 100 miles to
Huahine, which is a near neighbour of Raiatea, the island
usually identified with Hawaiki,[2] the legendary homeland
of the New Zealanders. Then would follow 500 miles to
Rarotonga in the Cook Islands,[3] passing between the rest
of the Lower Cooks some 400 miles *en route*. Finally
there would be the long stretch of open Pacific between
Rarotonga and New Zealand. The total distance of all
three 'legs' amounted to 2239 miles. Our object was to
find out by sea trial just how accurate and effective our
(book learned) version of the ancient methods was.

A word about experimental method and the mounting
of this trial may not come amiss. Any experiment necessarily involves isolating the factors to be investigated. Our
purpose was to test the accuracy of star and sun steering
by eye alone and the use of zenith (overhead or 'latitude') stars, in a situation where other relevant factors
were equivalent (but not precisely the same) as in a
prehistoric voyage. We were not concerned with such
matters as the structural stresses of a double vessel,[4] or

---

[1] See Lewis, 1967.

[2] The old name for Raiatea was Havaiki.

[3] Rarotonga, linked by language and legend with Tahiti on the one
hand and New Zealand on the other, would be a geographically logical,
as well as a traditional, staging post between them.

[4] The catamaran's resemblance to a double canoe was largely inci-
dental to an experiment whose purpose was wholly navigational. An
exception was that it provided a similarly stable platform for zenith star
observations, which a single-hulled Western vessel would not have done.

the lasting qualities of fermented breadfruit, nor were we attempting to throw light on the original finding of New Zealand by the Maoris. Following a sun course as we did, like using any other kind of sailing directions, implies that someone has not only found the destination, but returned home with a report of bearings and distance that would enable others to reach it too. Modern test voyages cannot, therefore, throw navigational light on original discovery. This must always be a largely accidental event, since the most an explorer could have to suggest the existence and bearing of an unknown land would be the clues afforded by drifting objects, migratory bird flight paths, and the like. But currents can carry floating branches in a circle and the first stop of migrating birds could well be Siberia.

All instruments—compass, sextant, radio, patent log, clocks and watches—were unshipped and stowed in the privacy of Priscilla's cabin, together with the charts. Her role was independent observer and safety officer; to keep account of our progress with the instruments and charts that remained throughout in her personal charge, to allow for subsequent comparison between our assumed and true positions; and to prevent our running into danger. She kept her knowledge strictly to herself and it played no part whatsoever in the actual navigation of the yacht. This was carried out exclusively by steering towards the setting points of stars, by maintaining an angle to the sun, swells, and wind and occasionally judging latitude by the unaided eye when a particular star was passing directly overhead.

Priscilla, however, was compelled on one occasion temporarily to interrupt the experiment in the interests of safety. I had unsuspectingly passed through the middle of the Lower Cooks and was heading out into the empty ocean beyond. The fault was my failure to recognise homing birds that had been plainly indicating the presence and whereabouts of nearby islands. The incident underlined, rather than otherwise, the effectiveness of the old Polynesian methods when practised by experts.

One aspect of the experiment that gave rise to misunderstanding was this. I needed data that were navigationally comparable, though perforce different in character to those of an old-time navigator, else the test voyage would have had little bearing on the past. It being obviously impracticable for me to spend years memorising star sequences and other material, I made use of a small-scale lifeboat chart of the South Pacific, a star identification disc, and sun bearing tables (Gatty, 1958). The main misconception was based on an exaggerated idea of the significance of latitude and longitude as indicated on the lifeboat chart.

Now latitude and longitude are convenient conventions for recording position, especially for subsequent comparison, but New Zealand is in exactly the same place relative to Tahiti whether located by crossed lines on a chart or by saying it is so many days sailing (at a given speed) in a particular star direction. Neither the Carolinian navigator Hipour nor I was the slightest bit discommoded during the 500-mile voyages to and from Saipan by Hipour's ignorance of the latitude and longitude of our objectives, for he mentally processed his data in the totally different terms that we will be discussing under 'orientation' in chap. 5. Judging by the early Tahitians' geographical knowledge, even as expressed in so unfamiliar an abstraction as Tupaia's map, I doubt very much whether the information on my little chart would have been anything like as comprehensive as that of an ancient Tahitian expert.

The star disc's information was much less precise than that of indigenous navigators I subsequently met and was necessitated only by my ignorance of astronomy. As to the sun bearing tables, these were entirely redundant since, as Hipour was to show me, the sun's point of rise and set can be regularly and accurately determined by reference to known stars.

How did the experiment ultimately turn out? In spite of our inexpert performance and second hand knowledge of the techniques we were using, the last and longest stretch, the 1630 miles from Rarotonga to New Zealand, culminated in a landfall whose latitude was only 26 miles in error. Some other lessons of this trial will be referred to later; current set and distance estimation in the section on dead reckoning; zenith star determination in chap. 9.

Apart from the test voyage itself, other Pacific territories were visited in *Rehu Moana* and information collected. These were Easter Island, Mangareva, Tonga, Fiji, New Hebrides, and Papua.

Learning from Indigenous Navigators, 1968-9

It was some months after the experiment we have been describing that encounters with practical star path navigators in Tonga and Papua, coupled with information that came to hand about contemporary Carolinian canoe voyaging, first brought home to me the realisation that parts of the sea lore of the ancient voyagers remained alive; that there still existed scattered among the islands a mosaic of fragments of a former Pacific-wide system (or systems) of navigational learning only waiting to be put together. But unless this were done soon the heritage of 2000 years would irretrievably be lost.

The upshot of many proposals and negotiations was that, at the conclusion of our circumnavigation in *Rehu Moana*, which began and ended in England, I was granted a research fellowship in Pacific History from the Australian National University to take up the investigation. We reluctantly parted from *Rehu Moana* because of the overriding requirement for a craft with a power range of something like 2000 miles to carry out a worthwhile research program in a limited time. The catamaran would have been unable to take on the necessary fuel, so the 39-foot auxiliary gaff ketch, *Isbjorn*, was purchased.

My wife and I, with our young daughters and my 20-year-old son Barry, set out in the ketch from England in March 1968 and reached Fiji six months later, visiting in the Pacific *en route* Nuku Hiva, Tongareva (Penrhyn), and Western Samoa. Leaving Barry in Fiji to cope with the yacht's antiquated motor, the rest of us flew to Australia, where I hurriedly photostatted a quantity of relevant material in Canberra, then rejoined Barry in Fiji.

The project, as it eventually took shape, involved concentration on selected localities. In those where ocean-going canoes still sailed we would join the voyagers. Where such craft were a memory and the learned captains too old for the rigours of open boat journeys we would seek a compromise. Navigators would be requested to take charge of an *Isbjorn* temporarily stripped of compass and other artificial aids and to demonstrate their methods at sea. Where neither of these alternatives was possible interviews would be conducted ashore.

The itinerary that was ultimately chosen is best followed on the endpaper maps.[5] From Fiji we proceeded to the Solomon Islands, only to retrace 300 miles of our course to the Santa Cruz Outer Reef Islands (Swallow Islands on some charts) to sail with the Outlier Polynesian Tevake. Tikopians, whose voyaging range overlaps that of the Reef Islanders, were interviewed independently in their settlements on Guadalcanal and the Russell Islands back in the Solomons proper.

Our next important stop was 1500 miles further north-west at the isolated Ninigo group of atolls in the Admiralty archipelago north of New Guinea.[6]

After travelling by canoe among these atolls, we set off for the Carolines. It was necessary to run 500 miles back eastward before the north-west monsoon until we could lay course direct for Truk 500 miles to the north across the north-east trades. We made a canoe journey from Puluwat in the same archipelago with the navigator Hipour and also sailed to and from Saipan in the Marianas without instruments in *Isbjorn* under his command.

---

[5] Our seemingly illogical clockwise route round the western Pacific, which was against head winds most of the way, was dictated by the need to reach Tonga before the winter solstice. King Tupou IV had invited me to observe the midwinter sunrise from the *Ha'amonga a Maui*, an ancient trilithon, which the King had found to be orientated towards the summer solstice and to bear markings indicating the winter one. The opportunity to meet him and the hereditary titled navigators of Tonga could not be missed.

[6] The Santa Cruz Outer Reef Islanders and the Ninigo people present problems of classification. Reef Islanders speak a Polynesian language, and in spite of Melanesian admixture approximate physically towards the Polynesian type (Neyret, 1962: 60, V, 34). Their navigational concepts are nearly identical with those of the indubitably Polynesian Tikopians, who share the same seaways. Thus despite the fact that their *te puke* voyaging canoes exhibit a *mélange* of Melanesian, Micronesian, and Papuan features (Haddon and Hornell, 1937: vol. II, 42; Neyret, 1962: 60, V, 36; Davenport, 1964: 136) and certain Melanesian cultural traits, I have chosen to group them with the Tikopians and Sikaianans as 'Outlier Polynesians'. Similarly the Ninigo Islanders appear to be essentially Micronesian, especially in language. Their canoes have a basically Micronesian hull form, though they carry oblong mat sails that derive from the north coast of New Guinea (Haddon and Hornell, 1938: vol. III).

The Gilbert Islands, which came after the Carolines/ Marianas in our itinerary, were a weary 1300 miles against the trade winds from Truk. A memorable event in the Gilberts was a canoe passage under the veteran Iotiebata between Tarawa and the neighbouring Maiana. Subsequently we called at four other islands of the group, interviewing altogether four out of the five surviving trained navigators. There followed a 1700-mile voyage south-south-eastward to Tonga, where the residual private lore of the Tuita navigator clan was divulged to us. The passage from Tonga to Sydney concluded the active or 'field work' portion of the investigation.

My son Barry was my only regular companion during the nine months the survey lasted. He acted as engineer-mate and it was only his stubborn refusal to be mastered by the obsolescent engine that ensured the project's continuation. We covered in all 13,000 nautical miles of western Pacific, equivalent to nearly two-thirds of the earth's equatorial circumference.

A major departure from the earlier *Rehu Moana* experiment was that there was no safety officer in these demonstration voyages, complete reliance being placed on the Island navigator in charge. So obvious was their competence that their sole responsibility for the security of the vessel and its crew worried me not at all. Not only were all instruments stowed away as before, but so were astronomical tables and every chart aboard.

In view of the alleged advantages of knowing latitude and longitude on the earlier experiment, I took the extreme step of purposely refraining from any prior consultation whatsoever of charts of the proposed voyaging areas. This occasioned some confusion, in that I had no idea how long the passages would take and whether favourable winds might be anticipated, with consequent difficulties over mail and supplies. It was not, however, navigationally embarrassing in view of the indigenous captains' comprehensive learning and skill.

Advantages of Using a Small Vessel   The advantages of using a yacht, quite apart from flexibility in arranging demonstration trips, were several. The least tangible but perhaps the greatest was that you encountered the sea, wind, and weather on the same scale as a voyaging canoe. Compared with a large ship, there were few sophisticated aids to isolate you from the elements.

An immediate fellowship of small-boat seamen was invariably apparent between us and the Islanders. The fact of having come so far to meet them was in itself a recommendation; at once an indication that we were reasonably familiar with the sea ourselves and a tribute to their status. The request that Hipour and Tevake take command of my vessel was rightly interpreted as a sign of implicit trust (which experience showed was never misplaced). Self-respect, so shaken by the arrogant European impact, was bolstered by the stranger playing the less familiar role of pupil. Our inquiry took place at a period in history when everyone realised that the ancient lore was on the verge of extinction without trace —unless recorded in writing. For all these reasons the navigators proved uniformly anxious to make sure that everything they expounded and demonstrated was grasped correctly. In presenting this book, therefore, I am conscious of a sense of responsibility in attempting to fulfil the trust they laid upon me.

Language and Related Problems

Problems there were many. Language varied in importance from group to group. At one end of the scale fluent English speakers were common in Tonga, while at the other, interpreters were always needed in Micronesia— the official ones being made available in the Gilberts and the Puluwat Island Council nominating Ulutak to accompany Hipour and me in the Carolines. In other places, like the Santa Cruz Reef Islands, we got along well enough; Tevake spoke some English and some Pidgin and his own tongue was a Polynesian one, in which the nautical and navigational terms at least were familiar.

It would be reasonable to ask how I can be at all sure of facts collected in face of such communication barriers. Mainly because the information we were seeking concerned techniques, about whose demonstration there could be no ambiguity. To take obvious illustrations: interviews concerning stellar courses were invariably held at night when the stars concerned could be pointed out; the manner in which waves were distorted by invisible atolls was shown to me at sea, as were the clouds that indicated land beyond the horizon. Once at Ninigo, the onset of persistent overcast brought star instruction to a premature close and left some important concepts in doubt. But what data had already been obtained had been demonstrated unequivocally on the night sky and could be relied upon. Again, in our voyages with Tevake and Hipour, the star courses and deductions about the effects of current set, leeway and the like were subject to the most rigorous possible proof of accuracy—the stern test of landfall.

An important subsidiary factor was the cross references often available either from the expositions of different experts or from historical sources. Four Gilbertese navigators, for instance, on separate islands, speaking through four interpreters, expounded what was clearly the same body of lore, often in near identical phrases.

While what was recorded did, I think, accurately reflect the precept and practice of the navigators, it seems probable that, through inability to communicate subtleties, additional material was forfeit. Thus the precise nature of Tevake's orientation concepts—the mental images in which he visualised his raw data—remain obscure.

Apart from the safeguards inherent in sea trial against unwitting misinformation,[7] it was not hard to see when an informant was tending to stray beyond his traditional knowledge and beginning to guess. This was because of the clear-cut boundaries of the 'closed' conceptual systems which typically composed his learning. Oral lore must of necessity be conservative in content and mode of presentation; it could not else be handed down undistorted over long periods. For instance, when a Carolinian captain listing star courses began to discuss them in terms other than of the 'movement' of reference (*etak*) islands (see chap. 5), he could be presumed to be nearing the limits of his indigenous navigational range.

---

[7] The navigators' extremely responsible approach to the knowledge of which they were custodians virtually precluded intentional deception. I have no hesitation in making this assertion, even though I am well acquainted with the Pacific Islanders' sense of humour and love of exaggerating personal achievements.

It was particularly conducive to confidence that, time and again, questions were answered with categorical negatives. Familiar phrases were Hipour's 'I have never heard of that' or Teeta's 'this is all I know about the subject'. The old man Teai from Sikaiana, in reply to a leading question about star courses, even went so far as to deny that his ancestors had used them at all, insisting instead that 'the evil spirits' had led them.

Every one of the navigators was unexpectedly capable of putting his concepts into words. Instruction would be given in the rather stereotyped phrases in which it had been originally memorised. Questions that interrupted such orderly exposition would not be well tolerated and often caused confusion; the thread was broken and the old man upset. This applied particularly to the Gilbertese Abera, whose material was every bit as highly organised as that of an academic lecturer.

One further notable feature of what we were told and had shown to us was that never once did anyone lay claim to any form of 'sixth sense'. A navigator had reason to believe that land lay over the horizon because he had observed certain signs that told him so—not on account of some vague intuition.

Two important conclusions emerged from field and documentary research. Firstly, there was the totally unexpected finding that nearly every important navigational technique and concept encountered in Micronesia was matched by its Polynesian counterpart. Differences seemed to depend much more on local insular geographical features than on major cultural-linguistic divisions. On the admittedly incomplete evidence available therefore, we would hardly seem justified in speaking of separate Polynesian and Micronesian navigational *systems*, though there may well have been some such distinction in the heyday of voyaging. What I think the facts at our disposal do strongly suggest is that the methods used in the two areas were productive of equivalent results—the precision of landfall they achieved was virtually the same.

The second conclusion was that the effectiveness of indigenous navigational methods substantially exceeded what recent scholarship would allow. Voyages that were accidental, deliberate or unclassifiable from the viewpoint of European motivation, all contributed to contact. Not only, therefore, must deliberate voyaging have been more extensive than previously thought, but also a higher proportion of fortuitous drifts must have ended successfully. The possibilities of inter-island population mobility were thus greater than hitherto suspected.

Part One

THE PUZZLE

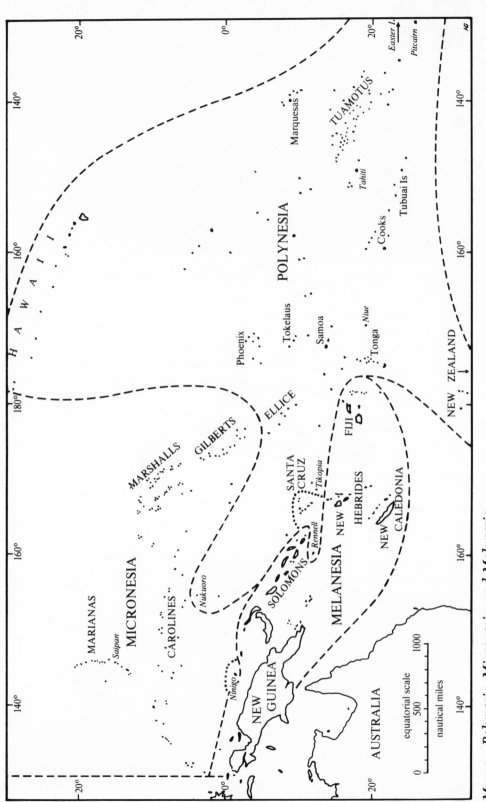

Map 1 *Polynesia, Micronesia, and Melanesia*

CHAPTER ONE

Rediscovery of a vanishing art

The Polynesians' and Micronesians' habitat is a primarily aquatic one, the proportion of dry land, exclusive of New Zealand, in the third of the Pacific where they dwell being of the order of two units of land for every thousand of water. It is understandable that few aspects of the history and culture of Oceania can be separated from sea-going. Ocean spaces can inhibit contact (though terrestrial features like mountain ranges may do so equally) but they become highways rather than barriers as marine technology—especially navigation—becomes effective. An understanding of what was and was not within the scope of the prehistoric navigator is crucial, therefore, to Pacific studies. The aim of this book is to make a detailed examination of indigenous navigational concepts and methods and to assess their efficacy and limitations.

The peopling of the Pacific basin, which occupies no less than a third of the earth's surface, was a unique maritime achievement whose details are lost in time, though archaeological, linguistic, and other studies are now laying bare a part of the process. The inhabitants comprise Melanesians, Micronesians, and Polynesians, whose territories overlap and intermingle. The Melanesians and Papuans of the larger 'continental' islands, despite some formidable voyages,[1] had less need to be sea rovers than their oceanic counterparts. These latter were the outstanding navigators.

The Pacific Islanders aroused the intense curiosity of Europeans from the very first. Where had they come

---

[1] These exceptions include the trading cycles of the Papuan Motu (Barton, 1910) and Mailu (Malinowski, 1915: 494-704; Saville, 1926: 130-41; Haddon and Hornell, 1937: 231) and the Siassi of New Guinea (Haddon and Hornell, 1937: 155). Then there were the fierce raids upon the Palau group of the Carolines, carried out from north-west New Guinea (Eilers, 1935: 708-10, 349). Again, though the evidence is conflicting, it seems not improbable that early Fijian voyaging was extensive. Wilkes, for instance, referred to Fijian voyages to Samoa, Rotuma, and Tonga (1845: vol. III, 347) and Neyret expounds their navigation (1950: 12). The contrary view, stressing the limited scope of Fijian captains, is advanced by Dillon (1829: vol. 2, 78-9).

from? This was one enigma. That their ancestors entered
Oceania from points in southern Asia is no longer in
doubt, the sole dissenting view, Heyerdahl's (1951) theory
of American origins, seeming no longer tenable in face of
the accumulated evidence. This is not, of course, to deny
the possibility of secondary contact having taken place
with the Americas, either by Peruvian *balsa* or Polynesian
canoe. We will not explore further the matter of ultimate
origins, however, since it is not the subject of this study.

The other puzzle concerns us more nearly. Men were
living on or had visited even the most remote specks of
land, and the Polynesians especially, though more widely
dispersed than anyone, exhibited an extraordinary uniformity of language and custom. Speculation immediately
centred upon the degree of isolation of the insular communities and the nature and extent of contact between
them. Plainly the finding of new islands in the beginning
must have been, like all discovery, essentially fortuitous.
Subsequent communication would be both by deliberate
voyages and involuntary ones. This much was obvious.
What was more obscure was the relative importance of
the two modes of contact.

Difficulty in interpreting the evidence, and we may
add, failure to gather it in the first place, bedevilled and
still clouds the issue. Language was an enormous barrier
initially. Less immediately apparent was the problem of
finding knowledgeable informants. Cook was uniquely
fortunate in encountering Tupaia, a dispossessed high
chief and navigator-priest of Raiatea (Beaglehole, 1955:
vol. I, 117n.) who was the *only* highly qualified Polynesian navigator who was ever interviewed at length by
Europeans.[2] By contrast, Quiros's most valuable 1606 informant about the voyages of the Taumakoans, the so-
called Pedro, was not a navigator at all, nor even a native
of that archipelago. He was a 'soldier-weaver' prisoner of

---

[2] The Tahitian navigator was known as *tata-o-rerro* (*tahata-orrero*) or
learned teacher (Forster, G., 1777: vol. II, 148, 155; Forster, J. R., 1778:
501, 530). Such men would probably be equivalent to the *tou tai*, or
professional hereditary navigators of Tonga, who were, according to
Ve'ehala, 'the recipients of knowledge handed down in their families for
generations'. They would be counterparts of the *tani borau* or 'men for
voyaging' of the Gilberts (Grimble, 1931: 197) and to the *ppalu* or
initiated navigators of the Carolines.

war from Sikaiana, which is 250 miles from Taumako (Markham, 1904: vol. II, 490). In these circumstances the extent of the information he was able to impart was nothing less than remarkable.

Not that men fully trained in these important arts would necessarily have revealed their knowledge even if asked. We have evidence from widely separated parts of Oceania that navigational lore was usually restricted to a few and often considered secret, so that in the Marshalls it was 'strongly and religiously forbidden to divulge anything concerning this art to the people' (Winkler, 1901: 505), and in the Tahitian area there were 'few men who preserve the national traditions' (Forster, G., 1777: vol. II, 148). It is questionable whether Tupaia himself would have been so co-operative had he not been in exile and deprived of his proper position.

Furthermore, the right questions to uncover the details of the techniques of navigation were generally not asked at all. At first sight this seems strange, because to us it is clear that the degree of navigational accuracy attainable is the central question for any consideration of trans-oceanic contact and the key to understanding what was possible, probable or unlikely in the way of regular communication. But the very idea that people without instruments, charts, or writing could have developed an elaborate and effective art (or 'pre-science') was so utterly foreign as not even to enter the minds of most Europeans. With few exceptions they were satisfied with rather vague statements about using the stars, sun, and waves as guide (though the vehicles of voyaging, the big canoes, were somewhat more closely studied).

Then again, the explorers' interests, in the main, lay elsewhere. In spite of Tupaia's impressive geographical horizons,[3] no one seems to have asked him *how* he orientated himself, nor what were his actual concepts and methods. Yet his ability in this direction was such that when he accompanied Cook in the *Endeavour* to Batavia

---

[3] Even allowing for all ambiguities and misconceptions his world included every major group in Polynesia except Hawaii and New Zealand (Hale, 1846: 122), and it extended for 2600 miles from the Marquesas in the east to Rotuma and Fiji in the west, equivalent to the span of the Atlantic or nearly the width of the United States.

'at more than 2000 leagues distance' from his home, and
despite the ship's circuitous route between 48° south
latitude and 4° north, he 'was never at a loss to point to
Taheitee, at whatever place he came' (Forster, J.R., 1778:
531).[4] A pertinent observation on the need to ask appropriate questions was made by the Russian explorer
Kotzebue. His informant, chief Lagediak, had omitted to
mention the existence of the Ralik chain (west Marshalls)
though he knew them intimately. This prompted Kotzebue
to write 'They never give any information on their own
accord, but merely answer questions, supposing that . . . we
know every thing' (1821: 197). Perhaps this partly explains why there is information on indigenous navigation
still to be collected in Oceania today—the navigators have
never been asked.

Later Europeans, despite enhanced facility with
language, were generally uninterested in inquiring about
the Islanders' beliefs and concepts. With notable exceptions, missionaries instructed but did not learn, traders
and sea captains were concerned with making their own
living, and so on. The cultures of Oceania became de-
valued in the eyes of the inhabitants and Westerners alike
by comparison with the spectacular achievements of
European technology. To complicate matters still further,
facts and ideas imbibed from the strangers became
incorporated into indigenous lore. Thus it is probable
that at times European knowledge of neighbouring
islands was responsible for new contacts and one may
sometimes recognise echoes of once current Western
theories in the midst of oral tradition. For instance,
certain accounts that I collected in Tonga (Kaho),[5] and
the Gilberts (Teeta) appeared to reflect the formerly
widely accepted migration beliefs of the late Percy Smith
(1915).

From the first, European ideas about Pacific dispersal

---

[4] It has been suggested that the ship's officers could not check Tupia's
assertions without elaborate trigonometry. In fact a piece of string laid
across a chart from the *Endeavour's* position to Tahiti would give the
rhumb line bearing exactly, or if a globe were used, the great circle one.
Calculation would have been unnecessary.

[5] Names in parentheses refer to my instructors in navigation, who are
listed at the end of this section.

and contact tended to polarise around *accidental* versus *deliberate* modes, which were usually seen (quite illogically) as mutually exclusive categories. When Quiros first encountered South Sea Islanders as pilot on Mendaña's 1595 expedition, he expressed very well, in a memorial to the Viceroy of Peru, the stark incredulity of so many Westerners about effective indigenous navigation and opted firmly for accidental drifts. ' . . . in losing altogether the land . . . it becomes necessary to understand at least the compass, which they have not', he wrote. 'Not to mention the contrary winds, currents, and other things, which may make them lose their right way'. The most experienced pilots 'losing sight for two or four days of the land, do not know, nor can determine their situation'. The instruments of navigation 'of these Indians' being their own eyes, the mutability of the sun, moon, and stars, which are 'not always present, nor in the same place' and often obscured into the bargain, constituted an added hazard. Quiros concluded that if accurate indigenous navigation were possible (adding that it was not), any voyages must have been short (Dalrymple, 1770: vol. I, 98). The information that Quiros obtained during his later 1606 voyage, however, demonstrated to him the remarkable voyaging range of the Santa Cruz Islanders —though he says very little about the techniques they employed (Markham, 1904: vol. I, 227-8, 490).

Cook on the contrary was, initially at any rate, impressed at how 'these people sail in those seas from Island to Island for several hundred Leagues, the Sun serving them for a compass by day and the Moon and Stars by night. When this comes to be prov'd', he adds but then deletes the parentheses '(which I have now not the least doubt of)', 'we Shall no longer be at a loss to know how the Islands lying in those Seas came to be people'd, for if the inhabitants of Uleitea have been at Islands lying 2 or 300 Leagues to the westward of them . . .we may trace them from Island to Island quite to the East Indias' (Beaglehole, 1955; vol. I, 154).

On a subsequent voyage, however, an encounter with Tahitian castaways on the Cook island of Atiu in 1777 convinced him otherwise. He felt that the incident

explained 'better than a thousand conjectures of speculative reasoners, how the detached parts of the earth, . . .
may have been first peopled' (Cook and King, 1784: vol.
I, 202). The real contact pattern would appear to combine both of Cook's speculations.

Later commentators have continued the debate on the
nature and volume of inter-island communication. Anyone following the controversies must be impressed by two
things: the adherence to rigidly defined theses; and the inadequacy and ambiguity of the few really original sources
(see Documentary Sources).

At one extreme we have the older traditionalists like
Percy Smith, who tended uncritically to accept the
migration legends of the Polynesians as if they were
literal history (1915). Andrew Sharp (1957, 1963) did
salutary service in demolishing the thoughtless assump-
tions of this school and firmly established the importance
of drift and one-way voyages. Unfortunately he attempted to lay down a new orthodoxy, which virtually denied
the Islanders any navigational expertise at all.

The conclusion is hard to avoid that the discussion has
become increasingly stultified by shortage of facts. This
point was realised by G. Ward (pers. comm., 1971) who
has made a computer analysis of ideal drifts and Finney
(1967), who has conducted paddling experiments in
Hawaii. Some leading anthropologists like Gladwin have
'opted out' by insisting that no general conclusions at all
should be drawn from their local field work (1970: 145).
It may perhaps be significant that the most heated pro-
ponents of opposing theories have rarely been navigators
and never small-boat seamen.

INTER-ISLAND CONTACT PATTERNS

It is worth digressing here for the sake of perspective,
to see what were some of the problems that prehistoric
navigators actually faced and what kinds of contact did,
in fact, develop. The vast stretches of the Pacific would
appear at first sight to present the navigator with insol-
uble tasks. Closer examination reveals, however, that it is
possible to sail to almost all the inhabited islands of
Oceania from South-east Asia, without once making a sea

crossing longer than 310 miles. The only exceptions are Easter Island, Hawaii, and New Zealand, though the most practicable routes between Eastern and Western Polynesia are also long. Such isolated lands apart, the majority of gaps between islands and even archipelagos are well under 310 miles and usually in the 50 to 200 mile range.[6] Since no one *wants* to cross more open ocean than necessary, it follows that most passages were of this order.

Starting from this indisputable fact, that indigenous sailing routes generally spanned only short (unbroken) stretches, for the very good reason that adjacent islands are rarely far apart, some commentators have assumed that navigational methods did not allow of longer voyages. This assumption is quite unwarranted, as our analysis of navigation in subsequent chapters will demonstrate.

Naturally, the shortest route was not necessarily always the most convenient, and in point of fact we do know of a number of deliberate voyages of something like 500 miles without intervening land that were being made around the period of first contact with Europeans. We will discuss some examples in later chapters. Some of these voyages were sporadic while others were relatively regular events. (The word 'regular' in the context of prehistoric Pacific voyaging does not exclude dallying ashore for indefinite periods, taking advantage of seasonal winds, etc.)

Prehistoric Oceania, from the viewpoint of communication, may be divided into zones of close contact, sporadic intercourse, and relative isolation. Map 2 (see p. 24) can at best be an approximation because the degree of contact fluctuated with the vicissitudes of trade and conquest; furthermore, the evidence on which it is based is generally indirect and often contradictory.

The limits of close contact seem to have been determined as much, or even more, by cultural factors as by inadequacy of maritime skills, and to have thus been less immutable than would otherwise have been the case. A particularly potent 'cultural' deterrent to travellers was

---

[6] Nautical miles are used throughout this book.

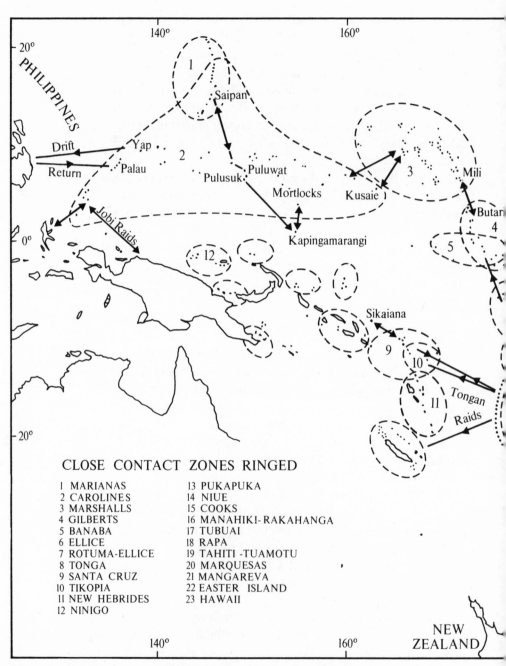

Map 2   Contact zones (after Lewthwaite, 1967; Neverman, 1923)

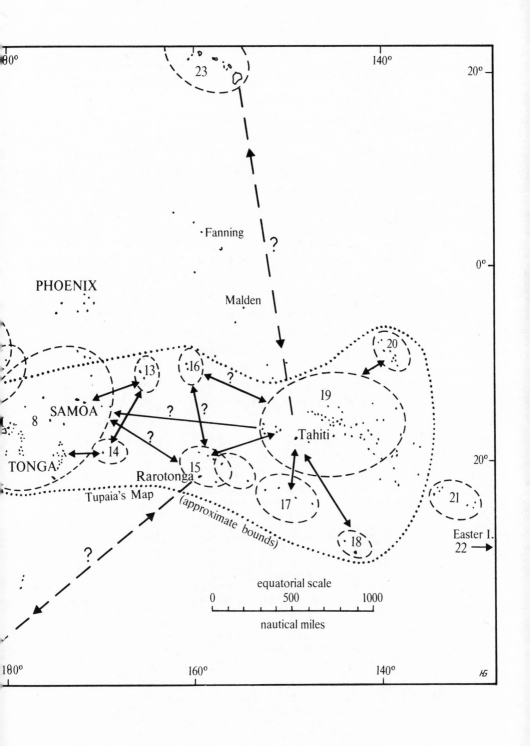

the widespread practice of killing new arrivals on sight.[7]

Save for the outposts of the Polynesian world and its major east-west divisions, the boundaries of the adjacent close-contact spheres were not very far apart. The importance of non-navigational factors emerges when it is realised that many voyages that were made regularly within zone boundaries exceeded in length and difficulty the more sporadic passages to neighbouring areas. For instance, the main Polynesian-Micronesian cultural 'frontier' is between the Ellice Islands, which are overwhelmingly Polynesian, and the Micronesian Gilberts further north. Yet the distance separating these groups is substantially less than several stretches within the Tongan close-contact sphere, which included the Ellice Islands.[8]

There is ample evidence that involuntary drift voyages continually took place, in addition to planned journeys, both within close-contact zones and between them. Deliberate and accidental voyages, far from being opposed, would seem to be complementary categories, and inter-island communication may perhaps best be apprehended as a combination of the two.

G. Ward's computer simulation of pure drifts (Levison, Ward, and Webb, 1972 and G. Ward, pers. comm., 1971) was undertaken in the belief that a drift hypothesis could

---

[7] We may mention Pukapuka (Beaglehole, E. and P., 1938: 406), Anuta, and Tikopia (Firth, 1954: 123), and the Tuamotus (Stimson, 1957: 61-3). As an example, the position in the Gilberts in 1841, after a series of wars had been raging for two generations, is described by Wilkes (1845: vol. V, 82): 'But so estranged have the inhabitants of the several islands become from each other, that if a canoe from one of them should visit, or seek, through distress, another island, the persons in it would in all probability be put to death, under the supposition of their being spies, or in order to procure their bones and teeth for the manufacture of ornaments.' Reasonable enough grounds one would think for restricting one's wandering. In an earlier more peaceful period, 'The grandfather of Tekere, the present king of Kuria, is said to have voyaged to every island in the group on a pleasure trip to see the world, about a hundred years since'. This rather suggests that the formidable barriers to contact of a later day were not navigational.

[8] The southern Gilbert islands of Arorae, Tamana, Nikunau, Beru, Onotoa, and Tabiteuea present overlapping 20-mile radius homing bird zones that make up a target arc of just over 30° from Nanumea, the northernmost of the Ellice Islands (the return voyage target is of the same order). The distance from Nanumea to the nearest Gilbert island, Arorae, is 185 miles and to Onotoa 230. Distances within the 'Greater Tonga' sphere include 255 miles from Fiji to Rotuma, 260 from Rotuma to Funafuti in the Ellice Islands, and 295 from Futuna to Rotuma.

provide a satisfactory explanation for the settlement of Polynesia. Contrary to expectations, the results showed that, while accidental advent upon a number of island groups was likely, drifts could not account for certain crucial contact stages. These were virtually impossible except as exploratory probes and subsequent deliberately mounted ventures. The probability of drifts occurring was negligible or zero across the following seaways: Western Melanesia to Fiji; Eastern Polynesia to Hawaii, New Zealand or Easter Island; Eastern Polynesian contact with the Americas in either direction. The probability of there having been drifts from Western to Eastern Polynesia and from Western Polynesia to the Marquesas zone was very low.

At any level of technology a proportion of even the most efficiently mounted marine enterprises is bound to suffer mischance. This will be so even where the highest navigational standards obtain, the absolute number going astray increasing with the volume of traffic. Naturally it is skilled captains of seaworthy craft who, when blown off course, are most likely to survive storms, keep their bearings, make fruitful use of land signs and ultimately return home. Such men, in the more distant past, would be the ones who brought back reliable tidings of any new lands they happened upon.

Accidental voyages involving inshore canoes and untrained Islanders must have occurred with increasing frequency as the general navigational level declined and specialised deep-sea canoes became obsolete. Rash adventurers in unsuitable vessels, and ill-equipped fishermen, would readily get blown away and often lack the skill to come again to land. In most of Oceania today confidence at sea and the urge to adventure have not diminished to anything like the same extent as has knowledge.[9]

[9] The banning by European administrations of inter-island canoe travel must have been a potent cause of navigational decline. Voyages were forbidden, for instance, in the Carolines in German times (Riesenberg, 1965: 164) and under Japanese rule (Lessa, 1950: 49). Itilon attributed the loss of traditional lore on Ninigo to the effect of the old German regulations. Prohibitions remain in force today in, among other places, the Tahiti group (Finney, pers. comm., 1970), and voyaging is strongly discouraged in the Gilberts. Not only must atrophy of knowledge have resulted but deliberate voyages had to be kept secret. Advent upon another island was invariably attributed to accident (Maude, pers. comm., 1969).

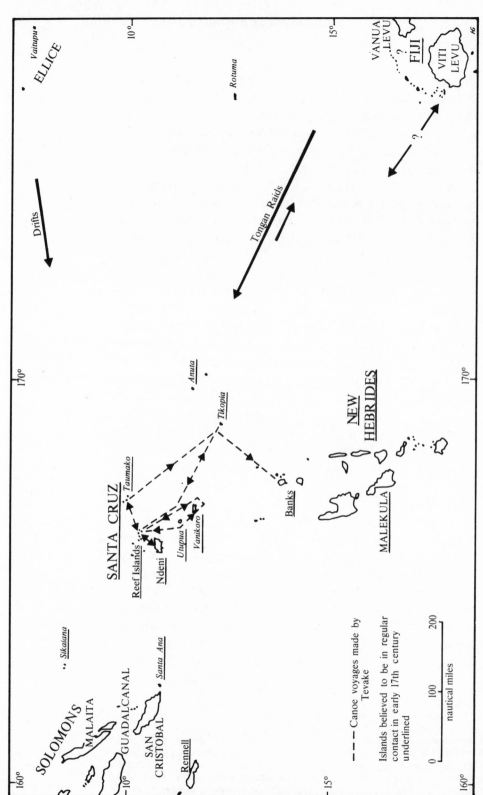

Map 3 Santa Cruz sphere

An example of the degree to which an intact navigational tradition prevents accidents comes from Puluwat in the Caroline Islands, where regular voyaging is maintained, yet the last time anyone from the atoll was lost at sea was in 1945, when a canoe with five occupants disappeared in a typhoon (Gladwin, 1970: 63).

PIECING TOGETHER THE MOSAIC

Though this work is in large part based on demonstration by contemporary navigators, it also makes free use of documentary sources. Since both categories of data are of necessity incomplete, it seems advisable here to comment on their general scope and limitations.

Demonstrations fell into three main divisions of exposition on land, open sea canoe journeys, and demonstration passages in *Isbjorn*. In neither the canoe nor the *Isbjorn* voyages were charts or instruments ever used.

Shore-based instruction was of considerable value, guiding star lore being expounded by Carolinians, Santa Cruz Reef Islanders, two groups of Tikopians, Ninigo Islanders, Gilbertese, and Tongans. Zenith star data were collected from the Tikopians and exotic matters, like the secret names of the zenith stars, were revealed by the Tûita navigator clan in Tonga.

Sea voyages in canoes were very informative. A number of short inter-atoll canoe passages were made among the Ninigos. In the Carolines I accompanied Hipour and five companions in his canoe on a return voyage between Puluwat and Pulusuk, a total distance of 95 miles. Some months later came the Tarawa-Maiana trip in the Gilbertese Iotiebata's canoe. In the course of all these canoe journeys 180 miles of open sea were traversed.

The most significant of the *Isbjorn* voyages were those made under the command of Tevake among the Santa Cruz islands and Hipour between the Carolines and Marianas.

The 'credentials' of the old Outlier Polynesian navigator Tevake are summarised under 'Instructors in Navigation'. He agreed to command our instrument-denuded yacht on demonstration voyages. Time did not permit us

Voyages with Tevake in Isbjorn: Santa Cruz Sphere

to undertake the longer ones he suggested (to Tikopia
and to the New Hebrides), so we confined ourselves to
return passages from the Outer Reef Islands to Taumako,
Vanikoro, and Ndeni, 60, 100, and 30 miles off respectively. The main subject demonstrated was star path
steering, though there was also an extremely impressive
example of keeping course by ocean swells during rain
and overcast and some significant examples of assessing
current set and of locating land by a type of underwater
phosphorescence. In all 335 miles of open sea were
covered.

The regular voyaging of the 40-foot *te puke* trading
canoes of the Santa Cruz group included, up to the mid-
1960s at least, the whole archipelago and associated
Taumako cluster (Duff Islands). Sporadic voyages were
made to Tikopia, and there was one by Tevake to the
New Hebrides, after he had learned the star course thither
on an earlier Tikopian visit.

It seems probable that this contact zone has shrunk a
little from what it was a century ago. O'Ferrall (1903)
says that 'Tepukeis have even been known to make their
way to the Solomon Islands', and the usually conservative
Lewthwaite includes not only Santa Ana Island, 200 miles
away off the southern Solomons, but also the far more
distant Rennell, in the Reef Islanders' range (1967: 63,
58-9, fig. 6). A more restricted scope, rather more nearly
coterminous with Tevake's own, is suggested by Davenport (1964a).

Extant Santa Cruz tradition would suggest that the
group's horizons never materially exceeded those of last
century (Davenport, 1964a). In this, however, tradition
is overly conservative, because we have independent evidence in the writings of Quiros, who visited the region in
1595 and again in 1606, that the range of the Santa Cruz
seafarers was then very much more extensive (Markham,
1904: vols. I and II).[10]

---

[10] Absence of a tradition of contact is no more conclusive negative
evidence than a positive tradition is necessarily acceptable *per se*. Certain
events may well be 'beyond the pale' of the society concerned, and so be
irrelevant to its 'memory bank'. Thus no memory has survived of Mendaña's particularly traumatic 1595 sojourn in Santa Cruz (Tedder, pers.
comm., 1968), nor of Quiros's in Taumako eleven years later (Daven-

Plate I Isbjorn *at anchor, Marquesas*

Plate II   Scale model of 40-foot te puke *as used by Tevake. Photographed at Taumako.*

That there was sporadic deliberate contact with isolated Sikaiana, 250 miles to the north-westward, seems
highly probable (Markham, 1904: vol. II, 490) and is
supported by Sikaianan tradition (Woodford, 1906: 167;
Teai, pers. comm., 1968), though not by contemporary
Taumakoan lore. Quiros saw at Taumako canoes that were
capable of holding 'fifty persons' (Markham, 1904: vol. II,
360), which were very much bigger than nineteenth-century models. Vastly more islands were known to the inhabitants than are today, for chief Tumai of Taumako indicated
the direction of no less than seventy islands that he knew,
'and a very large land . . . Manicollo' (or 'Mallicollo'), that
he told Quiros his people visited (Markham, 1904: vol. I,
227-8), would seem likely to have been Malekula in the
central New Hebrides, well outside the latter day Taumakoan world (Forster, J. R., 1778: 223, 228).

Size, bearing, and distance would seem to exclude identification of Manicollo with the nearby and familiar
Vanikoro. The suggestion that it was Vanua Levu in Fiji
has been made by Parsonson (1963: 49-50). Not only is
this unsupported by evidence, but the sea-going conditions involved would appear to conflict with the *te puke*'s
known poor weatherly performance (Tedder, pers. comm.,
1968). It is not unlikely, however, that Tongans staging at
Fiji might have told the Reef Islanders (including the
Taumakoans), the requisite star courses. A particularly
suggestive incident in this connection was when the Reef
Islander Bakapu and a companion, having been kidnapped
by 'blackbirders' and taken to Fiji, stole a small craft and
returned home across nearly 1000 miles of open sea directly
to their own island (Davenport, 1964a: 142). Their extraordinary voyage is most unlikely to have been guided by
other than traditional star courses and indigenous sailing
directions.

In order to complete the Santa Cruz contact pattern
we must include involuntary voyages, mainly from the
east. An island that Quiros calls 'Guaytopo' (Markham,

port, 1964a: 134-42). Quiros found evidence of contact between Sikaiana
and Taumako (Markham, 1904: vol. I, 490), yet the only remaining
Taumakoan traditions of such visits are of supernatural ones (Davenport,
1964a). Were it not for Quiros's writings, therefore, we would seriously
underestimate the size of the ancient Santa Cruz sphere.

1904: vol. I, 493), the place of origin of one such party that drifted to Taumako, was most likely Vaitupu in the Ellice group.

Voyages with Hipour in Isbjorn: The Carolines-Marianas Route

The demonstration voyages of the Puluwat (Carolinian) navigator Hipour were of a rather special character, in that the latest canoe journey from the Carolines to the Marianas appears to have been made around 1905 (Riesenberg, pers. comm., 1969), though one did take place more recently in the reverse direction (Lykke, pers. comm., 1969; Riesenberg, pers. comm., 1969).[11]

The voyages we made between Puluwat and Saipan in the Marianas in an *Isbjorn* once again freed from instrumental aids covered 1165 miles altogether. We staged at uninhabited Pikelot, 100 miles from Puluwat, on both the outward and homeward passages, leaving unbroken stretches of 450 miles to be covered in each direction.[12]

Hipour, like most of his highly trained contemporaries, is illiterate, his vast store of learning being entirely memorised. The Saipan sailing directions that he knew must have been handed down orally for at least sixty-four years, or two or three generations, since last put into practice; one of our main objects was to test their validity after such a period of disuse.

The question of the antiquity of Carolines-Marianas contacts is a matter very germane to Hipour's demonstration.

In 1686 the Spaniards conquered the Marianas, practically depopulating all the islands save Guam. Refugees fled in their canoes south to the Carolines, which were

---

11 Shamed by Hipour's Saipan voyage in *Isbjorn*, five men of Satawal, an island 130 miles west of Puluwat, led by the navigator Repunglug, sailed to Saipan and back by canoe the following year, 1970 (*Highlights*, May 1970; McCoy, pers. comm., 1970). Details of their exploit will be found in the section on motivation in chap. 11, under the heading 'Pride of Navigators'.

12 In the old days Puluwat canoes usually went to Saipan via Pikelot, just as Hipour did (Hipour; Beiong; Krämer, 1937: 82). An alternative route was via Magur in the Namonuitos (Ikééliman, quoted by Riesenberg, pers. comm., 1969). Satawal canoes made the voyage via Gaferut (Chamisso, 1907: 417-18), or West Fayu (McCoy, pers. comm., 1970). For routes from the Carolines to Guam, also in the Marianas, see Kotzebue (1821: 207) and Krämer (1937: 82, 123). These involved a shorter open sea crossing than the voyage to Saipan (320 miles as against 450).

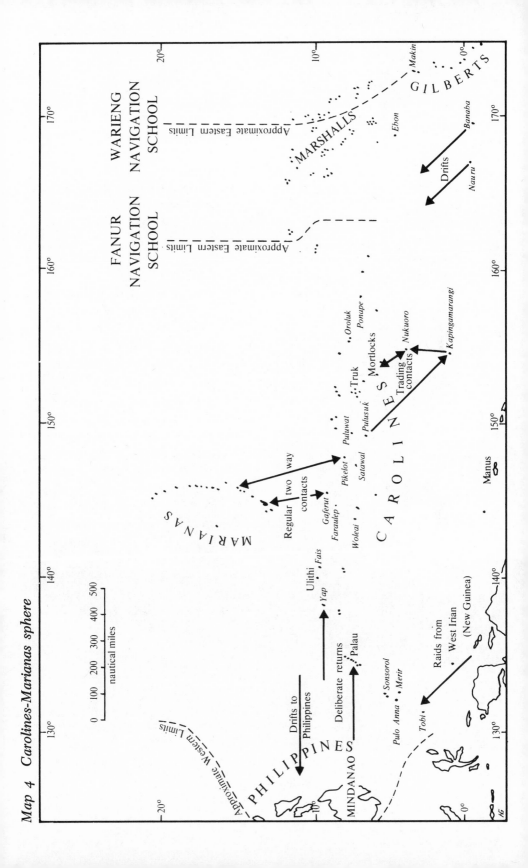

Map 4   Carolines-Marianas sphere

Plate III   Puluwat canoe bringing 250-lb turtle from Pikelot, 100 miles away

mercifully then unknown to civilisation. Burney (1967: 4) writes that 'it may be imagined that the islanders had a general knowledge of, and probably an habitual intercourse with, each other'. But henceforth connection between the two archipelagos abruptly ceased, to be cautiously resumed the following century by Carolinians in search of iron. It is from this latter period of contact that voyaging traditions today current on Puluwat and Pulusuk seem to derive. For instance, the Carolinian name for Saipan, *Sepi Puun*, or 'Empty Plate' is believed locally to refer to the island when bereft of its inhabitants by the Spaniards (Lykke, pers. comm. 1969).

What of the earlier pre-Spanish period? We have already noted Burney's opinion that Carolines-Marianas relations antedated the European advent. Kotzebue, who was in Guam in 1816, wrote that 'when in 1788, the Carolinians visited Guaham with several small canoes, . . . They said they had *always been trading* with the inhabitants of this island [Guam], and *only left off* when the white people settled here, whose cruelty they themselves had witnessed' (1821: 207, my italics). A more definite affirmation of the pre-European antiquity of regular contact between the archipelagos would be hard to find.

OUR INSTRUCTORS IN NAVIGATION, 1968-1969

The word 'informants' seems hardly appropriate, since so many of the accomplished men listed below were our teachers, who instructed us, mainly by demonstration, both ashore and afloat. The list is by no means exhaustive.

The majority were illiterate or could read and write only a little in the vernacular. Their degree of familiarity with Western instruments and vessels varied, but was usually slight. In practice it never proved difficult to recognise any (rare) intrusions of alien navigational concepts.[13]

The Micronesian Hipour and Outlier Polynesian Tevake deserve pride of place, since we spent so many weeks, covering hundreds of miles, under their tutelage.

---

[13] The navigators appear under the names by which they are generally known.

Outlier
Polynesians

Santa Cruz Reef Islanders. Tevake of Pileni atoll, now resident on nearby Nufilole, was trained in navigation by his father from the age of seven or eight onwards. He sailed for years in his 30-foot outrigger (*te puke*) on voyages of up to 320 miles, as far afield as Tikopia and the New Hebrides. This latter voyage was a forced one, during which Tevake retained his orientation and ability to navigate accurately. He was nearing Taumako from the Reef Islands (say 50 miles *en route*), when a sudden gale headed him. He altered course for Tikopia 163 miles to the south-east, which he fetched but was unable to land on because of the surf. Making use of what he had heard, during his previous *te puke* visit to Tikopia, of the New Hebrides and the star course thither, he set a new star course for the condominium. The distance was 110 miles and he arrived safely. Though his *te puke* has been wrecked these ten years, he cannot rest from the sea, and old as he is, and possessing no more than an outriggerless dugout, he still ranges ceaselessly among the islands.

Bongi of Matema atoll is Tevake's pupil and nephew, the main inheritor of the old man's sea lore. He himself has made *te puke* voyages throughout the Santa Cruz group, including Taumako. Matalau of Taumako is a less intensively trained pupil of Tevake. In 1968 he took his niece and two little boys on a 60-mile open sea passage (without intervening land) in an outriggerless dugout 'just for the ride'.

Tikopians. All were trained systematically by the old men of Tikopia, except Rafe, who as a child listened to them secretly, because loss of young men at sea had induced the elders to withhold navigational instruction.

Rafe has captained canoes from Tikopia to Vanikoro (about 112 miles) and to Mota Island in the New Hebrides (about 110 miles). He was interviewed on Guadalcanal.

Tupuai has navigated the Tikopia-Anuta return canoe voyage (71 miles each way).

Samoa has made the voyage to Vanikoro. These two navigators were both interviewed in the Russell Islands.

Sikaianan. Though Teai is not himself a voyager, this old man is a learned elder. He was seen on Guadalcanal.

Tongans. Hereditary titled navigators (*tou tai*) of the Tuita clan:

Hon Ve'ehala, Governor of Ha'a'pai, was formerly the leading spirit of the Tonga Tradition Department. Hon Sione Fe'iloakitau Kaho is the 88-year-old great-grandson of the famous blind Tuita navigator Kaho Mo Vailahi. He is the senior member of the clan. Hon Tuita is the present title holder.

All three expounded portions of the lore of the Tuitas, which was unique material, despite several generations of separation from practical sea going and astronomy.

Captains (*'eikivaka*). Cutter skippers who sail by the stars:

Kaloni Kienga was interviewed both in 1966 and 1969.

Ve'etutu Pahulu is a survivor of the Minerva Reef wreck epic (Ruhen, 1963).

Vili Mailau is a star path captain from Nomuka Island.

Sioni Mafi, also from Nomuka, is a blind ex-captain.

Carolinans. Hipour of Puluwat atoll is a trained and initiated navigator (*ppalu*) of the *warieng* navigational 'school'. He is a middle-aged man who has voyaged for years through the Central Carolines over an east-west range totalling something like 800 miles.

Beiong, the chief of Pulusuk, is an experienced canoe voyager though he is not a fully qualified navigator. He is particularly well versed in tradition.

Ulutak of Puluwat is a canoe man who accompanied us to Saipan as interpreter.

Homearek of Pulap is also a canoe man and was for a time our interpreter. He was once storm-drifted for a month in company with the navigator Sernous (Ullman, 1964: 69).

Gilbert Islanders. Iotiebata Ata of Maiana is a navigator (*tia borau*) who was taught by his grandfather and who makes frequent canoe passages between his home island and Tarawa. It was on one of these that he demonstrated cloud and wave signs to me. He was once five weeks storm-drifted, eventually locating land by clouds.

Teeta Tatua of Kuria is a *tia borau* who was trained in the classical *maneaba* tradition by his grandfather. He made wartime voyages without navigational aids through most of the Gilberts.

Abera Beniata of Nikunau is another navigator who was taught by his grandfather. He has made many canoe passages among the southern Gilberts.

Temi Rewi of Beru is a navigator who was instructed by his father with the aid of a hitherto unrecorded device —a so-called 'stone canoe'.

Micronesian-
Melanesian
(Ninigo Islanders)

Itilon, Papi, and Haidak are all canoe captains and practical inter-island navigators. They taught me both ashore and at sea in their canoes.

Melanesians

These were all interviewed during the earlier voyage in 1966.

Hanuabada, Papua. Frank Rei and Lohia Loa were participants in the *hiri* multiple canoe trading voyages of the Motu people across the Gulf of Papua (Barton, in Seligman, 1910).

Buin, Bougainville. Tonnaku has made the 60-mile canoe passage, guided by swells, from Rendova to the Shortland Islands.

DOCUMENTARY STUDY

One result of the combined literary and practical approach I have used in this book has been that it has proved possible to reinterpret a number of written accounts in the light of the teaching of contemporary navigators and of sea-going experience. For instance, one regular Carolinian voyage could be analysed and conclusions drawn as to permissible tracking error. Then again, fresh light is shed on the voyages of the Tongan Kau Moala (Mariner, 1817: vol. I, 317) by knowing the capabilities of canoes such as he used and by recognising his special status in the Tongan navigational hierarchy, as revealed by Tuita.

The Main
Documentary
Sources on
Actual Methods
of Navigation

For Polynesia these are unbelievably sparse. Significant *original* descriptions and examples number less than a dozen.

One of the few really outstanding accounts is that of the Spanish captain of the *Jupiter*, Andia y Varela, who was in Tahiti in 1774-5 (Corney, 1914: vol. II, 285). Then there are the writings of Cook's companions, especially Banks and the Forsters, for example Banks's *Endeavour* journal (ed. Beaglehole, 1962: vol. I, 368) and J. R. Forster's book (1778: 501-31). In Tahiti too the missionary Orsmond collected chants of astronomical and navigational significance, which were published by his granddaughter, Teuira Henry. They include 'The Birth of New Lands' (1894), and 'Birth of Heavenly Bodies' (1907). William Wyatt Gill, another missionary, has left us with a detailed picture of the Cook Islands' 'wind compass' orientation system (1876b: 319). The two Hawaiians, Kepelino (1932: 82) and Kamakau (1891: 142), despite the incorporation of some European ideas, provide valuable source material.

In the present century there has been Augustin Krämer's valuable though ambiguous report on Samoan navigation (1902: vol. II, 244-7), Collocott's work on Tongan astronomy (1922), the Beagleholes' series of relatively detailed star course sailing directions from Pukapuka (1938), and Raymond Firth's similar material from Tikopia and Anuta (1931, 1954).

For the rest, there are but snippets of information—a sentence here, a few words there, scattered through innumerable works.

Concerning Micronesia we are rather more fortunate, for in spite of the early discovery of at least one of the archipelagos (Magellan came on the Marianas in 1521), more intimate contacts tended to lag about a century behind Polynesia, so that much of the old lore survived. Happily for purposes of comparison, navigational accuracy in both the sections of Oceania seems to have been comparable.

In the Gilbert Islands uniquely detailed and comprehensive navigational data were collected by Sir Arthur Grimble (1924, 1931, 1943, and MSS. in possession of Maude and of Rosemary Grimble). There is also a solitary, but most valuable, account of a zenith star observation, that was recorded by Fr Sabatier (1939).

The Carolines are also well served. In the eighteenth century there was Fr Cantova (1728) and in the nineteenth Sanchez (1866). The observations of Krämer,

Hambruch, Sarfert, Hellwig, and their colleagues of the German South Seas Expedition of 1908-10 are a veritable mine of information (Hambruch and Sarfert, 1935; Krämer, 1935, 1937; Damm and Sarfert, 1935; Eilers, 1934). Even more detailed have been the recent studies of American anthropologists, notably Gladwin (1970), Alkire (1970), Burrows and Spiro (1957), Riesenberg (pers. comm., 1970 and MS. in preparation for *Journal of Polynesian Society*), and, in the field of astronomy, Goodenough (1953).

Marshallese navigation received mention in the sixties of last century from the American missionary Gulick (1862) and his Hawaiian counterpart Aea (1948), but the outstanding exposition was that of Captain Winkler of the German Navy (1901). This has been supplemented by Erdland (1914), Raymond de Brum (1962), and Davenport (1964b).

Documentary Sources on the Wider Aspects of Indigenous Sea-Going   The general field of voyaging, whereof the navigational arts proper are but a part, is much better documented. Compared with the strictly technical information we have been considering, the volume of data recorded in both Polynesia and Micronesia about particular voyages, contact patterns, and geographical horizons appears almost limitless. Indeed, the sources are so numerous that reference to even the most important would be quite impracticable and they will be left entirely to the bibliography.

We will, therefore, leave primary sources at this point and turn to some of the commentators whose role in the study of navigation has been primarily interpretive.

Commentators   Smith and Sharp have already been mentioned in the first part of this chapter as have the experimental studies of Ward and Finney. A symposium of Polynesian navigation was edited by Golson (1963). There are some works that are more than merely interpretive, like Makemson's review of Pacific astronomy (1941) and the canoe studies of Haddon and Hornell (1936-8) and Fr Neyret (1962-3 and 1965-6). Deserving of close attention are the views of the experienced master mariners Reche (1927), Hops (1956), Hilder (1959, 1963a and b), Heyen (1963, 1966), V. Ward (pers. comm., 1969) and Douglas (pers. comm., 1969) as well as those of the air-sea navigator Gatty (1943, 1958). The technical analyses of Frankel (1962), Lemaître's mathematical simulations (1970) and Akerblom's synthesis of documentary sources (1968) are significant.'

Our evidence has been discussed at such length to show how fragmentary it is and how imperfect must be the picture revealed by either documentary sources or demonstrations alone. The problems and methods involved in seeking sea-borne instruction needed to be described so that the quality of the results obtainable might be evaluated. All this becomes very relevant to the material presented in the following chapters, since the components of the navigational arts we shall be considering have had, for the most part, to be reconstructed from data of both kinds.

Plate IV
Hipour
steering his
canoe by the
sheet between
Puluwat and
Pulusuk,
Caroline
Islands

Part Two

DIRECTION

CHAPTER TWO

Steering by the stars

The first requirement of any system of navigation is to enable the voyager to take his departure and continue towards his objective in the right direction. The most accurate direction indicators for Pacific Islanders, still used in many parts of Oceania, are stars low in the sky that have either just risen or are about to set, that is horizon or guiding stars. You steer towards whichever star rises or sets in the direction of the island you wish to visit. In more technical terms the direction (bearing) of your objective, the course you must follow, is the direction (azimuth or bearing) of its guiding star, at rise if the course be an easterly one, at set if it be westerly. It seems appropriate, incidentally, to use the present tense in these descriptions, since the art is still a living one.

Although stars rise four minutes earlier each night—so that after six months one that had risen at 9 p.m. will be rising at 9 a.m. in daylight—the points on the horizon where they rise and set remain the same throughout the year. They do vary somewhat with latitude, and this will be discussed later under 'sidereal compass'.

As the earth rotates, each star appears to come up over the eastern horizon at its own special point, describe its arc across the sky and set on its precise westerly bearing. If it rises say in the north-east, the arc it follows is inclined towards the north and it will set in the north-west. In other words, it does not rise straight up from the horizon but at an angle, so that a few hours after it has risen in the north-east, as well as being higher in the sky, its bearing will have changed—perhaps to north-north-east. A horizon star therefore can only be used to steer by for a certain time. When it has risen too high for convenience or has moved too far to one or other side of the correct bearing, the next star to rise or set at the same point is used in its place. If a suitable substitute is not immediately available, course is maintained meanwhile by allowing for the original star's increasing displacement. 45

How high a star may rise and still be of use for steering, and therefore how many stars in succession need be followed during a night, will depend on the direction of the course and the latitude. For instance the northernmost star of Orion's Belt, whose declination (celestial latitude) is 0°, rises due east and sets due west from whatever latitude it is viewed. But while from the equator its apparent motion is vertical, so that it rises straight up and passes directly overhead through the observer's zenith, from high north or south latitudes it is seen to arch towards the south or north respectively. Thus on the equator one could hold an easterly course on Orion rather longer before substituting another star than would be practicable on the fringes of the tropics, and a good deal longer than if steering north-east by Deneb which, having a declination of 45°, would slant obliquely up from the horizon.

In practice, however, it is rare to require more than ten guide stars for a night's sailing—roughly twelve hours in the tropics. Firth (1954: 91) states that the star path from Tikopia to Anuta has nine stars. Now this course is 54° or about north-east-by-east, whereas for the passage from Ninigo to Kaniet (whose direction, 80°, is much nearer to east), only five stars are needed for the night's steering. (Statement by Itilon of Amich, Ninigo, 1969, who has sailed this course by stars.) The distances are virtually the same, being 66 and 71 miles.

Another example, like Tikopia to Anuta, of steering stars quickly changing their bearings is Vanikoro to the Reef Islands of Santa Cruz. We were making this passage under Tevake's command; the course was north-west. Tevake, drawing attention to how the stars in front were moving to the left at an angle to our course as they sank, explained that each one could only be used for steering for a very short while. However, he was so well orientated by these obliquely sinking stars that he was able to inform me during the evening that the wind had backed from south-east to south-south-east. I seriously doubted the accuracy of his observation until Canopus (*Trekapekau ki Ndeni*), topping the horizon on a bearing of 143° exactly in line with our stern, confirmed that we were in fact dead on course and that the wind *had* changed.

The star path, the succession of rising or setting guiding stars down which one steers, was known as the *avei'a* by the Tahitians (Ellis, W., 1831: 168), and since in Tahitian 'k' and 'ng' are replaced by ', this is analogous to the *kaveinga* of the Tongans and the *kavenga* of Tikopia, which latter island is two and a half thousand miles westward from Tahiti. Writing of Tikopian voyaging, Firth (1954: 91) explains that 'the major navigational guide is the Star-path, the "Carrier" (*Kavenga*). This is a succession of stars towards which the bow of the canoe is pointed. Each is used as a guide when it is low in the heaven; as it rises up overhead it is discarded and the course is reset by the next one in the series. One after another these stars rise till dawn . . .'.

Among the examples of star path steering that follow will be some from the Caroline Islands. Here the slightly more sophisticated concept of the sidereal 'compass' is used, in which stars indicate points or positions around the horizon as well as the bearings of islands. However, the steering procedure is exactly the same as when using the guiding star of an island, since it equally involves following a succession of stars rising from or sinking to the same point.

A legitimate question is how far do present-day star steering practices reflect the past. That they do is suggested by the most detailed of the early accounts, that of Andia y Varela who was in Tahiti in 1774.

When the night is a clear one they steer by the stars; and this is the easiest navigation for them because these being many [in number], not only do they note by them the bearings on which the several islands with which they are in touch lie, but also the harbours in them, so that they make straight for the entrance by following the rhumb of the particular star that rises or sets over it; and they hit it off with as much precision as the most expert navigator of civilised nations could achieve (Corney, 1914: vol. II, 286).

SANTA CRUZ REEF ISLANDS

Our first experience of steering by stars under command of an experienced Islander (Tevake) was on this *Reef Islands to Taumako* passage to a destination some 60 miles to the east-north-east. The course to the main island of Taumako was about 72°, but the navigator Tevake headed a little south of it lest we strike it only too accurately—in the darkness before dawn.[1]

We left for Taumako in the late afternoon. After nightfall Tevake directed the helmsman to steer by Betelgeuse (*Trekapekau ki Taumako*) rising ahead on a bearing of about 83°.[2] An hour and a half after sunset found us still steering by Betelgeuse and by keeping the newly risen Pleiades (*Fetu Mataro*) fine on the port bow. By about 20.00 two pairs of stars had come up, one pair on each side of Betelgeuse, and we were steering halfway between them. The northern pair were Castor and Pollux bearing about 60°-65°; the southern pair consisted of Procyon, which bore around 80°-85°, and a star I could not identify. (The pairs are both named *Taulua*, meaning 'two stars'.)

We were still heading between these pairs an hour later when a small constellation appeared between them called *Te Paikea*, the Crab, of which I do not know the European name, and we steered on that. By midnight, however,

---

[1] Since I had not consulted a chart prior to sailing with the navigators, nor had access to a compass until we had left their islands, distances and bearings between islands had to be measured later. The bearings given for horizon stars are approximate, but for the rather different reason that they varied according to the height at which the stars were actually observed. All times are estimates, since we had no clocks. My limited knowledge of astronomy is reflected in the designation 'unidentified', by which I mean that I was unable to identify a star by its European name. When the term 'unnamed star' is used, it implies that the Islanders either had no name for it or were ignorant of the name.

[2] Sirius (*Sino*) was also, Tevake remarked, a guide star for Taumako. How could this be so, I asked, sorely puzzled, since Sirius rises about 107°? How could two stars 24° apart both guide towards Taumako? You steer by Sirius, Tevake amplified, only when the wind is in the south, for then your canoe is close-hauled on the starboard tack (i.e. with the wind coming from the right, or starboard), when leeway plus wind drift of the surface water set it so sharply off course—he made a skidding gesture—that to compensate you must make this (24°) alteration of course to the southward.

Similar alternative star courses to allow for leeway are mentioned elsewhere. For instance, according to Ve'etutu Pahulu, the star course from Nomuka to Tongatapu, the main island of Tonga, is the equivalent of south-south-east with a free wind. If the wind backs from north-east to east, so that the vessel is close-hauled on the port tack, the star course is altered to the position where Antares rises, or south-east so allowing some 22° to counteract leeway.

the Crab had risen and moved away to the left and we were aiming at a small unnamed star that had come up over the horizon at the point where the Crab had risen earlier, a good way to the right of its present position.

We followed a succession of similar stars until 02.30 when Arcturus (*Tavau*) rose ahead on a bearing of 70°. This, like Betelgeuse, said Tevake, was a major identifying guide star for Taumako. By this time his nephews were searching the horizon fine on the port bow and it was on this bearing that the smudged outline of the island soon became visible.

This was a 100-mile passage with the island of Utupua lying in wait 60 miles *en route,* its 2-mile-wide fringing reef constituting a hazard that could claim a ship long before the island itself was sighted in the darkness.

Reef Islands to Vanikoro

The course, which was designed to make a cautious landfall on Utupua before rounding its western side, was 160°, and the major guide stars were two in number. First there was Canopus (*Trekapekau ki Ndeni*) which bore about 145° after rising, and continued to arch over towards the right until it set around 04.00 at 217°. The second guide was the position of the rising Southern Cross (*Kauvakorna*), about 160°. This position was only clearly defined around 23.00 when the constellation rose on its side; thereafter it was an imaginary horizon point whose position could be estimated only by the changing height and angle of the Southern Cross, which by the time it was upright had moved 20° to the right.

Since both 'stars' had big declinations, neither climbed too high to preclude using them, and Tevake continued to steer by them until Utupua was sighted about 03.00. It will be readily appreciated that neither guide star was easy to steer by, since in both cases knowledge of its bearing on rising had to be supplemented by an accurate estimate of its progress towards the right as the hours went by.

But, as if this were not difficult enough, there was an added complication in that the navigator deduced by the shape of the waves that a strong current had set in and was running to the eastward of north. He therefore altered course 1½-2 points (17°-22½°) to the right of the proper star course. That he was successful in maintaining this course of somewhere between 175°-180° with the sole aid of the mobile Canopus was proved when the Southern Cross topped the horizon at the correct position on the port bow an hour before midnight. That he was also correct in his deduction about the current was confirmed by Utupua duly appearing ahead as forecast, for had he been mistaken we should not have seen it at all, or else met its reef prematurely (see discussion of currents, chap. 4).

CAROLINES-SAIPAN VOYAGES

Several aspects of star path steering were illustrated in our passages without instruments under the Carolinian (Puluwat) navigator Hipour.

Puluwat to Saipan   The route we should follow, Hipour told me, would be via Pikelot, an uninhabited islet 500 yards long, 100 miles west-north-west of Puluwat. We would first head for the southern margin of a deep reef on the near side of the islet (Condor Reef, extending some 15 miles east from Pikelot at a depth of 13-25 fathoms). After identifying this reef we would alter to a more westerly course.

The first night, Hipour directed us to steer towards the setting Pleiades, though the constellation was still very high, something like 45° above the horizon.[3] By about 22.00 the constellation was setting, but as it was as often as not obscured by columns of cloud we maintained our heading in the main by using stars to one side with reference to parts of the rigging. Thus the rising Great Bear (*Daane Wole*) was kept in line with the main brace on the starboard beam and Capella further forward behind the starboard shrouds. Half an hour later Hipour was telling the helmsman to keep the Pole Star (*Fii He Magid*) towards the front of the wheelhouse doorway as seen from his position at the wheel (about 20° before the beam) and the sinking Pollux fine on the starboard bow (see fig. 1).

---

[3] See discussion on the optimum altitude of steering stars, p. 56.

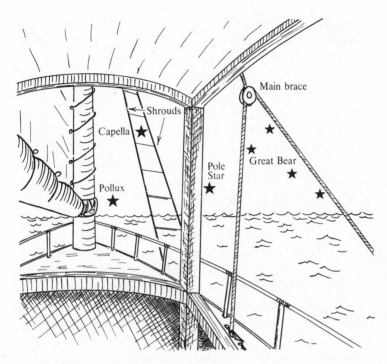

Fig. 1 Steering stars from Puluwat to Pikelot (from a sketch by the author)

Pollux set around one or two in the morning about 298°. Hipour described it (correctly) as setting on roughly the same bearing as the Pleiades and therefore being another guide star for Pikelot. He did not know its name. For the rest of the night we continued steering by Polaris 20° before the beam.

The sun and the swells enabled us to keep on course after daybreak and we continued in the same direction until a sudden alteration in the colour of the water announced that we were over the edge of Condor Reef, when we duly altered course towards the west. An hour later Pikelot hove in view.

This 100-mile passage to a tiny islet is commonly held to be so navigationally straightforward on account of this deep reef 'screen' that parties frequently set out towards Pikelot from Puluwat on the spur of the moment and when drunk on palm toddy. They always arrive (Gladwin, 1970: 43).

We set out for Saipan towards evening. At that time I knew Saipan's distance and bearing from Pikelot only very approximately, though I have since ascertained that

they are 450 miles and 344° respectively. Hipour correctly
indicated in which direction Saipan lay, a shade left of
the setting Little Bear (*Doloni Mailöb Bälefang*) or
about 345°, and said the passage in good weather with
fair winds used to take a canoe six or seven days, in
contrary winds up to twenty days. No canoe would
deliberately put to sea in such weather as we were
having, he said pointedly. He was not sure what *Isbjorn's*
speed would be since he was totally unused to such
vessels, but he expected we would arrive at a position
to windward of the Marianas island 'screen' in something like five days. The course, allowing for the constant west-going current that the traditional sailing
directions led him to anticipate, was towards the Pole
Star or due north. It was the practice, however, for canoes
setting out for Saipan in strong north-east winds such as
this, to head further east than the Pole Star to make up for
leeway. We would therefore steer for the rising Little Bear
(*Daane Mailöb Bälefang*) or 10°, for something like 100
miles, and then if the weather permitted alter to due north.

We duly followed this plan, or more precisely, since the
northern sky was obscured after sunset, we steered by
keeping Regulus (*Liligut*) before the beam to starboard,
since the star was rising at 80°. Only momentary glimpses
of the stars were available that night and the next day,
but each time a heavenly body did appear the helmsman
under Hipour's and Ulutak's guidance was found to be
maintaining an accurate course.

This brought home to me the importance of a navigator being able to know the whole sky so well that one
glimpse of a single star or constellation sufficed to give
him his bearings.

Thirty hours and about 100 miles from Pikelot, Hipour
duly altered course to north, but a day and a half later he
returned to the original track of 10° east of north and
continued to maintain a heading of somewhere between
5° and 10° until he judged Saipan to be nearly abeam.
This reversion was in consequence of renewed heavy
squalls and steep eleven-foot seas with breaking crests.
Strong winds generate strong currents and also increase
leeway, Hipour stated, demonstrating the angle between

the ship's course and her wake (the angle of leeway) by laying pencils on the chart table. It was customary in the Carolines, he said, to concentrate course adjustments for drift in the early part of a voyage as we had done over the first 100 miles, but in this weather we should be prudent if we resumed our more easterly heading to be sure of keeping to windward of our objective.

Four and a half days from Pikelot, after a night hove-to to avoid overrunning our goal, Hipour altered course again, but this time sharply westward towards the setting position of the Great Bear (*Doloni Wole*, 335°-340°), that we might cut the Marianas chain obliquely. Land was sighted the same evening.

We would sail south-east initially, towards rising Shaula, λ Scorpio (*Daane Mhäru*), about 127°, to compensate for the major part of current set and leeway in the first day or so. (The geographical course was 164°.) Hipour would later determine—depending on his estimates of current set, leeway, and distance made good in accordance with his mental image of islands 'moving' from 'under' one star point to another (see chap. 5)—when the time had come to change to a more southerly course.

Saipan Return to Puluwat (again via Pikelot)

In the event we made this alteration to the rising Southern Cross position (*Daanup*) or about 160° after 29 hours. I would estimate that from the place where we altered course the new track must still have been something like 10° to windward of the direct line, so that not all the compensation was made initially. Another example of this Carolinian practice of cramming compensatory course corrections into the first part of a passage is the former voyage from Truk to Ponape. Nowadays canoes sail no further than the 135 miles from Puluwat to Truk. The last canoe voyage to Ponape of which I have record took place about 1915, though it seems likely that others have occurred since.

Early in the first world war [writes Goodenough], the German governor of Truk in the Caroline Islands found himself unable to communicate with his superiors, all German shipping in the area having stopped. It happened that a canoe from Puluwat, ninety miles [sic] to the west, stopped in on a trading trip. At his interpreter's suggestion, the governor asked its navigator if he could get to headquarters on Ponape, 300 miles to the east. The navigator said he had never been there but was confident he could manage it. Not many days later he was back with replies to the governor's letters. The governor could well marvel that a simple loincloth-clad native could so confidently sail to a strange place without compass or chart and make the requisite landfall with pinpoint precision, . . . (1951: 105).

There were two routes from Truk to Ponape, Hipour told me, one via Lukunor in the Mortlocks and the other via Oroluk. The prevailing winds at present (early April) would favour the latter. Departure was taken from certain hills on islands in Truk lagoon, and you laid course towards where γ Aquillae rose (*Daane Baiifang*, 85°). Some time after you deemed to have passed an *etak* (reference) reef called Tuinmer (Minto Reef) lying far away to the north, you altered course towards the point where Aldebaran rises (*Daan Uun*, 75°). Precisely when you changed course depended on the state of the sea and the wind and your estimate of the distance covered. (The distance from Truk to Oroluk is 185 miles.)

The course for the remaining 145 miles from Oroluk to Ponape that Hipour gave me was towards Orion's Belt (*Daane Elüüel*) which bears 90°. This is a little too far north, presumably to allow for leeway from the prevailing north-east wind.

Use of Stars at an Angle to the Course   The voyage from Saipan back to Pikelot provided a very good example of using stars astern and at various angles to the actual course. Most of the time our heading was towards the rising Southern Cross, or about 160°. After dark, with the Southern Cross not yet risen, we kept Venus, whose bearing Hipour had checked at sunset and found to be west, abaft the beam to starboard, and the rising Saturn nearly reciprocal to Venus, before the beam to port. When the Southern Cross did rise about 20.30 the forestay exactly bisected it, proving that we were steering accurately. As the Cross rose towards an angle of 45°, it moved 10° or so to the right to become hidden behind the

Fig. 2 Steering by keeping the rising Southern Cross behind the headsail and Antares rising along the line of the shrouds (from a sketch by the author)

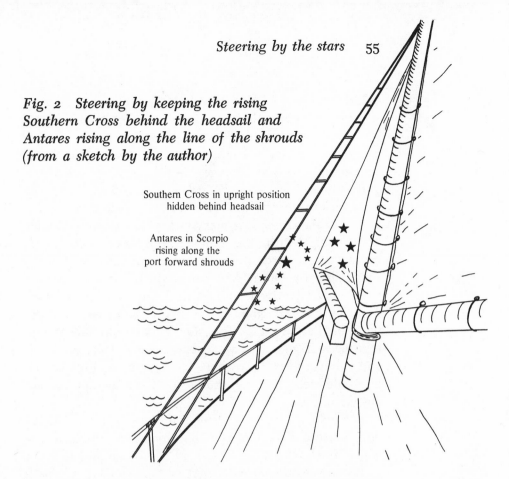

Southern Cross in upright position hidden behind headsail

Antares in Scorpio rising along the port forward shrouds

jib. Saturn by then was too high to use and Venus had set, so we held the Pole Star 20°-25° east of the stern and kept the Southern Cross tucked out of sight behind the sail in front.

Antares rose about an hour before midnight in line with the port forward shrouds. We were on the port tack, i.e. the wind was from the port side so the ship was heeled over to starboard. By coincidence the slope of the rigging on this tack matched the track of the star as it climbed obliquely up to the right, so that we were able to steer by it for hours (see fig. 2).

About two in the morning Altair (*Daane Mailöb*) emerged from a cloud bank low in the east on a bearing of 81°, and by this time the Southern Cross, tilting westward as it sank, had emerged from behind the sail on the starboard bow. We continued using Altair and the Cross, with appropriate adjustment for the latter's motion, until shortly before dawn, when Saturn sinking in the west provided an additional indicator.

In the Gilbert Islands the navigator Teeta replied to my question as to whether one always steered by the star in front by explaining that, 'we may use one to the side or astern for steering because from it we can tell the direction equally well as from one in front'.

Rafe made his 110-mile passage from Tikopia to the Banks Islands in the New Hebrides in a 27-foot mat-sailed canoe. He and his four companions left at midnight for reasons of stealth, the canoe having been stolen. The course was towards the south-west, but they guided the canoe first by Orion (*Arotoru*) which was sinking due west, and later by keeping the Southern Cross (*Rakau Tapu* or *Rua Tangata*) about south-south-east, over the point of the outrigger. The blind 83-year-old Vili Mailau told me in Tonga, that when guiding stars were obscured and only very big 'stars' shone through (including planets) he would steer by a big 'star' keeping it at an appropriate angle.

Not only is the practice of star steering often carried out by using stars abeam, behind or at any angle to the actual track, either in default of a suitable star in front or because clouds obscure part of the sky, but star path sailing directions may be couched in similar terms. For instance Tevake gave the course from Taumako to Vanikoro as 'Canopus and the Southern Cross, not ahead but on the port bow'. If such directions seem impossibly vague, it should be realised that they are taught by demonstration, the named star being pointed out together with whichever unnamed star should indicate the actual course; or else the angle between a named identifying star and the track to be followed being demonstrated by pebbles (Hipour), sticks or lines in the sand (Teeta).

Optimum Height of Steering Stars   Hipour's use of the Pleiades as a steering 'star' when still a full 45° above the horizon was exceptional and only possible because it was a nearly 'east-west' constellation that was sinking almost vertically. Horizon stars are generally used lower than this. In Tonga, Tuita practice was to 'steer by a star until it has reached a height the same as the sun has at 10 a.m. (*fangailupe hopo 'a e la 'a*), then leave that star and use a lower one on the same bearing' (Kaho). The Gilbertese navigator Teeta repeated to me his grandfather's instructions. 'A steering star has properly the bearing of an island at a slight but definite altitude, which is opposite the first or second beam of the meeting house (*maneaba*). The star at this slight height (of about 15°) marks the correct bearing of the island. When it rises or sinks too far another on the same bearing is used.' Teeta, like all older Gilbertese navigators, had been instructed in the *maneaba* whose beams and rafters were taken as representing the divisions of the night sky (Grimble, 1931: 197).[4]

Enough examples of star steering practice have been given, I think, to indicate that one must be careful not to equate the star course with the precise bearing of a star at the moment of its rise or set. The horizon rim in the Pacific is frequently obscured by cloud, so the guiding star is generally used anywhere from a little above the horizon up to the customary maximum, and therefore its precise azimuth when being steered by cannot readily be translated into an exact number of degrees. All azimuths of steering stars given in this book, therefore, should be as read as approximations only.

A single named star is commonly used to denote or identify a star course though, of course, it no more comprises the sum of sailing directions between two islands than would a simple compass bearing exhaust them in a European pilot book. Neither is it necessary to know the name of each unit of a star path, and in this respect the star path (*kavenga*) from Tikopia to Anuta, in which Firth (1954: 91) was told that the nine component stars were all named, is possibly exceptional. There has no doubt been some loss of star data since Firth's visit, so there could be an element of rationalisation in the insistence of all my Tikopian informants at Nukufera, one of whom had sailed this same voyage, that you did

Star Courses Identified by a Key Star

---

[4] Teeta was speaking through an interpreter. If he was referring to the roof-plate of the *maneaba* as the first beam, the height he was indicating could be the *nikaveve* (sacred enclosure) of the first beam above. This was a significant altitude in Gilbertese astronomy, since the appearance of the Pleiades here signalled the beginning of the year. Grimble takes it to be about 15° (1931: 193, 198, 200).

not learn the names of all the stars of a *kavenga*, only one or two key ones. Nevertheless the use of 'name' stars to represent star paths is widespread.

The Tongan practice was outlined by the 88-year-old Fe'iloakitau Kaho, the senior surviving Tuita.

'The new stars of the *kaveinga* in one line take their name from the star you first navigated by. The new star is called by the same name as the first although it is a completely different star.'

In the Carolines a question about a star course was usually answered with the name of a single star point. Further questioning elicited detailed sailing instructions about reference islands, currents and the best time of the year for the passage.

This convention in the naming or identifying of star courses has sometimes confused European investigators. Akerblom (1968: 117), for example, comments on Erdland's Marshallese star courses (1914: 80, 81): 'The information is incomplete, in so far as only one star has been allotted for each voyage'. Again, Akerblom (pp. 26-7) has doubts of the star courses to Samoa and Niue collected by the Beagleholes on Pukapuka (1938: 351-3), because 'the navigators were guided by only one star. This could only be used when it was low on the horizon, in other words for about one hour. How were they able to steer their course during the remaining 23 hours?' Leaving aside the problem of maintaining direction in daytime, which we will come to later, this formulation suggests failure to grasp the distinction between *naming* a star course and the procedure used in sailing it. In fact, as far as direction is concerned, if you are told to steer towards the setting Antares, the information has the same significance as telling a European navigator to steer 244° True. In the first case a series of suitable stars are chosen as they are needed, in the second the course is corrected to magnetic and aligned on the steering compass.

Star Courses and Allowance for Current   An important question is whether or not star courses should be assumed to allow for set and leeway.

Beiong in the Carolines told me that the course from

the Mortlocks to Pulusuk was 'actually towards the setting Pleiades position', about west-north-west. When I
asked him what he meant by 'actually', he explained that
you must sail a little north of this star point to counteract
southerly drift due to the prevailing wind and current
conditions. In other words, the course he had given me
was a geographical one that did not allow for current.

The Pukapuka-Niue sailing directions (Beaglehole, E.
and P., 1938) that we mentioned earlier, are discussed by
Akerblom (1968: 26) from this point of view also. He
writes that: 'if one plots the course steered on a chart one
comes so near to one's destination that the necessary
allowance for current simply cannot have been made'. It
is clear that in this instance, like the one above, the star
point identifying the course does not allow for west-going
current. Additional data, including that on currents trans-
verse to the track, would have been embodied in the
customary pilotage information, and this could not be
expected to survive in much detail after voyaging had
been discontinued.

An example of this dropping of detail in orally transmitted lore is the star course for the 465-mile voyage from
Pulusuk to Kapingamarangi, a navigationally hazardous
journey to an isolated landfall, but one which Krämer
(1935: 103) and Eilers (1934: 131), assure us was frequently sailed. Asarto, a navigator and the oldest man on
Pulusuk, gave Lykke (pers. comm., 1969) a course to
Kapingamarangi that was approximately correct—towards
the rising *Shaula* (λ Scorpio), or about 127°, and Gladwin
(1970: 157) was told the same course by one of his informants. But the necessary data about currents appears to
have been forgotten and the information that was added
about the reference (*etak*) island was a little equivocal.
However, if one adds to the bare statement of direction
given by Asarto, Beiong's point about southerly drift being
experienced on the relatively nearby Mortlocks passage,
or for that matter the current data on Admiralty Chart
781, this star course is seen to be a practical guide that if
followed would lead to the island. This is a case, then, of
a star course that *does* take currents into account.

Do star courses usually denote the geographically

direct route to an objective as in the Mortlocks and
Pukapuka examples, or is the more general practice to
indicate the course actually steered (Kapingamarangi)?
I think it must be fairly obvious that either method could
be followed (Gladwin, 1970: 161). When Hipour was
describing the route from Pikelot to Saipan, he indicated
first the direction in which Saipan lay, which was north-
by-west, then what we might call the course with
standard current allowance, due north, and lastly he laid
down the initial heading to be followed for a variable
time depending on leeway producing conditions, and this
was to the east of north. It will be recalled that Tevake
gave two distinct courses between the Reef Islands and
Taumako depending on whether the canoe was close-
hauled or running free, and Ve'etutu did the same in
Tonga. In the latter case there was no attempt to indicate
the geographical star bearing of Tongatapu from Nomuka
at all; only the courses to be steered were mentioned.

Abera of Nikunau in the Gilberts gave me a star
course which allowed for current set as the standard one
from Beru to Nikunau. (There was also another course
10° more southerly for when the north-going current was
strong.) On the other hand, Teeta of Kuria, also in the
Gilberts, listed for me a number of traditional star
courses, most of which he had himself sailed without
instruments, that were almost invariably geographically
direct and made no allowance for winds or set.

In other words we are dealing here with the practical
sea lore of mariners whose lives have been staked on its
accuracy. The wealth of detail that must needs amplify
any cursory statement of the bearing of an island will be
expressed in whatever form is most convenient for the
navigator to learn, the particular terms customary to his
teacher or those most suitable for describing any particular voyage. There can be no set rules for presentation of
data as in a European textbook. When a particular canoe
voyage was abandoned, so that the route became of no
more interest than the mumbling reminiscences of the old
men who had once traversed it, chance alone would
determine what version or fragment of the original complex sailing directions was retained.

The courses we have considered are usable only at particular seasons. Six months earlier or later all the stars composing them would be above the horizon only in daylight and a different set would be standing in the night sky. Tevake told me that the sailing season in the Santa Cruz group lasted all year round and that there were appropriate steering stars for each time of year. Similarly when Ve'etutu indicated the stars for the Nomuka-Tongatapu passage, he stressed that the ones he was showing me were usable only up to about September, after which new stars and sailings directions had to be used.

It follows that unless one stays at an island a full twelve months, it is impossible to have all the known star paths pointed out—and pointed out in the night sky the stars must be, if confusion is to be avoided. For this reason our data, especially from Tonga, Santa Cruz, and Ninigo, where voyaging continues through the year, are incomplete. In the Carolines and the Gilberts voyaging is in the main seasonal, generally from about March or April to September (Gladwin, 1970: 43; Grimble, 1931: 201, 202n.), so that the 'voyaging skies' were visible during our visits between the beginning of March to the end of May. Apart from inopportune massing of clouds, the other hindrance to the collection of star courses was the inability of elderly navigators to remain awake as the night advanced.

Seasonal Character of Star Courses

I discussed with Tevake, Hipour, Abera, Kienga, and Rafe the question of whether there was a standard time of the day or night for setting out on voyages. Everyone agreed that there was no fixed setting off time that applied to all voyages. Of course if very accurate back bearings were needed, unless the labour of lighting fires was undertaken, departure had to be in daylight. Apart from this, the hour of departure depended more than anything else on timing a voyage so as to make a daylight landfall.[5] Thus there was usually a customary time which

Customary Time of Departure

---

[5] 'Canoes may leave at any time of the day, or even at night, but most depart during the morning or at midday. This is especially true for those leaving on long voyages. The morning is not only available for the preparation of fresh food, but everyone has ample opportunity to learn of the departure and join in the farewells' (Gladwin, 1970: 51).

might be in the day or the night for beginning any particular journey.

THE SIDEREAL COMPASS (Carolines)

The Carolinian archipelago stretches 1800 miles east-west along a mean axis of 8°N. The Central Carolines language area occupies a good part of it. Here (and in Yap) has been developed an abstract system of orientation by the horizon points where chosen stars rise and set. This is spoken of as a 'star or sidereal compass' because

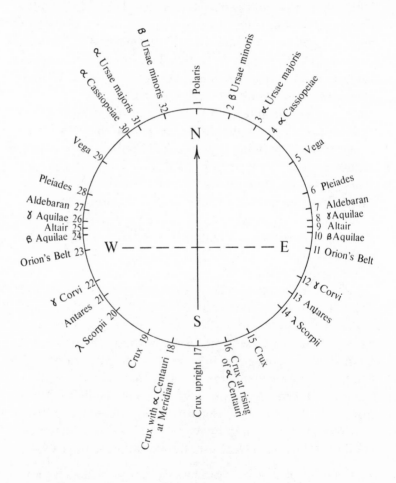

*Fig. 3   Carolinian star compass
(adapted from Goodenough, 1953)*

these star positions are in some respects comparable to the points of a mariner's compass (Goodenough, 1953: 2, 7).[6]

In most of the islands thirty-two points are named, though extra gradations seem to have been added to the standard compass in Sonsorol, Pulo Anna, and Merir (Goodenough, 1953: 5). This figure thirty-two has no connection with the thirty-two points marked on the card of a mariner's compass, for the star compass ante-dates the magnetic instrument in the Carolines and is not derived from it (Gladwin, 1970: 148). The apparent coincidence is explained when it is remembered that any symmetrical system of subdividing the horizon beyond the four cardinal points must progress through eight, then sixteen, then thirty-two. Thirty-two points was, incident-ally, the number into which the Cook Islanders divided the horizon in their so-called 'wind-compass' (Gill, 1876b: 320). The Tahitian 'sun-wind compass' had sixteen (Corney, 1913: 284).

We have seen that the bearings of stars at rise and set are symmetrical, so that if one rises, like Capella or Deneb, at 45° (north-east), it will set exactly at 315° (north-west). It follows that most of the stars incor-porated in the 'compass' will indicate two positions, at rise and at set. The exception is the Pole Star, known to the Carolinians as 'the Star that does not move'. Circum-polar 'stars' (constellations) like the Little Bear, Great Bear, and Cassiopeia, if observed from higher latitudes, would be seen to circle about Polaris without quite setting. Seen from the Carolines/Marianas, however, their pathways slant at a good angle but they do rise and set.

The stars making up the compass are often of quite small magnitude. Goodenough (1953: 3), writes: 'Position, rather than magnitude alone, is important in determining

---

[6] I have quoted extensively from Goodenough's work on Carolinian astronomy (1953). I carried a copy of the diagram a modified version of which is reproduced here (see fig. 3) to which I added the Puluwatan names for the star points, during voyages with Hipour, and it proved an invaluable aid to communication. Gladwin (1970: 147-55) gives a des-cription of the sidereal compass as used on Puluwat. Alkire deals in detail with the star compass, orientation and distance estimation systems and the training of navigators on the island of Woleai, which is in the same culture group as Puluwat (1970: 41-7).

which stars are named and which not', a feature of native astronomy also noted for the Marshall Islands by Erdland (1914: 78): 'It is surprising that many stars of first magnitude, such as Sirius and Rigel, have no name, whereas many of the constellations given names by the native navigators are composed of stars of from fourth to fifth magnitude.'

Of course the compass stars will not all be visible at the same time, and the times at which they rise and set will vary, so that at any given moment there will be a number scattered about the night sky. Their function is to indicate points around the horizon's rim, and these points remain fixed irrespective of whether the stars marking them are currently in the appropriate position or not visible at all.

It is not proposed to name and describe the individual star points, as these can be seen readily enough from Goodenough's amended diagram (fig. 3). We will go on to discuss certain features of the system.

The cardinal compass point and basis of the Carolinian navigational system is the position where Altair rises in the eastward. The 'remaining positions are usually listed from Altair north and then from Altair south, first in the east and then in the west' (Goodenough, 1953: 5). Altair has a declination of 8·5°N., so that it rises almost vertically and passes through or very near the zenith of the Carolines, which are strung out either side of the eighth parallel of latitude. But this declination of 8·5°N. means that Altair rises and sets this number of degrees north of the true east-west line, that is it rises at 81·5° and sets at 278·5°. True east and west would be indicated by one of the stars of Orion's Belt, Alnilam, with the declination of 1°S., coming very near it (see Appendix I).

Both Goodenough (1953: 5) and Gladwin (1970: 154) write of Altair bearings as being 'east' and 'west', and the discrepancy is immaterial to the Carolinian navigator because he knows the bearings of islands in star compass terms and is perfectly well aware at what precise points on the horizon Altair and the rest rise and set. If an island has a bearing of 81·5° from the navigator, he will describe it as being 'under the Big Bird', the rising Altair. No confusion therefore will arise between the European east which is 90° and the Carolinian cardinal bearing which is 81·5° so long as canoe navigators continue to sail star courses worked out by their forebears exclusively in terms of their own system. The discrepancy can, however, cause complications when a Carolinian navigator tries to compare his star bearings with European ones, or when a traditional star course is plotted on a European chart. We will return later to the significance of this fact in maintaining the integrity of the Carolinian conceptual system.

The north-south axis, the arc that divides the eastern from the western halves of the sky, is, unlike the east-west one, the same in both European and Carolinian systems. In the latter it is taken to be from the Pole Star to the point on the horizon directly below the Southern Cross in its upright position.

The Carolines being near the equator, the paths of the equatorially orientated stars are almost vertical. This makes for convenience in star steering but it is by no means essential to it. We have already seen examples from a higher latitude (11°S.) of steering north-north-west/east-south-east courses between the Reef Islands and Vanikoro by guide stars with markedly inclined tracks. In any case the paths of the northerly and southerly stars of the Carolinian sidereal compass slant too.

Gladwin (1970: 150-1) has drawn attention to the fact that the more northerly points of the Carolinian compass are marked by constellations rather than by individual stars (Little Bear, Great Bear, and Cassiopeia), and that no less than five southerly directions are indicated by the various positions of a single constellation, the Southern Cross (fig. 4). He adds that at least four of the positions will always be vacant since the constellation cannot be in two places at once. Drawing on his own experience at sea in Hipour's canoe, he concludes that in both northerly and southerly courses 'the configuration of the stars is sufficiently distinctive that one can estimate a course with considerable ease and accuracy' (pp. 152-3). This seems to be the correct interpretation of steering by large constellations and was borne out by the experience of our

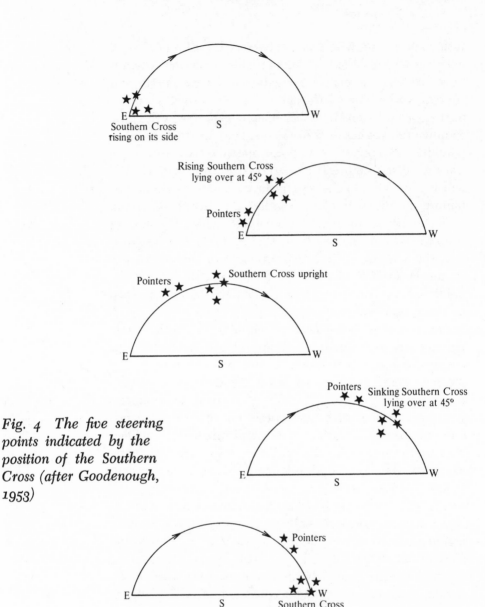

Southern Cross
rising on its side

Rising Southern Cross
lying over at 45°

Pointers

Pointers

Southern Cross upright

Pointers   Sinking Southern Cross
lying over at 45°

Fig. 4   The five steering points indicated by the position of the Southern Cross (after Goodenough, 1953)

Pointers

Southern Cross
setting on its side

long north-south passages when Hipour was always aware of the precise horizon position of his star points—even when only one heavenly body was available for orientation. The extraordinary precision of his landfall on Pikelot 450 miles south of Saipan, to be mentioned later, is a tribute not only to Hipour's proficiency but to the inherent validity of the system he was using.

A glance at Goodenough's compass diagram will reveal one very important feature—that the gaps between adjacent star points are far from being uniform. In easterly and westerly directions the points are crowded together, while further north and south they are spread widely apart. There could be several possible explanations for this bunching together of closely grouped star points around the east-west axis. Gladwin (1970: 154) concludes that 'it reflects the greater demands for accuracy that are placed on the navigation system as a whole by longer east-west passages'. However, the degree of accuracy required for the longest unbroken regular voyages made by the Carolinians, which were in fact those to and from Saipan, and Hipour's demonstration of how this precision could be attained in practice, throws some doubt, to my mind, on this explanation. A simpler one would be that the east-west stars are much the easiest to use, and pragmatic navigator-astronomers might be expected to take advantage of this fact.

Carolinian representation of the star compass may take the form either of a square or a circle (Goodenough, 1953: 5). In the earliest recorded description, Sanchez's informant insisted it be drawn in the shape of a rather irregular rectangle (Sanchez, 1866: 263-4). But the shape of the diagram is navigationally immaterial.[7] (See fig. 5.)

For a star compass to be a practical guide for navigators, the islands that lie along each particular axis must be known, their bearings and in fact all sailing directions being given in terms of the compass star points. Eiler's diagram reproduced in fig. 5 is, as Akerblom (1968: 107) justly remarks, 'merely an ethnographical reconstruction designed to explain the principle of navigation'. It is not a chart, an artifact that the Carolinians did not possess. All its information (and much more, for it shows approximate bearings only) would be carried in the navigator's head. It will be seen that the island of Tobi, for instance,

---

[7] Alkire describes the first step in training navigators as the laying down of small stones to represent the stars of the compass and states that these are always placed in the form of a rectangle (1970: 41). In a footnote to the same page, he adds: 'In part they justify this by saying it is a mnemonic device as the "corners" of the figure provide a ready reference system'.

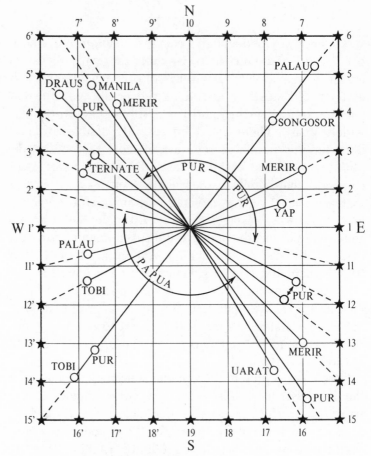

Fig. 5 Carolinian sidereal compass, customary rectangular presentation (after Eilers, 1935)

occurs twice in the lower left hand corner of the diagram, on the lines 15-6 and 12-3. In the former instance the courses to Pur, Songosor (Sonsorol), and Palau are all seen to be approximately north-west towards a star position that is presumably that of the rising Vega. In the latter, the course from Tobi to Merir is indicated as being roughly towards the rising Pleiades.[8]

---

[8] One of the most detailed stages in a navigator's training, writes Alkire, 'is the recitation of the location of islands correlated with star courses' (1970: 45). His own navigator-informants had in fact learned the courses radiating from eighteen islands, which amounted to some 270 separate items of information in this particular field of study alone (pp. 46, 47). Among further steps was the learning of 'islands and navigational reference points lying in a straight line beneath particular stars' (p. 49).

Alkire does speak of a Woleai diagram, very similar to the one from Pulo Anna reproduced here, as being an 'Island Chart' (1970: 45). I personally think this term confusing because the Carolinian concept is more of a plotting diagram in which the navigator always imagines himself at the centre.

We have already noted that if the sidereal compass is to be of practical value, the bearings of the islands to be visited must be known and incorporated in the system. We have also seen that the techniques are identical for sailing the star path of an island or a horizon compass star point that coincides with an island's bearing. The question arises, therefore, as to the advantage of having a sidereal compass at all.

Goodenough (1953: 3) states that the stars and constellations with specific names that go to make up the compass, including alternative stars for a good many positions, 'do not seem to exceed thirty or forty in number'. But by referring to no more than the thirty-two points that these stars denote it is possible to indicate the direction of an infinite number of islands. In other words the sidereal compass and related systems that will be considered below are flexible concepts that allow for the mental recording of a great deal of information in an easily applicable form. Nevertheless, the volume of information a navigator still has to memorise is formidable. For instance, Goodenough (1953: 7) quotes Damm and Sarfert (1935) as obtaining 'from a navigator on Puluwat a list covering several pages of fine print giving sailing directions in terms of his compass from every known place to every other known place. He gives each course both directly and with respect to a third island or reef to provide another point of reference . . .'.

The foregoing exposition of the characteristics of the sidereal compass leads us to the important question of the degree and nature of interaction between the Carolinian and European systems; the extent to which one could modify the other. Certainly ample opportunities have existed for 'borrowing' from Europeans. How is it then that this indigenous concept has continued in existence at all? This is a question that has implications for the whole field of prehistoric navigation.

It is submitted that the Carolinian sidereal compass persists in its apparently unaltered form to this day primarily because in three important respects it is incompatible with the mariner's compass. In the first place the star compass points are irregularly distributed around the horizon, secondly the east-west line is 8½° out, and thirdly sidereal compass bearings are true and not magnetic. Any one of these inconsistencies, except perhaps the first, could be compensated for by a correction, but taken together they place an insuperable barrier in the way of integrating the opposing systems.[9]

What is happening today on islands like Puluwat is instructive, for magnetic compasses are increasingly being carried on canoes but are used for secondary orientation only—in the daytime and thick weather (Gladwin, 1970: 155). In other words, the sidereal course is determined and the stars are followed, until, towards dawn or if the sky is clouding over, the magnetic instrument is taken out and compared with the star course being steered. The point on the compass rose corresponding to the star point is then followed, in preference to the more difficult practice of steering by swells, until direction can again be taken from the stars. This use of the instrument is now fairly general on Puluwat, Pulusuk, Satawal, and Pulap, though it is not universal, and I have heard navigators who indulge in it harshly criticised.

What may be expected to happen in the future? As the magnetic and sidereal systems of orientation are so nearly incompatible, and since charts and compasses are far easier to master than sea lore requiring half a lifetime of laborious study, it seems certain that the Carolinian system will ultimately disappear and be replaced by the European. The use of a magnetic compass for secondary orientation is probably about the limit of modification the Carolinian concept will stand; in default then of the possibility of incorporation, it must eventually be supplanted.

Such appears to have been the fate of the so-called 'wind compasses' in Polynesia. These will be considered below. The point I wish to make here concerns the significance of information given in terms of systems like sidereal or wind compasses, which are resistant to modification. Sailing directions and the like expressed in such indigenous terms are unlikely to have been influenced very much or at all by European concepts or knowledge.

---

[9] Alkire suggests that the circular representation favoured on Puluwat today is probably a Westernised conception (1970: 52n.).

This would apply to courses incorporating the concept of 'moving' reference (*etak*) islands, the sidereal compass itself, virtually every technique involving swell orientation, wave refraction patterns, deep phosphorescence, land loom, cloud lore, homing birds, sea marks, and zenith stars.

A related point is that the more sophisticated indigenous systems, requiring prolonged study and knowledge of astronomy and related disciplines, that functioned in intact social systems, were liable to be lost earliest. Simpler arts like star path steering, which can still be practised after the very names of the stars have been forgotten, remain extant for a much longer time.

One aspect of the Carolinian sidereal compass remains to be discussed; its validity over a range of latitude. Movement east or west will not affect its accuracy, but north or south is a different story. Not all star bearings alter to the same extent with change of latitude, however, and certain ones not at all, namely Polaris, the Southern Cross, and the east and west bearings of Orion. Apart from these, it is stars with the greatest declinations, i.e. the northerly and southerly stars, whose bearings (azimuths) vary most.

The following figures are taken from a table compiled by Frankel (1962: 42). Only northerly declinations are considered for simplicity, but southerly ones are exactly comparable.

A star of declination 75° at the equator will bear 15° at rise and 345° at set. The range of latitude over which its bearing error remains under 3° will be 9° north from the equator and 9° south from it. Stars with declinations of this order were used by Hipour for his Marianas landfall 8°30′ north of Puluwat, so this margin of error of up to 3° is clearly acceptable in practice.

The change of bearing for lower declination stars being much less, we find that a star with declination 45° does not exceed the 3° margin for 18° north and the same distance south of the equator; one with declination 30° for 23°. The 45° declination star's azimuth would be within an error margin that Carolinian navigators themselves

accept on Marianas voyages, for about as far south as the
Santa Cruz group.[10]

Even as far to the southward as Tahiti (17°S.) the
declination 30° star would not exceed the error limit by
very much. If we bear in mind too that the north-south
and east-west points do not alter at all, it can be seen that
the scope of the sidereal compass in unfamiliar latitudes
is considerable.[11]

Not only do star bearings change with latitude, but
familiar northern or southern constellations drop below
the horizon as you sail south or north. As Teeta says, 'The
sky is different from faraway places'. Fortunately the
change is gradual enough for the navigator to note the
direction of new stars in terms of familiar ones. As we
have already seen, Orion's Belt rises and sets due east
and west from wherever it is observed. The Southern
Cross remains visible over most of the Pacific voyaging
area. The same cannot be said of the Pole Star, however,
for it is lost to view soon after one crosses the equator,
though the Pointers of the Great Bear continue to indicate its position.

This is well known to the navigators. Teeta in the
Gilberts told me that the Pole Star could be seen from
Butaritari in the north of the group but not from Nonouti
(nearly 1°S.), but from there southward, the Great Bear
continued to show accurately where north lay.

Kaho, in Tonga (lat. 21°S.), very much further south,
mentioned the pointers of the Great Bear in connection
with voyaging to the Tokelaus. Nevertheless, north was
not the primary point of orientation for Tongan mariners,

---

10 7°30′N. latitude of Puluwat + 11°S. latitude of Santa Cruz =
18°30′. The axis of the Carolines is, of course, about 8°N., not the
equator.

11 A very experienced sea and air navigator sums up the practical
implications in these words: 'All the accuracy required in steering by the
stars will be obtained on *any course* between points which are between
30° North latitude and 30° South latitude' (Gatty, 1943: 119, his italics)
—in other words, all Micronesia and Polynesia except New Zealand. This
subject is dealt with in rather more mathematical detail by Dr Radhakrishnan in Appendix I. Of course, the fact that the star bearing of, for
instance, Tahiti might vary by perhaps 5° between the Carolines and
the Tahitian approaches would not incommode a navigator in the slightest
—provided his sailings directions were solely in star terms. His guide star
would occupy an intermediate position, representing the mean course,
and would lead him accurately to his objective.

who were wont to use the Magellanic Clouds for the purpose (Ve'ehala, Kaho, Ve'etutu, Kienga).

Tahiti's latitude is 17°S., 1000 miles from where the Pole Star can ever be seen, yet in a chant recited by an old woman called Rua-Nui in 1818 the Pole Star (*Ana-ni'a*) is described as being one of the 'Pillars of the Sky' (Henry, 1907: 101-4) and thus playing an important role in ancient Tahitian cosmogony, a circumstance that suggests that the range of Tahitian voyaging was once very wide (see chap. 9).

ANALOGOUS COMPASS SYSTEMS FROM POLYNESIA AND MICRONESIA

Before leaving the Carolines, it should be noted that the sidereal compass is not the only type ever to have been used there. A so-called 'wind compass' has also been reported.

Wind Compasses

In 1721 a large sailing canoe with twenty-four people on board, bound from Faraulep to Ulée (Woleai) in the Carolines, was storm-drifted to Guam in the Marianas. A Jesuit priest, Fr Cantova, who was interested in learning about their virtually unknown archipelago, spent much time with the castaways.

'I entertained such of these islanders as had more experience [than the others]', he writes, 'and, since they made use of a compass which indicated twelve wind-directions [*qui a douze aires de vent*], I learned exactly what wind-route they followed when they sailed from one island to another and how often they tacked [*ils mettent*] during their crossing[s]' (Cantova, 1728: 209-10). This tantalisingly brief account is supplemented only by Cantova's further comment on Carolinian education in which he notes that 'the only thing they learn there are some vague principles of astronomy to which most apply themselves due to its usefulness in navigation. The school-master has a globe [*une sphere*] where the principal stars are marked out, and he teaches his students the air-line [*le rumb de vent*] they should follow according to the different routes they hold to on the sea' (p. 237).

All this would seem very nebulous were it not for rather

more detailed reports of similar concepts from Polynesia. The Faraulep 'schoolteacher's globe' is reminiscent of Kaneakahoowaha's 'Instructions in Ancient Hawaiian Astronomy' as recorded by Kamakau in 1865, which begin: 'Take the lower part of a gourd or hula drum (hokeo), rounded as a wheel, on which several lines are to be marked (burned in), as described hereafter. These lines are called "Na alanui o na hoku hookele" (the highways of the Navigation stars),' . . . (Kamakau, 1891: 142).[12]

More to the point are the wind compasses that have been described from the Southern Cooks, Pukapuka, the Tokelaus, and Tahiti (see fig. 6).

Fig. 6 Cook Islands wind compass (after Gill, 1876b)

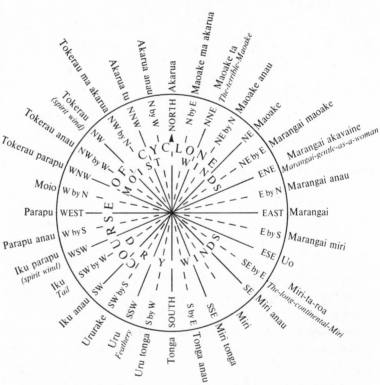

William Wyatt Gill was for many years a missionary in the Southern Cook Islands. This cluster, which was then termed the Herveys, includes Atiu, Mauke Mitiaro, and

[12] There is no reason to doubt this general tradition of Kamakau's, though certain of the lines he goes on to detail are open to suspicion of being derived from European sources. Kamakau had been a pupil at Lahainaluna High School.

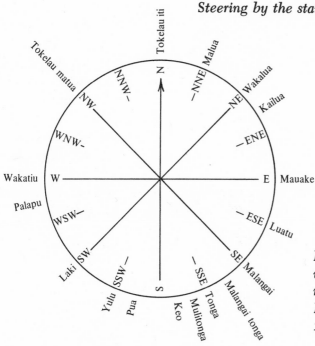

Fig. 7 Pukapukan winds and the directions named from them (after Beaglehole, E. and P., 1938)

Aitutaki. Pukapuka is isolated and only administratively part of the Cooks.

Subjoined is a plan of the winds of the Hervey Group from the lips of the ancient priests. With slight variations it will do for many other groups in the Pacific. The number of wind-holes in this plan exactly corresponds with the points of the mariner's compass. In the olden time great stress was laid on this knowledge for the purpose of fishing, and especially for their long sea voyages from group to group. At the edge of the horizon are a series of holes, some large and some small, through which *Raka*, the god of winds, and his children, love to blow . . . The vast concave above was symbolised by the interior of a calabash, in the lower part of which a series of small apertures was made to correspond with the various wind-holes at the edge of the horizon. (1876b: 319-21)

About a century after Gill was in the Cooks, the Beagleholes conducted a study of the Cook Island 'outlier' Pukapuka. The diagram they drew (see fig. 7) is not unlike Gill's, though by 1938 the names of only sixteen directions were remembered (Beaglehole, E. and P., 1938: 22).

From the Tokelau Islands comes the report that, 'The natives of the Tokelau group have the compass divided into twelve points, and have twelve names for winds from these quarters'. (Burrows, W., 1923: 147)

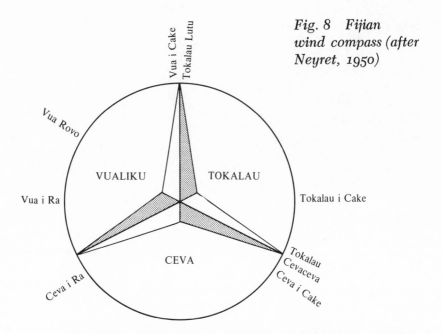

Fig. 8   Fijian wind compass (after Neyret, 1950)

Tongan influence was marked in the Lau group of Fiji. Fr Neyret's Fijian wind compass reproduced here (fig. 8) comes from this region. 'The terms', he says, 'primarily refer to the names of winds originating in the sectors and have been secondarily applied [*par extension*] to the sectors themselves' (1950: 11).

Andia y Varela, the excellence of whose descriptions we have already noted, wrote that the Tahitians 'divide the horizon into sixteen parts, taking for the cardinal points those at which the sun rises and sets'. After listing their names, he adds: 'When setting out from port the helmsman reckons the horizon thus partitioned counting from E, or the point where the sun rises' (Corney, 1914: vol. II, 284-5). The link with wind compasses is explained in a footnote to the list of direction names we have omitted. 'About half the terms here quoted are recognisable, allowing for differences in the spelling of some . . . They are the names of winds, according to the direction they blow from, and the force.' (Corney, 1914: vol. II, 285n.)

The sun orientation of this Tahitian system is further stressed by J. R. Forster's observation that the four cardinal points in Tahiti were all named after sun positions

(1778: 503). These Tahitian reports suggest the possibility that the wind compasses of the Cooks and Tokelaus
might also be based on the sun.

One might be tempted to a superficial conclusion that   *A Tongan Star*
the Carolinians were wont to orientate on the stars and   *Compass*
wind and the Polynesians on the sun and wind, were it
not for the data advanced by Kaho in Tonga. Unfortunately the Tongans have lost their names for the stars to
such an extent that Collocott (1922: 3) had to say: 'Few
if any living Tongans are able to point to and name more
than a very small proportion of the stars, and only in rare
instances have I been able to identify the stars named'.
Kaho listed for me eight stars that indicated directions
rather than the position of islands. The star paths, or
succession of steering stars, for these horizon compass
points he termed *kaveinga*, the same word that is used for
the guiding stars for islands. These 'compass' stars,
together with others that he has forgotten, had been
pointed out to him by his father, a navigator trained in
the double canoe era.

Here, then, would appear to be the remnants of a Polynesian star compass, and the fact that Kaho could not
identify the stars in the sky does not detract from this
supposition. One fact must give us pause, however; each
one of these Tongan direction-indicating stars has a different name, whereas we know that most stars will indicate two compass points, one at rise and the other at set.
These data are much too fragmentary to enable definite
conclusions to be drawn, but I find it difficult to imagine
what, other than some form of star compass, any system
of directions round the horizon indicated by stars could
be.

The only other reference from Polynesia that I know of
to stars being equated to a compass is William Ellis,
writing of Huahine. 'When setting out on a voyage, some
particular star or constellation was selected as their guide
in the night. This they called their aveia, and by this
name they now designate the compass because it answers
the same purpose' (Ellis, W., 1831: 168).[13]

---

[13] Correct spelling is *avei'a*.

DISCUSSION OF THE BASES OF WIND, SUN, STAR COMPASSES

The winds of the tropical Pacific are relatively steady in direction and their variation in response to fronts from higher latitudes fairly predictable. But in comparison with stars, the sun, or even ocean swells, winds at best can be but impermanent secondary indicators of approximate direction, that need to be checked frequently by more reliable phenomena. This checking could be from landmarks, the sun or stars.

The basing of a wind compass on shore landmarks would be impracticable on oceanic islands for any but restricted travel within sight of land or to give the most approximate bearings.

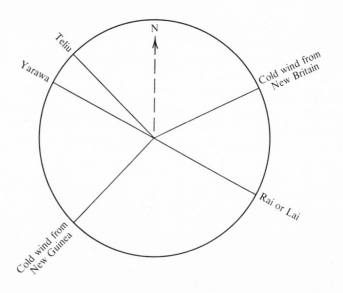

Fig. 9 Siassi wind compass (after Chappell, pers. comm.)

In Vitiaz Strait between New Guinea and New Britain, where the Siassi do use a 'compass' based on local geographical features, both these criteria of visible landmarks and short passages apply (see fig. 9). In the Cooks and Tokelau, however, the length of former voyages, and the fact that the Islanders share a number of compass point names,[14] seem to preclude their wind compasses from

---

[14] Pukapuka and the southern Cooks have eight equivalent names. (The *directions* they denote are often different.) Tokelau has seven words for bearings that also occur in one or both of the other groups.

having been constructed locally and independently, based on such directional features as trees or islets on the reef.

Orientation by the sun is the next possibility and the evidence does indeed suggest that the Tahitian wind direction system—and possibly that of the Cooks and Tokelaus—was immediately determined in this way. But since the place where the sun rises or sets varies even on the equator by 47°, it follows that some fixed points of reference are necessary on which to orientate the seasonally changing positions of the sun's rise and set. These are most conveniently provided by the stars.

The evening before we set out from Puluwat for Saipan, Hipour checked the bearing of the setting sun from his house by landmarks, the direction of which he had determined previously from the stars. He told us in sidereal compass terms that it bore 'Between setting Orion [270°] and setting Corvus [253°] a "little bit nearer" to Orion'. I noted in the log at the time that this would make it about 'half a point south of east'. This would be about 264½°, and I now see by the tables that for the date and the latitude of Puluwat the bearing was actually 264°.

Hipour did not demonstrably check the sun's bearings again until we were two days out at sea returning from Saipan, and then I think it was because I questioned him. 'You will be able to see for yourself this evening that it has not changed at all', he replied through Ulutak, and later proceeded to demonstrate the fact by the sunset and Orion. Subsequent reference to the tables showed that he was in error—by 1°.

There are examples from many parts of the Pacific of sun observations having been made, not only at the solstices when the direction of its north-south movement is 'reversed' but throughout the year.[15] The general character of Pacific Island astronomy suggests that the purpose was, in large part, navigational.

---

15 In the Gilbert Islands regular observations were made of the bearing of the rising sun by its relation to the Pleiades. There were specific names for the sun's positions at ten-day intervals (Grimble, 1931: 205-14). In the Carolines, the sun's bearing was noted in terms of Altair (Eilers, 1935: 84). In Tonga King Tupou IV demonstrated that the *Ha'amonga* trilithon was orientated on the summer solstice sunrise and

Throughout the islands astronomy was developed in close association with navigation and served it. There is not space in this book to deal with astronomy as such, and in any case there are excellent books on the subject (Makemson, 1941; Akerblom, 1968), so we will confine ourselves here to giving some examples to illustrate the foregoing assertion.

'In Micronesia, astronomy owes its development to the requirements of navigation. Knowledge of the stars, their names and movements, is very largely restricted to professional navigators' (Goodenough, 1953: 3). 'There is no specific word for "astronomer" in the Gilbertese tongue. If you would find an expert on stars, you must ask for a *tiaborau* or navigator' (Grimble, 1931: 197). 'The study of astronomy was treated by the Tongans as a branch of navigation' (Collocott, 1922: 3). J. R. Forster, remarking on the close connections of the three sciences of astronomy, geography, and navigation in Tahiti, says that 'knowledge of the two first has been made subservient to the last' (1778: 501).

It would be a reasonable enough deduction that the Carolinian wind compass was based on the well-known sidereal one. In Polynesia the sun seems to have had a more direct role in determining direction. But Kaho's description of what seems to have been a rudimentary or degenerate star compass, in the context of the similarity between Polynesian and Micronesian astronomical practice and the virtual necessity of checking sun bearings by the stars, suggests that in Polynesia too a sidereal compass may once have been the primary orientation system whereby all others were corrected and adjusted. Very

---

was likely to have been connected with yam planting (pers. comm., 1969).

References to systematic sun observations having been made in other parts of Polynesia, often from special structures, have been collected by Akerblom (1968: 16, 17). He instances Easter Island, where 'several *ahu* (temple platforms) were probably orientated with reference to the position of the sun at the time of the summer solstice or at equinox'; Mangareva where 'two stones were set up to form sights' as aiming points to determine exactly the sun's northernmost and southernmost positions, i.e. the solstices (Laval, 1938: 213, 214; Buck, 1938: 414, 415); Hawaii (Fornander, 1878: 127; Makemson, 1938: 375, 378); Pukapuka (Beaglehole, E. and P., 1938: 349; Makemson, 1941: 85); New Zealand (Beattie, 1918: 145).

likely nothing ever developed of comparable sophistication to the Carolinian compass, but circumstantial evidence
does seem in favour of Polynesian orientation ultimately
having been based on directional stars.

STAR AND MAGNETIC COMPASS STEERING COMPARED

An old Tongan cutter captain, according to Ve'ehala,
once averred that 'A compass can go wrong, the stars
never'.

Fe'iloakitau Kaho, speaking of his father, the blind
Tuita's grandson, at a time when cutters had replaced
double canoes, told me, 'There was on each vessel, a
compass, but he did not trust them and used only the
knowledge of navigation he got from his father Po'oi'.
Similarly Wilkes in 1845 (vol. I, 327) reported that the
Tuamotuans, who were becoming acquainted with the
magnetic compass, 'still prefer sailing by the stars and
sun'.

Sioni Mafi of Nomuka is the 82-year-old former captain
of an inter-island motorless sailing cutter. When he first
went to sea he had a compass, with the aid of which he
noted the bearings of the rising and setting stars. Thereafter he dispensed with it altogether, and for the best
part of half a century has guided his ship through dangerous reef-strewn waters exclusively by stars.

Of course, steering by horizon stars is every bit as
accurate as by magnetic compass and probably easier
than trying to follow the gyrating compass card of an
island schooner or a yacht. The snag is that, the navigator
using the stars as we should a compass, must be so
thoroughly familiar with the night sky that he can orientate himself when no more than one or two stars are
visible, an ability shown repeatedly by both Tevake and
Hipour.

The question arises whether today's navigators could
have gained any of this star lore from Europeans. It does
not seem likely, and early reports suggest that their
ancestors probably knew more. Thus the Tahitians of
1769 knew 'a very large part [of the stars] by their Names
and the clever ones among them will tell in what part of

the heavens they are to be seen in any month when they are above the horizon; they also know the time of their annual appearing and disappearing to a great nicety, far greater than would be easily believed by an European astronomer' (Banks, 1962: 368). This old lore would seem to have declined when Tyerman and Bennet (1840: 77), visiting the same group in 1840, remarked on the inhabitants' 'scanty ideas of astronomy'. However, traditionally educated men may well have been reluctant to air their knowledge in front of missionaries.

Frequency of   No navigator, no matter how skilful and how keen his
Overcast eyesight, can see stars through complete cloud cover. It is only total and persistent overcast that can seriously incommode a trained navigator, and the question naturally arises as to how common are such conditions? Some indication of their frequency may be provided by the number of days when we were unable to obtain sun fixes (two or more sextant sights) from *Rehu Moana* or *Isbjorn*. Out of 273 days actually spent at sea between Easter Island and the Carolines, position could not be determined on 7, or one in 39. It is important to note that on those days the sun was obscured at the desired sight time, not necessarily all day, nor were the stars always obscured on the corresponding nights. Judging from these figures, the frequency of obscured sky that we experienced when sailing with Hipour, Tevake, and Iotiebata was fairly typical of the Pacific and would constitute no major problem.

CHAPTER THREE

Subsidiary directional guides

We have discussed star steering at some length, but on any substantial voyage, the stars will be invisible for roughly half the time and other guides must be used. Thus our voyages with Hipour involved as many hours holding course by day as by night, so that the directional precision that was achieved depended on the accuracy of daytime steering as much as on that at night.

DAYTIME STEERING

Four points of the compass are indicated by the sun in the course of each day. These are the easterly and westerly bearings of sunrise and sunset (due east and west only at the equinoxes) that require periodic comparison with stars, and north and south that can be precisely determined at noon.[1] Both axes were determined by the sun in Tahiti, according to J. R. Forster (1778: 503). The directions due north and south of the sun at zenith on the meridian were called *to'erau* and *to'a* respectively.[2]

Keeping Course by the Sun

---

[1] We have seen that accurate determination of the sun's bearings at rise and set, by checking against stars of known azimuth, is a simple enough procedure whether ashore or afloat (Hipour before departure for Saipan and at sea, p. 79). Akerblom surprisingly asserts that, 'To achieve a satisfactory degree of accuracy when checking the course by means of the bearing of the rising or setting sun, the [Polynesian] navigator must necessarily have had access to some form of memorized table of the changes in the sun's azimuth' (1968: 43). All the navigator actually needs, of course, are his eyes and a knowledge of the stars; the sun-star comparison could be made twice in each day if one were so minded.

Akerblom (1968: 44) also takes Makemson to task for a statement that Polynesian navigators 'knew how to find the compass directions from its [the sun's] altitude and azimuth at any time of the day' (Makemson, 1939: 5). But of course this is just what the navigators did and still do, only the process is one of delicate judgment and interpolation, not measurement as the above terms tend to imply. The confusion here arises, I think, from such mathematically precise scientific terms being applied to the art of sun course steering.

[2] This north-south axis can be accurately ascertained at noon by the shadow of a vessel's mast, which points either due north or south depending on the latitude and the season. Davenport mentions the shadow having been so used at sea in the Marshall Islands (1960: 20). Kaho informed me that in Tonga the shadow of an upright tree was observed on land.

Knowing the sun's bearings at rise and set and its track across the sky, it becomes habitual with sufficient practice to make the almost automatic mental interpolations necessary for steering by the sun, especially for some three hours at either end of the day and during the period around noon. During the Saipan voyages, whenever Hipour or Ulutak were steering in the evening, the guide star invariably appeared at exactly the right place. The Tikopian Rafe explained how he had observed the sun, especially at rising and setting, noting which part of the canoe it was over.

In practice the navigator is naturally checking his bearings all the time from the swells and more temporally by the wind, as well as the sun.

It remains true nevertheless that daytime steering is less precise and demands more concentration to process mentally data of more than one order than holding course at night guided by a clearly defined pinpoint of light, and this of course is why Carolinian navigators are tending to resort to magnetic compasses for secondary orientation in the daytime.

Keeping Course by the Swells (Waves)   The procedure of steering by swells in the open sea should be distinguished from land-finding techniques based on the distortion of swells by islands, which will be discussed in chap. 7.

A few non-technical remarks about the nature of ocean swells may help explain their role in orientation. In the first place the word 'swells' denotes waves that have travelled beyond the wind systems that generated them, or that remain after the wind has died away. 'Waves', strictly speaking, are produced by contemporary winds. The two terms are frequently used as synonyms and indeed it is often impossible to distinguish one from the other at sea.

For swells to remain perceptible after travelling hundreds of miles, they must have their origin in regions of strong and persistent winds, the more important swells originating in 'permanent' weather systems such as the Trades. Trade wind generated swells tend to be from east, north-east, or south-east, depending on latitude and

*Plate V   Helmsman of Hipour's canoe on passage
between Puluwat and Pulusuk, Caroline Islands*

season. The other main source is the Southern Ocean belt of strong westerlies, whence long southerly swells sweep even beyond the equator. Largely seasonal swells originate in the monsoons of the western Pacific and others, more temporary still, are caused by tropical revolving storms.

Waves thrown up by the immediate wind tend to be temporary as well as having breaking crests and other recognisable characteristics. This distinction is well recognised by Pacific Island navigators and its importance was repeatedly stressed to me by Tevake and Teeta among others. The Papuans Lohia Loa and Frank Rei carefully explained that the swells they used were 'not wind waves', but were more permanent.

Swells from relatively distant origins are long in wavelength from crest to crest and move past with a slow swelling undulation, while wind waves and swells from nearby sources are shorter and steeper. The former are not readily abolished even by prolonged gales (see Iotiebata's experience, p. 124).

The ocean wave and swell pattern is almost always a complex one, with several systems that differ in height, length, shape, and speed moving across each other from different directions at the same time.[3] It follows that every Island navigator must select those swells that he considers most significant and reliable, and though there are patterns that are generally recognised throughout each navigational area, there can also be a personal element in this selectivity. In the Gilberts, for instance, it was certainly not due to confusion and ignorance that Iotiebata described the most important swell as coming from the east, while the equally accomplished Abera drew a diagram that showed it to come from the south, and Rewi asserted that the main swell was easterly but with a less prominent southerly component. The fact that

---

[3] Hilder has drawn attention to this complexity, writing that 'there are generally several swell series running at once in mid-Pacific . . . One day . . . I observed separate swells coming from four directions at once' (1963b: 188). The burden of the rest of the passage is, however, that this complexity would inhibit Polynesian navigators from analysing and making use of the swells, when actually, as the practice of Hipour, Tevake and others shows, the reverse is true.

these three navigators came from different islands either might or might not explain how their particular schools came to place emphasis on different swell components. However, wave patterns should not vary markedly in the archipelago. In any case there would be no confusion for a navigator sailing from one area to another because 'his' familiar 'main swell' would probably still be identifiable to a trained eye. Even should it disappear altogether, the prevailing pattern could readily be sorted out at sea from the sun or stars.

Holding course by swells seems always to be a matter more of feel than sight—which emphasises the value of the art on overcast nights. Tevake told me he would sometimes retire to the hut on his canoe's outrigger platform, where he could lie down and without distraction more readily direct the helmsman onto the proper course by analysing the roll and pitch of the vessel as it corkscrewed over the waves. In distinguishing swells, he stressed, you have to wait patiently until the one you want has a spell of being prominent and discernible. Rafe of Tikopia also spoke about 'feeling' the swell, and Gladwin (1970: 171) points out that Puluwatans too 'steer by the feel of the waves under the canoe, not visually'. One might perhaps be tempted to refer to keeping course by the swells as 'steering by the seat of one's pants', were it not for the more anatomically specific detail supplied by the veteran island skipper Captain Ward, who writes, 'I have heard from several sources, that the most sensitive balance was a man's testicles, and that when at night or when the horizon was obscured, or inside the cabin this was the method used to find the focus of the swells off an island' (V. Ward, pers. comm., 1969).

Examples of the practice of orientation by swells can be collected from virtually any part of the Pacific. Andia y Varela, for instance, gives one from Tahiti (Corney, 1914: vol. II, 285). Vili Mailau spoke of the swell from the south as being the most valuable for orientation in Tongan waters. Tonnaku of Bougainville described a canoe voyage down the 60-mile-long 'corridor', traditionally flanked by waves from the north and from the south, that extends between Vella Lavella and the Shortland

Islands. Ninigo informants also referred to using swells for direction. We cannot consider all these in detail, so will concentrate on the Santa Cruz and Caroline areas.

Santa Cruz Group. Three swells are considered to be present all the year round, varying in relative prominence with the wind, and one or other being sometimes difficult to detect, especially when overlaid by wind waves. Tevake insisted that they could be discerned even after long stretches of calm and that all three are generally present during both the north-west monsoon and south-east Trade seasons. Rarely the storm waves of a cyclone would temporarily abolish them all. They were:

Hoahualoa, the 'Long Swell', from the south-east.

Hoahuadelatai, the 'Sea Swell', from east-north-east.

Hoahuadelahu, from the north-west.

I would suspect these to originate from the south-east trades, the north-east trades (whose more common direction towards their southern limit is east-north-east) and the north-west monsoon, respectively. As to the likely geographical extent of this swell pattern, it would seem probable that it would be fairly general in the south-west segment of the Pacific, subject to the degree of interference by land. Further eastward but still south of the equator we might expect the effects of the monsoon to be lost and, once clear of the big Melanesian islands, for the Southern Ocean swell to sweep unhindered up from the southward. This indeed is the pattern in the Gilberts and Tonga, with their 'great swells' from the east and south.

Tevake demonstrated the three Santa Cruz swells on the passages between the Reef Islands and Taumako during December, the monsoon season of variable winds and calms. On this occasion the 'Long Swell' from the south-east was very low and hard to detect, the 'Sea Swell' from east-north-east was low and long and the north-west swell was very noticeable, having been reinforced by a recent cyclone. The north-west and south-east swells pass 'through' each other like the interlocked fingers of two hands, said Tevake, demonstrating. Some

time in the late afternoon a northerly swell from a recent
or nearby wind began to roll by, and for some hours
remained the most prominent.

Much more stress was laid by Tevake on the swells
than the sun for daytime orientation. It would be wrong,
I think, to conclude from this that Santa Cruz navigation
must needs incorporate the same preference as was shown
by this one particular Santa Cruz navigator. More
especially, since Tevake is virtually the sole surviving
exponent, must we be on guard against accepting his
personal practice as necessarily representative of the
whole area. A teacher's bias or his pupil's special apti-
tudes might be expected to give rise to differences
between the arts of different Island navigators, as we
have already seen in the three swell interpretations of as
many learned Gilbertese *tani borau*. Such individualism
is a characteristic of orally taught lore that we, who are
accustomed to all the data of a particular field being
systematically set out in a textbook, are only too apt to
forget.

The course towards Taumako was east-north-east,
directly into the 'Sea Swell' that came from the same
direction, though it was only present, or at any rate
detectable, occasionally. At such times it could be picked
out by eye and the ship rode up and over it (pitched)
without any roll at all, except when the steep northerly
wind-wave happened to coincide, when *Isbjorn* was
rolled to starboard at the same moment as she was pitching over the head-on 'Sea Swell'. In those long intervals
when the 'Sea Swell' was absent, the wind-wave rolled us
to starboard about once every five seconds without there
being any pitching component. I could feel little effect
from the south-east or north-west swells. After nightfall
we steered by the stars, the swells remaining unchanged
except that the wind-wave declined.

The return from Taumako to the Reef Islands was
commenced an hour before daybreak. The course was
west-south-west and the distance 60 miles. The wind
being south-east, the 'Long Swell' from that quarter was
much the most obtrusive and only occasionally could we
feel the stern being lifted up by the following east-north-

east 'Sea Swell'. Nevertheless, Tevake bade me disregard the roll imparted by the former.

From approximately 06.00, when clouds shut down, we had to steer exclusively by the swell. A violent squall came in from the north around 08.30 and over the next five hours the wind veered suddenly in turn to north-east, east-north-east, and finally south-east. Heavy overcast persisted with visibility remaining poor even between rain showers.

Tevake was piloting us by the east-north-east 'Sea Swell' from astern, he told me, but the steep northerly waves kicked up by the squall effectively prevented me from sorting out the pattern, and I only succeeded in doing so thanks to his repeated demonstrations. At each fresh wind change (which I by myself could not have detected at all) I became disorientated anew so that the laborious process of instruction had to be gone over again.

It was for eight solid hours that Tevake stood on the fore-deck with a plastic tablecloth decorated with roses or an umbrella palm leaf held over his head and a sopping *lava lava* flapping round his legs, gazing intently at the sea and only moving to gesture from time to time to guide the helmsman. Then around 14.00 something more substantial than mist loomed up through the murk fine on the port bow perhaps two miles off. 'Lomlom', said Tevake, with satisfaction. Very soon afterwards Fenualoa also became visible to starboard and it was apparent that Tevake had made a perfect landfall on the middle of the half-mile-wide Forrest Passage between the two, after covering an estimated 45 to 48 miles since his last glimpse of the sky.

The Central Carolines. The Puluwat navigators, like those of Santa Cruz, regard their swell patterns as permanent all-year-round phenomena, except when temporarily obliterated by typhoons. Once again three main swells are recognised, but in this western Pacific area north of the equator they are naturally different ones.

The 'Big Wave' from approximately east has special significance as coming from 'under the Big Bird'—Altair,

Plate VI   Tevake sheltering under a lo lop *palm leaf, between Taumako and Reef Islands, Santa Cruz*

the cardinal direction star in the Carolines. Probably it originates in the part of the north-east trade wind system beyond Truk, whose direction is nearly east. It was the only swell that Hipour had any reason to believe might possibly persist towards Saipan.

The swell from the north-east is the longest of the Carolinian swells, and was also the highest when we held it abeam *en route* from Puluwat to the deep reef on the near side of Pikelot. It may be assumed to be the product of the strong north-east trades of higher latitudes.

The swell from south-east was not demonstrable during Gladwin's visit, and I had it pointed out to me but once. If its source, as seems likely, is in the distant south-east trades, it could be expected to be often blocked by intervening weather systems, so that it would only reach 8° north of the equator in favourable circumstances.[4]

On the outward voyage from Pikelot to Saipan, the agitated seas built up by the squally east-north-east winds hindered Barry and me from making much use of swell patterns for steering, though Hipour and Ulutak found them informative enough.

The return journey provided calm enough conditions for Hipour to be able to demonstrate to me what he had worked out through prolonged and patient observation— the swell patterns of an unfamiliar ocean area. He studied them at frequent intervals for hours at a time, when necessary orientating them by the sun morning and evening, until he could recognise the shape and characteristics of each swell. Once they had been sorted out and mentally 'labelled', the different swells appeared to become as recognisable to him as people's faces. Questioned about his conclusions, Hipour answered that he had confirmed the tradition that the familiar 'Big Wave' from the east would persist north of Pikelot. All the rest were unfamiliar in direction and general character. He then pointed each one out to me, drawing attention to its height and profile, indicating the place on the ship's rail where it impinged and telling me in star compass terminology whence it came.

The four swells that he showed me were 'the "Big Wave" from Altair [a shade north of east], which was the longest and fairly high; a shorter and steeper swell from the rising Aldebaran position, or about east-north-east; one from true east, the rising Orion's Belt; a very short, low and occasional wave from the south-east [Shaula in Scorpio]'. This last was not the south-easterly swell known in Puluwat, but according to Hipour had its origin in a nearby wind.

---

[4] For the origins of these Carolinian swells, I have largely followed Gladwin (1970: 171-5). He also gives an interesting analysis of the motion of a canoe at various angles to the waves (pp. 177-8).

Here then we have an example of how complex swell patterns can be sorted out at sea with reference to the bearing of sunset, that had itself been determined at sea from the stars—and with the aid also of monumental patience.

The wind's inconstancy makes this the most inaccurate of secondary orientation methods, but the technique's simplicity renders it useful. Every helmsman under sail, whether he be a European or a South Sea Islander, must perforce be constantly aware of the direction of the wind in relation to his vessel, since even the slightest wind shift necessitates either a new course or the trimming of the sails. The only difference is that the Western steersman is made aware of the wind shift by his compass, his opposite number by the swells, sun, or stars. As the Tikopian Rafe put it: 'If the wind changes, I feel it by my boat on the waves'. The methods of estimating the direction of the apparent wind by pennants or merely the feel of the breeze on neck or cheek are too well known to require elaboration.

Keeping Course by the Wind

How variable is the wind in the open sea? Our own experience when sailing without instruments is probably a typical enough sample of what to expect, if the total thirty-nine weeks we spent under sail in Polynesian and Micronesian waters are anything to go by. Between Pikelot and Saipan in the north-east trade wind belt the wind altered six times on the outward and fourteen times on the homeward passage, most but not all winds blowing from somewhere in the north-east quadrant. We have already noted how four wind shifts in overcast conditions complicated Tevake's Taumako-Reef Island navigation in the area of the north-west monsoon. The month-long, 1600-mile passage to New Zealand without instruments, through the belt of Variables, in *Rehu Moana*, was marked by sixty-four wind changes (Lewis, 1967: 280). In all these cases swells were much less variable than the wind.

To indicate the direction of the wind the Tahitians used pennants. To quote Andia y Varela once more (Corney, 1914: vol. II, 286), 'since the wind is apt to vary

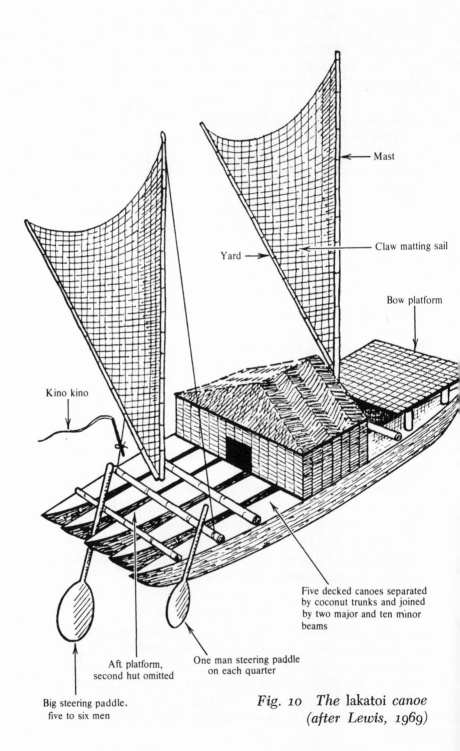

Mast

Claw matting sail

Yard

Bow platform

Kino kino

Five decked canoes separated
by coconut trunks and joined
by two major and ten minor
beams

Aft platform,
second hut omitted

One man steering paddle
on each quarter

Big steering paddle,
five to six men

Fig. 10   The lakatoi *canoe
(after Lewis, 1969)*

in direction more than the swell does, they have their
pennants [made] of feathers and palmetto bark, to watch
its changes by and trim sail, always taking their cue for
a knowledge of the course from the indication the sea
affords them'. Carolinian seafarers similarly fly strips of
inner bark from the end of the boom or have finer strips
streaming from the shrouds.

An ingenious method was used by the Motu of Papua
to note simultaneously the angle of the wind to the course
and the bearing of the steering star. This was a staff with
a long whip-like pennant at one end, called a *kino kino*.
Now the Motu trading cycle, the *hiri*, was seasonal, the
westward passage across 150 miles of open sea being
made with the south-east trades, and the return made
later in the year after the north-west monsoon had set in
(Barton: 1910). The clumsy *lakatoi* canoes, which might
consist of a dozen hulls lashed gunwale to gunwale, set
out across the Gulf of Papua with Venus sinking fine on
the starboard bow and the trades on the port quarter. The
kino kino was lashed in the starboard rigging in such a
position that its tip was aligned on Venus and the succession of stars that came down on the same bearing after
Venus had set, and the pennant allowed to stream out
before the wind. The slightest wind shift would be observed instantly by the responsible man in charge of the
kino kino, who would order trimming of the great claw
sails, and instruct as necessary the five or six men on the
steering paddle so that the *kino kino*'s tip might remain
fixed on the star. Should the star become obscured by
cloud, the angle between the staff and the pennant would
be kept constant (Lohia Loa and Frank Rei).

Two examples of crossings from Tahiti towards the
leeward islands of the same Society group, about 100
miles away, may serve to stress the necessity of checking
on wind changes by swell or other means.

When *Rehu Moana* made this passage without instruments in 1965, lengthy periods of overcast hid both sun
and stars for most of the time. The swells were difficult to
orientate by on this our first attempt. There were five substantial wind. shifts, some of which were only recognised
belatedly, but we corrected for our mistakes wherever

a break in the clouds afforded a clue, and cautiously hove-to for most of the night when none offered. In spite of this delay we made slightly better time than the commercial inter-island motor vessel.

In 1824 a group of Tahitian converts set out from Tahiti in the missionary John Williams's boat of 'about ten tons' (Dillon, 1829: 271), on the same journey. After losing sight of Moorea in a sudden rain squall they kept on, apparently steering by the wind for the sky remained hidden, all night and all next day, when not surprisingly they saw no sight of land. Their failure to determine wind shift from the swells, or to heave-to and wait for a glimpse of the sky, was incompetence amounting to idiocy, and the survivors were far luckier than they deserved to fetch up on Atiu 500 miles away (Threlkeld, 1853-5). It will be noted that in *Rehu Moana* we experienced almost identical conditions in the same waters but, in spite of our inexperience, had no real difficulty in reaching our destination.

This comparison is not intended to laud our own seamanship, which indeed was no more than the most elementary common sense, but is a reminder that by no means all Polynesians were navigators, and after even a short experience of civilisation many were not necessarily seamen either. The point needs making, I think, lest recurring accounts of skilful Island navigators make us lose our sense of proportion.

A situation meriting brief mention is when both wind and waves change direction under a clouded sky. Iotiebata showed in extreme conditions of this kind that the underlying swell would not be abolished by newer wind waves if only the navigator were skilful enough to detect it (see p. 124). Similarly, we have seen on p. 89 that it was precisely in such circumstances that Tevake was able to maintain perfect orientation. A less competent man like myself would certainly have become bewildered, but then I or any other sane seaman—I exclude from this category the unhappy Tahitian converts—would heave-to and wait for clear weather.

Part Three

COMPENSATION
AND ORIENTATION

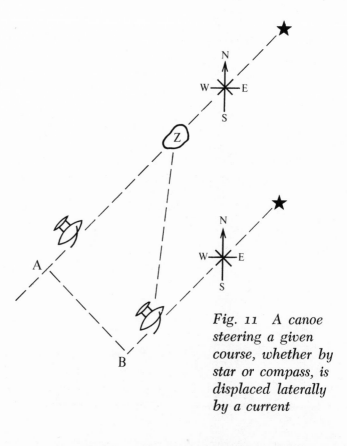

Fig. 11 *A canoe steering a given course, whether by star or compass, is displaced laterally by a current*

CHAPTER FOUR

Dead reckoning

What we have considered so far has all been concerned with maintaining a course or heading. Now we come to factors that displace a canoe from its proper track. The most important of these are current set, leeway (sideways wind-drift under sail), and gale-drift. All these have to be allowed for and, in addition, estimates of the canoe's speed will enter most calculations. Then there are orientation concepts in terms of which navigators visualise their positions, for in default of a scheme for processing their data they would quickly become bewildered in face of such complex orientation situations as tacking to windward beyond sight-range of land.

We shall therefore discuss in turn the factors responsible for tracking error, beginning with currents, and the arts employed to circumvent their effects; then go on in the next chapter to orientation concepts.

In fig. 11 a canoe is shown on passage towards island Z. Whether it is steering by a compass bearing or the azimuth of a horizon star is of course quite immaterial since both equally are directional references. (The size of the earth being infinitesimal compared with the distance to a star, the latter's bearing is virtually the same from a large part of the earth's surface.) Now if the vessel be drifted from A to B at right angles to its track, the same course will no longer fetch island Z, but only empty ocean. Should the navigator be aware of his drift and its extent, he can avoid this fate by altering to the new course BZ. This illustrates, I think, the difference between the course being *steered* and the course actually *made good* over 'the ground', which is the resultant track the vessel follows under the influence of the forces of sea and wind.

The next point is that, since when a current is flowing the entire ocean surface will be moving bodily along and bearing the canoe with it, a navigator cannot be certain, once he has lost sight of land, that the course he is steering is still towards his target. He must make estimates as to distance covered and course made good, taking account of leeway, current set and so on. From these he calculates his position and decides the course to steer. This procedure is termed *dead reckoning* and the most important thing to note is that it gives only a provisional position until land is sighted again or some astronomical or analogous confirmation becomes available (see chap. 10). In other words, the interim conclusions of dead reckoning are based on calculation and fine judgment and are subject to verification by landfall.

The arts of dead reckoning in primitive seafaring, the most ancient of all navigational methods, should not be underestimated—or the reverse. Some commentators have unjustifiably exaggerated the accuracy obtainable by non-instrumental techniques, while others, whose practical experience has either been non-existent or confined to large ships, have failed altogether to comprehend them. In an attempt to avoid either pitfall and to neutralise observer bias, we will keep as close as we can to the source of all our data—canoe navigators' theory and practice—and analyse actual voyages against the background of the winds and currents of the Pacific.

CURRENT SET

This presents a difficult and intractable problem of which Pacific Island navigators are only too well aware, as the variety of methods that are used to cope with it show. The situation is reminiscent of that which obtains in medicine, where it is axiomatic that a great variety of treatments for a single disease usually signifies that none is altogether satisfactory.

It is worth stressing once again that awareness of the very existence of a current is the navigator's first problem, for except at a meeting place of opposing streams, in default of some external reference, the craft's occupants are unaware of any motion at all. The situation is exactly parallel to that of a free balloon that is being swept along by the wind. To passengers in the gondola it appears to be floating in perfectly still air—until they see the ground sliding past below.

The currents of the tropical Pacific are mainly genera-ted by the trade winds and set towards the west or south of west. They are strongest near the equator (north and south equatorial currents) and decline steadily in strength further south (south subtropical current). North of the equator the same tendency to decrease in strength with higher latitude is manifested, though as the north-east trades are rather stronger and more consistent than the south-east it is less marked (see figs. 12 and 13 over).

The limits of Polynesian penetration were Hawaii in the belt of northern Trades and associated west-going current, and New Zealand in the extreme south. Between the latter country and the oceanic islands further north (Tahiti, Cook Islands, Tonga, Fiji), there stretches, in summer at any rate, a zone of weak and variable but generally west-going currents. These leisurely streams may for practical purposes be ignored by a navigator on passage say between the Cook Islands and New Zealand.[1]

The one important exception to west-going currents is the equatorial counter current. (I am leaving aside the strong and erratic streams that often run within sight of islands, and which, unlike true oceanic currents, are determined by local geographical effects. They are invari-ably well known to Island fishermen.) We have seen how the trade winds, by driving the surface of the ocean before them, give rise to the north and south equatorial streams. The end result is that water tends to 'heap up' off Australia-New Guinea and the Asiatic coasts. It is this body of 'heaped up' water that takes advantage of the relatively calm doldrum belt between the two trade wind systems to flow back towards the east and so form the equatorial counter current. It runs eastward at speeds up to two knots roughly between the parallels of 4°N. and 8°N. though, in the west especially, its boundaries are subject to marked seasonal fluctuation. Immediately north

[1] During the test voyage without instruments in *Rehu Moana* from the Cook Islands to New Zealand in November-December 1965 we simply followed the normal Pacific voyaging practice of aiming a little to the eastward of our destination to be sure of arriving up-current. The sub-stantial distance we had to traverse to the west after we had turned and headed towards land beneath our zenith star indicated that current deflection had been negligible for the 1200 odd miles since the trades (Lewis, 1967: 246-85).

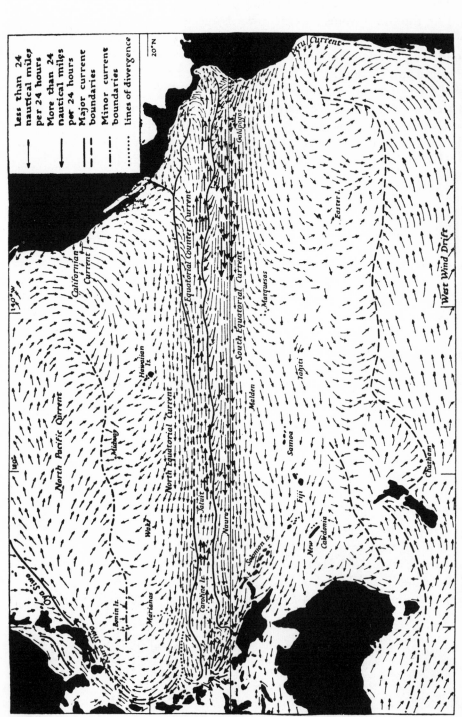

Fig. 12   Ocean circulation, northern summer (August to September). Variability is indicated by the lengths of arrows, the more variable the shorter the arrow. (Based on Schott, 1935, 1943.)

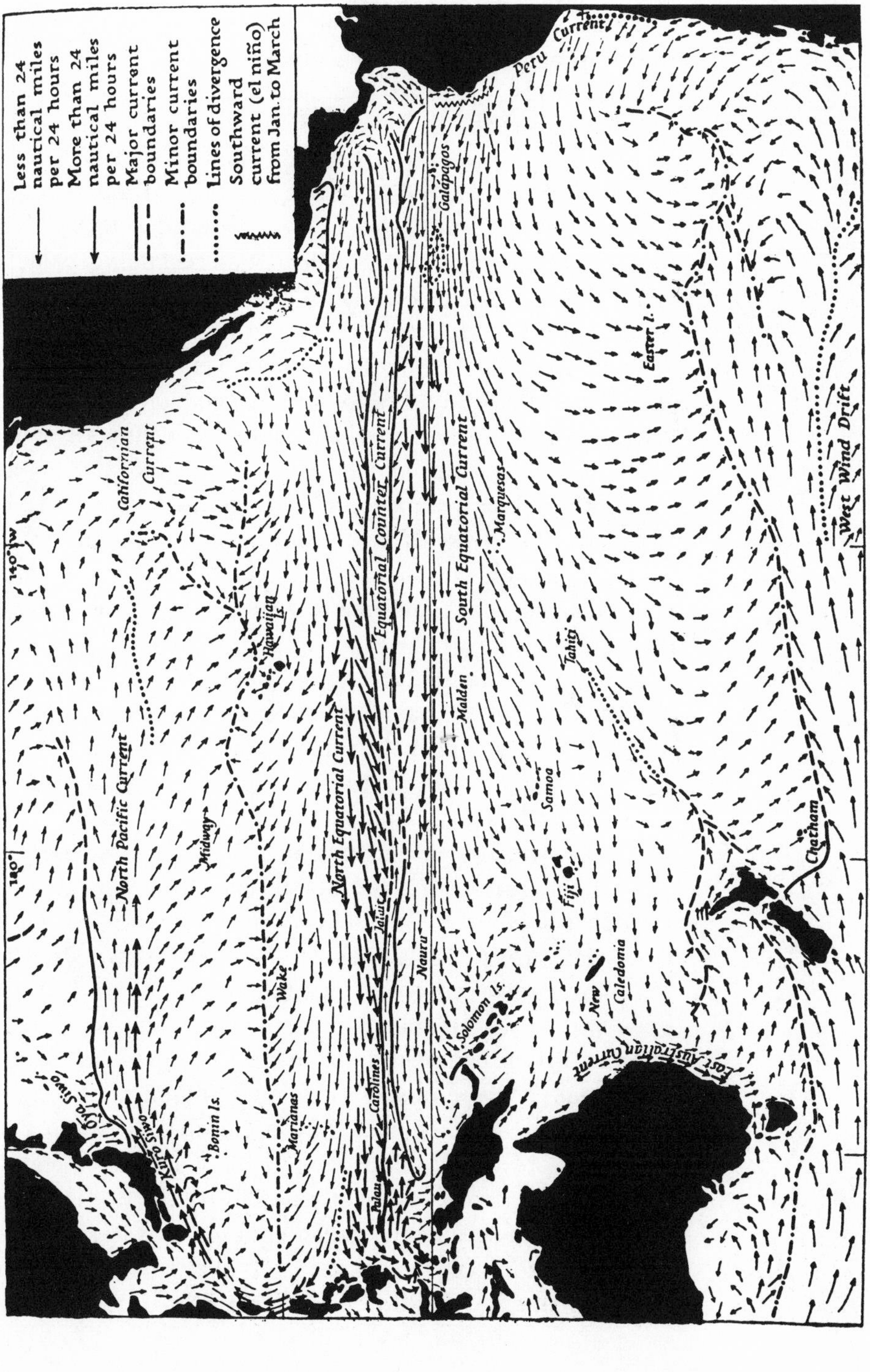

Fig. 13 Ocean circulation, northern winter (February to March). Arrows as in fig. 12. (Based on Schott, 1935, 1943.)

and south of it are the powerful opposite flowing equatorial currents.

The counter current is the only one whose existence and approximate direction cannot be deduced from prevailing winds. It affects the Carolines voyaging area, the Marshalls and the northernmost of the uninhabited Line Islands that lie to leeward of the Tahiti-Hawaii track.

One last general point, though an important one. All currents are subject to short-term variations in strength and direction which may upset dead reckoning calculations a good deal, especially on short voyages, whereas on longer ones the effect of day-to-day fluctuations will tend to cancel each other out. The principle is of great practical moment in that it applies to other aspects of dead reckoning as well—always provided that the estimates being acted upon are valid and have not neglected any important factor. For instance the daily estimates of distance sailed in the *Rehu Moana* test voyage were out by as much as 40 miles for a single 24-hour period, yet the total error for the 1600 mile month-long passage was only 77 miles (Lewis, 1967: 283).

In many an archipelago canoe fishermen, who today are devoid alike of the navigational skills of their forefathers and so much as a pocket compass, make their way (under power of a Johnson outboard like as not) to fishing grounds and islands hours out of sight of their home. Their knowledge of currents in all seasons is encyclopaedic, far surpassing in detail and accuracy that in European hydrographic publications; and while it is local, these data are by no means confined to inshore streams, for these canoemen go far enough from land to traverse open waters where only the true oceanic currents flow.

An old-time competent navigator, being familiar with such home centred observations and trained also in more general deep sea lore like the relationship between currents and prevailing winds, would be well able to couple together the two sets of data. His deductions would enable him to head out across unfamiliar waters with a reasonable idea of the current set likely to be encountered. In this he would be aided in no small measure by the aforementioned tendency for heading errors due to short-term current fluctuations to neutralise each other. (Naturally once a successful return had been made from any newly discovered island, the mean current set and stars for the passage would be known from the course steered and the precise place of arrival.) Some commentators have made very heavy weather indeed of currents, so that the subject has become not a little confused. The following sequence of misunderstandings is a good example:

A table was published by Frankel (1962: table 2) showing the sets observed during a yacht trip from Tahiti to Hawaii, compared with current predictions from the routeing charts. As might have been expected the rates varied a good deal, though unfortunately the method that was used to obtain navigational fixes (morning, noon, and evening sun sights only) could not have provided data of the precision claimed, so that the table is virtually meaningless.

Captain Hilder, however, accepted it and assumed that unrecognised currents 'would set a canoe 36 miles off track invisibly every 24 hours'. He concluded that after 1000 miles sailing at six knots 'the total error would be 250 miles' (1963b: 189); in other words, that the errors would be cumulative and all in the same direction, a presumption that the laws of chance alone would rule out. But chance would be supplemented by the exceedingly keen perceptions of a highly trained navigator, and of course, random errors would occur in all directions, not one. Therefore unforeseen deflections, even of the unlikely magnitude of 36 miles in one day, would be cancelled out on succeeding days by contrary deflections, so that the week's total error, far from amounting to 250 miles, might be expected to be of the same order as that for a single day —30 or 40 miles.

Sharp, referring to this embarrassing slip, went even further astray. 'In the light of Hilder's realistic analysis', he wrote, 'it is plain that the margin of lateral error on predominantly northing and southing courses was infinite and unknowable' (1968: 306).

The coincidence that three of the areas where we sailed with Island navigators should be plagued with about the most complex ocean currents to be found anywhere in the open Pacific is perhaps fortunate; what we were able to glean about their practice at sea may be the more helpful in this analysis.

The main Carolines voyaging area straddles the variable zone where either the north equatorial current or the equatorial counter current flowing the opposite way may hold sway, while the southern portion of the archipelago lies along the junction of the latter with the south equatorial current. The boundaries of these three currents are subject both to seasonal changes and short-term fluctuations, so that their precise point of juxtaposition may vary daily by as much as a hundred miles. Furthermore, transient north and south recurring eddies swirl between them.

The currents in the neighbourhood of the Santa Cruz group are also erratic, possibly because they are subject to complex monsoonal influences and interruptions of oceanic circulation by big Melanesian islands. On the way to join Tevake, Barry and I were once carried 18 miles south in 13 hours by a temporary set, the very possibility of whose existence was not even hinted at by the routeing chart.

The Gilberts, which lie on either side of the equator, are in the full flow of the powerful (west-going) south equatorial stream. To complicate matters for the seafarer, very strong aberrant sets in the opposite direction (east) or towards the north or south are occasionally encountered, which could not be anticipated from the routeing charts. Approaching Tarawa from the west at the beginning of May *Isbjorn* was set 24 miles south in 24 hours by such a stream. Burnett (1910: 65, 66) describes an encounter with a boat that had sailed and been drifted 700 miles east from Nonouti, and Captain Ward was once unexpectedly carried 40 miles eastward in the vicinity of Tarawa (pers. comm., 1969).

The custom of taking back bearings on the land when setting out on a voyage to align the vessel correctly on course and to check the direction and strength of the current, seems to be well nigh universal. For instance, Firth (1954: 91) says that in taking departure from Tikopia for Anuta the canoe is 'set carefully in the required direction by using marks of orientation on Tikopia. On the northern side of the island is a beach named "Mataki Anuta", "Looking on Anuta", i.e. facing in that direction. At the back of this beach a gulley runs up the mountain side; . . . When setting out for Anuta the crew turn the stern of their canoe to this gulley and keep it in sight as long as they can'.

A canoe captain, from Anaa in the Tuamotus, told how when leaving for Tahiti in 1826 'canoes were placed with scrupulous exactness in the supposed direction, which was indicated by certain marks upon the land' (Beechey, 1831: 230). Another account from early last century is that of the missionary John Williams, who succeeded in finding Rarotonga in 1823 only after the chief Roma-tane on Atiu had helped range his schooner by landmarks ashore (Williams, J., 1846: 82).

We have seen how opposing currents along the Caro- *Hipour's* lines navigation axis render it one of the few areas where *Practice* the average direction of set cannot be deduced from the *(Carolines)* prevailing wind. 'Compensation for these currents is an integral part of the package of instructions which comprise the sailing directions between island pairs', writes Gladwin (1970: 161), and in some cases it has been possible for Puluwat sailing directions to be designed to allow for this awkward phenomenon. From Truk, for instance, when setting out for Puluwat 135 miles due westward, you simply disregard the current's vagaries and head directly towards your objective. If there is a north-going stream you will sight not Puluwat but Tamatam 20 miles further north, which is what we did in *Isbjorn*. If the current is running the opposite way you will eventually come over the edge of Uranie Bank, a deep reef (12-33 fathoms) which extends about 20 miles south-east from Puluwat. Of course an east- or a west-going current will simply either delay or speed your arrival (see fig. 14).

Not all landfalls are so conveniently 'screened' by reefs

*Fig. 14   Current effects,
Truk to Puluwat. A. Course
made good in a north-
going current. B. Course
made good in a south-
going current.*

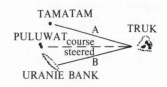

and other islands as to allow of such a simple practice,
however. The procedure then is to take back bearings
when leaving land to ascertain the direction of set and
rate of flow.

For instance when leaving Puluwat for Pikelot, on the
first stage to Saipan, Hipour carefully checked back
bearings on the land by eye to line up the initial course
and to assess current set, for in this area, he said, the
current changed direction literally from day to day. It did
not take long to decide that it was flowing north on this
occasion. How strongly it was flowing would determine
the course we must steer. If, said Hipour, it turned out on
further observation to be weak, we would head towards
the point where Vega set (about 309°); if strong, as
proved to be the case, towards the setting point of the
Pleiades (about 285°). Thus there were at least two distinct star courses traditionally laid down for this passage
and probably four to allow for strong and weak south-
flowing currents. (I omitted to inquire about this.)

On leaving Saipan on our return voyage to Puluwat via
Pikelot, Hipour carefully and repeatedly observed the
back bearings of Saipan and Tinian as they fell astern. He
made the significant comment that currents were always
strong near islands. 'You saw yourself what it was like
near the island close in', he reminded me, through Ulutak
the interpreter. Once we were well clear of the steep-to
islands, their transit showed a moderate west-going current to be flowing that could now be assumed to be
oceanic. Hipour would be entitled to anticipate, in accordance with the observations of Puluwat navigators of old,
that this same current would continue to dominate the
whole of the 450-mile sea lane to Pikelot. This assumption
was entirely justified in the event, for after crossing those
450 miles without sight of land he arrived at the precise

spot he was aiming for, an achievement that we will
discuss in chap. 8.

Hipour's earlier observation that strong winds reinforce
currents in the same direction was vindicated by the
outcome of the voyage to Saipan (see p. 52). The easterly
winds being very strong on that passage he made considerably greater allowance for current set (and leeway)
than was necessary on the equally successful return journey when the winds were very much gentler.

Currents must have been studied systematically by generation upon generation of Carolinian navigators for them
to have accumulated the huge amount of experience that
is embodied in their sailing directions. Not only are these
remembered for the nearby islands to which they still
sail, but also for such long abandoned and difficult ventures as from Puluwat or Pulusuk to lone Kapingamarangi. We have seen on p. 52 how the star course for this
465-mile stretch incorporates an allowance for current
which is correct regardless of whether the set be estimated from traditional sources or modern hydrographic
publications. Similarly the set and drift for the long
untravelled waters to Saipan were known to Hipour.

Now it would be possible for a skilled Islander to work
out the star course to an island previously unknown to
him from the deck of a European ship. Indeed Tevake
told me he had found the star course between Santa Cruz
and Santa Ana Island off San Cristobal in just this manner
while a passenger on the *Southern Cross*. But it would be
impossible to accumulate current data in this way. This
could only be done by traversing the area as ones' own
master, having all the necessary facts of the navigation to
hand. The point is mentioned as bearing on the perennial
question of the degree of European 'contamination' of
Micronesian and Polynesian navigational lore.

Clearly it was only through the trial and error of
innumerable canoe voyages that the Carolinians were
able to elucidate the most complex of Pacific currents for
a 1900-mile east-west span—more than the distance from
London to Kiev or New York to the Rockies—and about
840 miles south to north (from Kapingamarangi to the
Marianas).

Back transits were observed on our departure from the Reef Islands for Taumako and Vanikoro, both to align the yacht on course and to ascertain whether a cross current was flowing. The seasonal character of the Santa Cruz currents is apparent from the ocean circulation charts (figs. 12 and 13). In the August-September diagram they are seen to be west-going in accordance with the dominance of the south-east trades, while the February-March streams tend to flow towards the south-east before the north-west monsoon, but are in fact highly variable. While voyaging is continuous throughout the year, our personal experience was confined to the latter season.

Tevake is well aware of the relationship between currents and these major seasonal wind changes, but he did stress that the wind that happened to be blowing at a particular moment had no special bearing on the current (in the north-west season at any rate). His traditional sailing directions include current lore in the same way as do those of the Carolinians. However, his most interesting concept to my mind is that the *shape* of waves in the open sea can sometimes indicate the presence and direction of a current. Let us first describe his demonstration of this phenomenon and then discuss the possible explanations and implications.

We were bound from the Reef Islands to Vanikoro on a south-south-east course designed to intercept Utupua 60 miles away; the time was about 22.00. The 'Sea Swell' from east-north-east was detectable at intervals, the 'Long Swell' from south-east was a surge more felt than seen, while I failed altogether to make out the swell from north-west that Tevake tried to show me. By far the most prominent waves, however, the steepest and the tallest, were those thrown up by the brisk wind from the north-north-east which was then beginning to die rapidly away. Tevake indicated that we had altered course 18° or so to the right of our steering star Canopus because the steepness of the faces of the north-north-east wind waves was more marked than could be accounted for by the strength of the wind. The waves would only be rearing up in this manner if they were under the influence of a strong current flowing a little east of north. It was to counteract its effects that we had made such a substantial alteration of course. If there had been no such current as indicated by the waves, we should have headed directly towards the guiding star (Canopus).

The wind soon became imperceptible, but an hour and a half later the northerly waves remained steep and high and Tevake. again drew my attention to their abrupt profile, which even I, he said tactfully, should be able to observe now that the crests were no longer breaking, and realise that waves of this shape in the continuing absence of appreciable wind could only be caused by a current setting against the waves. We should therefore carry on along the amended track we were steering. In due course his deductions were borne out by our landfall.

We must have been some 20 miles from the nearest land at the time, and I found when I subsequently came to consult a chart that the rather scanty soundings in the area averaged around 800 fathoms (4/5 of a mile). The waves' shape, therefore, was no shallow water effect.

In discussing the probable cause of Tevake's phenomenon we must go back to first principles. The size of waves, other things being equal, is proportional to the strength of the wind causing them. Waves may be formed equally by wind blowing across the sea or by the sea flowing beneath still air and creating thereby relative wind. You are becalmed in the Thames Estuary at the turn of the tide, let us say. You wait knowing that in an hour, when the spring ebb has set in at 3 knots, you will experience a 3-knot relative wind from seaward. This 3-knot relative wind will form waves of exactly the same height as a true wind of 3 knots would have done.

When a wind is blowing one way and a current setting the other, the resultant waves will be higher than if there had been no current, since the wind producing them will be the sum of the true wind and the relative wind created by the flow of water. But their height and shape will be proportional to the total wind as experienced by the seafarer. The mariner afloat on the ocean's surface could not detect the current's presence.

How then could Tevake do it? I would suggest that the current we experienced was confined to the surface layers of the water. Flowing over deeper stationary layers that probably differed in temperature and salinity, the surface current was behaving exactly like a tide in the shallows, which often betrays its presence and direction (out of sight of land) by the character of its waves. I have seen this shallow water phenomenon very clearly displayed far out to sea during calms on the Nova Scotian banks in depths of around 30 fathoms.

Hydrographic research has revealed the nearly universal existence of such layers and the prevalence of subsurface currents flowing in directions contrary to the superficial ones. Current effects similiar to Tevake's have been noted by numerous seafarers. Slocum (1963: 194), for instance, wrote that approaching Cocos-Keeling in 1896 the force of the trade winds was lessening and he could see by the swells that a counter current had set in. This he estimated to be about 20 miles a day. Like Tevake he was able to confirm his deduction by his landfall. Some Atlantic currents are notable for such surface layer phenomena. Thus I noted that *Rehu Moana* was 'crossing patches of agitated water where the powerful upwellings of the Canary current created an appearance of tidal overfalls, though the sea was a mile deep' (Lewis, 1969a: 253). Again in the eastern mid-Atlantic north of the equator where the ocean was nowhere shallower than 2 miles, violent pyramidal confused wave conditions were seen that had also been recorded by Woodes Rogers and Dampier 250 years earlier (Lewis, 1969a: 262-3).

It seems to me, then, that Tevake's phenomenon is likely to have been something of this nature. There are many areas of unexplained wave agitation in the South Pacific that one notices from the deck of a small vessel a couple of feet above sea level that could well be the same, though the only analogous observations to Tevake's that we encountered were in the Ninigos and the Gilberts, and both were tenuous. Haidak, whose journeys had been to Maron Island (Hermit Islands), 38 miles from Ninigo, claimed to be able to detect a current at sea by the manner in which it could be felt 'pushing the canoe against the wind'. Unfortunately we only sailed together within the big Ninigo lagoon where there was no opportunity to demonstrate this. His description would fit conditions like those off Santa Cruz, though it is too vague to be certain.

The Gilbertese Iotiebata, aboard a canoe off Tarawa, pointed out a steep irregular lop through which the swell lines were detectable only with difficulty. It was caused, he said, by a current. We did not pursue the matter at the time as he was intent on showing me other phenomena. When I came to question him subsequently, he insisted on the primacy of the constellations that were in the ascendant in controlling currents, but that you could sometimes determine their direction at sea 'by the way the canoe was behaving', apparently meaning the motion as determined by the steepness and shape of the waves.

In default of more facts, there seems little to be gained in pursuing the matter further. Like so much else in the field of Polynesian and Micronesian navigation it retains its mark of interrogation.

The four *tani borau*, Iotiebata, Teeta, Abera, and Rewi, each offered different items of current lore, but were united in asserting the dominant role of the stars. 'The Gilbertese calendar, or rather, nautical almanac, is regulated by the observations of the Pleiades (Nei Auti) and the star Antares (Rimwimata)', writes Grimble (1931: 200). The two main divisions of the year depend on which of these stars is visible after sunset. The fine weather season of *Aumaiaki*, the time for voyaging, lasts from about mid-February to the end of August and, although it does not exactly coincide with the ascendency of Antares, this calm period is essentially that in which this star 'travels the sky in the evening' (Teeta). Similarly the stormy *Aumeang* season from about September to February is associated with the Pleiades.[2] Modern pilot books make a comparable division (*Pacific Islands*, 1943-5: vol. III, 307-8; Ward, E. V., 1967: 3-4).

Practice of the Gilbertese Navigators

---

[2] Details of the determination of these periods and also of the 16 *bongs* or 'months' into which the year is divided can be found in Grimble's 'Gilbertese Astronomy' (1931: 200, 202). He does not mention the specific terms *Aumaiaki* and *Aumeang* but does give the same limits for the sailing season as do Teeta, Abera, and Rewi.

The Gilbertese navigators explained that in the rough weather season when the Pleiades dominated the evening sky, currents were very strong and generally, though not always, west-going. In the fine weather season the current was weak, running sometimes east, often being absent altogether and always variable. They agreed that during the twice yearly periods when both constellations were visible at once (not coincident with the change from *Aumeung* to *Aumaiaki* seasons) they 'struggled for mastery' and the current was left free to move in any direction. It was certainly true that while approaching Onotoa on 19 May, at one such time of celestial conflict, we logged a change from a strong west-going to a weak east-going stream about 30 miles from the island.

How far is this lore of what amounts to seasonal variation in currents borne out by modern sailing directions? In general these lay more stress on the preponderance of west-going currents than the Gilbertese navigators seem to do (*Pacific Islands*, 1943-5: vol. I, Appendix 1, 545; Ward, E. V., 1967: 5). It would seem that where Gilbertese current traditions are not in complete accord with hydrographic data, the discrepancy is more a matter of emphasis than of disagreement.

Other Gilbertese current lore included an opinion on how far out to sea currents were influenced by land. This distance, said Abera, was 5 to 6 miles. For the 4 or 5 miles that remained before the atoll dropped below the horizon the streams were those of the 'great sea'. This observation seems reasonable enough.

The same navigator also discussed the sinuous lines of flotsam that collect at the junctions of opposing currents. This was a most valuable indication that could often be observed in certain areas, particularly in fine weather. Grimble (n.d.(a)) refers to similar 'Sea Marks'.

Clearly demarcated current junctions are well documented. Captain Heyen, mate of the topsail schooner *Samoa* in the Gilbert and Ellice Islands around 1922, master of the barquentine *Alexa* trading to Butaritari, and author of the 1937 Sailing Directions for the Gilbert Islands, writes:

During Te Aumeang, late November to the end of March, currents in the northern waters of the group are variable and the effect of the Equatorial Counter Current is sometimes experienced as far south as the equator. The fringe of this stream, where it meets the opposing Equatorial current, is sometimes visible for miles as a ribbon of disturbed water (1966: 11).

The familiar practice of taking back sights of land, to determine set, was mentioned in the Gilberts by Abera in connection with alternative star courses between Onotoa and Beru and between Beru and Nikunau that were to be used for different strengths of current. One last item of Gilbertese belief comes from Teeta. Flying fish, he said, provided they are not caught unexpectedly by a wave while in the air, always head into the current just before re-entering the water. Perhaps this is an accurate observation of what happens close to land, but I would think it unlikely to hold good on the open sea.

Tonga, Ninigo, and Tikopia

Nothing significant on currents was obtained from Tonga, where those who still steer by the stars do so essentially within the confines of their own archipelago. However, I may well have missed some data, as the greater part of my time in the kingdom was spent with men who, while guardians of a residue of esoteric navigational lore, were not themselves practical seafarers. Furthermore, an untimely stranding prevented at least one possibly fruitful interview with a Ha'apai captain.

In Ninigo, as has been mentioned, the shape of the waves was taken to define current (Haidak). The Pleiades (*Olaol*) was important in weather determination as in the Gilberts, but was not considered to affect currents in Ninigo (Itilon). The practice of taking back bearings to determine set was once more mentioned.

The senior Tikopians interviewed (Tupuai and Samoa) stressed that clear of land the currents followed the more permanent winds. Tikopia lies eastward of the Santa Cruz group well away from large islands and only on the fringe of the monsoon belt. For these reasons the streams have a generally regular oceanic character (see figs. 12 and 13).

LEEWAY

When the wind is before the beam, a sailing vessel of whatever type is not only impelled forward but is also driven bodily sideways through the water. The degree of this lateral wind-drift or leeway is determined by a number of factors, which include the efficiency of the keel or underwater hull at resisting displacement, how close to the wind the craft is sailed and the height and steepness of the waves. But for given conditions each type behaves in a characteristic way of its own that its captain learns to judge accurately.

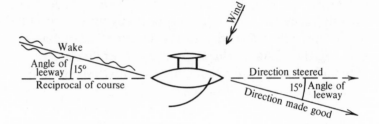

Fig. 15 Esti-mating the angle of leeway

Figure 15 shows how leeway is estimated by sighting back along the centre line of the canoe and observing the angle between the wake and this projection of the course being steered. The 15° leeway in the example would be a reasonable enough figure for an efficient canoe sailing not very close to the wind (a good full and bye), and this, as we will see in chap. 10, is the way Pacific Island canoes are normally sailed. But the exact angle in this hypothetical case is immaterial to our argument, which concerns the accurate estimation at sea of the angles' magnitude.

Aboard the utterly unfamiliar *Isbjorn* Hipour would patiently contemplate the wake, gazing astern and estimating the leeway angle and often calling me into consultation, though this was more a courtesy than anything else, since my 17,000 miles to date on the yacht had failed to equip me with an eye as discerning as the Carolinian's. Our successful landfall in the Marianas proved that his estimates for the combined effects of leeway and enhanced current due to strong winds, and the action he had taken to compensate for them, had been well judged.

Plate VII The author on board Itilon's canoe, which is doing 10 knots, off Ninigo

When Hipour was in his own canoe, as on the 48-mile run from Pulusuk to Puluwat, for the greater part of which we were close-hauled, he needed to do no more than glance occasionally astern to note the leeway. I doubt if any particular conscious effort of calculation was required in this familiar craft, whose every idiosyncrasy in all conditions was precisely known to him.

On only one of our trips with Tevake was the wind consistently before the beam. This was the 100 miles from Vanikoro to the Reef Islands. Tevake's method of estimating the leeway angle by peering astern from a point on the centre line of the yacht was identical in every respect with Hipour's and so need not be described further.

On the canoe passage in the Gilberts with Iotiebata we were close-hauled on both the outward run and the return. Iotiebata, like Hipour, would just look momentarily back from time to time. But again, his intimate experience of this type of canoe and his alertness to every change in conditions supplied the constant input of data about speed, points of sailing, wave shape and the like that accounted for his semi-intuitive continuous awareness of leeway. Several times he indicated the resultant course made good which so largely determined when we should reach our destination.

There is nothing I can usefully add about the Ninigo Islanders. The methods of the canoe captains with whom we sailed were identical with those described above.

ESTIMATION OF DISTANCE MADE GOOD

This amounts, of course, to deriving from the canoe's ever-changing speed an estimate of the ground covered in a given length of time. I want to stress the phrase 'ever-changing speed', for the wind fluctuates at short intervals in both strength and exact direction almost as much over the open ocean as it does near land. A small sailing vessel, therefore, seldom maintains the same speed for very long.

In default of some such instrument as a patent log it is mostly experience of a particular craft that enables one to gauge how fast it is moving at a given moment and so work out the mean speed and distance covered in a day.[3]

My own distance estimates on the Saipan journeys agreed generally with Hipour's, but I had been less successful in *Rehu Moana* when I underestimated our speed so that we passed through the Lower Cooks while I believed them to be still 70 miles ahead (see p. 4). We have already seen how on the longer Rarotonga-New Zealand section of the same voyage my daily distance calculations were often at fault, but the overestimates of one day were balanced by subsequent underestimation. This was natural, for if the art of dead reckoning be well learned and the sea signs accurately read, such unforeseeable factors as remain will mostly be random ones. An increase in wind strength, for instance, speeding up the canoe while the navigator is sleeping and a less experienced man on watch, would be unlikely to be repeated on

---

[3] One method of estimating speed that is more consciously arrived at, though I suspect no more accurate than an experienced Islander's 'eye', is by counting the seconds it takes a yacht to pass a patch of foam or bubbles. Three-fifths of a boat's length in feet, divided by the time in seconds, gives the approximate speed in knots. For example if a 40-foot canoe passes an object in four seconds, the speed will be $3/5 \times 40/4 =$ 6 knots.

his (the navigator's) next watch below. As far as lateral displacement is concerned, short-term variations in current strength also tend to cancel each other out.

Let us now put aside more theoretical considerations and turn to the ability at gauging speed at sea of the Micronesian and Polynesian navigators with whom we sailed. Tevake and Hipour were presented with a severe test of their ability when they took command of *Isbjorn* after their canoes.

During the passage towards Saipan I believe Hipour underestimated progress a little, though he denied this later, when discussing the voyage with navigators on Pulusuk (Lykke, pers. comm., 1969). On the return, when he knew the ship better, his judgment was exact. Tevake was also puzzled on our initial trip together, but after our first landfall he was able to gauge speed and progress with a good deal more accuracy than I could muster— for all my calculating from bubbles. In canoes, as might have been anticipated, Hipour, the Ninigo captains, and Iotiebata could not be faulted. They were aware of exactly how far they had gone in a given time.

How was this accomplished? They certainly did not deliberately count seconds while passing patches of foam as I sometimes did. Yet their results were far more reliable than mine. It would seem that, as in the case of leeway angle, the constantly varying rate at which the vessel passed through the water was apprehended through a multitude of indications—spray, turbulence, and wind pressure among them. And in much the same way this data was processed and analysed semi-consciously in light of a vast store of experience accumulated over years of study and sea-going. The distance covered in any particular period was thus appreciated with remarkable accuracy, so that questions as to progress on course were answered in exact figures which landfall later substantiated, often in terms of time, e.g. 'We will sight the island in four hours from now, at an hour before sunset'.

ESTIMATION OF TIME IN DEAD RECKONING

The extraordinary ability of the human brain to process environmental signals mediated by innumerable nerve impulses is embodied in 'learned' or conditioned reflexes that mostly function unconsciously. Among the factors that enter into activities like gauging a ship's speed is the estimation of time. I am not sure to what extent Hipour's, Tevake's, and Iotiebata's calculations are based on time or distance or both. I think it probable that both dimensions enter into their cognitive processes, and in Hipour's case we will be able to go rather deeper into the matter when we come to consider the concept of *etak* in the next chapter.

To return to 'time sense', considered for the sake of analysis as a phenomenon on its own. Is there in fact such an innate sense in human beings? For that matter is there some 'sixth sense' that civilisation has perhaps overlaid—anything akin to the exceedingly accurate 'biological clocks' and presumed inertial mechanisms that underlie the orientation systems possessed by certain birds, insects, and fish? (Ricard, 1969; Mathews, 1968). So far as our present knowledge goes, this latter suggestion must be answered firmly in the negative. I know of no evidence ever having been substantiated in favour of the existence of a human 'sixth sense'. Gatty examines this question rather fully and comes to the same conclusion (1958: 41-54). Time sense, however, is a very different matter and demands some consideration. It will be obvious that such activities as steering by the constantly altering bearings of the sun or judging the speed of a canoe must involve time discrimination. But since astro-navigation is concerned with heavenly bodies in continuous motion, the degree of accuracy that human beings can attain in estimating time and the nature of their 'biological clock' is of patent concern to us.

Neither Tevake nor Hipour was possessed of clocks or wrist watches nor were they accustomed to their use, though they understood their function well enough. Quite apart from navigational determinations there were several matters of sea-going routine—the length of spells at the helm, oiling the engine, meal times—that involved some rough estimation of the passage of time. Sunrise and sunset were references that were plain enough to us all and so, within half an hour, was noon. Whichever constel-

lation had just risen above the eastern horizon after dark
would move 15° across the sky each hour until it reached
the western horizon at dawn.[4]

After the test voyages in *Rehu Moana*, Priscilla Cairns,
the 'safety officer', told me that while my time estimates
were generally as close as 10 minutes they were erratic
and sometimes erred by an hour or more. I generally
seemed to be more certain of the time of night or day than
either Hipour or Tevake.

This leaves us with an apparent anomaly to explain, for
we have already noted the complex time/speed integra-
tions involved in their estimation of distance covered. A
moment's reflection will show that they are not the same
thing at all. On the one hand, we have sense of the
passing hours closely related to rates of solar and stellar
progression;[5] on the other, highly complex feed-back
mechanisms mediated by factors additional to indications
of time—the spindrift flashing past the canoe, for
instance. Moreover, the 'biological clocks' that control the
circadian rhythms of human physiological processes
(heart rate, body temperature, urinary output and so on)
appear to function on an automatic level. In other words
rhythmic timing mechanisms are intimately connected
with and probably part of the most fundamental bodily
functions, but a 'biological clock' is not a kind of time-
piece that can be extracted from some mid brain 'vest
pocket' to be consulted at will.

Gatty, I believe, confuses these two overlapping but
essentially dissimiliar things—automatic mechanisms and
the ability to gauge the time of day or night. For he
assumes Polynesian seamen to have possessed an innate
and apparently conscious time judging ability of high

---

[4] The complete rotation of the earth every 24 hours gives rise to an
apparent 360° movement of the constellation. In the 12 hours of the
tropic night it would 'move' 180° and in a single hour 15° (180 ÷ 12
= 15).

[5] Volunteers isolated under conditions of sensory deprivation underestimate the time they have spent and 'lose' as much as one day in four
(Vernon and McGill, 1963; Banks and Cappon, 1962). Other factors that
may affect the perception of time include temperature. Thus the rate of
counting of divers, whose body temperature varies with immersion in
warm or cold sea water, is correlated with temperature (Baddeley, 1966).
Capacity to code information in the storage banks of the memory also
appears to have a bearing on subjective assessment (Pollock *et al.*, 1969).

accuracy (1958: 41). Now while MacLeod and Roff's experiments, which Gatty cites, and much later work besides, leave no doubt as to the existence of a human biological clock in control of rhythmic functions, there is nothing to my knowledge to suggest that it is in any way qualitatively comparable to that possessed by migratory creatures. Their nervous systems are predominantly reflex and include specific navigational mechanisms connected with the migratory function. Any idea that the human time sense is of such a character that would allow longitude to be even roughly determined seems untenable. This is a matter we will be referring to again in chap. 9, when we touch on the impracticability of non-instrumental determination of longitude.

This apparent digression from the techniques of dead reckoning does in fact have a bearing on nearly all the arts that make up primitive navigation, not least the methods of orientation we shall shortly be discussing. Before we do so, however, there is one other matter to be considered.

GALE-DRIFT

Whole fleets of canoes have been lost through gales. For instance Winkler reports the worst disaster in the Marshalls to have been about 1830 when a flotilla of over 100 canoes set out on a voyage and only one survived. There were other major tragedies, but Winkler (1901: 507) points out how 'the testimony of Europeans' exaggerates their frequency![6]

In any society accidents are news, to be discussed avidly and sometimes exaggerated. It is not uncharacteristic for a drift to Pulusuk of five strangers in a canoe a century ago to be remembered and speculated upon end-

---

[6] Disasters might not have been unconnected with the gross overloading of some Marshallese flotillas. Winkler refers to canoes setting out on sea voyages so crowded with men that many times 'scarcely a decimetre was out of the water' (1901: 504). Aea, a Hawaiian missionary in the Marshalls, allowed a more generous freeboard of 'about three or four inches above the surface' (1947: 16). On the other hand such overconfidence suggests that the weather was usually reliable enough and navigation sufficiently accurate to allow of risks of this nature being taken with apparent impunity.

lessly to this day, while the feats of the long-distance voyagers who continually come and go are never individually recalled. It should be appreciated that the often dramatic and harrowing stories of storm-drifts have a special interest and therefore a differential survival value in Island folk tales—and also tend to appeal unduly to European minds unversed in the potentialities of indigenous seafaring.

To maintain a reasonable perspective about storm disasters it should be remembered that the Marshallese tragedies cited above were the outstanding ones of a century of frequent and extensive sea-borne intercourse. To regard them as the norm would be as wrong as to view modern maritime accidents with a similiar lack of proportion. For instance the following were among the losses of Pacific vessels due to capsize only, during the eleven years from 1953 to 1964.

Monique 240 tons, New Caledonia, no survivors, 120 lost

Elsie B 280 tons, Papua-New Guinea, no survivors

Melanesia 241 tons, Solomon Islands, no survivors, 45 lost

Muniara 300 tons, Papua-New Guinea, no survivors

Pollurian 339 tons, Papua-New Guinea, 29 survivors,
                                                                   82 lost

Kandavulevu 32 tons, Fiji, 2 survivors, 88 lost
                              (Couper, 1968: 21-2)

As another example, around the 1830s there were about one thousand new wrecks each year round the coast of Britain (McKee, 1968: 52)—yet we have always accepted the European merchant ship as a safe form of transport.

The Central and Western Carolines being about the only place where open sea canoe voyaging without instruments is still carried on on a large scale, the proportion of tragedies to volume of traffic may give an idea of the likely dangers of prehistoric travel in the rest of Oceania. The only figures I have are from Puluwat where there are fifteen large sea-going canoes. 'During the sixteen months from January 1966 through April 1967 the 15 big canoes made a total of 73 trips to other islands, an average of about five trips per canoe. One canoe made nine separate voyages during this period, another eleven . . . these voyages generally required two weeks or more for completion and involved in many cases stops at several islands en route' (Gladwin, 1970: 39). Yet no life has been lost since 1945 (Gladwin, 1970: 63). In most other parts of Oceania where fishermen lack both ancient and modern skills, the proportion of men doomed to what the Tikopians term 'sweet burial' (Firth, 1936: 32) is much higher.

We have been speaking of disasters caused by gales, but canoes are buoyant and resilient. Provided they do not break up they may remain swamped for days—indeed the Santa Cruz Polynesians sometimes swamp them deliberately so that they do not resist the waves—and still survive severe storms. The *navigational* problem that then arises is what has been the extent and direction of gale-drift and what is the canoe's present position.

An individual navigator would have to face the problem but rarely. Thus in all his years of sea roving Tevake has only twice been blown before gales. On the first occasion he made for Tikopia where he repaired his *te puke* before returning to a home island that had given him up for lost. The other time (p. 36) was when he ended up in the New Hebrides.

Iotiebata is the only present-day qualified Gilbertese navigator to have had a similiar experience. One November before World War II he had left Tarawa for Maiana with three companions when they were swept away by a north-west gale. The sky was never visible at first, but by the swell from the eastward that persisted despite the westerly storm, Iotiebata knew that the wind remained north-west for most of the first week and that he was east of the Gilbertese archipelago.[7] Subsequently the sun or stars appeared at intervals of days, and the gale alternated between north-west and west for the four more weeks that ensued before land clouds over Nikunau 260 miles south-east of Tarawa heralded the end of the ordeal. Once again, like Tevake, this skilled navigator was able to maintain his orientation and knowledge of the direction in which islands lay.

---

[7] 'The great swell was sweeping by unbroken by any land. Such swells continue to come from the east regardless of the direction of the wind, even a storm wind' (Iotiebata).

A canoe lies a-hull, with outrigger to windward, when it has been stripped of sail to ride out a gale. The mast is normally taken down to ease the motion. The full fury of a tropical revolving storm (typhoon, cyclone, hurricane) will probably destroy the canoe, but any ordinary gale it should survive. After the gale has blown itself out the canoe captain must try to estimate his position. We will assume the most navigationally unfavourable circumstance, total overcast throughout the storm, for otherwise he would know the direction of his drift and could calculate its amount easily enough. In the Carolines the canoe captain 'usually made the assumption when the storm was over that he was roughly in the area where he had been when the storm began unless he had reason to believe otherwise' (Gladwin, 1970: 176). At first sight such an assumption is patently absurd. The canoe could not possibly still be at its starting point since it would obviously have been wind-drifted and probably set by current as well. However, an analysis of the gales in which we ourselves had been involved resulted in a surprising vindication of the Carolinian navigators' practice.

In all the 273 days and nights we actually spent at sea in the voyaging zones of the Pacific aboard *Rehu Moana* and *Isbjorn* there were no gales except for a cyclone encountered in *Isbjorn*. After 27 hours hove-to land was sighted in our lee and we thankfully ran for shelter. A voyaging canoe would have done precisely the same. Atlantic and Indian Ocean data on *Rehu Moana*'s gale-drifts come from areas less renowned for good weather than the trade wind Pacific. The behaviour of the relatively heavy 40-foot catamaran would be exactly analogous to that of a double canoe or large outrigger when lying a-hull, except perhaps that the canoe's drift would be lessened by the taking down of the masts.

The questions at issue are: how far did severe gales drift the catamaran away from her intended track; and how much of this drift was in an unknown direction, i.e. under wholly overcast skies? One qualifying remark must be made on these data. The figures are based on the vessel's positions when she lay-to and when she made sail again, and since neither of these usually coincided with sun or star sights, an element of dead reckoning perforce entered into their location. Such errors would be unlikely to exceed about 3 miles. For the Cape of Good Hope gales the figures are exact, as bearings were taken on the land.

The list below is confined to the most severe contrary gales we encountered in four years of voyaging in *Rehu Moana*. In favourable gales *Rehu Moana* or a voyaging canoe would run down-wind under bare poles.

North Atlantic   Off north-east Iceland in 66°N., force 8-9 on the Beaufort scale (34-47 knots), drift 10 miles.

Off south-east Iceland, force 9 (41-47 knots), drift 20 miles.

Off Bay of Biscay, force 9-10 (41-55 knots), drift 20 miles.

South Atlantic   Off Argentine Patagonia in 47°S., force 10-11 (48-63 knots), drift 20 miles.

Indian Ocean   Off Cape of Good Hope, 3 south-west gales, all force 8-9 (34-47 knots), drifts 23, 13, 16 miles.

In every one of these gales the sky was visible for a proportion of the time. None of the gales set directly across our course, so the maximum deflection at right angles to the course was probably in the region of 10 miles and that in a direction that would have been largely known without the aid of a compass. For a canoe navigator a lateral displacement of this order would not be too serious. The sight range of an atoll is around 10 miles, to which the reliable zone of terns and noddies, deflected waves and cloud signs add another 10, giving a target 40 miles in diameter for the smallest atoll. The Carolinian assumption would therefore appear reasonable after all, and when the facts are looked into a little, gale-drift is seen to be a less intractable problem for the Pacific Island navigator than commentators have sometimes supposed.

CHAPTER FIVE

Orientation concepts in dead reckoning

It is hoped that this section may, *inter alia,* go some way towards explaining how the prehistoric discoverers of distant lands like Hawaii could have gathered the navigational information needed to regain their home islands. Of course the precise character of long migratory voyages that took place a millennium and more ago must remain uncertain, and no serious investigator would dream of beginning an analysis of navigation with speculation about such remote events—he could assert almost anything, there being few facts to disprove him. Our more modest aim is to investigate and try to reconstruct what we can of the ancient arts, so as to form an estimate of their usefulness. Only when we have assessed the available data can we usefully apply our tentative conclusions to the necessarily debatable subject of the part conscious navigation may have played in early crossings of the vast spaces of the Polynesian triangle (see chap. 12). Not least in importance in explaining how the bearings of home islands can be retained, despite the vicissitudes of prolonged voyages and bad weather, is an understanding of what is known about orientation systems in Oceania.

The most detailed facts about a Pacific orientation system come from the Caroline Islands in Micronesia, where it may be studied in operation today. Unfortunately no systems of comparable sophistication have survived or even been described elsewhere in Oceania. This is not very surprising since voyaging was discontinued in most of Polynesia much earlier than in Micronesia and very little was ever recorded about navigational concepts from Polynesia proper. Techniques, yes—star path steering, maintaining course by wave and wind, hind marks; even wind compasses and suggestions about zenith stars and something of astronomy have come down to us. But there has been virtually nothing about the terms in which the navigators themselves conceived their position in relation to islands beyond the horizon.

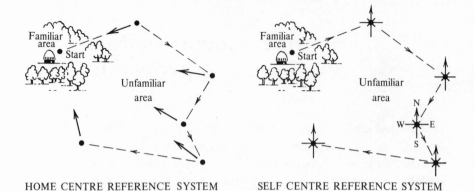

HOME CENTRE REFERENCE SYSTEM   SELF CENTRE REFERENCE SYSTEM

Fig. 16   Home centre system and self centre reference system (after Gatty, 1958)

As mentioned on p. 17, not a single word was recorded as to how Tupaia was able to retain his bearings during his voyage with Cook. That he could do so, however, is in line with what we know of the potentialities of home referenced orientation systems, of which the concept that survives in the Carolines is but a specially sophisticated example.

It is possible to orientate oneself with reference to such geographical points as one's home, an island, river or coast or else by astronomically derived directions like north and south that, as it were, radiate out from one's self. In practice mixed criteria are generally used. Thus in some seaside city our sense of direction might be based on a simultaneous awareness of the lie of the coastline and the fact that the main street ran north and south.

The clearest treatment of the subject that I know of is by Harold Gatty, whose diagram is reproduced in fig. 16 and from whom I have quoted extensively in the following paragraphs.

'As early peoples ventured forth in search of food', he writes, 'they maintained a constant anxiety about their home and would often look back to see where they were in relation to their point of departure. Each time they went out more territory would become familiar to them; and they would proceed further . . . never once loosing the thread'.

Gatty compares this practical method of orientation with our complicated self-centre system, in which modern man

considers himself (wherever he is) as the centre. He divides
the horizon into north, south, east and west . . . He involves
himself in an intricate network of calculations and, even with
the aid of a compass, often looses his way. At each point when
he stops to refer to the points of a compass, he may sever his
connection with the previous place at which he did the same
thing. All too easily, in this way, can he lose the thread which
tied him to his original place of departure.

A better system than the 'self-centre system' combines it
with the home-centre system. We may call it the 'local reference system'. Under this system directions are related to some
local prominent feature—a range of hills, a river, a coastline,
a lake front. Some primitives have used this system: it is the
basis of very accurate maps by Greenland Eskimos discovered
by European explorers (Gatty, 1958: 45-7).

I have had this ancient form of orientation drummed
into me in the African bush when following tortuous
game trails through flat, featureless scrub country where
the sun was the only external reference. At each change
of direction my companions would require me to point
out the direction in which our camp lay, until in a day or
two I was doing this automatically and re-orientating at
each major twist of the trail without conscious thought.

Both the Carolinian system of *etak* and Tevake's ability
to point out the location of invisible islands while at sea
whenever he was required to do so are examples of this
mixed system of Gatty's and there is little doubt that Tupaia's orientation would come under the same heading.

Now an important difference between the two systems
when applied at sea (or the component parts of the
mixed one), is that the self-centre system uses external
references like the star position of Altair or the north-
pointing compass needle. The home-centre reference
system, on the other hand, when used on the ocean, is a
cognitive concept, a method of working out and visualising the relationship of the vessel to distant places that
adds nothing to factual input. This is a very good reason
for the Islanders combining elements of both systems. In
the Carolines directional data from the sidereal compass
is combined with the mental concept of islands 'moving'
from beneath one star position to the next that is called
etak.

What little we know about Polynesian orientation amounts to fragmentary facts about systems in the first category, like the wind compasses in Tahiti and the Cook Islands that were referred to in the second chapter, but conceptual constructs analogous to *etak* have disappeared.

The primary reference points for Tongan orientation are those two faint opalescent galaxies that revolve around the South Pole, the Magellanic Clouds (*'Onga Ma'afu*). They were the guiding centre but not necessarily the actual centre of the heavens (Ve'ehala, Kaho, Tuita, Mailau). Unlike the Pole Star, commonly used for the same purpose in the northern hemisphere or Altair in the Carolines, the Magellanic Clouds must themselves be orientated by reference to the Southern Cross to obtain accurate bearings. It is of interest that Buck (1932: 4) notes that the Islanders of Manihiki and Rakahanga in the Northern Cooks also used the Magellanic Clouds (*na mahu*) for guides.[1] Likewise the Polynesian Reef Islanders use the same galaxies (*luamafu*) as guide stars. It is unfortunate that scattered items of information like these should make up a good part of what little we know about Polynesian orientation.

During our test voyages in *Rehu Moana* we began by recording our positions in terms of the home-centre, or rather the mixed reference, system. For instance the noon position on 5 October 1965 was logged as: '135 miles west-south-west of Huahine, and 295 east-nor-east of the Lower Cooks'. It soon became obvious that this method did not lend itself to subsequent comparison with Priscilla Cairns's latitudes and longitudes, so we abandoned it as a way of recording estimated noon positions in favour of the conventional method. But we continued to visualise our relationship with the objective in such terms as by saying that New Zealand was 'over there', indicating a couple of points off the starboard bow, for instance.

No subsequent comparisons would be available after the star path voyages with Tevake and Hipour so positions were logged exclusively in terms of the home-centre mixed reference system.

---

[1] A scholar, who shall be nameless, has cited this statement of Buck's as an example of the Polynesians using clouds to locate land!

In the second chapter we saw how this Outlier Poly-nesian navigator steered his course by the stars. It is less clear in exactly what terms he visualised his changing position along his track, but since he is wholly unacquain-ted with charts and the use of the mariner's compass, it is at least certain that he did not mentally pinpoint his position in terms of latitude and longitude. His ability to point out the direction of invisible islands whenever he wished is presumptive evidence that he was thinking in terms of some form of home-centre reference system.

It is a matter for very real regret that our rather limited ability to communicate prevented me from ques-tioning Tevake in any depth about this complicated subject that seems to have been entirely neglected by the earlier European investigators in Polynesia. One cannot say, therefore, whether or not Tevake's orientation con-cepts resemble the Carolinian one of *etak*. All that we can be certain about the picture that his mind composes of the changing relationships of islands 50 and 100 miles from his course is that it is of a similar order of accuracy and enables him to point out the direction of invisible islands in the same manner.

For instance, as we sailed through the night from the Reef Islands towards Taum-ako, Tevake showed me the guiding stars for Ndeni, Utu-pua, Vanikoro, and Tikopia both as they would be from the Reef Islands and from Taumako. Now the bearings of these islands were very dif-ferent from the two starting points, yet *en route* between them Tevake was able to indi-cate where each island lay from any point on the way. Figure 17 will make this clearer. For simplicity only Utupua is shown, Vanikoro and Tikopia being omitted.

Tevake's Orientation

Fig. 17 Tevake's orien-tation (from Admiralty Chart 2901)

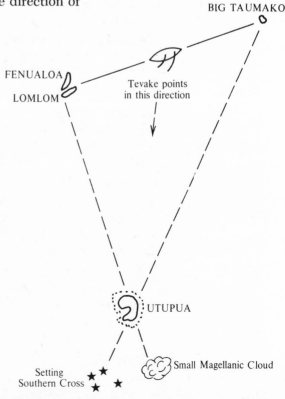

BIG TAUMAKO

FENUALOA
LOMLOM

Tevake points in this direction

UTUPUA

Small Magellanic Cloud

Setting Southern Cross

Having neither chart nor compass available while I was with Tevake I could not be sure he was indicating exactly the right direction. All that can be said is that subsequent checking of geographical and star bearings showed that if he was not, he was pointing very near to it indeed.

Another example of Tevake's orientation in relation to islands was on the passage from Vanikoro to the Reef Islands. The old navigator had been dozing during the early afternoon while Bongi steered by the swells. When Tevake awoke I asked him in what direction the island of Ndeni bore, and without hesitation he pointed over the port bow. None of us (not excluding Tevake who had been asleep) had sighted Ndeni up to this time, but peering through the haze in the direction he had indicated, there it was.

Today Tevake and perhaps Bongi are the only Santa Cruz men capable of such orientation, for they are the last representatives of an ancient tradition that is fast dying out. Nearly a hundred years before we sailed with Tevake three Santa Cruz boys were travelling aboard the missionary vessel *Southern Cross*. It was noted that the eldest was

teaching the names of various stars to his younger companions, and [I] was surprised at the number he knew by name. Moreover, at any time of night or day, in whatsoever direction we might happen to be steering, these boys, even the youngest of the three, a lad of ten or twelve, would be able to point to where his home lay; This I have found them able to do many hundreds of miles to the south of the Santa Cruz group (Coote, 1882: 152-4).

We are not able to re-create the conceptual framework within which Tevake organises his data any more than we are able to do so with the boys who were his countrymen, or with Tupaia, who must have orientated in broadly similar terms. However, though we lack understanding of their outlook, there is evidence enough of their ability to achieve results. Quite apart from normal voyages, we have seen how Tevake's orientation was put to test by storm, how the Gilbertese Iotiebata maintained his sense of direction in even more trying circumstances, and we will come later to analogous Carolinian and Tongan examples.

THE *ETAK* SYSTEM

Etak, or *hatag* as it is pronounced on Woleai (Alkire, 1970: 51), is a concept of dividing up a voyage into stages or segments by the star bearings of a reference or *etak* island.[2] A navigator's position at sea is defined in *etak* terms and the concept also comes into play in maintaining bearings when tacking or when driven off course. It must be re-emphasised that we are dealing with a method of visualising where the navigator is and of processing the data already in his possession, no new facts being involved.

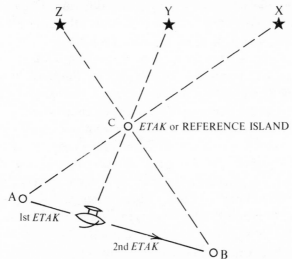

Fig. 18 A very short voyage of two etak *from island A to island B*

Let us take the simplest case of a voyage that proceeds direct from island A to island B. A third island C is chosen as reference island (see fig. 18). Ideally it should be equidistant from the other two and located to one side

---

[2] I have drawn extensively on Gladwin (1970: 181-95) and on Alkire (1970: 51-5) for material incorporated in this section as well as for diagrams that I have adapted, and of course those passages specifically cited. Gladwin's manuscript accompanied us to the Carolines and was invaluable in giving some understanding of *etak* before ever I sailed with Hipour.

An *etak* island is a reference island. Confusion has arisen through early observers referring to them as emergency or refuge islands (Sarfert, 1911: 134-6; Akerblom, 1968: 107). Whether this was ever even a subsidiary meaning of the term is a little doubtful, for as Gladwin points out, 'It is in the nature of the system that in order to know where the etak reference island is the navigator must also know where all the islands around him are. Therefore if he were in trouble he would flee to the most accessible or most useful of these, not necessarily the etak island. Many reference islands are actually quite useless for refuge. Some are tiny and uninhabited, others difficult to approach in bad weather, and a few are actually reefs or shoals with no dry land at all' (1970: 186).

of the line between them. In practice it is the exception
to find one so conveniently sited.

The navigator knows how the reference island bears
from island A (and also from B, it having been part of
his training to learn the direction of every known island
from every other one). In Carolinian terms he has learnt
'under which star' C lies when visualised from A. In fig.
18 it lies under star X.

When the voyage commences towards the objective B,
the bearing of island C alters until, when the canoe has
reached the position shown in the diagram, C has come
to lie beneath star Y, the next point of the sidereal compass. The canoe is then said to have travelled one *etak*
and this is expressed by saying that the *etak* island C
has 'moved' from one star point to the next, in this
instance from 'under' star X to 'under' star Y.

This is the essence of the concept—that one *etak* along
the course corresponds to the apparent 'movement' backwards by one star point of the reference island.

By the time the navigator arrives at his destination
island B the reference island C will have 'moved' under
the next star point Z. Since the voyage is only two *etak*
long, very much shorter than a real one would be, he will
be at his destination after covering only these two *etak*.

In other words, the canoe is conceived as stationary
beneath the star points, whose position is also regarded as
fixed. The sea flows past and the island astern recedes
while the destination comes nearer and the reference
island moves 'back' beneath the navigating stars until it
comes abeam, and then moves on abaft the beam. (It can
be appreciated from fig. 18 that if a voyage is undertaken
in the opposite direction, the 'movement' of the *etak*
island past the stars is simply reversed.)

Naturally the Carolinians are perfectly well aware that
the islands do *not* literally move. For instance Ulutak was
at very great pains to make sure I realised that all the
islands concerned with a voyage 'moved' under the stars.
He and Hipour insisted that I could never know where I
was at sea unless I appreciated this fundamental concept.
Yet in the same breath Ulutak said laughingly 'Of course
we know that islands stay in the same place'.

It is rather like sitting on a train and looking out the window [writes Gladwin]. In your little world you sit and talk while the scenery slips by. In the distance there are mountains which for long periods of time seem to pace the train. Looking at them you are distracted by nearby houses which flash backwards between you and the mountains. The mountains are the stars and the houses the islands below (1970: 183).

And at sea,

You may travel for days on the canoe but the stars will not go away or change their positions aside from their nightly trajectories from horizon to horizon . . . Back along the wake, however, the island you left falls farther and farther behind, while the one towards which you are heading is hopefully drawing closer. You can see neither of them, but you know this is happening. You know too that there are islands on either side of you . . . Everything passes by the little canoe— everything, except the stars by night and the sun by day (p. 182).

There is another point to note from fig. 18. The *etak* island C is not equidistant from the other two, being nearer A, so the distance from the first island A to the canoe's position as shown will be shorter than the second *etak* from the canoe to island B. In general an attempt is made so to choose reference islands that the segments are of roughly equal length, and something of the order of 10-20 miles is considered the optimum.

Let us now consider an actual case, the 117-mile voyage from Woleai to Olimarao. The island of Faraulep 70 miles to the northward, and almost equidistant though a little nearer the former, makes a nearly ideal *etak* (see fig. 19).

This journey is divided into six *etak* of approximately comparable length averaging around 20 miles. As the navigator travels towards Olimarao, Woleai falls astern with respect to his canoe and Olimarao begins to come nearer. Faraulep, which at the beginning of the voyage lay beneath the rising Great Bear, after one *etak* has been traversed now lies beneath the rising Kochab. As the voyage continues it passes progressively beneath Polaris, Kochab setting, the Great Bear setting, Cassiopeia setting; and when Olimarao is reached the *etak* island lies beneath the setting position of Vega (paraphrased from Alkire, 1970: 53).

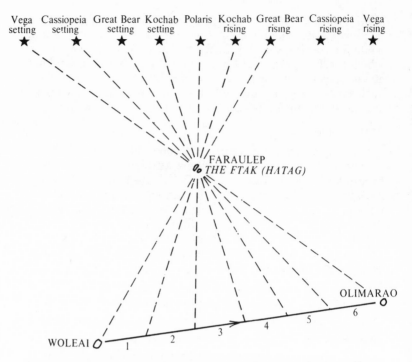

Fig. 19   *Voyage from Woleai to Olimarao (from Alkire, 1970; position of islands from Admiralty Chart 763)*

We have already seen that if the reference island forms an uneven triangle with the starting point and destination, the length of the *etak* segments will be uneven. This effect is intensified if the reference island is very near, in which case the initial and final *etak* will be longer than those when the canoe is abeam of the reference island (Gladwin, 1970: 186).

WEST FAYU
O

LAMOTREK
O
          O
SATAWAL

Fig. 20   *The islands of West Fayu, Satawal, and Lamotrek (from Admiralty Chart 763)*

The clustering of the sidereal compass stars east and west and their sparsity north and south (see p. 67) is another cause of inequality. Gladwin (p. 187) gives the example of the roughly equal triangle of islands West Fayu, Satawal, and Lamotrek. The distance between each pair is a little over 40 miles, and to the third of the trio, the *etak* reference island, it is the same (see fig. 20).

For the seaway between Satawal and Lamotrek the *etak* is West Fayu, which 'moves' during the passage under the sparse northern stars from the setting Little Bear to the rising Cassiopeia, so dividing the voyage into four segments. Between Satawal and West Fayu, on the other hand, the reference island Lamotrek passes under the crowded western star positions from setting γ Aquilae to setting Southern Cross, dividing the voyage into seven segments. This is nearly twice as many as for the other voyage of the same length.

The two Puluwat navigational schools of *fanur* and *warieng* (*faluch* and *wuriang* on Woleai) do not always choose exactly the same reference islands, *warieng*, for instance, preferring to use two on passages as long as about 150 miles. These details need not concern us. One complication that we must tackle, however, is that of the initial and final pairs of *etak*.

The first two and last two *etak* are known as the 'etak of sighting' and the 'etak of birds', and differ fundamentally from the rest. We have seen how an *etak* is a segment of a voyage and that its length varies both from one voyage to the next and from one part to another of the same passage. The first and last pair of *etak* stages are exceptions to this rule (Alkire, 1970: 54; Gladwin, 1970: 188). They are only approximately equated with the passage of the reference island beneath the first and second star points, and their actual length is based on criteria of a quite different order. The *etak* of sighting, as its name implies, is completed the precise moment the carefully watched island is seen to dip below (or rise over) the horizon. Its length is taken to be 10 miles. The second *etak*, that of birds, is also considered to be 10 miles (of course, birds are equally present in the 10 miles where land is visible), for 20 miles is the distance that terns and noddies may be relied upon to indicate direction of land from their morning and evening flight paths.

Thus only these two *etak* are of fixed length, and only in their case may the term '*etak*' be translated as 'zone'—'zone of visibility' and 'zone of birds', whereas we have seen that all the other *etak* of a passage are segments and the *etak* island a reference one.

Before we go on to the special applications of *etak* to tacking up-wind and setting course after a storm-drift, let us re-state the nature of the system itself. The concept, to paraphrase Gladwin, is a convenient way to organise and synthesise the information the navigator has available in order to make his judgments readily and without confusion. The picture he uses of the world around him includes all the islands he knows and the places of rising and setting of the navigational stars. It can give him no new objective facts. Knowledge of the bearings of *etak* islands is attained through study of the little diagrams of islands and stars shown by pebbles on the canoe house floor during the years of instruction. The reference island on one voyage may of course be the objective on the next. Thus in fig. 18, if the voyage were made from B to C, island A would function as the *etak*.

The system is workable only because of the vast number of star courses and other items of information stored in the navigator's memory. This has to be coupled with his skilled judgment—thus his reckoning of the canoe's speed will mainly determine his estimate of the number of star points past which the reference island has 'moved'.

Etak, then, provides a framework 'into which the navigator's knowledge of rate, time, geography and astronomy can be integrated to provide a conveniently expressed and comprehended statement of distance travelled'. It is a tool 'for bringing together raw information and converting it into the solution of an essential navigational question, "How far away is our destination?" ' (Gladwin, 1970: 186).

Etak *and*
Tacking   'My informants', writes Alkire, 'emphasised that mastery of this step [tacking] separated the good from the mediocre navigators' (1970: 55n.) and Gladwin points out that tacking up-wind over a long distance with only the logical construct of the moving island for guidance 'places the greatest demands of any routine navigational exercise upon the judgment and skill of the navigator' (1970: 189). The following account of *etak* when tacking follows Gladwin's closely (1970: 189-95).

We will consider the simplest case for orientation, which is when the canoe has to tack directly up-wind. Let us say that the distance from island A to island B is 100 miles and the objective B lies 'under' Altair, that is it bears 8° north of east or 82°. We assume the canoe to be

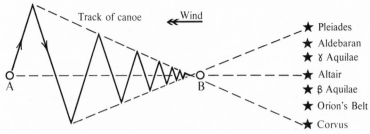

Fig. 21 Tacking directly up-wind and etak *(after Gladwin, 1970)*

able to make good 72° from the true wind (probably better than it could do in practice), the wind in this instance blowing straight from Altair and so being directly contrary. Carolinian procedure is to make the initial tacks long and gradually shorten them each time a change is made so that near the end they become quite short. 'In this way near its destination the canoe courses back and forth on successively tighter tacks to assure that it will intercept the island'.[3]

Let us suppose the navigator chooses to make his first tack towards the north (see fig. 21). His guidance comes from his estimate of the 'movements' of the destination island B, which is more or less on his beam and behaves as if it were an *etak* reference island. That is it 'moves' south beneath the navigation stars. (The usual *etak* island is disregarded during a tacking voyage since the destination island has virtually assumed its role.) 'A tack which moves the destination island three stars away, the equivalent of three segments in the etak system, is frequently the length selected', says Gladwin (1970: 192). In our example island B in moving from under Altair to a position under Corvus three stars away would travel through an arc of about 25° which would require an initial northbound tack of the order of 40 miles, requiring perhaps twelve hours.

The navigator now comes about and heads east of south, and island B moves back north until it passes Altair and eventually comes under the Pleiades three stars beyond. This second tack will be about 75 miles, but the

---

[3] The procedure was the same in the Marshalls. 'The navigator at first makes extended tacks, perhaps six hours long, then gradually shorter' (Winkler, 1901: 507).

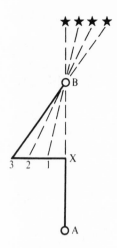

*Fig. 22 Etak
when blown
off course and
wind later
reverts to a
favourable
direction
(drawn under
Hipour's and
Beiong's
direction)*

next north-going one will be only 55 miles. The tacks become successively shorter as the canoe closes island B because it always ends each tack on the same bearing of the destination. On the ninth or tenth tack the island should come into view. The 100-mile journey has required nearly 350 miles of sailing, during which time the navigator has had to keep in mind 'estimates of rate, time, bearing, drift and some complex visual images of canoe, islands, and stars. Of all these he can only see the canoe, the water, and at night the stars' (Gladwin, 1970: 193).

In practice a voyage would normally be delayed until the wind was no longer dead ahead, so allowing one or other tack to be the more favourable. The journey in such circumstances would be shorter—a wind at 45° to the course requiring a canoe actually to cover some 170 miles (instead of 350 in a dead head wind) to traverse a 100-mile passage. But with tacks of uneven length and at different angles to the direct track, orientation would be more complex, though in no way different in principle.

While, like all good seamen, Carolinians and other Islanders prefer to await favourable winds before putting to sea, I was astonished at how readily the Puluwatans undertook the 135-mile open sea voyage to Truk when the wind was but 20° or so from being dead ahead. They cheerfully allowed about a week for this passage during which the navigator would have to zigzag up-wind with never a sight of land, except perhaps Tamatam, all the while maintaining his bearings as he visualised his objective moving back and forth beneath the stars and slowly drawing nearer. The usual reason given me, incidentally, for these arduous ventures was to buy cigarettes—of course the government steamer was available, but what star navigator would so demean himself. . . .

Etak *when
Blown off
Course*

In the first case a canoe on passage from island A towards B is storm-drifted at right angles to its proper track for three *etak* to the left (in a westerly direction. See fig. 22). When the gale has subsided and the wind has freed so that the captain can lay his objective, he must steer three star points (corresponding to the three *etak* he was displaced) to the right (eastward) of his original star course.

But there is one important modification. He should so adjust his course from 3 to B that he rejoins the original course *before* the destination, so that he *can be sure from which side* he is approaching it.

This method, or perhaps principle is the better term, is widely applied in navigation. Instead of heading directly towards the objective, the navigator incorporates in his course a small deliberate bias in a pre-determined direction, so that as he comes near he *knows* in which general direction the destination lies. Thus in the diagram it must be to the north of him, it cannot be either north or south. Similarly Hipour deliberately kept to the east or windward of the Marianas, so that he could eventually turn down-wind towards the island chain confident that it was in our lee. Again, Tevake added a slight southerly bias to the proper star course in anticipation of a night landfall on Taumako. The same principle comes into windward landfall, which we will refer to in chap. 9. It was also used by Chichester in his approach to Norfolk and Lord Howe Islands on the first New Zealand-Australia solo flight (pers. comm., 1961)

Figure 23 shows a canoe that had reached the half way point from island A to island B before being gale-drifted at right angles to the course, from X to Y. In this instance, though the wind moderates so the canoe can make sail again, it fails to free and continues blowing from the direction shown. The captain then gets under way and sails parallel to his original track. His dead reckoning tells him that he had completed half the voyage before the onset of the gale, three *etak* say, and so would have had three more to go. When he has covered three *etak* on this parallel course and reached 3, he will be opposite B, which will be east of him. He still cannot head directly towards it because of the head wind, however, so must continue in the same direction until he is able to do so, in this case to 5. Since 5 is two *etak* north of B, the latter will bear two star points south of east from 5 (corresponding to the two *etak* the canoe had to sail beyond B).

Naturally, once again the proviso applies about adjusting this final approach course to make landfall on a pre-determined side of the objective. This is not indicated in the diagram.

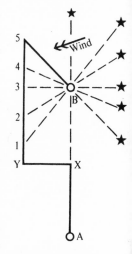

Fig. 23 Etak when blown off course and wind remains unfavourable (drawn under Hipour's and Beiong's direction)

Again for the sake of simplicity, the *etak* island for the course A-B is omitted from both diagrams. This *etak* island in fact becomes conceptually immobile all the while the canoe is being drifted, because this drift is equivalent to proceeding along a course X-3 or X-Y, when B and A act as *etak* (as in tacking). After the canoe takes up its original or modified course towards its destination the *etak* island resumes its former role.

Some Implications of Etak

Etak is a poly-dimensional system that involves direction and time and therefore movement. The *etak* conception of moving islands is an essentially dynamic one that is not easy to fit into the framework of the abstraction that to us is so familiar—the static two-dimensional chart. It is easy for us to forget, because of its familiarity, how much of an abstraction a chart really is. Whether Mercator, gnomic or any other projection be used, it is impossible to depict the surface of a sphere in a flat plane without distortion. The proverbial man from Mars would scan the ocean in vain if he expected to see marked there the same figures denoting fathoms and lines indicating shoals that a chart so prominently displays.

Hipour and Beiong found attempts to reconcile the two concepts to be just as difficult as we should. On one occasion I was trying to determine the identity of an island they named Ngatik—there were no charts to be consulted of course—that lay somewhere south-west of Ponape. It had not been visited by Central Carolinian canoes for several generations but was an *etak* reference island for the Oroluk-Ponape voyage and as such its star bearings from both these islands were known to Hipour. On his telling me what they were I drew a diagram to illustrate that Ngatik must necessarily lie where these *etak* bearings intersected (see fig. 24).

Hipour could not grasp this idea at all. His concept is the wholly dynamic one of moving islands, and possibly this is why he several times asked me how islands got on charts. I think he can visualise islands as static when thought of from the start or end points of a voyage, provided there is no tacking and the course between is a straight line: but he certainly cannot conceive of them as

Fig. 24　The location of Ngatik

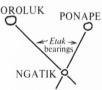

being static when they are conceived of as fulfilling their
etak function. Beiong, who is less highly trained in navigation, and though profoundly steeped in tradition has a
more original mind, had exactly the same difficulty as
Hipour. However, he eventually succeeded in achieving
the mental *tour de force* of visualising himself sailing
simultaneously from Oroluk to Ponape and from Ponape
to Oroluk and picturing the *etak* bearings to Ngatik at the
start of both voyages. In this way he managed to comprehend the diagram and confirmed that it showed the
island's position correctly.

It appears, therefore, that in the *etak* conception we
have another system which, like the sidereal compass, is
virtually incompatible with the corresponding European
abstraction—in this case the static chart. Like the star
compass the *etak* system can probably be little modified
by European concepts; it may be expected to remain
essentially intact until it is ultimately replaced and
disappears.[4] It follows, I think, that geographical-
navigational data expressed in terms of star course and
etak are likely to have been only marginally influenced by
European knowledge.

Contact with European seamen has not enabled navigators like Hipour to abstract data from European charts
and incorporate it effectively into their own system. It is
quite possible for some star courses to distant islands to
have been updated or even extended through the observations of Island navigators travelling on Western ships,
and perhaps even more by their talking to fellow navigators on the islands they visited.[5] However, it is very
doubtful if such accretions (I am talking of detailed star-
etak bearings, not vague approximate courses) to the body
of tradition would do more than balance the decline in

---

[4] Minor modifications are likely to have occurred. For instance Alkire
points out that there seems to be a tendency on Woleai towards making
hatag segments of more equal length that could have resulted from
familiarity with Western charts. He considers it more than coincidence
that the 60 miles between Woleai and Eauripik are divided into six *hatag*
and the 95 miles between Faraulep and Olimarao into nine (1970: 54).

[5] Some sailing directions in the far west of the Carolines from Sonsorol
to Tobi are said to have been 'updated and corrected in Warieng a few
years ago when a navigator of that school served for a short time on a
government ship which plied between them' (Gladwin, 1970: 202).

oral navigational lore that has accompanied the steady shrinking over several centuries of the voyaging sphere.[6]

An element in the survival of indigenous navigational concepts like *etak* and the sidereal compass is that they are essentially 'closed' systems that, by their very completeness, as well as the nature of their concepts, have been resistant to the incorporation of data from outside sources. Another example of this conservatism is the height of the Pole Star. I was aware that this must almost exactly double from about 7½° at Puluwat to 15° above the horizon at Saipan. Clearly even the roughest method of estimating when the star had attained this higher altitude would have been of inestimable assistance in judging when a canoe was abreast of the Marianas.

It was extremely difficult, without asking very leading questions, to find out if Hipour was aware of this phenomenon, since the name of Polaris in Puluwatese is 'The star that does not move'. Eventually he realised that I was inquiring about upward not lateral displacement. He did know through the navigational traditions taught in the *warieng* school that the star was going to rise higher. But by how much he had no idea, nor had he heard of any method of making use of this observation for navigational purposes. So during all the centuries that canoe fleets had regularly crossed this empty expanse, none had apparently thought to draw practical conclusions from this striking finding, that when the Pole Star doubled its altitude your destination must lie under one of the positions of the cardinal reference star, Altair, i.e. west or east of you.[7] The requirements of the navigation system do not include innovation.

A further example of a navigator being highly com-

---

[6] For former seafaring in the Carolines, see Krämer (1935: 103). For decline of Woleai voyaging, see Alkire (1970: 45).

[7] I added the qualifying 'apparently' as there must have been aspects, probably sophisticated ones, of Carolinian navigation that are now forgotten. Fr Cantova's eighteenth-century reference to a Faraulep 'wind compass' (1728: 209, 210) that we noted on p. 73 is one piece of evidence. Even more suggestive is the nineteenth-century report of a canoe arriving at Tinian (neighbouring island to Saipan) from Elato in the Carolines with a navigational bamboo cane filled with water which was apparently used to determine latitude (Sanchez, 1866: 263). This will be referred to again under zenith stars in chap. 9. See especially p. 242.

petent in his own 'closed' tradition but unfamiliar with the concepts of an alien one—in this case compasses and charts—comes from the Gilbert Islands. Teeta of Kuria is a *tia borau* trained in the classical manner and probably the most learned navigator in the Gilberts today. During the war, to get food for New Zealand coastwatchers, he sailed from Kuria to Nonouti by canoe (60 miles) and then in a launch visited Tabiteuea, Beru, Nikunau, Onotoa, Abemama, and Maiana. There was a small boat compass which was stowed away and never used and no chart (which in any case he would not have known how to use).

EXAMPLES OF *ETAK* AND ANALOGOUS ORIENTATION

This took place about 1961 or 1962. There is a written record by Ullman (1964: 68-75), which is supplemented and corrected in minor detail by the account of Homearek, our first interpreter in the Carolines, who was a member of Sernous's crew. Their home was Pulap, an island some 20 miles north of Puluwat, and it was from there that the sailing canoe with its complement of five set off. They were bound for the uninhabited islet of Pikelot 100 miles to the westward to catch and bring back turtles for a feast to celebrate the completion of a new church. (This is one of the few discrepancies between the accounts, Ullman asserting that they were going to Truk 130 miles in the other direction for cigarettes. Homearek says that this was an earlier voyage.) The venerable canoe captain Sernous, who has since died, was a highly qualified and respected navigator.

Sernous's Voyage

The canoe was driven past its objective by gale force easterly and later northerly winds. (In these waters a string of tropical depressions or revolving storms away to the north-east would be the probable cause of such prolonged severe easterly and northerly weather.) They lay a-hull, that is without sail, in the worst squalls and attempted to tack back towards the west in the lulls. There was ample rainwater to drink and they managed to catch about a fish a day. After thirty days at sea without sight of land Sernous still retained his orientation in spite of the intermittent drifting and tacking. He judged, according to Homearek, that the resultant track had been a little south of west, so that their starting point of Pulap would havé 'moved' very far astern indeed and would lie beneath the rising γ Aquilae. Sernous may have been helped to know the direction of drift during overcast periods by what Ullman describes as 'the rusted wreck of a compass'. Homearek says, however, that the sky was rarely obscured for long and the east and north-east swells remained discernible throughout. Furthermore Sernous believed the compass (probably with reason, as the alcohol had leaked out) to be broken, and did not use it. The nearest land, Sernous told his crew, would now be the island of Ifalik, which had 'moved' to the setting point of Vega, or north-west, and should not be so very far away.

This estimate would mean that they had been driven some 300 miles west of their starting point. The wind had come round to the north and was too strong to allow more than a rag of sail to be carried; they were inching their way north-westward through enormous seas towards Ifalik, bailing continuously, when the motor vessel *Chicot*, on which Ullman was a passenger, encountered them.

After some shouted exchanges, the five agreed to be taken aboard *Chicot*, provided their canoe accompanied them. Ullman mentions his astonishment when the light craft had been hoisted onto a hatchway, because its occupants insisted on bailing out the water, spreading the sail to dry and testing the lashings before agreeing to go to the galley for a meal.

They were not lost, Sernous assured the ship's captain, they were blown away. The navigator went on to explain how long and how far they had drifted and in which direction. Ullman writes (1964: 74), 'When we picked them up they had been hoping to reach the atoll of Ifalik, in the district of Yap. "Is that way", he [Sernous] said, pointing off to the northwest. And the captain and mate nodded in bemused agreement. Ifalik was indeed "that way"; thirty-five miles by the ship's chart, from where we had sighted them.' The peculiar navigational interest of this story lies not so much in the orientation ability displayed being in any way exceptional in a trained Pacific Island navigator, but because of the coincidence of meeting with *Chicot* that enabled this orientation to be independently confirmed.

Sernous's ability to maintain his bearings in difficult conditions is comparable to that of the Gilbertese Iotiebata when gale-drifted east of his islands for more than a month (see p. 124). Another instance was Tevake's success in finding Tikopia and the New Hebrides in gale conditions. What exactly did this entail? He was nearing Taumako from the Reef Islands, though, his destination not being visible in the thick weather, he only had his own estimate to tell him where he was, when the 'big wind' came down upon him. The *te puke* being unable to stand into the gale, he ran off for Tikopia over 160 miles away; when it came into view he had covered something over 210 miles on two angled courses without ever having seen land—no small navigational achievement. *Tevake and Iotiebata, Similar Examples*

On leaving Saipan to return to the Carolines Hipour told me that he aimed to arrive a little up-current and to windward (east) of Pikelot and that he hoped to locate a deep reef within the islet's 20-mile radius bird zone. Our *etak* would be the island of Gaferut, which was not ideally placed, being opposite the southern part of our track.[8] After nearly four days had passed since we last saw land and we judged we had covered a little over 400 miles, Hipour and Ulutak asked if I could point out the positions of our destination Pikelot, the *etak* Gaferut, and another island Satawal. I indicated that the first was now due south of us and the third about south-south-west. The *etak* Gaferut, I said, bore a little south of west. This last statement caused much amusement. Yes, I had been quite right about Pikelot and Satawal, but the *etak* island had already passed the beam and fallen astern of us. It now lay under the setting position of Aldebaran—about west- Etak *Bearings with Hipour*

---

[8] Gaferut is 148 miles west-north-west of Pikelot. An alternative *etak* for this voyage, according to Beiong, is Magur in the Nomonuitos, 100 miles east-north-east of Pikelot, which is no better situated.

by-north rather than west-by-south as I had so mistakenly thought. We all agreed, however, that we should reach the bird zone that afternoon, and so in fact we did.

From our Pikelot landfall the next day and the chart I later consulted (in Australia), I calculated that at the time of the incident Pikelot had indeed been about 40 miles due south of us, Satawal 130 miles south-south-west and the *etak* Gaferut 90 miles west-by-north, just as Hipour had said. It is significant, I think, that it was not only the trained navigator Hipour, but also the ordinary island canoeman Ulutak, who had such utter confidence in his bearings—after a 400-mile four-day passage across an unfamiliar sea.

A Polynesian Example of Orientation   One of the very few individual voyages to have been recorded from early last century was made by the Tongan chief Kau Moala. We owe this record to an English youth, Will Mariner, a survivor of the taking of the privateer *Port au Prince* at Ha'apai, who was adopted by the Tongan chief Finau. Kau Moala was one of the specially accomplished navigators known as *kaivai*, or 'water eaters' (Ve'ehala). He was also a son of Akau'ola, High Navigator of Tonga. I think this tradition may be accepted the more readily as it was told by members of the Tuita, rivals to the senior Akau'ola. It would have been a different matter had they claimed the well-known 'adventurer for their own clan.

Kau Moala was returing from Fiji towards the Tongan island of Vava'u, a passage of 250 miles of open sea, and he had sighted his objective, when the 'wind becoming unfavourable to land, and the sea running very high', he was obliged to change course and run for Samoa, which is over 300 miles from Vava'u, 'but the wind soon increasing to a heavy gale, drifted him to the island of Fotoona, situated North West of Hamoa' (Mariner, 1817: vol. I, 316). Futuna is about 300 miles from Samoa and 340 from Vava'u, and this is the only stage of the chief's travels where chance is at all likely to have played any part in the landfall.

His canoe with its load of sandalwood was taken from him and a new one built according to normal Pacific

Island custom. About a year later he set out once more with thirty-nine companions, who included four Futunans who had 'begged to go with him that they might visit distant countries'. They touched at the solitary island of Rotuma, 295 miles to the westward, and thence sailed 255 miles south to Fiji. Ultimately Kau Moala returned to Tonga (Mariner, 1817: vol. I, 316-17).

All the islands visited or aimed for by Kau Moala were well within the Tongan close-contact sphere; some, like Rotuma, paid tribute to Tonga as late as the 1820s (Dillon, 1829: 295; Diaper, 1928: 111). The fact of his calling at them is not, therefore, in any way remarkable when we consider the capacity of his vessels—compare the complement of forty after Futuna with Sernous's probable limit of seven or eight. It is only the accident of Mariner's presence on the scene when Kau Moala returned that was so exceptional.

It seems evident from Kau Moala's personal reputation as a navigator, his background, and the courses he followed, that he was aware of bearings of islands like Samoa, Futuna, and Rotuma from different starting points. But what variety of home-centre or mixed reference system he used is unknown, for the manner in which Polynesian navigators conceived the geographical relations of the archipelagos within their ken was, as we mentioned at the beginning of this chapter, never recorded. However, just as some form of sidereal compass may once have underlain the Polynesian wind compasses, it seems likely that an orientation system of comparable accuracy to the Carolinian once obtained. What we cannot assume, of course, is that the same or a similar concept of moving reference islands ever developed in Polynesia. But from such examples of orientation capability as those of Tevake and Kau Moala, I think we may safely deduce that Polynesian concepts were also of the home- or local-centre reference type and that they did produce results of a comparable degree of accuracy to the Carolinian.

We have touched on compensating for current and leeway and estimating distance by the arts of dead reckoning, and also considered methods of orientation. In theory we should now draw conclusions as to the accuracy attainable. In practice, however, the accuracy of any navigational system must be closely related to the spread of the target. We shall therefore postpone consideration of the accuracy attainable in dead reckoning star path courses until we have described in the following chapters how the target is 'expanded'.

Part Four

EXPANDED TARGET LANDFALL AND POSITION

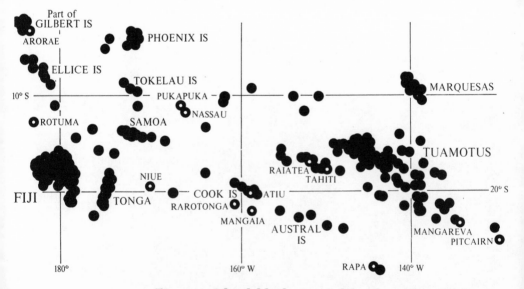

Part of
GILBERT IS

ARORAE

PHOENIX IS

ELLICE IS

TOKELAU IS

10° S

PUKAPUKA

NASSAU

ROTUMA

SAMOA

MARQUESAS

NIUE

FIJI

TONGA

COOK IS

ATIU

TUAMOTUS

20° S

RAROTONGA

RAIATEA

TAHITI

MANGAIA

AUSTRAL
IS

MANGAREVA

PITCAIRN

180°

160° W

RAPA

140° W

Fig. 25   Island blocks formed by drawing a circle of
30 miles radius round each island; heights have been
ignored (from Lewis, 1964b)

CHAPTER SIX

Island blocks—birds—clouds

Techniques for 'expanding' the size of the target are an integral part of Polynesian and Micronesian navigation. The concept is a crucial one because star steering and dead reckoning systems would be less than adequate did they not incorporate methods for the qualitative transformation of tiny into sizable objectives. The idea applies to two situations. In the first an isolated atoll is appreciated as being surrounded, far beyond sight range, by a zone of land indicators. In the second, the gaps between the islands of a group are 'bridged' by the overlapping zones round individual islands so that the whole archipelago becomes a target for landfall. Both applications depend on the observation of such land signs as homing birds, clouds, or wave patterns.

The term 'expanded target landfall' refers to individual atolls as well as to groups, while the phrase 'island block landfall', is more or less restricted to archipelagos. The latter term seems a convenient description of the transformation of discrete island units into destination blocks.

ISLAND BLOCK LANDFALL

Any figure that may be advanced for the average extent of zones wherein land indicating signs may be relied upon is of course the merest approximation, since the distance will differ from one island to another and for the same one day by day. However, Frankel (1962: 40) estimated that there was a 'very good chance' of making land within 30 miles of a low-lying target. This seemed a reasonable enough abstraction in 1964, and still does in the light of experience. The following paragraphs are paraphrased from an earlier paper.

If we draw circles with 30 miles radii round each Pacific island, we find that the circles overlap over vast areas, giving rise to 'solid blocks', i.e. islands separated by not more than 60 miles, passing between which a canoe could not be more than 30 miles offshore (see fig. 25).

Attention has been drawn to the danger of canoes passing between chains of islands in the dark (Hilder, 1963a: 90-1), and contemporary Carolinian and Santa Cruz navigators are only too well aware of it, as evidenced by Tevake's and Hipour's practice of heaving-to when in the slightest danger of over-running an island at night. The island block chart and the list of dimensions of the major blocks given in the table below both neglect the height of land, and so tend to give an unduly pessimistic indication of the likelihood of successful locations of islands. That this factor can be a substantial one is shown by the fact that Tahiti, 7400 feet high, has been sighted over 80 miles away and its standing clouds still further.

EXTENT OF SOME 'ISLAND BLOCKS'

Name of island group forming block	North-south extent	East-west extent
Tonga	260 miles	140 miles
Fiji	370 miles	330 miles
Samoa	110 miles	260 miles
Tuamotu	550 miles	500 miles
Society (including Tahiti and Raiatea)	160 miles	310 miles
Marquesas	210 miles	180 miles
Southern Cooks (excluding Rarotonga and Mangaia)	120 miles	200 miles
Ellice	250 miles	200 miles

The Hawaiian chain extends for more than 1000 miles in a west-north-west to east-south-east direction. Of this, 340 miles consist of high islands rising to 13,000 feet, with active volcanoes. The whole chain is marked by islands, atolls, reefs, shoals, wind shadow and wave interference phenomena (Lewis, 1964b: 369).

The extent of these blocks is such as to be able to absorb considerable tracking and dead reckoning error and render arrival in the block navigationally certain— in so far as certainty exists for small vessels on the open sea—even from a very great distance. Of course landfall among unfamiliar reef-girt islands with unknown currents would have its dangers, but it would present far less of a problem to canoes drawing a foot or two of water and filled with powerful paddlers than it would to deep draught motorless European sailing ships. Within the blocks, no one has questioned the feasibility of regular voyaging.

After learning something of Pacific navigators' actual ideas about 'island blocks' and having seen demonstrated some of the methods they use to expand their targets, I at first formed the intention of modifying fig. 25 to make it reflect reality more closely. With this end in view I looked up the species of birds roosting on each group with their feeding ranges and seasonal habits. I had begun working out and plotting the sight ranges of the higher islands when I stopped, because I realised that the exercise was becoming artificial. The model, which at best could only be an approximation to reality, was in danger of being mistaken for the real thing; the construct was becoming isolated from the realm where it belonged, that of practical seamanship.

It might indeed be possible to construct a representation of the Pacific archipelagos at a given moment in time, showing exactly how each island deflected the swells, modified the clouds above, was visible from a certain distance and was surrounded by a flight range of birds that rested there. But every one of these signs is ephemeral. By the very next day they would have changed to falsify yesterday's exact picture.

We might with advantage dwell for a moment on this mutability of land signs, for we who are accustomed to the absolutes of sextant and chronometer position fixes can easily forget that we are here dealing with arts: techniques for evaluating accumulations of circumstantial clues that, taken by themselves, are all too often tenuous, transitory, and unreliable. Thus the sight range of high islands varies with the visibility; as an example, the mountains of Mangareva and those of Truk should be discernible 45 miles away yet because of overcast, our first sight of both islands was not the peaks, but the low islets on the intervening barrier reef. And again, terns and noddies generally fish within 20 miles of an island, booby-birds 30, yet storms, breeding seasons or migratory urges

may profoundly influence the behaviour of particular
bird populations. Land clouds may be absent or else
obscured in general overcast. A storm may abolish wave
patterns. On rainy nights the deep phosphorescent 'lightning' called *te lapa* may indicate the direction of land 60
or 100 miles off to the Santa Cruz Reef Islanders; in fine
weather it is absent. And finally, low islands may be
unwittingly passed in the darkness, if through faulty dead
reckoning a navigator has neglected to heave-to at dusk
when approaching them.

We must beware, therefore, of oversimplifying the arts
involved in identification of distant land and of under-
estimating the problems involved. Unambiguous signposts
are noticeably absent from the open ocean, and it helps
not at all towards an understanding of the careful observations and prodigious learning of trained Island navigators to pretend that they exist.

So far we have based our discussion on what, when first
put forward in 1964, was no more than a theory. Subsequent experience of the concepts and practice of Island
navigators has confirmed and amplified it and provided
the justification for the assertion that expanded target
techniques are an integral and important part of Polynesian and Micronesian navigation. What is the nature of
these indigenous 'island block' conceptions?

Tongan   A Tongan aphorism expresses the 'island block' idea
Concepts   very plainly. Expounding Tuita navigator clan lore and
coming to the subject of returning to Tonga from distant
lands, Ve'ehala averred that it was customary not to aim
for a specific island. He then quoted the navigational
proverb:

'It is enough that we strike *the row* of Puko trees'.
The meaning of this was, he said, that 'Vava'u and
Ha'apai are like a row of these very high trees, and one
only needed to hit the row not a particular tree. In the
same way a canoe captain would aim for the middle of
the group instead of for an individual island'.

Ve'ehala went on to discuss the applications of this
concept to the cases of landfalls on Tonga from Niue and
from Fiji. Later measurements brought out its value.

From Niue in the east to Ha'apai in the middle of the Tongan chain is 250 miles of open sea, and from the closest of the Fijian Lau group to the central Tongan islands is about 200.[1] But we have already seen that the north-south extent of the Tongan landfall 'block' is 260 miles—a veritable forest of Puko trees which would be exceedingly hard to miss.

This saying about the Puko trees and its interpretation by Ve'ehala was the only formulation of the idea of landfall on a whole archipelago that I was offered in Tonga. However, this Governor of Ha'apai, being the chief traditionalist of the Tuita, was a particularly authoritative source.

Tongan captains who still sail by the stars like Ve'etutu, Kienga, and Vili Mailau, voyage only within the confines of their own reef-studded archipelago, and are therefore most concerned that their star courses, dead reckoning, and landfalls should be precise. These present-day captains have no experience of either visiting other archipelagos or returning to their own. Nevertheless, the other application of the concept, that of helping to locate individual islands, is part of their repertoire, for they do make free use of land signs to 'expand' their targets within the group. Such indications as cloud signs, deflected waves, deep phosphorescence (Ve'etutu), and wave patterns (Kienga) are used, and will be referred to in the appropriate sections.

Carolinian Concepts

As in so many aspects of navigation, current Carolinian usage may be studied directly, whereas in other areas only vestiges and aphorisms remain. Expanded target landfall is no exception. The range at which it is possible to home in on an island of destination determines the amount of error allowable in any navigational system. Navigation en route must be able to get the canoe close

---

[1] The passage from Tonga to Fiji was customarily begun from Vatoa in the Lau Group, according to Neyret (1950: 12), and it was here that canoes awaited suitable weather. Vatoa was the point of departure of Finau's double canoe in which Diaper was a passenger (Diaper, 1928: 114). The distance from Vatoa to the nearest Tongan island, Tofua, is only about 180 miles and to Ha'apai itself, 225 (not 300 miles, as Diaper says).

enough to its destination so that the navigator can find it
with the techniques at his disposal' (Gladwin, 1970: 195).
Homing birds and the recognition of deeply submerged
reefs are the favourite Carolinian techniques of this
nature, and on long voyages a navigator simply heads into
a 'screen of islands, reefs and birds' (Gladwin, 1970:
200).

The 'blocks' of islands surrounded by their indicator
zones, that were first postulated theoretically, are for
living Carolinian navigators 'screens'—a more practical
expression of the concept, since it implies what is most
important to the seafarer, the interception of the aberrant
or unfortunate canoe. Such men as Hipour, Ulutak, the
Puluwat chief Manipe, Homearek from Pulap and Beiong
from Pulusuk, continually made use of this figure of speech
in discussing voyages. Thus the degree of 'screening' of a
particular island was considered to be the major safety
consideration in making a voyage there.[2] The metaphor
came up in connection with currently undertaken passages,
with discontinued long voyages in general and those we
made ourselves to and from Saipan. (In chap. 8 we will be
describing Hipour's expanded target landfalls with which
these latter voyages culminated.)

It is worth mentioning here that our Carolinian informants were agreed that the length of a voyage was much
less important in terms of navigation than the size and
efficacy of the screen of islands, deep reefs, and bird zones
that made up its objective. Indeed, the longer voyages
that used to be made in the past to such places as Saipan
and Ponape were considered to have been tests of en-
durance and ability to withstand hardship rather than as
especially difficult navigational exercises. Gladwin also
touches on this point (1970: 61).

Some of the screens important in Puluwat navigation

---

[2] After Beiong had given me the star course for the voyage from the
Mortlocks to Pulusuk, he added that it had been sailed direct on several
occasions since the war by Pulusuk and Puluwat canoes (250 miles of
open sea). The course was not unduly difficult because there was a good
'screen' of islets, deep reefs, and bird zones in the neighbourhood of
Pulusuk. When I asked Beiong about the course in the reverse direction
(from Pulusuk to the Mortlocks), he gave it to me, but then explained
that the passage in this direction was in fact almost invariably made via
Truk, since the Mortlocks were an 'unscreened' target.

are described by Gladwin. If one visualises a 20-mile radius of safety surrounding each of the islands the

resulting overlapping circles, each 40 miles in diameter, will be seen often to stretch across the sea in long chains or screens able to intercept a canoe crossing them at any point. One such screen extends north and south with only one short gap, from Magur at the northern end of the Namonuito Atoll over one hundred and fifty miles south to Pulusuk. The gap results from the sixty-mile span of open ocean between Ulul and Pulap. This leaves an area without homing birds perhaps twenty miles across. However, a canoe sailing west through this area would almost certainly pass soon after over Gray Feather Bank and thus locate itself. . . .

A far longer screen emerges if the islands of this area are viewed as they would appear from the north. This view is of some historical interest because it is the view from Saipan. Seen from the north there is a continuous screen of over-lapping bird ranges extending for three hundred miles from Gaferut on the west to Pisaras on the east. If one will concede to the longer-ranging boobies of East Fayu a capability almost to close the sixty-mile gap east of Pisaras, the screen can be extended more than a hundred miles further east to Murilo in the Halls. This screen was used deliberately on the return from Saipan in the past when that voyage of over five hundred miles was occasionally made (Gladwin, 1970: 199-200).

As we shall see, Hipour used it too.

Teeta gave the clearest expression to the island block *Gilbertese* idea that we encountered in the Gilberts. 'If I were *Concepts* heading for somewhere far away I would go in the general direction and then look for signs of land', he explained. He stressed that stars gave you the course to travel but that landfall was determined by the very important land signs, especially clouds, waves, and birds. He repeated this point several times during our discussions, saying that on a long voyage he would head for a cluster of islands, then locate one of them by land signs. For example, the star course from the northern Gilbertese island of Butaritari to the Marshalls was 'just to the left of where the Great Bear shows the North Star to be'.[3] The

---

[3] This would be geographically correct for Mili, I noted subsequently, but if followed exactly without allowance for current set, would be more appropriate for the Ralik chain further west in the same group. However, he did not remember whether this course, which his grandfather had taught him, was meant to allow for current or not.

instructions had been that after proceeding on this northerly course for some days the navigator was 'to look out for the land signs'.

Teeta was unacquainted with Western charts, which he told me he did not understand; his knowledge of the location of islands, like his star lore, came from his grandfather's teaching in the *maneaba*, yet he could indicate a course that, whichever way it was interpreted, would certainly bring him into the Marshalls, and he could explain how he would then find land. (The methods are considered below.) That these vague sailing directions for a long discontinued voyage to a foreign archipelago were valid enough to have taken him into the thick of the cluster, and that once there he could be absolutely confident of making a landfall, is a striking exposition of the importance of the island block concept. The most exact star courses and dead reckoning instructions would be of less service to a navigator than the simple plan of sailing into the midst of an archipelago and then applying the skills and techniques we are about to consider to locating the nearest island.

THE LAND-FINDING METHODS THAT 'EXPAND' THE TARGET

Before we examine these systematically there are some general considerations to be taken into account. The available data must of necessity be incomplete, since in many island groups little of the old arts has survived, and what was earlier recorded was often minimal and rarely represented coherent bodies of knowledge, chance determining that an item of bird lore, say, should be noted in one place, and wave refraction in another. Then our own contacts with navigators in the places we visited were often hurried, while most islands perforce remained unvisited altogether.

Now all these qualifications apply equally to other branches of indigenous navigation, but it is land-finding techniques above all that might be expected to exhibit the greatest degree of purely local diversity. The configuration of the ocean floor in the vicinity of an archipelago, the presence of upwellings of nutrient-rich water, to name but two factors, will affect wave patterns and the feeding habits of birds. It would be logical to suppose, therefore, that methods for expanding landfall would fully reflect the variety of the phenomena associated with the targets. I myself had not seriously questioned this assumption.

But perhaps the geographical diversity of islands is more apparent than real, for they all deflect waves, provide resting places for seabirds and influence the clouds drifting above. Such effects will certainly vary in degree and relative importance from one island to the next, but in kind they need not differ at all.

The random records that connected a technique with a particular area tended to obscure the fact that several methods might be used in each place. This was the situation that we time and again encountered. To give but three instances. Similar conceptions of wave interference phenomena to those that have been described in the Marshall Islands were found to be an important element in navigation not only in the nearby Micronesian Gilberts, but also in distant Polynesian Tikopia. Deep phosphorescence was encountered as a land direction indicator in Santa Cruz, the Gilberts, and Tonga. The species of birds most highly esteemed for their reliable homing qualities were found to be the same in the Carolines as in the Santa Cruz Reef Islands. All three examples, incidentally, straddle the cultural gap between Micronesia and Polynesia.

The influence of particular features of the immediate environment must clearly not be discounted. They will cause techniques to be modified, and help determine which ones are preferred as most suitable to an area. Together with historical and cultural factors, they will be instrumental in determining the relative importance of methods from place to place. Thus the Carolinians prefer to trust in their reliable bird zones and to make much of submerged reefs, while the Gilbertese order of preference is for clouds, waves, and birds. Yet though the Carolinians do not think much of cloud signs, they do study wave interference phenomena (Gladwin, 1970: 195). And the Gilbertese for their part include reference to deep reefs in their sailing directions (Grimble, n.d.(a)), as do the Tongans (Ve'etutu, Kienga). Similarly it is the importance assigned to wave pattern methods that is so characteristic of the Marshalls, rather than anything unique in the methods themselves.

Precise usages vary with conditions in different localities of the same region. For instance within the Carolines boobies roost only on certain islands, in whose vicinity the significance of bird observations must necessarily differ from areas with shorter-range birds. Such variations inside groups seem to be as important as those between one archipelago and another.

So in the field of expanded target methods, where we should have anticipated local differences to have been most manifest, inquiry has revealed similar and often identical practices in widely scattered areas. The situation is the same, in fact, as for navigation in general. The question arises whether these similarities might have developed independently in response to similar conditions.

There are but a finite number of possible land signs, so it is inevitable that seamen in one place should sometimes happen upon the same observation as their counterparts 1000 miles away. But the correspondence that we actually find between highly elaborated systems is a little too close. Not only are practical concepts involved but also some that could not have been derived from observation of natural phenomena. These include mythological beliefs, magical practices, and fallacious star weather lore. All in all, it seems unlikely that fortuitous convergent development has played a significant role in promoting an apparent uniformity in navigational theory and practice.

One last generalisation. From the admittedly uneven and fragmentary evidence that is set out in the following pages, it would appear that the 'frontier' between Micronesia and Polynesia was navigationally not very significant. Techniques vary quite as much between adjacent archipelagos of similar culture.

Homing Bird Lore   'Birds are the navigator's very best friends', stated Teeta. He went on to elaborate. 'Birds are very useful up to twice the sight range of an island from a canoe'. He added, in response to my question, 'The sight range of land is about ten miles and that of the birds twenty. The birds which are most significant are terns and noddies'.

Every word of the foregoing[4] could equally well have been spoken by Hipour or any of the Puluwat navigators.

Precisely how do birds indicate to the voyager the direction of invisible land? Any Pacific traveller is familar with the large flocks consisting in the main of certain species of tern, with possibly a few tropic-birds and a solitary frigate-bird or booby often seen very far out at sea. They fly purposefully from one shoal of tuna to another but obviously have no interest in land at all. Even less do truly pelagic species like petrels and shearwaters have any connection with islands.

Noddy

But within 30 or perhaps 50 miles of shore, boobies in threes and fours, often accompanied by a predatory frigate-bird or two, are extremely common. Closer in still, when the nearest atoll is 20 or 25 miles off, mixed flocks of white terns and noddies will be encountered busily searching for fish. And once again, they show no more interest in directing the wayfarer than a busy New York policeman.

The first thing we must do if the birds are to teach us anything is to discard the pelagic species that roam at will over the open ocean, and concentrate exclusively on birds that are land-based, that habitually return to land to roost. The most important of these are terns and nod-dies, which have relatively short daily ranges, and boobies and frigate-birds, which fly further out. The latter are unable even to alight on the sea at all as their feathers quickly become waterlogged. Now we must make the proviso that, although the presence of these varieties in large numbers suggests that land is not very far away, the direction of that land is not shown by the bird's behaviour during the day.

White tern

It is in the early morning when the seabirds fly out to their fishing grounds and towards evening when they

---

[4] The formula for the sight range is: square root of the object's height in feet, added to square root of the observer's, and multiplied by 1.15, gives the distance away in miles the object can be seen above the horizon (Gatty, 1943: 82).

The distance at which the palms of a typical low atoll break the horizon as seen from a canoe's low deck seems to be taken by common consent as about 10 miles (Hipour, Iotiebata, Abera, Tevake, Ninigo and Tongan captains). Coconut palms being around 75 feet high, this is in accord with the above formula.

Fig. 26
Pacific seabirds
(after Gatty,
1958 and King,
1967) See
pp. 163-7

return home again, and at these times only, that their flight paths indicate the direction of land. Towards evening, the frigate-birds, for example, will be seen to abandon their leisurely patrolling, climb even higher and set off in one direction, probably homing by sight. About the same time the boobies will tire of their inquisitive inspections and fly low and arrow-straight for the horizon. As the noddies depart they will weave slightly in and out between the crests of the larger waves, while the terns will be flying a little above them, but all will be following a very exact path towards their home island.

Gilberts. Noddies and white terns were named, as we have seen, by Teeta of Kuria. Abera of Nikunau remarked that these species 'leave the land in the early morning and return in the evening. You observe them at sea morning and evening for the direction of their flight. Of course there are many kinds of bird that do not go home at night and so are of no use to us'.

Booby bird

The two navigators differed in the exact identification of the sub-groups of these seabirds.[5] The important point for the navigator, however, is that their habits were the same; they provided reliable and consistent land indication morning and evening up to 20 miles offshore, or twice the sight range of an atoll.[6]

Before we leave terns and noddies, there is one other aspect of their behaviour to be noted, an exception this time to the rule that they can only be useful navigationally at dawn and dusk. According to Teeta two groupings of these birds visit passing canoes at night.

---

[5] *Te io* or *te kunei*, according to Abera, was the noddy, which he correctly described as being black with a white patch on its head. Grimble (1931: 201) also says *te kunei* is the common noddy. In Abera's view *mankiri* is a smaller noddy-like bird with no white patch. Teeta on the other hand said *mankiri was* the noddy and that it *did* have a white patch, and that *te io* was not the noddy at all but the sooty tern which is slightly larger. The white tern was named *matewa* by Teeta and *kiakia* by Abera. None of these differences is particularly significant, for it is clear that closely related sub-groups are being described.

[6] A modification of this statement as to range is that during the month named *Te Kunei*, late November to 8 December, the noddy 'is said to be a better mark for navigators than at any other period, as it flies higher over the land and farther out to sea than usual' (Grimble, 1931: 201). It is of interest that Beiong on Pulusuk in the Carolines told me exactly the same thing: around the end of the year noddies conducted their fishing operations much further from land than at other times.

'They are like coastwatchers', he said. 'They are very
interested in everything that passes even miles away from
the island. When there is any object out at sea they go
out to look at it and then fly straight back to land'. The
groupings (*manikuru* and *maningonigo*) are distinguished
from each other according to which section of the coconut
palm frond they are believed to favour for roosting and
the times when they are most wakeful.

Boobies were less familiar to the *tani borau* we met
than were the birds we have been discussing.[7] They did
mention them, however, and Grimble may have been
citing a reference to the characteristic behaviour of boobies when he referred to a species of seabird that is said to
'mount high in the air and cast about to different points
of the compass . . . The navigator will steer in the direction they ultimately take, for that way lies terra firma'
(1924: 128). But in a footnote to the same page he says
that these birds, which he had been unable to identify,
were called *maningoningo*, which we recall as being the
name Teeta applied to the second wave of 'coastwatchers'.
The identity of these particular birds is therefore an open
question.[8]

Frigate bird

One more topic deserves mention before we conclude
our discussion of the remaining traces of Gilbertese bird
lore. This is the question of the use of tame birds as land-
finders. All over Polynesia and Micronesia one keeps
coming across legendary references. Certainly frigate-
birds and tropic-birds are not difficult to tame and they
are not uncommonly fed by hand. But stories of their use
in land-finding to come my way have been vague and
non-specific. None of the present day *tani borau* had
definite knowledge of this practice. There are, however,
specific references to birds carrying messages between
islands from Polynesia as well as Micronesia. The missionary George Turner in his journal of 1876 mentions that
when he was at Funafuti (Polynesian Ellice Islands)

---

[7] Boobies are scarce in the Gilberts probably because they are easy to
catch and are eaten by the Gilbertese (Maude, pers. comm., 1969).

[8] The word *maningongo* (not *maningonigo*) is translated by Sabatier
as *un oiseau de mer* (1954: 525). Child calls the grey-backed tern
maningongo (1960: 6).

a frigate bird arrived from Nukufetau, it bore a note from Sapolu, the native teacher of that island. The note was placed in a light piece of reed, plugged with cloth and fixed to the bird's wing. Formerly the natives had sent pearl fish-hooks from island to island by these birds. There were perches on most of the islands and the birds were treated as pets and fed with fish. (Turner, 1876)

Carrier pigeons proved unable to maintain communication between Nauru and Banaba, although before phosphate operations were commenced in 1900 the Banabans and Nauruans had already exchanged some messages by means of their tame man-of-war hawks (frigate-birds). A well-authenticated record exists of the 160-mile journey having been done by one of these birds in two hours (Ellis, A. F., 1935: 173-4).

Captain V. Ward (pers. comm., 1970) says that there are traditions of land-finding frigate-birds and that within living memory they were used as messengers. He adds that tame frigate-birds are kept today at Butaritari, Makin, Marakei, Onotoa, Arorae, and Tamana in the Gilbert Islands.

Carolines. It is perhaps indicative of the importance of birds in Carolinian navigation that it should have been a magic *kuling* (a species of plover) that first revealed the secrets of navigation to mankind. Surprisingly, this momentous event is said to have taken place not on dominant Puluwat, but on the inferior subject atoll of Pulap (Beiong).

For the Puluwat navigator the observation of seabirds overshadows all other techniques for homing on islands that are out of sight (Gladwin, 1970: 195).

Hipour and his colleagues stressed that white terns and noddies were the commonest and most widely used birds and that they wandered within 20-25 miles of the land during the day and headed directly homeward at dusk. This as we have seen is exactly in accord with the Gilbertese situation as outlined by Teeta and Abera.

Boobies are the most favoured of all bird guides. They characteristically display great interest in any sailing vessel, circling about and trying to land on inappropriate parts of the rigging, down which they slither with alarmed squawks. They cannot help but be noticed and eventually fly unerringly towards home. Their range is further than that of the terns and noddies (Hipour gives the figure of 30 miles) but unfortunately they are common on only one island in the neighbourhood of Puluwat: East Fayu.

Tropic bird

Apart from our bird-confirmed landfall in the Marianas, which will be described after discussing other target expanding methods, we encountered boobies twice during the Saipan voyages. At daybreak on 22 March about 90 miles south-east of Saipan two boobies appeared from a little north of west, flying straight and level. We assumed that they had come from Guam, which at that time should have 'moved' to a position somewhere under the setting Altair (278°). Plotting our track and approximate position on a chart in Australia later, I found that Guam had indeed been about 10° north of west and about 60 miles away.

Two days later we came across another pair of boobies. This was around noon when their direction of flight was not apparent, but we took them to come from our *etak* island of Gaferut, which must have been just about west of us and something like 70 miles off (this estimate was also subsequently confirmed).[9] The sighting had tended to confirm a dead reckoning of which we were confident in any case. It is worth noting, however, that had we entertained serious doubts as to our position it would only have been necessary to heave-to until dusk to be

---

[9] I had always assumed that bird populations would be overwhelmingly larger round uninhabited islands. It was unexpected, therefore, to find on sea trips with Hipour and Homearek, when we were especially sensitive to the presence of homing species, that their numbers did not seem to vary appreciably off different islands. They seemed just as plentiful in the waters surrounding Puluwat, Pulusuk, Tamatam, Truk, Saipan, and Tinian, for instance, as in the neighbourhood of the uninhabited Farallon de Medinilla in the Marianas and Pikelot in the Carolines.

A case of birds indicating the existence and direction of an undiscovered uninhabited archipelago is when Kotzebue in 1816 failed to discover the Phoenix group by a few miles. He saw 'a great quantity of sea-birds, which after sun-set flew to the south . . . we could not doubt, from the great number of birds, that we were near many uninhabited islands and rocks. and, if time had permitted, I should have followed the direction of the birds to the S.W.: but, as it was, the current took us every day from between 33 to 45 miles to the N.W.' (Kotzebue, 1821: vol. I, 169).

able, by observing the direction in which our visitors departed, to verify just how far south we had come.

Sooty terns are made use of but considered more erratic in their flight paths than the foregoing; *kuling* warn of approaching land at night by their cry; frigate-birds may be sighted up to 75 miles from land but are unevenly distributed throughout the area. (I once counted seventy soaring over Pikelot at one time but in other parts they are rare.)

Specialised Carolinian navigation certainly is, and unique in being virtually an intact system. But analogues of most of its features are found elsewhere, as we have already seen in connection with star and wind compasses, swell orientation, dead reckoning and so on. Bird lore is another case in point. We have already noted how Teeta's and Abera's tern and noddy usages were practically identical with Hipour's and how Beiong and Grimble both referred to the increased range of noddies in the latter part of the year. There seems to be correspondence also between the booby observations of Hipour and Tevake.

Santa Cruz Reef Islands. Boobies are known to indicate land 'not very far away', according to Bongi and Tevake. The birds are watched carefully morning and evening to learn the direction of their flight, exactly as in the Carolines. Tevake and I experienced some difficulty in comprehending each other's conceptions of distance, so this 'not far away' is the nearest thing to a flight range I was able to obtain. Neither terns nor noddies are as common in this group as in Micronesia and the rest of Polynesia. White terns do not breed in the Santa Cruz at all and certain of the noddies are rare (King, 1967: 82, 83, 84), so the most useful short-range guide birds of the Gilbert and Caroline Islands are not readily available to these Outlier Polynesians. The old Santa Cruz navigator regarded his namesake the tropic-bird (*tevake*) as too erratic in its range and homing characteristics to be of much use to seamen. Hipour shared this view.

Tikopia. We were never at sea with Tikopian navigators, so it was virtually impossible to record any worthwhile data about homing birds. For unless birds can be pointed out, preferably in their normal ocean habitat, there is little to be gathered that will not be ambiguous and uncertain. So all that can be said here about Tikopian practice is the definite statement by Rafe that there were some species of birds that remained in the 'middle sea' and other kinds that came out from and returned to the shore. The first group were of no service, but the second were to be looked for when coming out from land in the early morning to fish and again when they flew homeward before dark. Of the types of birds concerned or the ranges up to which their presence could be relied upon, I learned nothing definite.

Tonga. The same circumstances obtained as had with the Tikopians. There is, however, a tradition from the distant past that may be of interest. Two brothers, Gaseata and Gaseana from the village of Nofoalii on Upolu, Samoa, had a tame tropic-bird. One day she was restless and kept flying out. The brothers thought she must be fishing a new area or have found land, so they followed her in their canoe. They came first to Vava'u and then to a fishing ground off Tonga called Fakanoaloto and finally to Ha'apai where they settled to become the founders of the Tuita clan (Ve'ehala).

Another story concerns a chief of Eua, in pre-Christian times called Hama, who also had a tame tropic-bird. He used to send her out to find bonito. She would return and call and Hama would follow in his canoe (Ve'ehala).

A number of estimates have been put forward as to the probable distance from land indicated by the sighting of a given number of birds of any particular species.[10] The purpose of such bird range tables was to give survivors their earliest intimation of how far away and in which direction land might lie. But the aim of the indigenous navigator in increasing his arc of landfall by the use of birds is quite different. He is no castaway, but a highly

Discussion of Bird Techniques

---

[10] The best known publications to deal with this question have been *The Raft Book* (Gatty, 1943) and *South Sea Lore* (Emory, 1943). Both authors wisely stress that reliance should not be placed on isolated sightings.

trained expert making deliberate voyages within the conservative framework of his navigational system. Although he may be glad of a bird clue far at sea after a storm or similar emergency, his primary purpose is to use homing bird ranges confidently to expand his target. All his navigational methods are prudent and allow for safety margins, and his bird-enlarged target must be no exception. It must be reliable. He 'is not concerned', writes Gladwin (1970: 196), 'with how far out he might conceivably see a given species of bird. Instead he wants to know how far out he can rely on seeing that same bird any time he needs it'.[11]

The ranges suggested below are put forward as being those at which different species of birds may be expected with reasonable confidence to be present in good numbers; in other words where they give the navigator a trustworthy expanded target to aim for. They are less in general than those published in the survival handbooks.

Noddies and white terns as we know are consistent land guides to double the sight-range of atolls, or 20 miles offshore, and this applies throughout the Carolines and Gilberts. That it holds good elsewhere is suggested by the observations of Captain Anderson, who was born on Fanning Island and who gives the same figure of 20 miles for noddies, though a much greater one for white terns (Emory, 1943: 17). Hawaiian data seem to indicate that these ranges apply there also (Emory, 1943: 19, 20). It seems reasonable to suppose, therefore, that the fishing zone of the noddies is the same in Polynesia as it is in Micronesia, and that of the white terns at least as big and possibly larger.

All authorities agree that the daily range of boobies is greater than that of noddies, something like 30 miles being Hipour's estimate, and one that was supported by the presence of sizable flocks at about that distance off

---

[11] During the *Rehu Moana* test voyage from Rarotonga to New Zealand, I was ignorant of the relatively restricted bird ranges actually used by indigenous navigators. Consequently I drew the unwarranted conclusion from a bird sighting that we were passing the distant Kermadec Islands, although I knew from dead reckoning that these must have been a good 150 miles off (Lewis, 1967: 278, 279). It is obvious enough now, in the light of instruction from experts, that the birds were pelagic, indicative of shoals of fish rather than land.

the Marianas. Anderson gives the same 30-mile radius for brown boobies (Emory, 1943: 17). King says that this variety is rarely seen more than 50 miles from the nearest land (1967: 52) and Gatty that the sighting of six or more brown boobies denotes that land is usually within 30 miles (1943: 35, 36).

There are two other species of booby, the red-footed and the blue-faced or masked. These wander rather further than the brown variety, a tendency most marked in the sub-adults. King puts the range of the majority of red-footed adults at 50 miles, and rather suggests that the blue-faced scatter is wider (1967: 50, 52). Anderson on the contrary allows blue-faced boobies 50 miles and red-footed 100 (Emory, 1943: 17). Gatty avers that a sighting of three or more of either species suggests the presence of land within 75 miles, six or more within 50 (1943: 35).

For purposes of expanding one's target, then, a reasonable estimate would be that brown boobies would generally be encountered up to 30 miles out and the other two species to 40 or 50. As to the distribution of these useful birds, the brown booby breeds on or visits every group except the New Hebrides and Easter Island, and the red-footed is almost as widespread. The masked is absent from the Carolines and from Melanesia except Fiji, but is present in the rest of the tropical Pacific including the Marianas (King, 1967: 50, 52). At least one of these varieties occurs in every archipelago.

Frigate-birds may be sighted 75 miles from land according to Hipour (Gladwin, 1970: 197) and I myself have come across individuals as far as 150 miles from the Marquesas. Puluwat navigators consider them a little erratic in their homing and of limited practical value, since the navigators' miss-distances are so very much less than 75 miles. Gatty considers that six or more suggest that land is within 75 miles (1943: 36), Anderson restricts the birds' average range to 50 (Emory, 1943: 17) and King says they are 'most abundant within 50 miles of their breeding and roosting places but individuals may be found any distance from land' (1967: 56). Once again there is fairly general agreement on the birds' habits.

Their distribution, like that of the other species we have been considering, covers the better part of tropical Oceania.

A point that will be referred to later in connection with Hipour's bird-assisted landfalls (see pp. 217-22) is so important that it deserves mention here as well. It concerns acuity of observation. The number of birds logged by a man casually on watch will bear absolutely no relation to the number picked out and identified by keen-eyed Islanders, who search for them hour after hour with absolute concentration, as their destination draws near.

Migrating   The suggestion has been put forward by Gatty (1958:
Birds 31-6) and Hornell (1946: 142-9) that migrating land birds might have provided the early Polynesians with clues to the existence of undiscovered islands. Among the possibilities Gatty cites the September migration of long-tailed cuckoos from tropical Polynesia to New Zealand and the Pacific golden plover from Tahiti northward (1958: 35). Sharp disagrees, exhibiting a diagram of a blank circle which he labels 'Courses by Following Migratory Birds' (1963: fig. 4).

Any supposition that very early voyagers may have followed flights paths must be highly speculative and we can do little more than discuss whether such procedures would be practicable. Given the meticulous observation of natural phenomena habitual to Pacific Island navigators, the annual migrations of land birds would certainly be noticed and the rather obvious deduction made that another unit of land was their destination. The direction of the birds' flight would be perceived in star compass or analogous terms, just as we might say that the birds flew towards the south-south-east or north-west. But as to how far off the birds' destination lay, there could be no indication at all.

This drawback would not necessarily prevent curious voyagers from casting about along the star path the flocks had taken. A 50-foot double canoe could cruise a very long way, especially north or south across the trade winds, when it would have a virtual guarantee of fair winds for the return to its own island. The orientation and dead reckoning procedures with which we are familiar would be applied as on any other voyage and there is no navigational barrier to such hypothetical probes having taken place.[12]

A tradition of Pacific Islanders deducing the presence of a previously unknown island by the behaviour of birds, and following a star in the direction of the flight-path to discover and settle the new land, comes from Bougainville in the Melanesian Solomons archipelago and was related by Tonnaku in 1966.

The people of Buin (Southern Bougainville) originated further south, he said. At one time they were settled on Rendova Island. They realised from the manner in which birds kept flying out in one direction that land must lie that way. This was beyond the offshore island of Simbo (making the birds' track something north of west). They followed in their canoes the direction taken by the birds, and also made use of a small star, to discover and settle Treasury Island and later Buin on the Bougainville mainland (Treasury is 65 miles west-north-west from Simbo).

A Tuamotuan chant or *fangu* called 'Pathway of Birds' refers to 'the migrating bird' revealing 'the road of the winds coursed by the Sea Kings to unknown lands' (Stimson, 1957: 74).

These isolated traditions notwithstanding, I want to stress that hypotheses about following migratory bird paths remain entirely speculative. This is in total contrast of course to the role of birds in expanding landfall.

We will refrain from discussing clouds in weather forecasting, an art in which Abera and Rewi, among others, were adept. For while meteorology is vital to seamen, it does not properly form part of the science of navigation. In this section, therefore, we will confine ourselves to

Clouds as Indications of Land

---

[12] Marcus considers it possible that avian migrations were land clues in the early stages of the Viking expansion over the Western Ocean (1953: 128) but once again such ancient episodes are necessarily shrouded in myth and legend. There are many examples, however, of the use of seabirds for landfall on the regular voyages that followed discovery and settlement (*Erik's Saga*, *Faereyinga Saga*, and *Biskupa Sogur*, cited by Marcus, 1953: 128, the *Orkneyinger's Saga* and Hornell, 1946: 145, 146). A saga legend of the use of tame land-finding birds is cited by Gatty (1958: 37, 38).

clouds in their role as indicators of the presence of invisible islands.

Reports of 'land clouds' indicative of islands below the horizon are common enough from all parts of Oceania. Most are either observations by ships' officers unversed in indigenous navigation, or else rather vague statements about Islanders making use of the clues clouds afford. The most they suggest is that the practice of studying clouds as aids to landfall was once widespread.

Gilbert Islands 'Land Clouds'. In this archipelago cloud signs are the preferred method of locating islands (Teeta, Abera), just as in the Carolines observation of homing birds is the technique of choice, and in the Marshalls the pattern of swells. While individual Gilbertese navigators remarked on particular phenomena or had the opportunity to demonstrate some special sign, the consensus was such that they were obviously expounding generally accepted concepts.

We will therefore discuss the observations of Abera, Iotiebata, Teeta, and Rewi, indicating where appropriate any points specially stressed by one or other, and then go on to describe Iotiebata's demonstration of some of these phenomena from a canoe at sea.

Let Abera introduce the subject. Clouds move rather slowly over an island, as if stuck, he said. When they are past the land they move faster. This is a distant sign, and it is one that illustrates, incidentally, the dynamic nature of cloud lore.

Much nearer land, perhaps 15-17 miles, you begin to see colours in clouds that stand over land, quite different from clouds that are over sea. Iotiebata explained that the colour of clouds is useful for detecting land in fine weather. Colour becomes apparent when you are nearing land which is still well below the horizon. When you are going from Tarawa to Maiana, for instance, you first see a dark rain-like cloud, but it does not indicate rain or bad weather. (He later demonstrated this dark cloud to me about 17 miles out from Maiana.) Then as you come nearer, you see bright clouds over the invisible island, when it is perhaps 15 miles off. 'Brightness' seemed to be

the operative word, and more significant as a sign of land
than particular colours, which vary with the kind of
terrain. About 15-16 miles seems an average distance for
brightness or colour to become manifest. Before going
into detail about the colours involved and their significance, let us continue our consideration of more distant
signs.

In a storm it is much easier than in fine weather to
detect far away land, Iotiebata asserted. Referring to the
cloud signs over Nikunau, recognition of which saved his
life on the occasion of his five-weeks storm-drift, he was
able to describe the appearances only as 'a clearing of
the storm over where the land was'. Beyond this phrase,
he could not put into words the exact nature of the
phenomenon he had so providentially recognised. He
explained that in very windy weather, but when there
was no gale, clouds dispersed out in all directions from
where land lay, no matter whether it was morning or
afternoon. When only the normal trade wind was blowing,
clouds tended to pile up over atolls, while neighbouring
clouds moved on.

As you approach land from a distance, said Abera, the
'land cloud at first lies on the horizon like other clouds,
but as the hours go by, you notice that it stays in the same
place, or else reforms continually over that place'. This
process, which was to be demonstrated at sea by Iotiebata, brings out the importance of prolonged observation.
For it is the movement of clouds, their formation and
break up, that counts as much or more than their static
appearance.

Abera mentioned two special signs. The one occurs
when it is calm and there are no other clouds. If you look
carefully, he told me, you may see a pair of clouds low on
the horizon of the type called *te nangkoto*, which are like
a pair of eyebrows.

The second sign is to be observed in the presence of
wind and other clouds. A vee-shaped cloud then indicates
the presence of land below the horizon (see fig. 27).

This phenomenon, he explained, is quite unmistakable.
The clouds round about drift but the vee does not. Or
rather, as the clouds pass over the land's position they

*Fig. 27 'Eye-
brow' and vee-
shaped clouds
indicating land
(after Abera)*

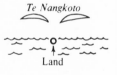

Te Nangkoto

Land

form the vee, then as they drift on and dissipate it is re-formed by the clouds following after. It may therefore be seen in either form shown in fig. 27. In the middle drawing the vee is just forming; in the bottom one it is being blown away from the land and is beginning to disperse, while its successor has not yet taken shape.

Grimble describes the same thing. 'When a mass of cumulus towers over an island, some draught, caused probably by the refraction of heat, bends over the pin-nacles of the cloud, so that it dips towards earth. Twice, while at sea, this phenomenon has been pointed out to me by a native, and in both cases it proved a true com-pass' (1924: 128).

The colours that begin to appear closer to land vary with the make-up of the island. There are three kinds of island with corresponding clouds, Teeta says. Above lagoon islands the cloud 'roof' tends to be greenish; over extensive areas of white sand or surf, the cloud or a portion of it will be brighter (more white) than the rest; the clouds above a wooded green island will be darker than their neighbours. Abera referred to a pink tinge over reefs and green above lagoons. Rewi likewise said that lagoon islands reflect green, and ones without lagoons a reddish colour. Islands with no lagoons like Kuria, said Iotiebata, reflect a dark colour that must be distinguished from rain cloud, which appears very similar. Islands with big stretches of dry reef or mangroves have bright coloured clouds above them. Given the fact that these *tani borau* were interviewed on different islands, that the services of four separate interpreters were involved and that such subtle phenomena are not readily put into words, the correspondence between all these descriptions is remarkable.

We come now to the 'land clouds' demonstrated by Iotiebata from a canoe between Tarawa and Maiana. There was a brisk trade wind and the sky was about half covered with fine weather cumulus. When we were a few miles south-west of Betio Island on the rim of Tarawa Atoll, and Maiana was still well below the horizon, about 17-18 miles off, Iotiebata showed me the clouds that were forming over Maiana. He bade me note how they formed and massed thick and high over the invisible atoll, and how they eventually broke up as they drifted away to leeward.

I found the building-up over Maiana much harder to pick out than the disintegration of the clouds when they had moved away down-wind. Towering cumulus forms readily enough over the open ocean, and it required an informed and practised eye—not a seaman's so much as a trained land-searching Islander's—to appreciate the extremely subtle changes in colour, shape, and manner of development that constitute the all-important signs.

A little later Iotiebata drew my attention to a phenomenon that had become apparent, the bright reflection of big, shallow lagoons onto the columns of drifting cumulus. The whole of Tarawa's triangular lagoon up to its apex 18 miles away was delineated. Maiana was much further off than the nearer part of Tarawa, 17 miles or so. But above it also, sections of cloud were brighter, though the lower levels were more darkly shadowed than open sea clouds. The under surfaces of the Tarawa clouds were distinctly green. As we came a little nearer to Maiana, within something like 15-16 miles, the darkish under-shading progressively assumed a more greenish tinge.[13]

The colour was so striking over Tarawa that I was puzzled at Iotiebata not mentioning it. I put a question through the interpreter, to which he answered after a little hesitation:

'I did not wish to embarrass or insult you by mentioning this green. For after all, you are a navigator, of a kind, yourself—and even Europeans notice this obvious sign!'

The clouds broke up for a short time around 10.00.

---

[13] The sign occurs wherever large shallow lagoons exist. For instance, we observed it about 11 miles off Onotoa. It may well have been visible earlier, but we had not been keeping watch.

On a previous voyage we saw Ashmore lagoon, Arafura Sea, tinting green the clouds above it when the near rim of the reef was about 17 miles away (Lewis, 1969a: 160). In describing the incident I was in error in implying that the observer had to be in a certain relationship with the sun and the atoll. Betwen Tarawa and Maiana the sign did not alter with the height or angle of the sun nor with the bearing of either island.

Another area from which this phenomenon has often been reported is the Tuamotu archipelago, most frequently in connection with the atoll of Anaa (*Pacific Islands*, 1943: vol. II, 194; Buck, 1954: 186).

What would happen to the signs now, I asked? Iotiebata counselled patience. Land signs were not present all the time, he said, but if one watched carefully, and knew what one was looking for, they would be seen again sooner or later.

This seems to me to be a most significant formulation of the general attitude of Micronesian and Polynesian navigators towards the arts of elucidating tenuous and transitory natural signs—and such indications as the ocean provides of interruptions in its continuity by invisible islands are elusive in the extreme. They are almost as variable as the moods of the sea itself. Five minutes' careful inspection of the sky (or of sea swells) would tell even the most knowledgeable Islander very little. One hour or two hours intent study of the relevant phenomena are more like what is required. This is particularly true of cloud signs, which so much depend on processes of change. As to Iotiebata's insistence on knowing what one is looking for, it is worth noting that apart from the green reflection, by myself I would have appreciated none of the signs he showed me.

The period during which the clouds disintegrated proved very brief. Apart from this gap of about half an hour, they remained as signposts for both islands virtually the whole day through. That is, from about 09.00 to 16.00 or 17.00.

Cloud Signs in Other Islands. In Tonga Ve'etutu asserted, rather to my surprise, that the most reliable cloud indication of land below the horizon was to be seen in overcast weather (see fig. 28).

The overcast may either be general or limited to the sector of the sky you are studying. A blacker, thicker cloud or a darkening and thickening of the overcast over the position of the invisible island indicates where it lies.

The examples we have been considering have referred almost exclusively to low atolls. Higher land may give rise to standing wave clouds in addition to convection clouds.

During the non-instrumental voyage of *Rehu Moana* we were on the lookout for Rarotonga in the Cook Islands. About 09.00 on 10 October, 'an odd-looking lenticular

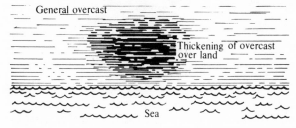

Fig. 28 Cloud formation indicating land (after Ve'etutu)

cloud could be made out off the starboard bow. We turned in its direction and kept our eyes on it. Soon dim mountain buttresses began to take shape beneath it. It was Rarotonga some 30 miles away' (Lewis, 1967: 263). An interesting point is that the 2110-foot island should theoretically have been visible some 50 miles off. Yet we only sighted its standing cloud about 30, and the peaks themselves a little nearer. Haze was present only to a degree common enough in the Pacific Trades—a reminder, I think, that visibility at sea is often restricted.

Another cloud phenomenon reported from the Cooks is that landfall on canoe voyages between Mauke and Atiu was facilitated by characteristic clouds. These were said to extend down-wind from the islands 'like flags' and to be present early in the morning. The relevant altitudes are Mauke 100 feet and Atiu 270 feet (Mills, pers. comm., 1965).

There is a reference to land clouds in a voyaging chant from the Tuamotus, a *fangu* entitled 'The Road of the Winds'. Stimson points out that 'Even to-day it is everywhere regarded as tantamount to sacrilege to alter a *fangu*'. The line concerned is 'May the peaks of Havaiki be banked in clouds!' (*Kia kohu te mata o Havaiki!*). Mataiti, a Maifano of Takume Island, explained this meant 'that when the vessel was thought to be approaching land a sharp lookout was kept for motionless clouds near the horizon—for these were supposed to be caught upon the tops of mountains' (Stimson, 1932: 181, 188, 133).

This is a technique that I have heard reported only in the Gilberts. It is mentioned by Grimble and was explained to me by Abera and his colleagues on Onotoa. Unfortunately weather conditions (persistent heavy cloud) prevented its demonstration.

Grimble's account, with which I was unacquainted when I met Abera, reads as follows. 'Another sign of land for which he [the navigator] watches is its "loom" upon

The Loom of Invisible Land

the horizon. This I have many times seen myself; it is quite unmistakable. The white sand and the still lagoon of an atoll reflect the tropical sun-glare upwards, so that a pale, shimmering column is shot into the air over the island, whose presence is betrayed at great distances' (1924: 128).

When there is no cloud at all [said Abera], look carefully round the horizon and you may see a brightness coming up over the horizon at one point. This is called *te kimeata*[14] and is not marked at all, it is just a little different from the rest of the horizon on *close* inspection. You can see this appearance in any direction, but most easily when the sun is high around midday.

It is actually easier to make out the sign when there is some cloud about. It is best seen above islands with plenty of reef and lagoon. Nevertheless, if an island is covered entirely with vegetation one may see a dark line (not a cloud) in the sky above it in the same way.

Te kimeata may be detected up to about 30 miles or a little more. You can 'see' the position of Tabiteuea from Onotoa in this manner [32 miles from where he was speaking]. Tamana, however, is a little too far to locate by this means [45 miles].

All the islands mentioned are low and are only visible 10 miles from a canoe or from ground level.

The loom of an island may also be seen at night. To quote Abera once more: 'You can observe *te kimeata* when there is no moon or only a small one. When there is rain over the island you are looking for, you see the loom clearer because the wet island is reflected on to the rain clouds like a mirror. Thus rain or overcast helps bring out the sign, although an intervening rain shower or murk, of course, hides it'.

Abera assured me that the loom seen at night was nothing to do with the lights of people living on the island. 'It is equally noticeable', he said, 'above islands with no inhabitants'.

'On dark nights when it is raining at Tabiteuea you can see its loom from Onotoa more than 30 miles away', he continued. 'Actually you can make it out much easier if you are in a canoe clear of land'. Abera ended with the warning that practice was needed to detect *te kimeata*.

---

[14] '*Kimeata*　Lueur dans le ciel (reflet d'une terre)' (Sabatier, 1954: 446).

CHAPTER SEVEN

Swell patterns and phosphorescence

SWELLS DISTORTED BY LAND

This is an important means of detecting the presence and bearing of land afar off and so enlarging the destination zone. It needs to be distinguished from using the alignment of swells in the open ocean to maintain direction that we discussed in chap. 3. The techniques we are now considering concern swell interference patterns, whereas ocean orientation is dependent on the opposite phenomenon—swells that are free from land interference.

Though the two arts are different in every other respect they have one thing in common. They both involve the analysis and interpretation of swells and waves, therefore certain similarities in method must obtain. What was said on p. 86 about navigators selecting swells to suit their purpose applies with even greater force to land swells, whose patterns are rendered more complicated because of the interference by islands. Navigators individually, or according to school, choose those patterns that they find most significant or readily determined.

Let us consider what happens when an island obtrudes into the even run of the open ocean swells. There are two distinct effects—refraction and reflection (see fig. 29).

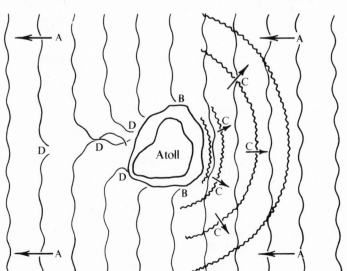

Fig. 29 Refraction and reflection of ocean swell. A. Direction of swell. B. Refracted swell. C. Reflected swell. D. Shadow of turbulence. (After Davenport, 1964.)

181

Swells are *refracted* when land friction impedes and slows their inshore ends, which bend more and more until they are in line with the coast. The ocean swell being divided by the island, these refracted portions move round both sides to meet in its lee, and there cross each other and give rise to an area where, as the Gilbertese say, the waves 'move up and down'.

The other process involves waves that impinge directly onto a weather coast, and are *reflected* back the way they came. Since the reflected waves differ in wavelength and other characteristics from the primary swell, besides moving in the opposite direction, they can be detected far out.[1]

Gilbertese Land   Among the Gilbertese the preferred patterns of different
Swell Concepts   navigators varied. Abera considered the long low swell from the south to be most significant, Rewi and Iotiebata the trade-wind-generated swell from the east.

> We come to waves now, near land and far out [said Abera].
> The main swell, *nao bangaki* [*nao*—wave or swell] comes from the south; it is big long and low and does not break; it is independent of the trade wind. If you are in a canoe bound from Onotoa to Tabiteuea [about north-north-west] you feel it as a slow heave that rolls the canoe a little from the port side. This swell can be detected over all the seas.

This long swell rolling up from the zone of strong Southern Ocean westerlies is indeed apparent all over Oceania, except where deflected by land like the Melanesian Islands in the west and the Tuamotu archipelago in the east (see p. 88). Finney draws attention to its use by Hawaiian surfers (pers. comm., 1970). Cook (1777:

------

[1] A word about figures. Figure 29 shows only a single swell system. This, of course, is an oversimplification. We have been speaking of selection from among a number of swells, and we have seen how Hipour separated out four distinct components at sea from those that were running at the time. Of the diagrams that follow, Abera's shows one primary swell, Rewi's two, and Iotiebata's drawing of the pattern round the solitary island three. (His other sketch illustrating interference between swells bent by two islands assumes but a single main swell.) The Marshallese base their concepts and their 'stick charts' on four swells, while the Tikopian diagram reproduced in fig. 34 shows one, and is concerned with reflection only. Naturally the navigators are well aware of this selectivity and do not believe that only one or two or even four discrete swells are all that are running.

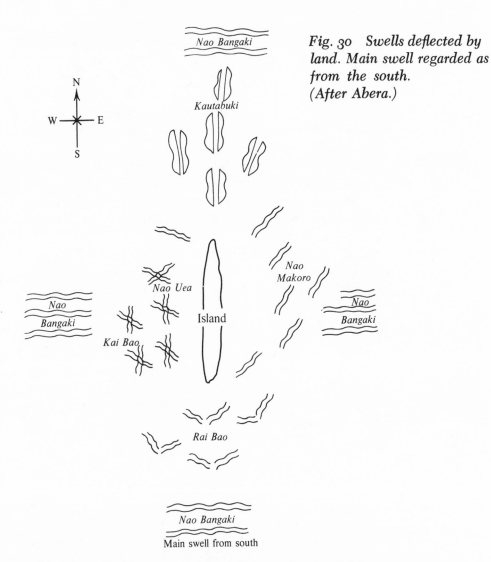

Fig. 30 Swells deflected by land. Main swell regarded as from the south. (After Abera.)

Main swell from south

316) noted how it was cut off as soon as he passed into the lee (north) of the Tuamotus. I logged the same phenomenon west of Nuku Hiva when no less than 400 miles north of the Tuamotuan chain. There are several points that may be noted from fig. 30.

The bending of the southerly swells as they impinge on the island is indicated.

Kautabuki, the rough northern sector, is shown by both Iotiebata and Rewi in the same position, despite their regarding the swell from the east and not from the south as the most important.

Nao uea is the area of cross seas in the lee (west side) of the island. Abera says that the intersecting waves concerned are the refracted main swells moving up from the south, 'waves that come out from the land' and that component of the swell from the east (not indicated in the diagram) that has passed round the northern end of the island.

No mention is made by Abera, incidentally, of waves *reflected* back to windward. Teeta was the only *tia borau* I encountered to draw attention to these. Grimble, however, says that when a man sailing at night 'passes from a beam-sea into a swell that lifts first the stem and then the stern of his craft' he knows he is approaching land (1924: 128). This is a plain enough description of a canoe headed shorewards pitching into the waves reflected back from the coast.

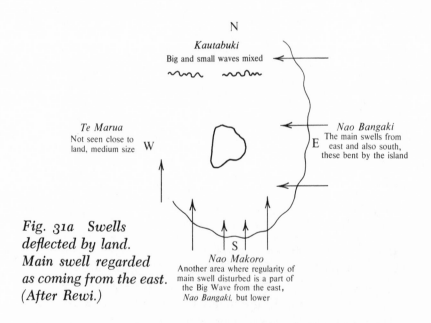

Fig. 31a Swells deflected by land. Main swell regarded as coming from the east. (After Rewi.)

It is of interest that Abera, Teeta, Iotiebata, and Rewi considered that the distance out to sea at which ocean swells began to be appreciably affected by land, or to re-form after passing it by, was anything from a little out of sight to double the sight range (about 13-20 miles). These distances are about the same as those given by the Tiko-

Plate VIII   Temi Rewi's instructional stone canoe, Beru, Gilbert Islands. Left hand stone represents swell from east, lower right northern sector.

pian Tupuai, but a good deal shorter than the ones put forward by Marshallese and the Tikopian Rafe. A possible explanation for the discrepancy would be the small size of the atolls in the Gilberts compared with those in the Marshalls, or with the high island Vanikoro, that Rafe was discussing. Tupuai was referring to the smaller Anuta and Tikopia. Other features, like depth and contouring of the ocean floor, being equal, one would expect more disturbance of open sea swell patterns by large islands than by small.

Temi Rewi, the Beru navigator, drew the next diagram. It is seen to be based on an assumption of the primacy of the swells from the east, but also to allow for the effects of a secondary southern swell (fig. 31a).

It will be most convenient if we introduce the 'stone island' or 'stone canoe' at this point, for this instructional device shows Rewi's wave concepts very clearly (see fig. 31b and plate VIII). It is regarded variously as an island or a canoe according to its role at any particular time. When the model is being used to illustrate wave lore it is seen as an island, the triangular stones at the four corners representing by their size, shape, and angle the waves characteristic of each side of the island.

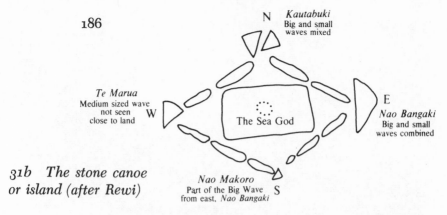

31b The stone canoe or island (after Rewi)

N Kautabuki Big and small waves mixed

Te Marua Medium sized wave not seen close to land **W**

The Sea God

E *Nao Bangaki* Big and small waves combined

Nao Makoro Part of the Big Wave from east, *Nao Bangaki* **S**

The tallest triangular stone represents *nao bangaki*, the major swell which Rewi regards as coming from the east. The small southern stone is *nao makoro*. This is the zone where the easterly and southerly main swells, which are both bent (refracted) by the land, affect each other particularly. We note that it is transposed from Abera's east to the south side. The difference may be more apparent than real, however, for Rewi, if I understand his meaning aright, regards this area as belonging to the big swell from the east, though to that part of it that has been bent round towards the south and has intermingled with the southern swell.

On the west side is the medium sized stone *te marua* which stands for a wave form of moderate height encountered only at some distance from land. It occurs further offshore than Abera's westerly *nao uea*. They are not the same thing at all and it is probably analogous to Abera's *kai bao*.

On the north side, two stones of different sizes set at an angle to each other represent the choppy *kautabuki* sector, where big and small waves are mixed.

The stone teaching device is aligned astronomically to facilitate learning about the stars. At such times the pupil sits on the rectangular stone in the centre as if he were in a canoe. The bearings of the southern Gilbert Islands are taught in terms of the rising and setting points of navigational stars.

Underneath the rectangular stone seat and hidden from most angles, is a rounded lump of brain coral. This, the navigator revealed, represented the sea god, 'who is most important of all. He helps us sail over the sea because he rules the sea'.

It is perhaps of interest that Rewi, who is the youngest

of the *tani borau*, being about 45 years of age, is teaching navigation to his son in the same way that his father and grandfather did before him. The structure in the yard of Rewi's house in Nuka village which is illustrated was constructed by his father who copied it from one on the eastern coast of Beru built by the present navigator's grandfather, Tebotua.

Tebotua, whose home island was Beru, built a similar one on Tabiteuea South. Another was constructed on Arorae by one Otang, who copied it from Tebotua's on Beru. Rewi is not aware of any elsewhere, nor of earlier date.

We have seen how, when Iotiebata was storm-drifted, he could still detect the underlying easterly swell after a month of westerly gales. It is not surprising to find that he regards this swell as the most important in producing significant wave patterns round islands. His first diagram is complicated, however, because he takes into account the very long, low swell from the south and a subsidiary one from the north as well. Moreover, he noted how these react with the components of the easterly swell that are separated by the island and sweep past it to the north and south (see fig. 32).

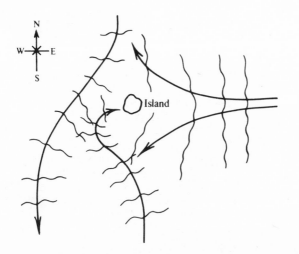

Fig. 32 Swells round a solitary island. Three primary swells are indicated. Arrows show axes of swells. (After Iotiebata.)

The *swell from the east* is divided by the land, one part going north round the island and the other rounding its southern side. The portion deflected north about is the

rougher, forming waves that are steep though they do not
break. It comes up against the swell coming down *from
the northward* and forces it over to the westward. The
southern component of the easterly swell, and the swell
coming up from the south, are both gentler than their
northern counterparts. These combine to travel in a circular manner round the south side of the island and when
they come to the western side they are called the 'western
waves', as Iotiebata put it. In this sector they meet the
swells coming from the north, the two systems clash and
the southerly waves bend *in towards* the western shore of
the island. The waves from the north, on the contrary, are
deflected *away from* the land out towards the west. They
continue south-westward until they are clear of the land,
when they turn back southwards once more.

*Fig. 33 Intersect-
ing swells between
two islands (after
Iotiebata)*

In fig. 33 Iotiebata ignores the north and south swells, which indeed would be largely cut off by the two islands, and concentrates upon the swell from the east. The islands concerned are about 20 miles apart and the refraction effects are detectable up to about that distance. The navigator demonstrated them from a canoe on passage between the atolls.

The fresh wind, south-easterly in the morning and north-easterly in the afternoon, set us well to westward of the direct course between the islands, necessitating hours of tacking on the return. In view of the delay occasioned by the capricious wind we did not land on Maiana. The round trip occupied about 13 hours.

About 3 miles from the south-west tip of Tarawa Iotiebata let fly the sheet and brought the canoe to a standstill to show how the swells from the east, sweeping round the southern shore, were being bent. Further out from under the land the swells gradually straightened out, although they remained at a very distinct angle, perhaps 15°, to what Iotiebata judged would be their direction in the open ocean. They did not appreciably alter their angle any more after this until no longer discernible some 18-20 miles from Tarawa.

We hove-to again at point A in fig. 33 about 8 miles out from Tarawa, which was by now only intermittently visible from the higher wave crests. Maiana would not come up over the horizon for some hours since we had been forced so far to leeward. Iotiebata pointed out tiny but distinct waves that were crossing the backs of the main swells. The explanation was that the main swell from the east, bent (deflected) by Tarawa until it was moving towards about 15° north of west, was being crossed by a minute swell of equal wave-length, that was a part of the primary swell from the east that had been bent by the northern coast of Maiana so that it was travelling in a direction 15° south of west.

As we progressed, the 'Maiana wave' got bigger and bigger while the Tarawa one shrank progressively in size, though the angle between the two and their wavelengths remained unaltered. By the time we reached B in fig. 33 the 'Maiana wave' was the larger. No land was visible

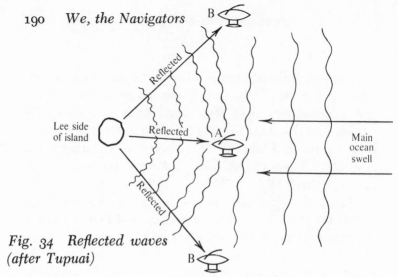

Lee side
of island

Reflected

A

Main
ocean
swell

*Fig. 34 Reflected waves
(after Tupuai)*

from shortly after we left position A to about two hours'
sailing beyond B, when Maiana topped the horizon on the
weather bow. By this time the 'Tarawa wave' was very
small (though still plainly discernible), the swell refracted from Maiana having become unequivocally dominant.

Tikopia. Wave   Figure 34 was drawn at the Tikopian settlement at
Reflection   Nukufera in the Russell Islands in the Solomons, by
Tupuai. Samoa and several other navigators were present
and concurred with what was being demonstrated.
'Waves are different when you get near land', Tupuai said.
'The change takes place about 15-20 miles offshore and is
due to the wave reflected back from the shore. The reflected wave is called *te ngaru fenua*, the land wave. It is
faint when far from land and needs an expert to detect'.
It is, he stressed, a particularly valuable sign in thick
weather. He then drew attention to two sets of circumstances that he illustrated by the diagram.

In the first case a canoe is at the position I have labelled
A. It is running down the axis of the primary swell and is
headed correctly for the island. The main swell goes right
up to the land and hits back directly from in front of the
canoe up to 15-20 miles out to sea. Thus it confirms that
the destination lies dead ahead.

The second case is that of a navigator aiming for the
island who, while still sailing down the axis of the primary
swell, has been set at right angles to his course to one of the
positions marked B. He is steering in the same direction
as the canoe at A, but having been displaced later-

ally, his track will by-pass his destination. But 15-20 miles offshore he encounters the waves reflected back from the land, which this time impinge on the canoe at an angle, so that he will know which side of the island he is on, and will turn in towards land by heading directly into the reflected swell.

Tupuai made the significant admission, 'If you go past the island down-wind, you just sail on and miss it, for I have no knowledge of the seas on the leeward side'. This would seem at first sight to indicate a hiatus in the wave lore of Tikopian Polynesians compared with Micronesians. But such a formulation can hardly be sustained. The gap is in the admittedly residual knowledge of some present-day informants. To what extent their information represents the picture in former times we have no way of knowing.

The Tikopian Rafe, whom I saw on Guadalcanal in the Solomons, discussed land waves with special reference to his canoe voyage from Tikopia to Vanikoro. When an island was still a long way off, he averred, out of sight unless it was a very large island, the swells changed character from those in the 'middle sea'. 'I feel the sea hit the canoe—shake him like move him go back', he said, expressively miming the sharp slap of the reflected waves and the pause and jerk in the canoe's forward motion.

On the Vanikoro voyage he encountered these reflected waves shortly before dawn on the day of arrival. The island itself came into view at daybreak, but so far off that they did not get in until after nightfall, 12-13 hours after the reflected land wave had first become perceptible.[2] The average speed over the whole trip was 3.5 knots or a little under so the reflected wave must have been recognisable around 35 miles offshore.

The Tongan wave patterns that were explained to us, and that we ourselves encountered at sea, were confined to the 80-mile stretch between Tongatapu and Ha'apai. This is an area full of islets, reefs, deeps, and shoals that

Tonga.
Land Swells

_____

[2] Vanikoro is 3000 feet high so theoretically visible more than 60 miles in clear weather.

must to a large extent condition the swell patterns. The material we were able to gather, therefore, has limited general validity.

This assessment does not necessarily apply to extant Tongan wave lore as a whole. Such distant units of the kingdom as Tafahi, 170 miles north of Vava'u, are still visited by cutter captains who use compasses rarely and charts never, and who make use of swell phenomena to facilitate landfall on their isolated targets (Ve'etutu, Kienga, Vili Mailau). It is a matter of regret that time did not permit me to accompany Ve'etutu in his cutter on a Tafahi voyage, when these wave patterns might have been demonstrated.

We are left with the various 'seas' between Tongatapu and Nomuka 60 miles further north as described by Kienga and Ve'etutu. We followed the former's wave directions at night in *Rehu Moana*, when they enabled us to keep constant track of our progress by alterations in the vessel's motion (Lewis, 1969a: 40). Three more recent passages amplified those observations.

From Malinoa, the northernmost reef of Tongatapu, an area of confused seas extends several miles northwards. (This would appear to correspond to the Gilbertese rough *nao bangaki* sector on the north side of an island.) Beyond this disturbed zone the seas become relatively calm and a short, low easterly swell prevails.

These pleasant conditions continue for some 26 miles until the Hunga Islands come abeam to leeward, when long, high seas roll in from the east. These are ocean swells funnelled through a deep that cuts through the Tongan chain at this point. They have some of the characteristics of their oceanic origin, except that, being compressed, they are higher and wilder than swells far from land.

Once across this deep, the waves resume their former character until Kelefesia island and reef come abeam to windward. There is then a change due to the easterly swell being bent round until it comes from the south-east (Kienga). The rest of the way to Nomuka is marked by small cross waves that appear to be derived from swells divided by islands some 10 miles to windward.

Wave diffraction techniques are less used in the Caro-   *Carolines.*
lines than in the other islands we have been considering.   *Land Swells*
On the one hand bird landfall overshadows other ex-
panded target methods. On the other, irregularity of
currents is likely to be a complicating factor.

Crossing the 450-mile gap between the Carolines and
the Marianas across wind and current, it was of course
vital to decide whether we were in fact up-wind of the
Marianas as planned. When the time came for us to alter
course to cut the Marianas' chain obliquely, Hipour knew
by the swell that we were indeed to windward (east) of
that archipelago. 'The height and form of the long swell
from the east makes it most unlikely that any land lies to
windward', he said.

One point merits consideration: the pronounced effect   *Swells in*
of such a substantial land mass as New Zealand on swells   *Lee of New*
in its shelter.   *Zealand*

New Zealand lies in the westerly belt of the Southern
Ocean swell. Its lee side, unlike other Polynesian lands, is
therefore the east. *Rehu Moana* approached New Zealand
from this direction. The winds were mainly very light
easterly, but as we moved further southward, a low
westerly swell became perceptible. At a distance later
estimated at between 150 and 200 miles east of the land
this swell disappeared (log *Rehu Moana*, 7-11 December
1965). About the same time a deal of flotsam was noted.

The art of locating islands by 'land waves' appears to   *Marshalls.*
have developed further in the Marshall Islands than any-   *Land Swells*
where else in the Pacific. However, since we do not know
how much has been lost without record elsewhere, we are
hardly entitled to be dogmatic on this point. What is
certain is that in the person of Captain Winkler of the
German Navy, Marshallese navigation, and particularly
wave lore, has been favoured with an inquirer, Winkler,
of almost unique calibre.[3]

---

[3] The account that follows will draw heavily on Winkler's classic study
(1901), supplemented by observations by Krämer (1906), and Erdland
(1914) and more recent sources like de Brum (1962), son of one of
Winkler's informants, de Laubenfels (1950), Davenport (1960, 1964b),
and Akerblom (1968).

It is important if we are to keep a sense of proportion to remember that Marshallese navigation, like that in the rest of Oceania, was based on star steering (see Akerblom, 1968: 116). Some of Winkler's informants, rather surprisingly, denied this, though Winkler cites the trader Capelle as having witnessed the use of stars by a Marshallese chief at sea (1901: 504). However, the Hawaiian missionary Hezekiah Aea, in an account written thirty-six years before Winkler's paper, seems to infer that stars were the primary guide for Ebon navigators in the Marshalls. Meinicke, about the same date, also suggests the use of navigating stars (1875: 342). Nor can all star knowledge have quickly been forgotten, since Erdland as late as 1914 (80, 81, 85, 89, cited by Akerblom, 1968: 117) described Marshallese guiding stars in some detail.[4]

Four main swells go to make up Marshallese swell patterns and all are present throughout the year, but only two, the ones from the east and west, are actually shown in fig. 35. It is only necessary, however, to rotate it through 90° to represent the north-south picture which is analogous in every way.

The 'Backbone Swell' (*Rilib*) is from the east. It is the strongest and most noticeable.

The swell from the west (*Kaelib*) is less obvious. 'Unpracticed persons are able to detect the Kaelib only with the greatest difficulty', writes Winkler (493).

The swell 'Coming from the South' (*Bungdockerik*), is next in prominence to the east swell, and may equal it, especially in the southern Marshalls.

The swell 'From the North' (*Bundockeing*) is weak everywhere, though most developed in the northern portion of the group.

This symmetrical picture of four main swells suggests a more complete and systematic version of the rather varied concepts of contemporary Gilbertese navigators. It would be reasonable to speculate whether the Marshallese custom of depicting swell patterns in the relatively

---

[4] The following section, summarising features of Marshallese swell techniques, is largely based on Winkler. As it would be out of place for a comparative study such as this to go into very great detail, the reader with special interest in the subject is referred to the studies mentioned in the introductory paragraph.

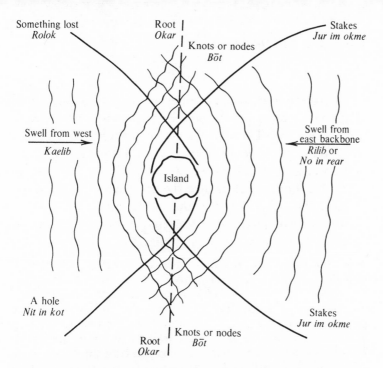

Fig. 35 *Marshallese swell patterns (based mainly on Winkler, 1901). Only swells from east and west are shown.*

permanent form of 'stick charts' might not have helped preserve their system while the Gilbertese, Tikopian, and Tongan declined.

Each primary swell is reflected back in its respective quadrant (Bryan, 1964: 3; Playdon, 1967: 159, 160; Winkler, 1901: 493), for Marshallese swell analyses take account of both reflected and refracted waves. The patterns in the different zones are usually complexes of both phenomena.

The distance offshore that these 'backwash waves' can be perceived is more than 20 miles according to de Laubenfels (Bryan, 1964: 3). De Brum says the land effect is appreciable 25 miles to leeward (west) of an atoll and at 40 miles it is no longer felt. On the windward (eastern) side, however, a vessel approaching an island begins to pitch into the 'land wave' some 50 miles out to sea (de Brum, 1962: 6). Exactly what proportion of this disturbance is due to reflected waves and how much to crossed refracted swells from the opposite quadrant is uncertain, since de Brum includes all 'cross waves' in a single category. These distances are considerably in excess of those accepted in the Gilberts and Tikopia, with the exception of reflected swells from the large island of Vanikoro.

Let us now consider the quadrants a little more fully.

The northern and southern ones are very ill defined, and as de Laubenfels points out, their names really denote wind directions. Their swells are only slightly out of line 'as if they were being held back a little at one edge' (Bryan, 1964: 3). However, as we shall see later, these rather featureless sectors, like the other pair, are traversed by guidelines (the 'roots' shown in fig. 35).

The eastern quadrant is the 'backbone' (*rilib*). Of it de Laubenfels writes (Bryan, 1964: 3),

A *rilib* pattern means that the land is off in the general direction toward which the waves are travelling. The reflected waves are coming back against the main series, and interfering with them, but the secondaries are parallel to the primaries. The *rilib* area is a quadrant, and the navigator does not know whether he is in the middle of it, or to the left or right of center, but he has a first general direction which he takes.

Now he watches for a line which he calls (in Marshallese) *Jurrinokamie*; there are two such, at about 90° apart, with the island at the apex and the *rilib* in between [see fig. 35]. At the *Jurrinokamie* the reflected waves are no longer parallel to the primary swells, but at such an angle that they form a choppy interference pattern. When he sees it, the wise old native turns parallel to the *Jurrinokamie* and follows it neatly to land.

The correspondence with Tikopian wave lore as expounded by Tupuai is almost uncanny.

We come now to the western quadrant (*kaelib*), the leeward one in terms of the trade wind and the dominant eastern swell. Here the main easterly swells that have passed each side of the island come together and cross each other. This is the zone called by the Gilbertese *nao uea* (see fig. 30). The pattern is complicated by the presence of the swell from the westward and the reflected waves produced by its impact on the coast. Like its eastern counterpart, this quadrant is bounded by lines exactly equivalent to the *jurrinokamie*, but called in this case *rolok* and *nit in kot*.

The Four Lines of Remarkable Swells
(Winkler, 1901: 493)

Let us consider these lines in more detail. These form the boundaries of the quadrants we have been discussing. They radiate out from islands towards the north-west, south-west, north-east, and south-east. Though included in fig. 35, they are indicated in fig. 36 on their own.

The *rolok* and *nit in kot* of the left hand side are both parts of the *rilib* or backbone swell from the east that have become curved from reflected wave pressure and refraction against the coast. They would appear to be the innermost of these easterly swells to maintain their momentum and integrity in face of the forces of refraction. The swell lines are reinforced and pushed up into breakers by two sets of waves that impinge against them; the reflected western waves radiating out from land, and the zone of leeward crossed seas.

The *jur im okme* (both have the same name) shown in the right hand side of fig. 36 are analogous. They differ from the left hand pair of swell lines only in the relative importance of their wave components. The boundary line is made up of the innermost bent but intact *kaelib*, or swell from the west. It is weaker than its eastern equivalent, and the reinforcing intersecting seas beyond (east) of the island are also less prominent. On the other hand the waves reflected back from the land by the impact of the easterly swell radiate out conspicuously and probably play a major part in delineating the *jur im okme*.

The names of these four quadrant boundary markers are indicative of their significance for navigators. Thus the western pair are labelled 'something lost', meaning, says Winkler (1901: 493), 'that you are out of your course'; and 'a hole', which he points out signifies 'a cage or trap'. In other words, an encounter with these leeward swell lines is a warning that the canoe has overshot its objective and is in danger of being lost down-wind. On the contrary the name 'stakes' given to the windward (eastern) swell lines simply refers to an obstruction, an approach route to land that is yet invisible.

We will now turn to quite a different set of linear wave phenomena.

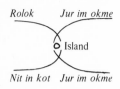

Fig. 36 The four lines of 'remarkable swells' (after Winkler, 1901)

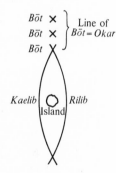

Fig. 37 'Knot' and 'root' swell intersections (after Winkler, 1901)

The 'Knots' (Bōt) and the 'Roots' (Okar)

It will be seen from fig. 35 that these extend roughly north and south from an island and are formed by the intersection of the refracted easterly *rilib* swells with the westerly *kaelib* ones. There are corresponding 'roots' on the east and west as well, which are omitted from figs. 35 and 37.

The 'knots' or 'nodes', *boot* or *bōt* (Winkler, 1901: 493), *buoj* (de Brum, 1962: 2) are the points where individual pairs of swells cross. A line of 'knots' makes up a 'root' (*okar*). In Winkler's phrase, 'As the root, if you follow it, leads to the palm tree, so does this lead to the island. Okar is the continued series of Boots. When you have found the first Boot, then you get to the island by following the Okar' (1901: 493). Winkler stresses the importance of these 'roots' in inter-island sailing. The navigator's 'highest art', he says, 'would consist in keeping on the Okar, between Rilib and Kaelib, or between the Bungdockerik and Bundockeing' (pp. 505, 506).

Fig. 38 How the angles at which swells interlock at the knots vary with distance from land

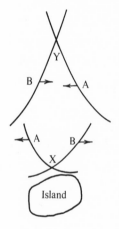

We described the 'roots' as extending roughly north and south (and east and west) from an island. Winkler points out that 'the course of the Okar is not as a rule straight, but through the influence of currents the Okar is set to one side or the other' (p. 497). This is why, he explains, stick charts represent them by slightly curved palm ribs.

The swells that interlock at the 'knots' impinge upon each other at an angle that varies according to the distance from the shore. Figure 38 should make this clearer.

Easterly swells A and A1 intersect with westerly swells B and B1 at 'knots' X and Y, close to the island and some miles offshore, respectively. It is plain that the angle of intersection at X is larger than that at Y. Thus by following a 'root' and observing whether the angle is becoming larger or smaller, the navigator is able to determine whether he is nearing the land or moving further away from it (*vide* Akerblom, 1968: 120).

If I correctly understand de Brum, he asserts that the angle between swells at a 'knot' a few miles out to sea would be about 45°, and 30-40 miles offshore would have decreased to around 25° (de Brum, 1962: 4, 5, 6).

Raymond de Brum's Concepts

Raymond de Brum (son of one of Winkler's informants, Joachim de Brum), published his article on Marshallese navigation in 1962. When an editorial mis-orientation[5] of

---

[5] 'Always the long wave at the top of the [stick] chart represents the wave from the east side' (de Brum, 1962: 3). The diagrams referred to are indeed oriented this way, but the top has been incorrectly labelled 'north' instead of 'east'.

east and north in his illustrations (1962: 4) has been corrected and some differences in terminology elucidated we have a comparable account separated from Winkler's by more than 60 years. Since the elder de Brum was instrumental in translating and explaining a good part of Winkler's material, I think we may take it that the latter's paper represents his views. It is necessary to go into the younger de Brum's concepts a little more closely before we are able to make a comparison between the two.[6]

Raymond de Brum uses the term *non rear* to describe the main swell from the east, the one that Winkler calls *rilib* or 'backbone wave'. There is no discrepancy in using the word *non rear*, since Winkler also gives *no in rear* as meaning 'swell from the eastward' (1901: 494).

The situation is different, however, in respect to de Brum's use of the word *drilip*, which he too translates as 'spinal wave'. For he applies it, not to the main east swell but to short *cross waves*. He apparently includes under this heading reflected waves, intersecting waves in an island's lee and waves from the north and south as they relate to the east and west swells (1962: 2). Thus de Brum lumps together a number of different elements into his category of spinal cross waves or *drilip*.

The words for 'knot' or 'node', *bōt* or *boot* (Winkler) and *buoj* (de Brum), are synonymous, but de Brum extends the meaning to include the four lines of 'remarkable swells' that radiate towards the north-east, south-east, north-west, and south-west, as well as the strings of 'knots' extending in the cardinal directions that are classified as *boot* by Winkler.

Apart from these essentially simplified usages, de Brum approaches his data differently; not as someone analysing concepts, but from the point of view of the practical seaman he is. Thus he describes swell phenomena largely in terms of a vessel's motion, how it pitches and rolls

---

[6] Winkler pays tribute to the help he was given with his other informants by Joachim de Brum (1901: 489, 490). It is characteristic of the secrecy that used to surround the teaching of navigation in the Marshalls that, as Joachim's son Raymond writes, 'it was seldom that a "common man" was allowed to learn navigation. My own father had a difficult time obtaining permission, but as he spoke fluent English and some German, . . . he finally was given permission to be taught' (1962: 1). He in turn instructed his son.

when it encounters waves at particular angles, in various sectors and at distances up to 50 or 60 miles from land (de Brum, 1962: 6, 7). All this is too detailed to be considered here, but we may remark that it adds something of a new dimension to previously published studies of Marshallese wave lore.

We are now in a better position to compare Raymond de Brum's concepts with his father's of half a century earlier. They are not always exactly the same, and as might have been anticipated, have generally become simpler with the passage of time. However, the son is a navigator actually using swell techniques, so the element of personal selectivity that has been noted elsewhere will be likely to come into the picture. Thus a part of his simplification of concepts may well be individual idiosyncrasy. What seems most significant is that the essential integrity of this swell lore, so foreign to the usages of European navigation, has been preserved. It has been maintained, moreover, in face of such cultural challenges as the disappearance of big sailing canoes, atomic bomb testing in the group and the pseudo stick chart trade.

As in other archipelagos, swell motion in the Marshalls is felt rather than observed. Here is de Brum on the training of future navigators: 'These elder skippers, first of all would take the younger man out to the ocean. They would be in a boat, but they would lay the young man

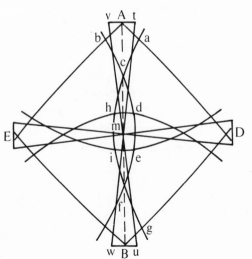

Fig. 39
Mattang *stick chart (from Winkler, 1901)*

in the water, on his back, and tell him to float and relax so that he would get to know the feel of the waves as they came along' (1962: 1).

Aea (1948: 17), writing in 1862, is plainly referring to Marshallese 'feeling' the swells when he says 'the navigator lies down in the canoe pressing his right ear on the floor for several minutes, then he would say to those on board, "Land is behind us, on one side or before", and so forth'. The 'right ear' may be disregarded, I think, since Marshallese navigation was secret (Winkler, 1901: 505), and a missionary would be the least likely recipient of explanations of practices he observed.

These constructions of palm ribs bound by coconut fibre with shells as islands were first reported by the missionary Gulick in 1862 (Akerblom, 1962: 117). Their existence gave the impetus for Winkler's investigation of swell techniques (1901: 487), and had it not been for these artifacts, such techniques might well have gone as little recorded as Marshallese star or bird lore was.

Marshallese Stick Charts

The stick charts are not charts in the Western sense, but instructional and mnemonic devices concerned with swell patterns (Winkler, 1901: 490). Neither are they essential navigational tools, de Brum, for instance, never having used one (de Brum, 1962: 3).

Three types are known (see figs. 39-41):

Mattang. Instructional and mnemonic.

Meddo. Shows swell patterns in relation to a few islands.

Rebbilib. Covers the whole or a large part of the archipelago and seems more concerned with islands than swells.

Our discussion will concentrate on the *mattang*, which is an indigenous construct devoid of European features, whereas the *rebbilib*, and possibly to some extent the *meddo*, seem likely to have been influenced by Western models.

In the *mattang* illustrated in fig. 39, A, B, D, and E are islands. The borders of the chart are to hold all together, but also to represent swells. Thus AD and DB make up the *rilib* or east swell for island D, and EA and EB the

kaelib or west swell for island E. tM is the southern half
of the *rilib* or east swell for island A, and vM is the southern portion of its *kaelib*. Similarly uM is the northern
section of island B's *rilib* and wM its *kaelib* (Winkler,
1901: 496).

The purpose of these straight lines is to show how
'among islands near together and under simple relationships, one comes from A to B in straight lines, if he holds
himself always between Rilibs and Kaelibs' (Winkler,
1901: 497).

ac is another *rilib* for A and bc another *kaelib*; gf and
ef have a corresponding relationship with island B. These
lines are to show how the *rilib* and *kaelib* of A come in
contact at the 'knot' c, and those of B at the 'knot' f. If
there were no current a further series of 'knots' or crossings would follow along the line cf. But the 'root' not
usually being straight, the curves cdef and chif are to
indicate its course in easterly and westerly currents
respectively.

The corresponding *bungdockerik* and *bungdockeing* are
represented by the similar ED complex of lines.

We have followed Winkler in orientating this *mattang*
and the other figures after the Western manner, i.e. with
north shown uppermost. If we were to adhere strictly to
Marshallese custom, of course, the upper border would
be regarded as easternmost (de Brum, 1962: 3).

The *mattang* differs in principle from the European
chart in at least three important respects. There is first the
obvious fact that it is constructed for the purpose of
indicating swell lines which these charts ignore. Then the
attached shells are able to represent *any* islands, and the
stick chart may be orientated at the angle most convenient for the particular circumstances being illustrated.
And thirdly, *mattang* are utterly individual artifacts,
constructed by navigators to suit their own requirements.
As Winkler puts it, without 'the maker of the chart himself
as explainer; another, even an entirely competent navigator, can not under any circumstances read the deliver-
ances of a chart which he himself has not made' (1901:
495).

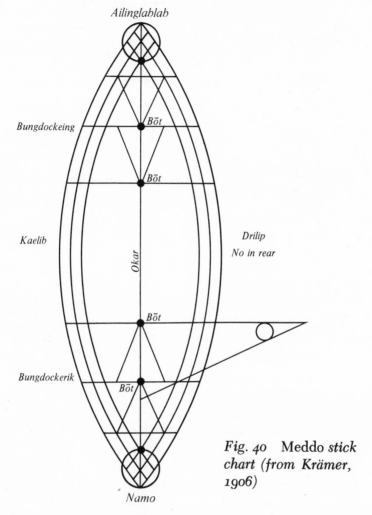

Fig. 40   Meddo *stick chart (from Krämer, 1906)*

Captain Playdon judges the *mattang* to be a device 'of limited antiquity' (1967: 166). In spite of his having been advised by a member of the ubiquitous de Brum family, who was a student at the University of Hawaii (pers. comm., 1968), one can hardly accept this assessment.

The Age of 'Stick Charts'

Akerblom has put the relevant facts very clearly, I think, and I cannot do better than paraphrase his presentation (1968: 129, 130). The principles underlying the swell phenomena that were expressed in stick charts were illustrated and explained to Winkler by Marshallese navigators in 1898, long before Europeans had formulated and explained these phenomena theoretically, which was not done until during the twentieth century.

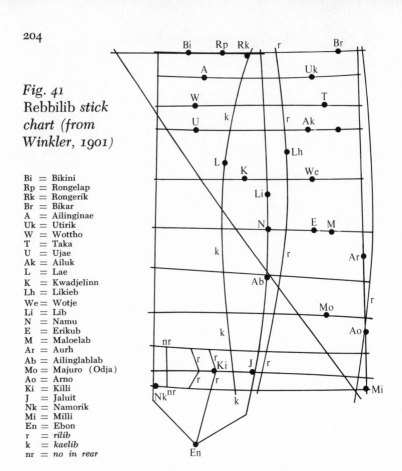

Fig. 41
Rebbilib *stick
chart (from
Winkler, 1901)*

Bi = Bikini
Rp = Rongelap
Rk = Rongerik
Br = Bikar
A = Ailinginae
Uk = Utirik
W = Wottho
T = Taka
U = Ujae
Ak = Ailuk
L = Lae
K = Kwadjelinn
Lh = Likieb
We = Wotje
Li = Lib
N = Namu
E = Erikub
M = Maloelab
Ar = Aurh
Ab = Ailinglablab
Mo = Majuro (Odja)
Ao = Arno
Ki = Killi
J = Jaluit
Nk = Namorik
Mi = Milli
En = Ebon
r = *rilib*
k = *kaelib*
nr = *no in rear*

The instructional *mattang* is a purely theoretical model of swell phenomena, and in it one cannot trace any influence from European cartography. Europeans had no corresponding graphic representation of these phenomena, and could not have had any, since the underlying principles were not generally known.

Coming to the *meddo*, its function, unlike that of Western charts, is to indicate the position of islands relative to observable swell phenomena, the true distances and directions between the islands being of only secondary importance.

Akerblom concludes that stick charts are of independent Marshallese invention and the *mattang* developed without outside impulse. He considers it possible that the *meddo* and *rebbilib* underwent certain changes as a result of contact with European navigators, and that this would apply particularly to the *rebbilib*, on which the islands are given a relatively correct geographical position.

I am in agreement with the above common sense analysis, including the proposition that the *rebbilib* must remain suspect. But while this is true of its development or modification, it does not necessarily apply to the original geographical concept. In fact we have evidence of the ability of early Marshallese navigators correctly to depict the positions of the islands of their archipelago at a date when it was they who had to instruct the geographically uninformed European explorers.

The Marshalls consist of two parallel island chains called Ratak and Ralik. In 1817 Kotzebue was aware of the existence only of part of the former. It was the old chief Langemui, whom he encountered on Ailuk atoll, who first told him there was a second chain 130 miles to the west. Langemui proceeded to represent the islands of both groups by means of stones set out on a carpet (presumably a mat).

'As his account of the clusters of Radeck (as far as we knew them) was correct, his account of Ralick also deserves confidence' wrote Kotzebue. 'The chart of the chain of Ralick, which will be found in my atlas, I sketched from Langemui's account', he stated (1821: 167-8). Just how accurate was the chief's knowledge can be seen by comparison of this chart, based entirely on the data the chief supplied, with the appropriate section of Admiralty chart 781. Both are reproduced in map 5.

GENERAL REMARKS ON SWELLS

Are the selections, made by navigators from complex wave patterns, characteristic of those individuals, or are they functions of the general practice of particular archipelagos? Both, it would seem. Continuity in the transmission of oral lore as well as geographical factors would tend to lead towards conformity.

But we cannot assume more than this. We have seen the great differences in theory and practice that exist between different Gilbertese *tani borau*, and in the Marshalls between the concepts of a son and the father who taught him. The Tikopians expounded a coherent fragment of what has previously been generally regarded as being 'Marshallese wave lore'.

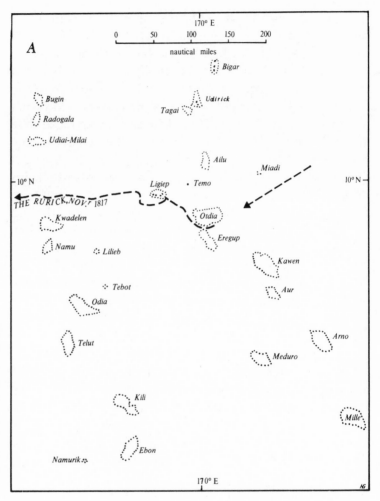

Map 5
The Ralik
chain. A. As
drawn from
Langemiu's
account (after
Kotzebue,
1821).
B. From
Admiralty
Chart 781

If there had been the account of only one of the de
Brums to go on, or that of but a single *tia borau,* we
should naturally have assumed them to represent their
national navigational 'schools'. In all probability the
Tikopian wave concepts told to me represent only one
part of the whole, other portions of which could be known
to living Tikopians, or have formerly been known to
earlier generations.

This should serve to remind us to be very careful in
drawing hard and fast conclusions from the incomplete
data at our disposal on what constituted the different

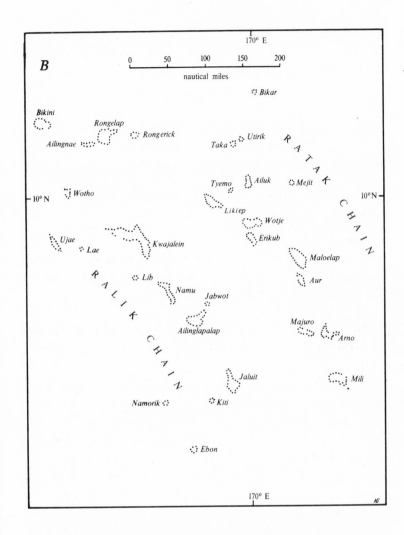

B

170° E

0   50   100   150   200

nautical miles

Bikar

Bikini

Rongelap

Rongerick

Ailingnae

Taka   Utirik

RATAK

Tyemo   Ailuk   Mejit

Wotho

10°N   Likiep   10°N

Wotje

Erikub

CHAIN

Ujae   Kwajalein   Maloelap

Lae

Aur

RALIK   Lib

Namu

Jabwot

Majuro

Ailinglapalap   Arno

CHAIN   Jaluit   Mili

Namorik   Kiti

Ebon

170° E

navigational systems of Oceania in their heyday.

The other important point about swell techniques concerns their indigenous nature. Their purpose in general is to expand the range at which islands may be located, a concept quite foreign to exact instrumental navigation, and one most unlikely to owe anything at all to Western influence. Swell pattern analysis is thus in the same category as star compasses, orientation systems, cloud, loom, and deep phosphorescence techniques; none of these arts was of European origin.

There are certain elements of Western geographical

knowledge that are likely to have dispersed across the Pacific via Islanders serving aboard European ships, but it seems in the highest degree improbable that concepts of the type mentioned were among them. These systems of ideas are too ancient and secret and deeply imbedded in their communities' culture. In origin, development, and dispersal (where this has occurred) they would appear to be largely independent of outside influences.

DEEP PHOSPHORESCENCE INDICATING DISTANT LAND

This sign is of particular interest. Firstly because it has not to my knowledge previously been recorded, and secondly since it is known in widely separated areas in Polynesia and Micronesia.[7]

Santa Cruz
Reef Islands.
Te Lapa
Phenomenon
of Tevake
and Bongi

Te lapa[8] has nothing in common with ordinary surface or subsurface phosphorescence (save that both can be seen best on dark nights). This point was stressed repeatedly. Tevake described the former as *under water lightning,* and I think this is an excellent analogy. It comprises streaks, flashes, and momentarily glowing plaques of light, all well beneath the surface. Exactly like lightning, it flickers and darts and is in constant motion. It occurs a good deal deeper down than common luminescence, at anything from a foot or two to more than a fathom.

The phenomenon acts, in Bongi's words, 'all same compass to show where land is', for its flashes dart out from the directions in which islands lie, or else flicker to and fro in line with these bearings. It is best seen 'in the "middle sea", 80-100 miles out', but it invariably indicates the direction of land. As you approach land it becomes scanty and finally disappears by the time the island (if an atoll) is well in sight.

The particular kind of motion is said to be related to distance offshore. Far out at sea it moves relatively slowly;

---

[7] I have used the familiar term 'phosphorescence' in lieu of the more exact 'luminescence' to avoid any unwarranted assumption of precision. The nature of this phenomenon is uncertain.

[8] Demonstrated at sea by Tevake and Bongi on two occasions.

when land is near, say 10 or 20 miles away, it takes on a rapid to and fro jerking character. A further complication is that *te lapa* 'from' reefs is slower moving than that 'from' islands the same distance away.

The phenomenon is so marked on dark rainy nights that it is then customary to steer by it. Unfortunately such conditions did not prevail at any time while we were at sea with Tevake. Nevertheless, when *Isbjorn* was hove-to for three hours awaiting daylight on 31 December, the 'near-land *lapa*' and the 'reef *lapa*' were both discernible and only the slow moving 'distant-land *lapa*' was absent.

'Land *lapa*' was seen to be darting to and fro along two distinct bearings which were both plain enough for me to see despite the clear night and the comparative nearness of the islands. One series kept flashing from a direction which Tevake averred was that of the volcano Tinakula. The other, he said, was 'from' the island of Ndeni. Morning revealed the high islands of Tinakula and Ndeni, each about 20 miles away, and respectively west and south of our position. These were the directions that the old navigator had indicated.

'Reef *lapa*' which came 'from' the extensive Matema reefs a few miles away I found much harder to distinguish. The glows and flashes from that direction were so infrequent that I cannot honestly claim to have observed that their rate of movement was any different from the rest. There was no doubt at all, however, as to the directions indicated by the three *lapa* 'streams'.

What can be the nature of this phenomenon? It seems probable that it is related in some way to deep swell movement, perhaps to 'ground swell' or 'backwash waves' reflected from land or reefs. This speculation leaves unanswered the reason for its being seen more clearly at such surprisingly great distances from land, a characteristic that distinguishes it from all other swell phenomena—if indeed it can be so classified.

Te lapa, dynamic, transient, and deep in the water, is in all these respects quite distinct from ordinary phosphorescence. Moreover, their distribution is not the same. Common phosphorescence is most profuse within a mile or so of reefs and coasts, whereas *te lapa* does not begin until 8 or 9 miles offshore. It is the former to which Gatty refers when he says, 'At night, increasing luminescence, due to organisms in the water, constitutes a warning that you are approaching a reef or shore line' (1943: 65).

It is interesting that the Tikopians, whose voyaging range overlaps that of the Reef Islanders and who are also Polynesians, do not know of *te lapa*. Perhaps it would be more correct to say that those I interviewed were unaware of it. Ordinary phosphorescence (*te poura*) was familiar enough. This, they said, was seen mostly in unpleasant rainy weather. It told nothing useful.

Gilbert Islands.   This is not the phosphorescence caused by a canoe's wake
The Te Mata   [said Abera], but it is best seen when a canoe is travelling very
of Abera of   slowly. *Te mata* moves; the longer movement away from land,
Nikunau   the shorter towards it. It shoots out quickly in one or other of these directions rather than going back and forth. It is like lightning. We see it about eighteen inches below the surface and lower down. When land is near by, there is a lot of phosphorescence about; this is nothing at all to do with *te mata* and is of no use whatsoever for indicating the direction of land.

There is really no comment to be made on this Micronesian navigator's description of *te mata*. It is clearly analogous in every respect with the Santa Cruz Outlier Polynesians' *te lapa*.

The usually well informed Teeta was unacquainted with the phenomenon. This suggests caution in drawing conclusions, based on the knowledge of a single navigator, that a concept is unknown in a culture area. Compared with a written discipline, even the most systematically taught body of oral lore is bound to be differentially apprehended by its individual practitioners. Teeta knew only of ordinary phosphorescence (*buatono*). This did not move in any particular direction, was found right up to land and disappeared well offshore. It was most noticeable among the stirred-up seas near reefs on rainy nights.

Tonga. The   Phosphorescence on the surface of the water means
Ulo Aetahi   nothing except that it is likely to rain, said Ve'etutu. But
of Ve'etutu   'deep down flashes of light show the way land is'. At the time he was unable to remember the name. A little later

he recalled it as *ulo aetahi*, the 'glory of the seas'. Despite the brevity of the description, it fits in perfectly with *te lapa* and *te mata*, and with nothing else I know of. Once again the distinction is made between the deep, darting, land-indicating 'lightning' and superficial phosphorescence.

Te lapa, *te mata*, *ulo aetahi*, is a phenomenon as far as I know without European definition, and its use in land-finding a wholly indigenous art. While its application is limited to night time and restricted by weather conditions, it provides a very distant land indication indeed—that is if Santa Cruz Reef Islands experience is generally applicable. Since we now have knowledge of it from two Polynesian and one Micronesian area, the results of inquiries elsewhere are awaited with interest.

OTHER METHODS FOR 'EXPANDING' TARGETS

It is probable that this list could be extended substantially and doubtless further investigation in Oceania will bring more methods to light and also amplify the brief descriptions below.[9] Not all the techniques mentioned are likely to be valid. But if we hope to gain any insight into the outlook of Pacific voyagers of an earlier age, we must appreciate how much their practical arts were hedged around with unfounded beliefs, and their confidence enhanced not a little by magic. Of the methods mentioned in this section, the first would appear doubtful, the next few practical enough and the last group frank superstitions.

Sun's Rays

Abera of Nikunau asserted that on calm cloudless days, when the sun is nearly overhead, this sign is to be looked for: you peer down into the sea and observe the sun's rays. Some rays will be long and some short. The shorter rays point towards the invisible land.

Drift Objects

All manner of drift objects apprised us of the presence of a substantial land mass to windward when we were 150 to 200 miles off the New Zealand coast in *Rehu Moana*

---

[9] Variations in the distribution of marine life, reports of diving down to 'sample' sub-surface water, scents of land and land breezes all spring to mind. I have no worthwhile information about any of these.

(Lewis, 1967: 281). Gladwin (1970: 195) mentions the attention Puluwat navigators pay to freshly broken branches found floating at sea after storms. Abera answered a question about the significance of drift objects or seaweed evulsed from reefs, by saying, 'They do not tell you how far off land is, but they do indicate its direction, provided that you know the direction of the currents, or if the object be high out of the water, the recent or prevailing wind'.

Deep Reefs   These, as we have seen, are important to Puluwat navigators for extending the 'screens' between and around islands. Hipour demonstrated how the sea's colour alters when you pass over the edge of a reef 20 to 30 fathoms down. There is a distinct change from deep blue to a lighter, greener tint. In good weather, steep, short waves revealed the presence of the reef at a little distance, he said. It was never calm enough during our stay in the Carolines for this to be seen.

A Polynesian report of homing on a very isolated reef fishing ground comes from Samoa. Stair (1895b: 617) says that expeditions were made at certain seasons of the year to a reef midway between Wallis Island (Uvea) and Savai'i. Pasco Bank, the reef referred to, lies a little over 80 miles west of Savai'i at a depth of 8 to 13 fathoms. No portion of it protrudes above the surface.

Canoes in   A report of this practice—canoes sailing abreast a mile
Line Abreast or two apart to facilitate landfall—comes from the Marshalls (Erdland, 1914), but it seems not improbable that it is a misunderstanding of Marshallese practice. The Marshallese commonly travelled in flotillas 'usually of 25-30 canoes', under command of their chiefs. The latter, wishing 'to hold this knowledge [of navigation] for their sole benefit, . . . stayed together on one canoe, the pilot boat, the other canoes following this' (Winkler, 1901: 505).

It seems then that far from fanning out, the vessels remained together for the very good reason that they must keep in touch with the boat carrying the navigators. To this end they sailed one behind the other. Winkler refers to a report of canoes abreast, only to say that it has not been confirmed, 'although it may have been practicable.

From the explanations received by me, the canoes always followed their leader in single file' (p. 505).

References to flotillas from other parts of the Pacific seem to do with war expeditions, ceremonial visits, trading ventures or migrations, but to bear no relation to land-finding.

Gladwin puts the matter in a common sense light when he says: 'Usually canoes travel alone. Sometimes they sail in convoys of two or three, but hardly ever more than four. In addition to companionship the other canoes add an element of safety'. Mentioning the emergency spars and lashings always carried on Puluwat canoes, he adds that salvage and repair operations are much safer and 'easier if another canoe is standing by to help' (1970: 58).

The same point of safety in numbers was made on Ninigo where, in default of local timber, the canoes are built of drifted logs that have been months or even years at sea. The timbers of even the most recently built craft are therefore invariably less than sound.

Only a very few examples will be given. 'When utterly gone astray at sea, having tried all other expedients in vain, the native naturally resorts to that everlasting prop of his race—magic' (Grimble, 1924: 128). *Magical Beliefs and Practices*

Gladwin refers to another use of magic—the destruction of canoes by sorcery. To bring about disaster to a canoe at sea one had to know the secret names of the seaways upon which it would be travelling. Although this practice died out in the 1930s, he found that the awe associated with seaway names made navigators lower their voices when pronouncing them (1970: 209).

The spread of Christianity has sometimes tended to foster the belief that old time practices were inspired by the devil. Thus an elderly Sikaianan, Titus Teai, when asked how two famous early navigators had found their way, answered, 'They did not use the stars to steer by, but were directed by evil spirits'.

A versatile technique was mentioned by Makea Nui Ariki, High Chieftainess of Rarotonga in 1965. The canoe man at sea plucks out an eyelash. If it comes away easily, land is near. The identical procedure is adopted by his wife ashore to ascertain if the food in the earth oven is cooked. If her eyelash is easy to pluck, the meal is ready.

Often, however, the border between the practical and magical is much more difficult to delineate than in the above instances, a given practice not infrequently combining elements of both. Sometimes, too, reports are so vague that the character of a technique cannot be determined. For instance an administrative cadet's description of the weather lore of the late Teimarane, a Gilbertese navigator, leaves in doubt which items he considers practical and which 'idolatrous rites' (Roberts, pers. comm., 1969).[10]

---

[10] Weather lore is essential to seamanship but marginal to navigation proper. We will therefore limit consideration to the few comments in this footnote.

Observations of animal habits are only a small part of Gilbertese weather forecasting, which includes a wealth of cloud and sea signs. Grimble mentions some of the former, including the behaviour of ants, spiders, and starfish (1924: 127, 128). Abera demonstrated them to me on Onotoa. Space forbids more than a single example: 'Before setting out on a voyage you must consult the sea signs', said Abera. 'In considering sea signs we will start with crabs. There are two sorts of crab; one digs a hole straight down and him we will consider. The other kind digs a spiral and him we reject. The crab does one of four things:

1. He may block the mouth of his hole and scratch the sand down flat across the opening leaving marks like the sun's rays. This means wind and rain within three days.
2. He may level the excavated pile but not block the mouth of the hole. There will be strong wind but no rain.
3. He blocks the hole but does not scrape the mound flat. There will be rain but no wind.
4. He leaves the excavated sand piled in a mound. This indicates fine weather.

On inspection above the tide line we found all crabs except one to be expecting wind but no rain (no. 2). The solitary pessimist anticipated both (no. 1). Unfortunately we had to leave Onotoa before either prophecy had time to be fulfilled.

A quite different aspect of weather lore is prediction by the stars. Its validity is necessarily limited to seasonal patterns, but more interesting than the beliefs themselves are their wide distribution. Such erroneous deductions as to cause and effect could hardly have been made independently in separate parts of Oceania.

For instance Cook (Cook and King, 1784: 144) and Andia y Varela (Corney, 1914: vol. II, 284) mention star weather divination in Tahiti. In Ninigo, the three stars Canopus, Sirius, and Procea (together called *Maan*) were pointed out to me by Itilon as being controllers of wind direction and weather. Gladwin records fallacious star weather forecasting in the Carolines, and remarks that the forecasts of the two navigational schools, *Warieng* and *Fanur*, are more often contradictory than congruent (1970: 212).

But once again we must exercise caution. Not every star weather sign is erroneous. Ve'etutu in Tonga and Abera in the Gilberts both instanced marked twinkling of stars as a probable precursor of rain and wind. Their detailed descriptions left little doubt that they were referring to thin cirrus haze heralding the advent of a front.

In fact Teimarane's study of the behaviour of crabs and other creatures was but a prudent weather forecasting procedure, while the making of shell talismans against storms would appear doomed to futility.

Magic and shrewd observation are in all probability combined in certain Gilbertese *betia* or 'sea-marks'. What is one to make of the following, for instance? 'Between Tarawa and Maiana were porpoises in pairs whose heads always pointed in the direction of the passage into Tarawa lagoon at the place called Bairiki'. Grimble evidently thought it could be a valid observation, because he added in parentheses that it was 'quite probable that these porpoises would be feeding on some sort of food swept out of Bairiki passage by the tide race of the lagoon at falling water' (Grimble, n.d. (a)).

Similarly, the Carolinian lists of 'sea-life' said to be found between pairs of islands, are 'ambiguous, but intriguing', in Gladwin's words (1970: 207). Since they include such things as a shark, two tropic-birds and the like, he points out that the great majority, but not all, of these inventories are of phenomena that would not by their nature be likely to stay long in one place.

CHAPTER EIGHT

Expanded target landfall in practice

LANDFALL ON THE MARIANAS

On our voyage from the Carolines Hipour aimed to arrive in the vicinity of the Marianas to windward (east) of the island chain. They were high islands, according to tradition, and from Tinian and Saipan they stretched away in a long line to the northward. There were 450 miles of open ocean to be crossed from Pikelot in the Carolines. By the evening of 16 March we were nearing our objective. The navigator judged it prudent that we heave-to to await daylight.

Our reckoning of the distance covered was uncertain, because the vessel was totally strange to Hipour and because bad weather had rendered impossible accurate estimation of progress. We did agree, however, that we must be roughly opposite Saipan or a little beyond it.

The other problem, whether we were indeed to windward of the Marianas, was easier to determine since Hipour had had no alternative but to over-compensate. Thus the probability was that we were quite a distance to weather of Saipan, perhaps 40 miles. There was strong support for this supposition in the character of the sea that was running. Hipour, who had been studying the waves all day long with more than ordinary intentness, gave it as his opinion that the height and form of the long unbroken swells from the east made it most unlikely that any land lay to windward. If we had in fact erred and gone down-wind of our destination, he added, we could not have done so by very much, and either land would have been visible that afternoon or it would at least have 'blanketed' the free running easterly swells.

After a night hove-to, dawn on the 17th brought (as anticipated) no sign of land. Hipour had definite ideas as to procedure. We were agreed, he said, that our position was almost certainly to windward of the southern end of the chain of islands that extended north from Saipan. He had been given to understand that the Marianas were

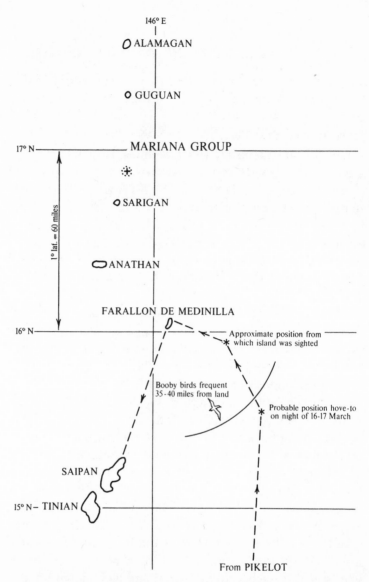

146° E

O ALAMAGAN

O GUGUAN

17° N————————— MARIANA GROUP ————————————

✴

O SARIGAN

◯ ANATHAN

FARALLON DE MEDINILLA

16° N—————————————— ⌀- - - - - ←- - — Approximate position from —————
                                              ✱ which island was sighted

1° lat. = 60 miles

Booby birds frequent
35-40 miles from land

                                              ✱ Probable position hove-to
                                                 on night of 16-17 March

SAIPAN

15° N– TINIAN —————————————————————————————

From PIKELOT

Fig. 42
Landfall on
the Marianas

inhabited by homing birds in abundance, although deep
reefs were said to be absent. The height of the islands, and
the relatively short distances between them, ensured that
birds and land would form a continuous 'screen' in our lee
(see fig. 42).

We would proceed on such a bearing as to cut through
this 'screen' at an acute angle. A very careful watch would
have to be kept all the time for signs that might indicate
the presence and direction of land. If night should fall
without our having sighted an island or significant birds,

we would heave-to again. Alternatively we might range back southward in the night something west of our track today, so as to be in position to begin another parallel sweep north-westwards tomorrow. For the moment the course would be towards the setting Little Bear (350°) for two hours, and thereafter until dark towards the setting Great Bear position (335°-340° or north-north-west). We got under way at 09.00.

Hipour and Ulutak payed the greatest attention to occasional noddies, terns, and boobies that appeared during the next two hours. At 11.00 we passed five boobies fishing together. Around noon two separate pairs of boobies and a noddy were seen. By 15.00 another group of three boobies and a single bird had been sighted. All of us were keeping a close and continuous lookout by this time. Visibility was only moderate with some haze and we were sailing slowly north-north-west with a light beam wind. We estimated that by dark we would be no more than 20 miles west of our 09.00 position. A flock of twelve boobies appeared about 16.30. Land was obviously near. None of the cumulus clouds seemed to be forming at a special place or to be particularly heaped up over any one spot. Then, after a further hour, Ulutak, at about 17.30 sighted an undulating featureless hill to the west which was later estimated to be 16-18 miles away.

It was now near dusk. Almost immediately after the sighting three boobies flew off low and straight towards the land in a manner quite different from their fishing flight. Half an hour afterwards another booby was noticed streaking low towards the island. We hove-to for the night shortly afterwards, supposing the island to be one of the Marianas north of Saipan.

This was correct, for on closing the land next morning, we found it to be small, barren, and uninhabited. It was Farallon de Medinilla, 250 feet high, 1½ miles long, the first island north of Saipan. Throughout the whole of the 48-mile open sea crossing to the latter, seabirds in much greater profusion that the previous afternoon remained in evidence. Now, save for one slightly larger gap between two 3000-foot high islands 200 miles north of Saipan, this was the longest break in the whole Marianas chain. It would be quite impossible, as Hipour had foretold, to cross this avian concentration (in daylight) and cut the 'screen' unawares. A navigator who was unsure of his position would only have to wait until evening to ascertain the bearing of the nearest land.

It is worth noting that the meteorological conditions at the time of our visit by no means favoured an easy landfall. The weather had been exceptionally bad during the voyage and none of the convection clouds associated with normal trade wind conditions had formed over Farallon or Saipan. Even more unfavourable was the haze. Farallon was sighted about 17 miles off when it was already high above the horizon. In clear weather Ulutak would have been able to pick it out from his perch in the rigging at 23. Saipan, which is 1555 feet high and theoretically detectable 47 miles away, materialised at little more than 20.

LANDFALL ON THE CAROLINE ISLANDS 'SCREEN'

Returning from the Marianas, Hipour's announced intentions were to aim up current and a little to weather of Pikelot so as to cross the margin of a deep reef east of the islet and within its 20-mile radius bird zone. There was a 'screen' of underwater reefs and almost contiguous bird zones, he reminded us, around the low islands of our destination area—Pikelot, West Fayu, Satawal, and Lamotrek. We should be able to 'cut' the submerged reef at the desired point, but if we were careless enough to go astray, this 'screen' would catch us. It is worth noting that Hipour was intending to make his landfall within a stretch of 20 miles to one side of a 500-yard-long islet—after 450 miles across wind and current. This confidence he retained throughout and it proved justified (see fig. 43).

By the morning of 25 March nearly four days had passed since we had last seen land—Saipan, 410 miles to the north-north-westward. This was the time, as mentioned on p. 147, that Hipour questioned me about our *etak* orientation and was so amused at my reply, though I judged correctly that Pikelot must be about 40 miles due south.

We were sailing in a south-south-easterly direction. No birds had been seen at sunrise, nor had any been expected

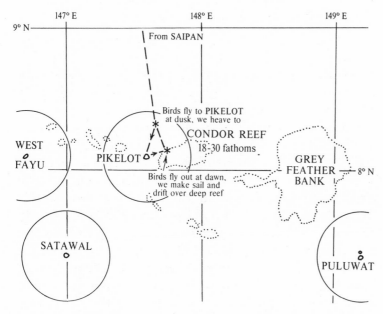

*Fig. 43 Landfall on the Carolines. Circles show 'screen'
of bird zones and dotted lines submerged reefs.*

so far from land. The sea was rough. Heavy masses of
thunder cloud towered round the horizon; visibility was
only moderate.

The first flock of birds appeared at noon. It was a sizable one, consisting of nearly a dozen terns and one or two
noddies. All were fishing industriously.

Half an hour later we sighted a bigger group of 20, mostly noddies this time. Then at 17.30, as evening approached,
the event we had so anxiously been awaiting took place:
two birds broke off fishing to fly away low and straight
south-by-west. In the next 30 minutes five more ceased
circling and diving and flew off in exactly the same direction; then a single bird, next a pair. All headed south-by-
west or 190°. There could be no further doubt. We had
arrived in the bird zone of Pikelot. Landfall on this occasion was by terns and noddies. There were no boobies.

Hipour and Ulutak's tense watchfulness now relaxed
completely. Such birds as were still circling about were
now regarded only as indications of shoals of fish. A fishing
line was put over the stern and Hipour gaily spun the
wheel and set off in pursuit of the nearest swooping flock
—without a care for the course he had previously been
following so meticulously. It was hard to realise that this
mood of relief and celebration after four days and 450

miles of steering only by the stars, sun, and waves with
never a sight of land, had been induced by the behaviour
of a few score tiny seabirds.

When the ship had eventually been snugged down for
the night Hipour proceeded to explain his deductions about
our position. The birds had flown towards the Southern
Cross angled 45° sinking, the bearing called *Majemeledo*
(190°), so Pikelot must lie in that direction. It was between
10 and 20 miles off; if it had been less than 10 we should
have seen it; if more than 20 there would have been few
birds or none. The large size of the flocks suggested that
the islet was nearer 10 than 20 miles away. We could now
relax for the night but must look out for birds next morning
since we had sailed some way south after their departure
for home and currents might set us in any direction during
the next eleven hours.

Hipour and Ulutak were on bird watch before dawn,
but it was not until the sun had risen that the first groups
of noddies and terns appeared. All came from the direction of the setting Antares, that is from the south-west,
showing that we had indeed been set some distance south
of our position the evening before.

(A matter touched on earlier is worthy of repetition
since it has bearing on all aspects of navigation by natural
signs. It is that I had not before realised how many birds
and other phenomena could be observed and analysed by
the keen and practised observation of men whose lives had
time and again depended on the acuity of their apprehension.)

While getting under way at 07.30, Hipour pointed over-
side to where the colour of the water was changing from
blue to green, indicating that the ketch was drifting over
the edge of a submerged reef (subsequently identified as
Condor Reef, 18-30 fathoms deep). We followed the direction whence the birds had come. Half an hour later Pikelot topped the horizon on the starboard bow.

THE ARC OF LANDFALL

We are now in a position to discuss the degree of accuracy to be expected from non-instrumental methods of
navigation, by analysing individual voyages in an attempt

to deduce which arcs of (expanded) landfall would be relatively safe, risky or too small for safety (see fig. 44).

Fig. 44   An arc of landfall. A. Starting point. B. Objective. Circle is zone of location of B, either sighting or expanded bird range.

Any such estimates can only be the roughest approximations, since in reality the accuracy attainable must vary with the characteristics of the seaway concerned. Unusual meteorological and sea conditions may convert the most prosaic passage into a desperate venture. While these qualifications apply to seafaring everywhere, they are particularly relevant to voyages navigated by relatively transient natural signs.

Navigational accuracy is not a function of length of voyage (if anything the longer passages providing the greater opportunity for random sea effects and judgment errors to cancel out). Thus if a 15° arc of accuracy, for example, can be attained over 300 miles, it is just as navigationally feasible over 1000. The special problems of the longer journey concern such factors as food supply, man power, motivation, and strength of the vessel—not navigation.

It is not very difficult to work out the degree of accuracy achieved by Hipour on the Saipan to Pikelot voyage. His objective was the middle of the 20-mile bird-flight arc on one side of the islet or 10 miles out to sea. As we saw he reached the seabird zone 15 miles or less from Pikelot. Five miles out in 450 corresponds to a tracking error of under 1°.

Could anything like such precision be consistently relied upon? I rather doubt it. The voyage *to* Saipan is less amenable to exact reconstruction, as Hipour deliberately overcompensated for the factors displacing him to leeward. If we assume he was aiming 20 miles up-wind of the target and actually was 40, the error would be about 3°. Clearly

then, great accuracy *can* be attained, and in conditions
that are far from being ideal. However, we shall see from
the examples below that the 'expanded' objectives of Pacific voyagers appear generally to allow a much greater
margin than this.

THE PUKAPUKA VOYAGES

A wealth of voyaging traditions and star courses from
this isolated atoll between Eastern and Western Polynesia
has been collected (Beaglehole, E. and P., 1938). The des-
tinations, where identifiable, were generally in the west,
the Tokelau Islands, Tonga, Niue, and Samoa being frequently visited (p. 410). (See fig. 45.) The reasons for
voyaging included the procurement of basaltic stone adzes.

We saw how the Pukapukan star courses were geogra-

*Fig. 45 Some
Pukapukan
voyages*

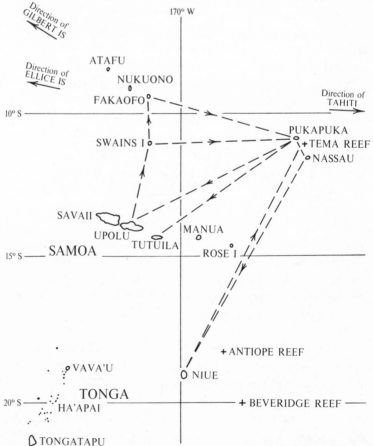

phical bearings rather than sailing directions allowing for drift.[1] They are adapted to appropriate times of the year. For instance a Centauri, the course star for Niue, sets in the early part of the night and is thus readily available for bearings during July, August, and September, months when the winds are most favourable for the voyage. The same applies to Antares for Samoa (Beaglehole, E. and P., 1938: 352). Again, 'the Orion's Belt course from Swains Island [Olosenga] to Pukapuka is peculiarly advantageous as these stars are visible to the eastward during the early part of the hurricane season when the winds are favourable for the return voyage' (Beaglehole, E. and P., 1938: 353).

However, our particular concern is with the conditions of landfall.

Pukapuka to Samoa. The star for Upolu is Antares (*Melemele*) which bears 245° when 15° above the horizon. The course is 243°. The distance is 370 miles and the arc of landfall on Samoa, mostly by sight of high islands, is 22°.[2]

Samoa-Swains Island-Pukapuka. This was one of the common return routes from Samoa (Beaglehole, E. and P., 1938: 353). Alternatively they 'sailed first to the Tokelau Islands, waited there for the hurricane season and, . . . sailed back to Pukapuka with a beam wind'(Beaglehole, E. and P., 1938: 410-11).[3] The arcs of landfall for the two legs of the route via Swains Island are these:

---

[1] There is nothing unique about the Pukapukan star courses, as has sometimes been suggested. Others of equally demonstrable validity and sometimes equivalent length have been collected on Samoa (Krämer, 1902: 245, 246), Tikopia (Firth, 1954: 91), the Carolines (McCoy, pers. comm., 1970; Riesenberg, pers. comm., 1970) and the Santa Cruz, Admiralty, Gilbertese, and Tongan archipelagos (Lewis, 1970). Furthermore, their correspondence with known Pukapukan voyaging patterns and their adaptation to sailing seasons render post-European influence most unlikely.

[2] The two most recent voyages were made after the coming of the missionaries. Yipouli had been fined for stealing nuts and was so ashamed of being labelled a thief that, together with a few friends, he sailed his double canoe to Tutuila and later Upolu. He navigated by Antares. The second voyage was a little later, about 1880. Some young men reached Tutuila in a stolen canoe. They wrecked it to avoid detection but all except one, Yolomili, were eaten by sharks; a punishment by the old gods, thought the Pukapukans, for stealing the canoe (Beaglehole, E. and P., 1938: 409).

[3] This is a typical pattern in Oceania—roving, circuitous routes taking full advantage of seasonal weather and allowing ample opportunity for prolonged visits. Tevake and Hipour were most reluctant to cut short our stops as my timetable unfortunately dictated. They considered such haste to be totally at variance with custom.

Samoa (Upolu)-Swains Island. The distance is 170 miles and there is an expanded landfall arc of 15° with the bigger Tokelau 'screen' in the background and to leeward. Fifteen degrees may well be an underestimate for the island is well known for its seabirds (p. 352).

Swains Island-Pukapuka. The guiding star is Orion's Belt (*Te Tolunga-Maui*), bearing 88°. The distance to Tema Reef, midway between Pukapuka itself and Nassau 40 miles further south, is a little over 300 miles. The expanded arc is 14°.[4]

Pukapuka to Niue. The guiding star α Centauri (*Na Mata-o-te-tokalua*) bears at set 209° from Pukapuka and 207° from Niue. The course from Pukapuka is 205°, but if, 'as some of the Pukapukans claim, Nassau was used by the old navigators as a point of departure, then a canoe headed for Niue would fetch up within 12 miles of the land' (Beaglehole, E. and P., 1938: 352). The distance is 530 miles from Pukapuka and 510 from Nassau. The expanded landfall arc of Niue, assuming boobies with a 30-mile flight range, is 8°-9°. (Sight range of Niue from a 9-foot canoe mast is itself 22 miles, giving a 5°-6° arc) (see fig. 45).

Rose Island, a haunt of boobies (*Pacific Islands*, 1943: vol. II, 676), lies approximately half way, a little to leeward of the course, but close enough for canoes from Pukapuka to pass through its bird zone. Antiope Reef, which breaks, is 40 miles to windward near Niue, and Nicholson (Beveridge) breaking reef and lagoon 125 miles beyond Niue is also to windward. The winds at the appropriate season are fair, so leeway would be negligible, and the current would be a weak westerly drift (*Pacific Islands Pilot*: vol. II, 4; vol. III, 15, 16). It will be recalled that Hipour was able to make much more accurate landfalls than this after voyages of comparable length in much worse conditions.

---

[4] In this connection Frisbie (Beaglehole, E. and P., 1938: 33) gives an exceptionally clear exposition of expanded target landfall. 'In case the canoe missed Tema Reef, due to bad steering or cloudy weather, it would still be likely to come within sight of Nassau or Pukapuka; and even if it missed all three landfalls, it could scarcely fail to come within a point 30 miles to the north or south of one of the islands, which point would be within sea-flight of the white terns—the sign of land'. Hence 'the navigator has a cross section of ocean . . . 110 miles long, in which to make his landfall'.

Niue return to Pukapuka. The expanded landfall arc is 10°-12°, and a particularly good one, with Pukapuka to one side, Nassau on the other and Tema Reef in between.

Pukapuka to Tokelau and the Ellice Islands. The guide star is the setting Altair (*Tolu*) bearing 279°. Almost any course between 277° and 300° would take a canoe close to one of the islands (Beaglehole, E. and P., 1938: 353). The distance to the Tokelaus is 320 miles and their bird zones give an arc of 14°-15°. The Ellice Islands, 850 miles from Pukapuka, give a comparable arc that overlaps that of the Tokelaus on the south, just as the Gilberts, further away still, overlap it on the north.[5]

Fais-Ulithi. Tribute voyages from the Central Carolines to Yap in the west were formerly annual events (Lessa, 1950: 48). Canoes from the Puluwat area called at Woleai or Faraulep before traversing the long open stretch to Fais and Ulithi, whence local canoes took over (Fritz, 1907: 660). Fais is 107 feet in altitude, so can be seen 14 or 15 miles away from a canoe's mast. Ulithi, which lies 42 miles further westward, is more extensive, but being an atoll, is lower. Given the 20-mile bird ranges customarily accepted in the Carolines, the expanded arc of the combined islands, when approached from Woleai, would be 14°. The distance is 244 miles from Woleai to Fais; 296 from Woleai to Ulithi. The distances from Faraulep are nearly the same (248 to Fais), though the expanded landfall arc is a little smaller, being 10°. Incidentally Ulithi, 600 miles west of

Tribute Voyages to Yap

---

[5] There is a point to be raised touching the validity of these voyages towards the north-west. When the Wilkes Expedition visited the Tokelaus in 1840, the Islanders they encountered were said to lack knowledge of any other island groups (1845: vol. V, 8-9). The Ellice Islanders, on the other hand, were much better informed. They knew of the three Tokelaus and pointed out their direction. They mentioned 'Oloosinga' and appeared acquainted with Tonga and Rotuma, though surprisingly enough they 'did not understand the name Samoa'. They referred to an island called 'Pokopoka' that Wilkes was unable to identify (Wilkes, 1845: vol. V, 43).

This knowledge of Pukapuka could, it may be argued, have resulted from accidental drifts, and indeed their occurrence would be probable. The survival upon Pukapuka of an accurate star course for the Tokelaus, and the use made of the group as a staging point on the way back from Samoa, is strong evidence of deliberate voyaging. There is nothing incompatible, of course, between these two forms of contact whose frequency seems often enough directly related.

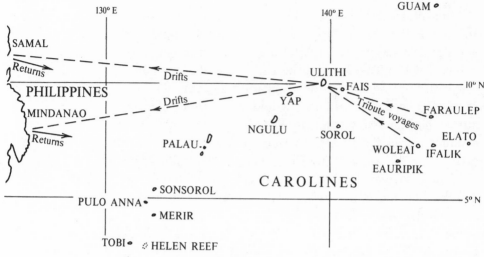

Fig. 46   *Tribute voyages to Yap via Fais-Ulithi. Drifts to Philippines and return.*

Puluwat, is the most distant island Hipour has visited in his sailing canoe. He went via Woleai.

This seaway, then, was formerly traversed repeatedly by large numbers of canoes and, though a proportion are known to have missed their destination and finished up in the Philippines (usually it appears on account of gales), the landfall arc involved seem practicable enough.[6]

Gilberts-Banaba   Gilbert Islands to Banaba (Ocean Island) arcs. These
Voyages   voyages appear to have been sailed during two periods and later abandoned (Maude, H. C. and H. E., 1932: 266, 267). The arc of landfall on the solitary Banaba was a relatively small one (in the opposite direction the whole central Gilbertese 'screen' was the target). Contact was primarily between Beru and Banaba, but it would be reasonable to suppose that departure was actually taken from the island nearest the destination, namely Nonouti.

Banaba is 280 feet high and 2 miles across from north to

---

[6] To take only two examples from opposite ends of the time scale: Fr Serrano tells us that in 1664 alone, 30 canoes were drifted from the Carolines to the Philippines. This must have been an exceptionally stormy year, for in 37 years in the Philippines, he had seen boats drift in only eight times (Lessa, 1962: 328).

A sailing canoe with six men left Ulithi for Fais in 1963. They missed, returned to Ulithi and reset their course, only to be overtaken by a typhoon. They ran for Yap, then Palau and finally steered for the Philippines, where they landed at Samar (Riesenberg, 1965: 164).

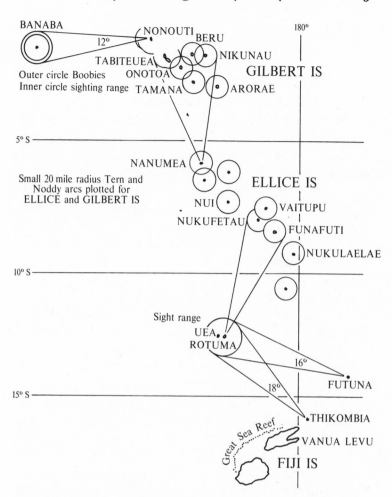

BANABA
NONOUTI
BERU
180°
12°
TABITEUEA
NIKUNAU
Outer circle Boobies   ONOTOA
GILBERT IS
Inner circle sighting range   TAMANA
ARORAE

5° S

NANUMEA
Small 20 mile radius Tern and
Noddy arcs plotted for
ELLICE and GILBERT IS
ELLICE IS
NUI
VAITUPU
NUKUFETAU
FUNAFUTI
NUKULAELAE

10° S

Sight range
UEA
ROTUMA
16°
FUTUNA
18°
15° S
THIKOMBIA
Great Sea Reef
VANUA LEVU
FIJI IS

Fig. 47   Some landfall arcs in Tongan and Gilbertese spheres

south. From the island's centre the sighting radius is 24 miles and the booby flight range 31. These give arcs of 8½° and 12½° respectively. The distance from Nonouti is 274 miles.

Thikombia (Fiji) to Rotuma. This Fijian island is ideally placed, by reason of the direction of the prevailing wind and current, for voyages to Rotuma. It is perhaps suggestive that there are several Rotuman settlements in nearby parts of Vanua Levu (Reid, pers. comm., 1969).

Some Landfall Arcs in the Tongan Voyaging Zone[7]

[7] References to the Tongan sphere include Dillon (1829: vol. I, 294-5; vol. II, 103-4), Diaper (1928: 112), Mariner (1817: vol. I, 316-17) and Cook (Cook and King, 1784: 368-9).

Rotuma is 840 feet high and a smaller island, 6 miles further west, 860 feet. The summits would be visible in favourable conditions 40 miles east or west and 35 miles north or south (where one island would 'blanket' the other) of the islands. Birds would not in general fish so far offshore, so would be unlikely to be of use. From Thikombia to Rotuma is 255 miles and the arc of landfall by sight (in clear weather) is a substantial one—18°.

From Futuna to Rotuma is 295 miles. The arc of sight landfall is just under 16°. The even higher Futuna gives a similar arc on the return.

From Rotuma to Vaitupu (Ellice Islands). Here we have a 'screened' landfall. Voyages were made to Vaitupu and Nui (Dillon, 1829: vol. II, 103), but we can safely assume that the nearer Ellice Islands would be the first to be encountered. They are 40 miles apart, so their tern and noddy ranges would bridge this gap and extend at least 20 miles beyond the two atolls. To one side of this 'screen' is Nukulaelae and behind lies Vaitupu. The primary 'screen' by itself, however, gives an 18° expanded arc at a distance from Rotuma to Funafuti of 260 miles. From Funafuti to Rotuma the arc of sight landfall is 18°.

We saw in the footnote to p. 24, how the distances within the 'greater Tongan sphere', mentioned above, like the landfall arcs, are substantially less than those between the Polynesian Ellice Islands and the Gilberts, which are part of Micronesia.

Four Illustrative Landfall Arcs   Mauke to Nurotu (Maria or Hull Island). The Southern Cook Islanders of Mauke were wont to visit this uninhabited western outpost of the Tubuai archipelago for the fishing (Lucett, 1851: 122).[8] We may assume birds to have been good land indicators for the Maukean fishermen because people from Rimatara go to Nurotu even to-

---

[8] The possibility that the Maukeans may have got their information about Nurotu from the visit of a whaler has been raised (Dening, 1963: 126). The tradition, however, was an old one when Lucett visited Mauke in the forties of last century. 'They have only traditionary accounts respecting it'. It was their 'ancestors [who] used occasionally to resort thither to fish', he said (1851: 122). Nurotu was first reported by the whaler *Maria* in 1824 (Sharp, 1960: 208); not much time, one would think, for the story of fishing expeditions to be elaborated and incorporated into Maukean tradition.

day for young seabirds (*Pacific Islands*, 1943: vol. II, 238).
Given a 30-mile booby flight range, the atoll would present a 17° expanded target at 182 miles, the distance from
Mauke. Without this 'expansion' the isolated atoll would
have been very hard to find indeed.

Pulusuk to Kapingamarangi. This 465-mile voyage over
open sea to a large but totally isolated atoll was clearly
rendered practicable only by the bird arc of 7½°. It is
tempting to surmise that, for such a difficult passage
(across variable currents) and devoid of any additional
reef or other safety 'screen', this 7½° expanded landfall arc
might represent something like the limit of navigational
feasibility.

Savai'i (Samoa) to Pasco Bank. It is salutary to remember that not all landfalls are subject to 'expansion'. Indeed,
in this case there was no dry land to be found at all. The
Samoans, after covering more than 80 miles, had to find
an objective that is entirely under water and could not be
apprehended until a canoe was practically on top of it.
The 8° arc that the bank itself presents could not, therefore, be exceeded.

Puluwat to Satawal. Among voyages now commonly
made from Puluwat, Gladwin writes, 'the greatest accuracy thus demanded is on the passage from Puluwat one
hundred and thirty miles to Satawal, which is less than ½
a mile across. An error of 10 miles at the end of this journey would result from an angular deviation of less than
4½°'. He reminds us that this is through an area of ocean
with strong cross currents (1970: 202). In another context Gladwin implies that a Carolinian navigator would
expect his courses made good to exhibit something less
than a 5° error (p. 156).

At first sight there appears to be a discrepancy between
this figure of 4°-5° and the landfall arcs, often of the order
of 15° or more, that we have been considering. The explanation is that, as Gladwin says, the dead reckoning
system is so accurate that most landfalls are made visually
within the 10-mile sight-range of an atoll, the seabirds
(and the other 'expansion' techniques we are familiar
with) constituting a safety factor and an insurance against
disaster (Gladwin, 1970: 202).

Summing up the material presented in the last three chapters, we may conclude, I think, that the widespread acceptance of Oceania as being made up of 'blocks' of islands with surrounding zones of land signs may well have contributed to the confidence at sea so characteristic of Polynesians and Micronesians. Rafe the Tikopian, for example, was not being obtuse when he failed to understand a question about what he would do if he should miss his home landfall. 'I know the way my island is', he said. 'It is my island. It is where I follow the stars where to go—I cannot miss *my* island!' His certainty was reinforced because, in addition to guiding stars he knew signs such as reflected waves and seabirds that would guide him to Tikopia.

CHAPTER NINE

Position fixing at sea

The preceding chapters have been concerned with course, dead reckoning, and landfall, and although competent navigators have made innumerable voyages solely by these techniques, they are not the sum of indigenous navigation. The special arts that we now come to were very possibly limited to highly trained specialists. They were 'secrets that only I and the devil know', in words attributed to the blind Tuita of Tonga. They go beyond the inspired guess-work of dead reckoning in an attempt to 'fix' some component of position.

The most significant of these methods was determination of what we call latitude by means of overhead or zenith stars. This concept, its navigational implications, and data from several archipelagos concerning it will take up the bulk of this chapter. Some ill-understood high star techniques and certain oceanic phenomena like water temperature occupy the remainder.

ZENITH STARS

A star's declination is its celestial latitude. It passes directly above all places whose latitude equals its declination as it progresses from east to west across the sky. Thus if Sirius traverses the zenith of Vanua Levu, a navigator, noting that this star was directly overhead, could deduce that he was in the same latitude as the island (lat. Vanua Levu and dec. Sirius are both about 17° S.). He would, however, have no means of knowing by the zenith star whether, or by how much, he was east or west of the island (see fig. 48).

A clear distinction must be drawn between the zenith star of an island—the 'star on top', as the Tikopians term it—and directional or steering stars, which we have seen to be low on the horizon. The point is stressed because of claims by Reche (1927: 214-19, 266-71) and Gatty (1958: 39-41) that it is practicable to steer with great accuracy towards an island's zenith star (apart from using it to de-

The Concept

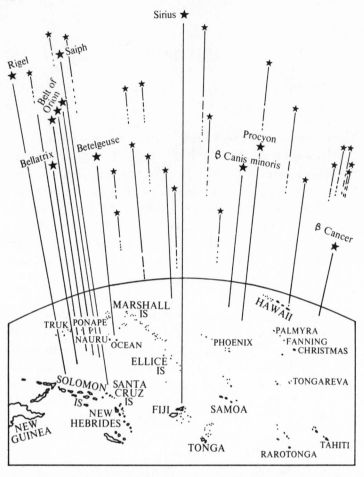

Fig. 48 Zenith star passing over Fiji (after Gatty, 1943)

fine latitude). Frankel (1962: 44) has exposed the fallacy of this view by pointing out that a navigator only 2° south and 2° east of his target, and thus about 170 miles from it, would, if steering towards a zenith star, be guiding his vessel by an object whose bearing (direction) was changing by 3° every minute. Even were he able to judge time to the nearest four minutes (an unattainable degree of precision) his miss-distance would be of the order of 120 miles.

There are, however, certain circumstances when a zenith star may provide approximate directional guidance. As it reaches the summit of its arc it will stand directly above its island. But this can only be perceived if the distant observer is due north or south, when the star at its highest point will indeed momentarily indicate the island's bearing. The other case is when the zenith star is east or west, though its bearing will then be less accurate.[1] There is evidence to suggest that the Tongans, on very long voyages, did make some limited use of zenith stars in this manner—for rough initial bearings.

It must be reiterated, however, that by far the most important function of zenith stars is to indicate, when they are directly overhead, the latitude of the observer.

Determination of longitude, unlike that of latitude, depends upon accurate knowledge of Greenwich mean time. This cannot be found by any amount of watching the sun or the stars, because their motion reflects local time only. As Gatty (1943: 134) puts it, 'There is no practicable way of finding out how far you are east or west on the surface of the earth by the sun, moon or stars without the use of a watch showing Greenwich time'. This statement conflicts with the same author's theory of using zenith stars as guides for accurate great circle sailing. Such procedure would entail time discrimination of an impossible order. The fallacy of equating automatic rhythmic and reflex processes with conscious time estimation has been discussed in chap. 4, and need not be referred to again here. What should be stated categorically, however, is that there is no known indigenous method of ascertaining longitude by celestial observations. We shall see below, under the heading 'windward landfall', how this problem is tackled, and in part circumvented in practice, by the navigators of the Pacific.

Evidence as to the Use of Zenith Stars

As might be anticipated from the nature of the subject, references are fragmentary and usually vague.[2] Moreover, the technique, unlike star path steering, is no longer in use anywhere in the Pacific. Nevertheless, the accounts that we do have include extant tradition and come from such widely scattered parts of Polynesia and Micronesia that the sum of evidence is far from negligible.

Tonga. The data are former secrets of the Tuita navigator clan, wherein the meanings attached to certain words and star names were restricted to members. An example of

---

[1] See Appendix I.

[2] Akerblom (1968: 34, 40), basing his argument exclusively on published sources, even regards the whole concept as hypothetical.

such private meanings is the term *fanakenga*. Tongans divide the sky into three zones or *fanakenga*, the northern, middle, and southern, and this is the commonly accepted meaning of the word (Collocott, 1922: 4). There is an additional secret one, however, not generally known outside the circle of Tuita navigators, of a *fanakenga* star being the overhead (zenith) star of an island (Ve'ehala). It is significant that even King Tupou IV, who is noted for his knowledge of tradition, was ignorant of this special meaning.

Ve'ehala gave me a very clear exposition indeed of the zenith star concept. A *fanakenga* star in Tuita usage was 'the star that points down to an island, its overhead star'. *Fanakenga* stars were used to indicate the direction of an island at a great distance by observing the star when it pointed down to the island. When such a star was overhead it indicated that you were reaching the island.[3]

The present Tuita, whose knowledge is much less detailed than Ve'ehala's, referred to *fanakenga* stars as being overhead ones that divided the heavens into three parts. Returning to Tonga from far places you followed a star as a rough guide (it was not clear whether an overhead or a horizon guiding star was meant). As you drew nearer you changed course to other stars. Imprecise as this statement is, it plainly refers to some method other than dead reckoning, for in the latter an exact course must be maintained from the outset.

Ve'ehala's definition of *fanakenga* stars as ones that pointed down towards islands and his statement that they indicated when overhead proximity to the corresponding inland, are both tantalisingly brief. Nevertheless they are definite and specific, and in view of his standing as the greatest living exponent of Tongan tradition, they are uniquely valuable. Ve'ehala's main informants were an old

---

[3] Ve'ehala listed what he thought were *fanakenga* stars for certain Tongan, Fijian, and Samoan islands. All were in the central division of the sky (*Fanakenga faka lotu langi*). However, the present-day Tuitas are two generations removed from sea-going and as far back as 1922 the Tongans could not confidently identify any star by name (Collocott, 1922: 3). It is not surprising, therefore, that Ve'ehala's star names were virtually useless. Six appeared, from other evidence, to be directional or horizon stars, three could not be identified and only one, Sirius, could be fully accepted.

woman, Makelesi Lokoti, who had been taught the lore in the form of chants by the grandfather of the present Tuita, and his own grandfather Ve'eto, who was over 90 years old when he died in 1959.

Tikopia. Two separate groups of Tikopians were interviewed; Rafe at Honiara on Guadalcanal and Samoa and Tupuai at Nukufera in the Russell Islands. In both places the information was the same.

'The star on top is different from the guiding star [*kavenga*] for an island, it is a different thing', said Rafe. 'The star on top for Tikopia, the star for the island, is *Manu*' [Rigel was pointed out]. 'The star on top for Vanikoro and Anuta is the same *Manu*'. There was a different star for the Banks Islands, he continued. The one for Rennell was *Fetura Manu* [unidentified]. There was an 'on top star' for Sikaiana that had been known to his grandfather, but he himself did not know it.[4]

Samoa and his colleagues at Nukufera emphasised that the 'star on top' was no use at all for steering by. The star that passed over Tikopia was *Manu* (Rigel was again identified). 'When this star is on top, up above, we know we are near land', they said. 'What land?' I asked. 'Tikopia'. Rigel was the only zenith star they personally knew, though they said that some old people were acquainted with 'on top stars' for other islands.

All the above would be plain sailing, were it not for the fact that Rigel, whose declination is 8°15'S., does *not* pass through the zenith of Tikopia, whose latitude is 12°17'S. The discrepancy is no less than 4° or 240 miles.

Certainly in the course of centuries stars' declinations alter to varying degrees. Thus in 1000 A.D. Rigel's declination was 9°52'S.[5] But even then the discrepancy would be 2°25' or 145 miles.

No definite conclusion is possible on the evidence be-

---

[4] The latitude of Tikopia is 12°17'S. Anuta and Vanikoro are both 40' (40 sea miles) further north. The northernmost of the Banks Islands, that Rafe said had a different star, lie in about 13°40'S., 1°23' or 83 miles south of Tikopia. The unidentified *Fetura Manu*, the zenith star for Rennell, could well be Rigel itself, since Renell is in the same latitude as Anuta and Vanikoro.

[5] All the 1000 A.D. declinations quoted in this chapter have been worked out by Dr Radhakrishnan with the aid of a computer.

fore us. A hypothesis which is purely speculative is that Tikopian zenith star observations may have been made (as mine were) by sighting along the mast. Throughout the south-east trade wind season, which is favourable for Tikopian voyaging, the wind would incline a canoe's mast north of the vertical regardless of the tack it was on. In a moderate breeze the angle of heel would be 3°-4° so that Rigel would, in fact, be above the masthead when the canoe was in the latitude of Tikopia.

Hawaii.[6] The mid-nineteenth-century scholar Kepelino seems to be referring to a zenith star in a brief passage of one sentence (Kepelino, 1932: pt 13, 82, 83). The key phrase is rendered by Makemson (1941: 13) as stars 'which are suspended in turn over each land', which does suggest the zenith concept. Beckwith's translation, on the contrary, is stars 'that rise over each land', which would seem more like a reference to horizon steering stars. Fortunately Beckwith gives the Hawaiian text, which is translated by Professor Samuel Elbert, co-author with Pukui of the Hawaiian-English Dictionary (1957)[7] as follows:

Part 13. The Protecting Stars

'These are the stars that are suspended (kau) severally over the various lands, such as Hoku-lea in the Hawaiian islands, and the Southern Cross over the lands of Tahiti, etc.'

Hoku-lea appears to be Arcturus, though Aldebaran is a possible alternative identification.[8] Since the main Hawai-

---

[6] A myth which has been an 'unconscionable time a'dying' has been that Hawaiians once used a calabash filled with water as a kind of primitive sextant. The story derives from an account by Admiral Rodman who was shown by King Kalakaua a gold-banded container with a series of holes through the margin. The curator of the Bishop Museum, which possesses the specimen, explained that the calabash was, in fact, 'a modern replica of one of the clothing containers . . . It stands about 3 feet high and a foot in diameter, and would require at least 10 or 12 gallons of water to fill it up to the holes . . . The holes round the brim were used for tying on the cover' (E. H. Bryant Jr, letter to Captain Haug, 22 September 1923). The then director of the museum, Sir Peter Buck, wrote to the same inquirer (12 March 1948) that '. . . there is no information from Hawaiian sources that such an instrument ever existed.'

[7] Consulted by Dr Finney on my behalf (pers. comm., 1969).

[8] Makemson (1941) makes both identifications. Bunton and Valier (1963), Akerblom (1968), and Finney (pers. comm., 1969) favour Arcturus. Aldebaran would hardly have been a zenith star. Its present declination is 16°25', but in 1000 A.D. it was only 14°.

ian islands extend from 18°50′N. to about 23°N. and the declination of Arcturus is 19°27′N., it would seem at first sight to be an ideal zenith star. However, the only long voyages likely to have been made by the Hawaiians were to Tahiti,[9] and these ceased a long time ago—perhaps a millennium. So the present-day declination of Arcturus is of less significance than its earlier one. In 1000 A.D. its declination was 24°39′N., or a hundred miles north of the archipelago.

However, Arcturus would still have been a much more suitable overhead star for Hawaii than Rigel was for Tikopia. It seems reasonable to suppose that, exactly as with star path courses, the name of the identifying star had to be supplemented by further detailed instructions, which would be unlikely to long survive the discontinuation of voyaging.

A problem raised by Akerblom (1968: 39, 40) is that Makemson (1941: 13) omits the last part of Kepelino's sentence, that dealing with the Southern Cross and Tahiti. Since the Cross has a declination of about 60°S. and Tahiti's latitude is approximately 17°S., it could not possibly be a zenith star for that island, but only a directional guide. I myself doubt whether reference to zenith stars and horizon stars in the same sentence necessarily invalidates a millennium-old tradition, in which it would be naive to expect navigational precision. Moreover, the second part of the sentence, unlike the first, bears an indication of European influence. The word 'Tahiti' appears in the Hawaiian text, whereas the Hawaiian name was actually 'Kahiki'.

Tahiti. The only indication that zenith stars may have had meaning for the navigator-astronomers of this group is an indirect one. It is a chant called 'Pillars of the Sky', recited in 1818 at Borabora by an old woman called Rua-Nui.[10] The sky was said to be propped up from the earth by star pillars. It may be entirely coincidental that the 1000 A.D.

---

[9] See Hawaiian traditions collected by Fornander (1880: 6-58) and Finney's review of the evidence (1967: 163).

[10] The stars named were identified by Paora'i of Borabora in 1822. The account was recorded by the missionary J. M. Orsmond and published by his granddaughter Teuira Henry (1907: 101, 102).

declinations of most of the stars concerned are close to the latitudes of certain islands north and south of Tahiti.

Should this tentative interpretation of the chant be correct, it indicates the extreme limits of Eastern Polynesian (Tahitian) settlement, Hawaii and New Zealand. To the southward the zenith star for the Tubuai archipelago, a logical stage *en route* to the latter country, is delineated. Phact was the overhead star for New Zealand that we ourselves made use of during the *Rehu Moana* test voyage. Northward from Tahiti stars over the Line Islands (to leeward of the long Tahitian-Hawaiian route) appear to be prominent in the list.[11] All save Aldebaran would be of the greatest navigational assistance to the voyager on this long and featureless journey.

The last two stars, Polaris and Dubhe (part of the Great Bear), are of a different character from the rest, being clearly directional. Dubhe gives a fair approximation of north from Tahiti. Polaris would, of course, be more precise, but it is not visible until nearly halfway to Hawaii, 1000 miles from Tahiti. That this distant star was known to the Tahitians, and moreover had such a place in their cosmogony, suggests that long deliberately navigated voyages were once made far northward from Eastern Polynesia. The occurrence of Raivavae-type structures on Malden in the Line Islands supports this view. Tahitian knowledge of the Pole Star remains significant irrespective of the correctness or otherwise of our speculations about the other 'pillars'.

Gilbert Islands. An Abemaman tradition, referring to the use of what could only have been an overhead star, is related by Fr Sabatier (1939: 94-5). The semi-secret arts of navigation were usually handed down from father to son, but in default of male offspring, a daughter was often trained. Such a one was Paintapu, the woman navigator of a flotilla that was returning from Tarawa to Abemama

---

[11] The Line Islands were uninhabited when discovered by Europeans, but a number show signs of earlier Polynesian occupation. Of particular interest in the present context are the ruins on Malden which 'reveal remarkable agreement in plan and detail' with those on Raivavae in the Tubuai archipelago (Emory, 1934: 1-4, 37-40). Raivavae is 300 miles south of Tahiti, while Malden is 800 miles beyond Tahiti in the opposite direction, to the north.

Table of 'Star Pillars' and Islands

European name	Star Pillars Tahitian name	Dec. 1000 A.D.	Islands and latitudes
Antares	*Ana-Mua*	23°37′S.	Rurutu 23°20′S. Rimatara 23°40′S. } Tubuai Tubuai 23°50′S. } archipelago Rarotonga 21°10′S.
Aldebaran	*Ana-Muri*	14°0′N.	No land. 5° south of Hawaii
Arcturus	*Ana-Tahu'a-Ta'ata- Metua-Te-Tupu-Mave*	24°39′N.	Close (100 miles) north of Hawaii
Spica	*Ana-Roto*	5°46′S.	Starbuck, Line Islands (Ellice Islands far to the westward)
Alphard	*Ana-Henheu-Po*	4°41′S.	Malden, Line Islands.
Procyon	*Ana-Tahu'a-Vahine- O-Toa-Te-Manava*	7°15′N.	A little north of Kingman Reef, Line Islands (Marshalls far to the westward)
Betelgeuse	*Ana-Vara*	6°38′N.	Kingman Reef, Line Islands (Marshalls far to the westward)
Phact	*Ana-Iva*	35°47′S.	North Auckland, New Zealand
Polaris Dubhe	*Ana-Ni'a* *Ana-Tipu*	90°0′N. } 62°0′N. }	Directional, indicate north

somewhere around 1780. The incidents of the expedition
are outside our province, but they partly hinge upon Paintapu's navigational methods, which were unfamiliar and
strange to her uninitiated companions. She lay in the bottom of the canoe for hours gazing up at the heavens
(*recouche . . . face au firmament*), giving orders when to
tack, for the wind was contrary. In due course they reached
Abemama.

Caroline Islands. Towards the middle of last century a
canoe from the Carolinian island of Elato arrived at Tinian
in the Marianas 450 miles to the northward. Captain Sanchez y Zayas, who interviewed the navigator, wrote (1866:
263) that if a canoe is forced to lay-to by storm, 'three
days are necessary to get to the eastward what they have
lost. Then they have recourse to their observations: they
fill a cane with water and observe the stars in the zenith,
and thence study the position of the vessel'.

Once again we are faced with unanswerable questions.
The reference to 'stars in the zenith' is definite enough.
How then was the cane used? It is tempting to assume
that it served as a kind of spirit level to define the vertical,
for this would be a practical and helpful aid. But we have
no proof of the matter.

Akerblom (1968: 112, 113) suggests that the height of
the Pole Star might have been meant, but the mention of
zenith stars is quite specific. Nevertheless, there is nothing
to prevent both methods from having been used. The altitude of Polaris exactly doubles from 7°30'N. at Elato to
15° at Tinian. Our 1969 voyage from Puluwat with Hipour
was between the same latitudes. Hipour told me that, while
he knew from tradition that the Pole Star would rise, he
did not know by how much, nor was he aware of any
application of the knowledge (see p. 144). The following
year he informed Professor Edwin Doran Jr (pers. comm.,
1970) that Polaris was 2 *naf* high at Puluwat and 5 *naf* at
Saipan. (A *naf* in this context is the forefinger to thumb
distance at arm's length, or about 10°.) This is erroneous,
since the star is less than one *naf* high, not two, at Puluwat
and 1½, not 5, at Saipan, though the proportional rise is
not so far out.

The inaccuracy of Hipour's statement is at variance with the customary precision of Carolinian navigational instructions, but may well reflect an ancient technique. This supposition is supported by evidence from the island of Satawal. In 1970 the navigator Repunglug made a canoe voyage to Saipan. He has had no contact with Western navigators. He said that the height of Polaris was thought of on his island in terms of *ee-yass* (breadfruit picking poles). Polaris was said to be 1½ *ee-yass* high at Satawal and two *ee-yass* at Saipan (McCoy, pers. comm., 1970). This is more nearly correct than the Puluwat lore but still too inaccurate for practical navigation. McCoy points out, however, that Carolinian navigators never completely confide in foreigners. His own opinion is that 'it is a traditional part of their schooling to navigate by the height of Polaris' (pers. comm., 1970).

Bougainville (Melanesia). Brief mention must be accorded a statement made to me by Tonnaku of Buin, Bougainville in 1966, that his ancestors from the south made use of 'a small star nearly at right angles to Venus, which goes over southern Bougainville'. The phrase 'goes over' seems to refer to a zenith star rather than a horizon one.

Windward landfall seems a more appropriate term than 'latitude sailing'. The latter was the method used by European seamen prior to the late eighteenth century, that is, before a practical method of ascertaining longitude had been developed. Akerblom (1968: 47) correctly points out that though, theoretically speaking, it was possible for the Polynesians to have navigated by latitude sailing, there is not an atom of proof that they ever did so. (The exception would be east or west voyages, when the actual course to be sailed would lie coincidentally along a parallel of latitude).

Windward Landfall

We do have ample evidence, however, that standard practice in Oceania was, and is, to make landfall to windward and up-current, on a known side, usually eastward, of an objective. Examples include Hipour's strategy on the voyages to and from Saipan (see pp. 217, 220), Tevake's approach to Taumako (see p. 48) and *etak* practice after gales (see p. 141). On long voyages spanning several degrees of latitude this procedure is entirely compatible with the use of the zenith star. Dead reckoning ensures an up-wind approach to the destination, preferably, according to Hipour, at a distance well under 50 miles. Confirmation by a zenith star that one was then opposite one's island would be an inestimable boon.

It will be recalled that both Ve'ehala in Tonga and the Tikopian elders used almost identical phrases to the effect that, when the zenith star was overhead, the island was nearby. Such a formulation would be incompatible with latitude sailing in the European manner, for the destination would not necessarily be near at all, only in the same latitude. It would be fully in accord, however, with the windward landfall navigational procedures actually used by the Pacific Islanders.

Let us sum up the principles involved in using zenith stars. For distant targets on cardinal bearings, the Tongans at any rate seem to have regarded the destination's zenith star as a rough indication of direction (Ve'ehala and Tuita), though they would certainly have done their actual steering by the usual horizon stars. The course would be set a little to a known side of the objective, preferably so as to hold it in one's lee. Once the zenith star was overhead the navigator could turn directly towards his island. This seems the logical navigational interpretation of the statements made by Ve'ehala, Tuita, and the Tikopians and of the practice of Hipour and Tevake.

Methods of Making Zenith Star Observations and the Accuracy Attainable
There is no definite information about the actual method or methods of making zenith star observations that were used. Paintapu seems to have gazed straight upwards without sighting along the mast, which is raked and canted in Gilbertese (and Carolinian) canoes. Lying on one's back in this way appears to be a practical enough technique, especially if the craft is paddled in a circle (Gatty, 1943: 129; 1958: 41).

We have suggested that a cane filled with water might have been used in the Carolines to indicate when a star overhead was vertically above the navigator. This seems a reasonable enough supposition as far as the Carolines are concerned, but there are no reports of any such artifact as the cane described by Sanchez having been used in other archipelagos.

My own method was developed through trial and error on the *Rehu Moana* test voyage. When the zenith star was seen to be nearing the summit of its arc I would ask someone to steer east or west by the stars. Then, lying down at the foot of the mast, I would sight along it. The masthead would be describing an elipse even in the finest weather, so the mean position had to be judged. Allowances had to be made too for the mast's slight rake and the catamaran's angle of heel, factors that I would already have estimated against the horizon before darkness fell.

It was easy enough to decide whether the star was passing to the north or the south, though if it were much more than 5° from the vertical I could not judge its angle to nearer than a degree. When the star was more nearly in the true zenith greater accuracy was possible.

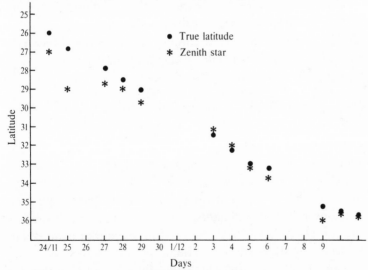

Fig. 49 Comparison of latitude by zenith stars and true latitude on Rehu Moana *test voyage (after Lewis, 1966b)*

Of course there was no way at all of confirming *en route* the degree of accuracy that was being achieved. Only when we reached our destination and Priscilla Cairns's true positions were compared with the zenith star ones did I know whether or not the exercise was futile. Gatty claimed that this method, which he himself had tried out, could give latitude to the nearest whole degree (1958: 41) or even better (1943: 129). Our results were similar. In good weather and with practice, an accuracy of ½° or 30 sea miles could be anticipated—from the deck of a stable catamaran, double canoe, or large outrigger. The latitude of our New Zealand landfall, for instance, was 26 miles in error.

Figure 49 shows our real latitudes compared with those estimated by zenith stars. The second result was inconsistent with the rest. That of 9 December was estimated when the star, which had been obscured by cloud, had passed the zenith. It was also discarded. The consistent southerly error in the first four observations of between ½° and 1° may have been due to insufficient allowance for the heel of the catamaran in the trades. The last six observations, leaving aside the poor one of 9 December, were in error by an average of only 12′ (12 sea miles).

The great extent of many of the 'expanded' targets in Oceania renders such results fully adequate for navigation and even where a solitary island is the objective, careful observation of land indicating signs should ensure a successful outcome of the voyage.

HIGH STAR TECHNIQUES OF UNCERTAIN NATURE

There are intriguing and ambiguous accounts of non-zenith star practices that appear to make use of stars at considerable altitudes. Krämer (1902: 244-6) refers to Samoan techniques that involved lying supine in a canoe and observing star clusters. His informants laid stress on groupings of three stars, though the manner of using them was not satisfactorily explained.[12]

The assumption that this was a zenith star technique is precluded by specific mention of Orion's Belt, which culminates about 1°S., while the mean latitude of Samoa is

[12] Samoan knowledge of 'star formations and their meaning had become somewhat uncertain through long neglect of this art', Krämer pointed out, and also admitted to his own failings as an astronomer. An ingenious explanation of Krämer's three-star groups has been supplied by Reche (1927: 214-19, 266-71). He does not appear, however, to have gathered fresh data from Samoans. There seems no evidence whatsoever to support the 'three star triangle' he postulates.

around 13°S. It seems more probable that the three stars of the Belt were used in some way for steering.

Indirect confirmation of the supposition comes from the Tokelau Islands, which are culturally akin to Samoa. In this archipelago the three stars of Orion's Belt (*Tolu*), in their zenith, were said to be a direct guide from Nukuono to Atafu (Macgregor, 1937: 90). Here again Orion is very far from being a true zenith star.

A somewhat similar technique seems to be practised in the 'para Micronesian' island of Ninigo. The three stars in line, Canopus (*Maanihaiup*), Sirius (*Maanifono*), and Procyon (*Maanitola*) were together called *Maan*, said Itilon. They were of prime importance in all navigation and they also indicated the direction of the wind.[13] You were near the island when Sirius was 'right in the middle of Ninigo', and the indication that Sirius was in the correct position was when a line of small southern stars called *Tieti* pointed towards it. Heavy clouds obscured these small stars before they could be identified and this cloud cover did not lift during the remainder of our stay. The best Itilon could do was to draw the curved paths of the stars in the sand.

Again the concept of *Maan* is not a zenith one because the declination of Sirius is 17°S., Procyon 5°N., and Canopus 53°S., while the latitude of Ninigo is 1°S. A star in Orion's Belt would actually be in the island's zenith, yet Itilon was emphatic that Orion's Belt (*Apahilipohin*) did 'not stop on top of Ninigo'. My failure to elucidate this matter is particularly galling because Itilon was obviously conversant with his facts and had often used the methods he was trying to explain to me on his own voyages.

We are left with the unsatisfactory assumption that the inconclusive accounts from Samoa, the Tokelaus, and Ninigo probably point to the existence of ill-understood high star methods—a reminder of how little is really known about indigenous navigation.

---

[13] This is difficult to understand. During the north-west monsoon season the line of the stars trends south-west/north-east in the early evening, gradually rotating to west-north-west/east-south-east before setting. At the time of the south-east trades the stars' axis is south-east/north-west after dark, but works round to west-south-west/east-north-east.

OCEANIC PHENOMENA USED TO DEFINE POSITION

*Water
Temperature
and Salinity*

A flotilla of double canoes, returning from Samoa to Tonga in the 1820s, lost their way. The king's *kalia* had on board Akau'ola, the High Navigator of Tonga, and Ula, the next in rank. The blind Kaho Mo Vailahi, who held the lower title of Tuita, was navigating one of the smaller vessels with the assistance of his son Po'oi. The other experts having confessed their bewilderment, Kaho is said to have dipped his hand into the sea, tasted the spray and bade his son tell him the position of certain stars. He then averred the water was Fijian and the waves from the Lau group, where they duly arrived the next day (Ve'ehala, Kaho, Kienga).

There are several possible interpretations of this story. It is fairly obvious that the blind Tuita was using stars as described by his son and perhaps also feeling the waves reflected back from the land as they passed beneath his canoe (Kienga). But his action in touching the water with his hand (and lips?) seems likely to have been to obtain information about the sea's temperature.[14] This would be a method that could be used to define approximate position.

'Navigators', said Kaho, 'could feel which *fanakenga* they were in.[15] The northernmost was the warmest and the southernmost the coldest. My father, the son of Po'oi, said any true sailor knew when he had crossed any of these *fanakenga* because of the temperature'.

This seems reasonable enough in the context of the great north-south extent of the Tongan world and the size of the archipelagos therein (see p. 229). Tafeedoowaia (Tabiteuea) in the Gilberts, that the Tongans told Cook had at one time been under their domination (Cook and King, 1784: vol. I, 369), is 19½ degrees of latitude or 1170 miles north of Tongatapu. The difference in mean sea surface

---

[14] The 88-year-old Kaho had an additional explanation. 'My great grandfather put his hand in the water to feel the movement of the waves and how hot they were. But more important was to get in touch with the devil'. The latter, he explained, was the 'old god of the sea'.

[15] *Fanakenga*. The three latitudinal zones, north, middle, and south, into which the sky and the sea beneath were divided (see p. 236). Kaho was alone in describing them as dividing lines between the zones rather than the zones themselves.

temperature between the two islands is 6°F in summer and 8°F in winter (*Pacific Islands Pilot*, 1956-7: vol. II, 25.

The term 'sea mark' (*betia*) is a Gilbertese one but the   *'Sea Marks'* conception is not unique to that archipelago or to Micronesia. For instance, Carolinian navigators learn sequences of what they call 'sea life'. These, much more frequently than their Gilbertese counterparts, are transitory phenomena such as sightings of certain fish, and the like. Some, however, like a whirlpool on Uranie Bank, have real and permanent existence (Gladwin, 1970: 205).

Grimble recorded a number of 'sea marks', of which we will give one example.

There were certain traditional signs by which navigators judged their distance westward of the land. The safety limit to leeward (i.e. westward in the trade season) was called the Fish Wall of Kabaki. It consisted of a line of leaves and rubbish scattered over the sea from Makin to Samoa far to the westward of the land. This is possibly quite true, the rubbish being carried by some current (n.d.(a)).

In another manuscript (R. Grimble, pers. comm., 1970), he added, 'It is said that by following this line a navigator could reach as far South as Samoa, but would find great difficulty in beating up to the land from the point where the drift began to fail him'.

Most other sea marks of this type are much less extensive than the Fish Wall of Kabaki. Their exact location and their very presence would probably depend upon seasonal currents and they would be detectable only in calm weather. Nevertheless, knowledge of sea marks would be a valuable addition to a navigator's repertoire.

This discussion of position fixing concludes our survey of the actual concepts and methods of Polynesian and Micronesian navigation. We will go on to consider subjects peripheral to the navigational arts proper—canoes and the relevance of navigation to communication within Oceania.

Part Five

THE LONELY SEAWAYS

CHAPTER TEN

Voyaging canoes

I propose in this chapter to discuss the abilities and limitations of the ocean-going vessels in which Polynesians and Micronesians made the more planned of their long voyages. The analysis will touch on constructional features only in so far as they effect function—manoeuvrability, speed, windward ability, strength, carrying capacity, and provisioning.[1]

The word 'canoe' is rather misleading in the present context, conjuring up as it does a picture of some tiny craft hollowed out from a tree trunk. The vessels with which we are here concerned (and which have, in the main, long since vanished from Pacific seaways) deserve the appelation 'ship' rather than 'canoe'. As an indication of their size, some were longer than Cook's *Endeavour* (Haddon and Hornell, 1936: 326; 1938: 43).

Of course, small dugout and sewn plank inshore canoes would always have been many times more numerous than their sea-going counterparts—and would, incidentally, contribute a high proportion of involuntary castaways. There were many distinct varieties of these little craft (especially in Polynesia) that were adapted to particular fishing techniques, lagoon transport, and in short, every purpose except long deliberately mounted voyages.[2]

The voyaging craft proper of Oceania were generally double canoes in Polynesia and canoes with an outrigger on one side in Micronesia.[3] Big outriggers were also used

[1] Design and construction are treated very fully in Haddon and Hornell's classic *Canoes of Oceania* (1936-8) and in Fr Neyret's 'Pirogues Océaniennes' (1962, 1963).

[2] Some confusion has been caused by ignoring this distinction. For instance, the missionary William Ellis's poor opinion of certain Tahitian double canoes has been cited as evidence of the inadequacy of the Tahitian *pahi*, or twin-hulled voyaging canoe (Sharp, 1963: 56). A glance at Ellis's book is enough to show that he was referring, not to *pahi* at all, but to *va'a motu*, which were unstable and fragile coastal craft (Ellis, W., 1831: 160-5).

[3] Canoes with outrigger floats on both sides (double outriggers) were used in Indonesia and the Indian Ocean but not in the open Pacific. The type extended eastward only as far as the Torres Strait Islands and the extreme north-west of New Guinea (Hornell, 1932: 131-43; Haddon and Hornell, 1938: 15-19).

in some parts of Polynesia, as in Pukapuka (Beaglehole, E. and P., 1938: 171) and the Marquesas (Mathias G[arcia], 1843: 233) but the only place in Micronesia where double canoes have definitely been recorded has been the Carolinian island of Truk (Haddon and Hornell, 1936: 408). Hornell (Haddon and Hornell, 1936: 439) considered the Micronesian vessels to be 'probably the finest outrigger craft ever built', but he believed them to be 'less suitable for prolonged voyages' than the double canoes of Polynesia because of their more limited carrying capacity (p. 440). However, as we shall see later, the big outriggers would seem to have been well able to accommodate crew and ample provisions.

Throughout Oceania the preferred size of vessel for deep sea voyaging seems to have been in the 50-75-foot range.[4] This was probably because, as Banks (1962: 366) said of the Tahitian and Raiatean voyaging canoes (*pahi*), 'the middling sized ones' were least liable to accidents in stormy weather.

The long distance ships we are speaking about, whether Micronesian or Polynesian, were not hollowed out from tree trunks. They were essentially planked vessels, with broad strakes fastened to each other and to ribs and keel by stitching or lashing with coconut fibre (coir or sennit).[5] The keel was generally adzed out from solid logs and was composed of several sections fastened together. The width of the strakes or planks, their number and their length varied with the particular design. A vee-shaped cross-section was the norm in all the plank built types, except in Fiji, where the round-bilged Melanesian hull form was apparently retained when numerous Micronesian features were adopted.

Hornell (1935) has drawn attention to striking similarities between Polynesian and Micronesian voyaging

---

[4] See Wilkes (1845: vol V, 94) for the Gilberts; Nozikov (1946: 139) citing Lutké for the Carolines; Winkler (1901: 504) for the Marshalls; Haddon and Hornell (1936) under the appropriate sections, for the main Polynesian archipelagos.

[5] For Tongan design details see Anderson in Beaglehole (1967: 937) and Haddon and Hornell (1936: 268, 280). For Tahiti and Raiatea see Banks (1962: 319, 320) and Cook (1893: 99). For the Tuamotus, Gilberts, Marshalls, and Carolines see Haddon and Hornell (1936: 79, 345, 366, 377). For Fiji see Wilkes (1845: vol. III, 347).

canoes and pre-Viking Scandinavian craft. So close were the two types that they differed in construction only in the Norse ships being clinker (lapstrake) rather than carvel built and the lashings being of leather instead of sennit. Both were extremely flexible. The major design difference was, of course, the narrowness and consequent need of stabilising devices like double hulls or outriggers on the Pacific models.

The planked construction of voyaging canoes seems to have been a very ancient feature and no recent innovation. Haddon and Hornell (1938: 40) cite facts suggesting that 'vessels used by the proto-Polynesians had frames and were plank-built, rather than ordinary dugout hulls with strakes'. They mention the persistence of frames or spreaders in Hawaiian and Niuean dugouts and the ribs used in the Tuamotus and elsewhere. Some of these, often vestigial, structures they considered to be 'truly marginal, as in Hawaii and the Tuamotus, and . . . thus presumably ancient'.[6]

New Zealand, Hawaiian, Marquesan, and some Cook Islands double canoes would be exceptions to the rule that Polynesian voyaging craft were vee-sectioned and plank built, were they not clearly specialised inshore paddling craft with auxiliary sail, and not voyaging canoes at all. As we noted above the true Polynesian voyaging canoes,

---

[6] An uncritical application of marginal diffusion theories to ocean-going craft, like the assumption that 'the most widely distributed form is likely to be the oldest in time' (Finney, 1967: 145), seems to have led to the idea that Hawaiian and New Zealand coastal craft represented the earliest Polynesian models. Thus one writer (Whitney, 1955: 17) makes the groundless assertion that Polynesian voyaging canoes were primarily 'man powered'.

Haddon and Hornell (1938: 12, 13) warn against the mechanical application of such theories. Efficient and seaworthy vessels may have reached distant lands across seaways impassable to less able craft. But even these authors fall into the same trap by arguing from similarities between New Zealand canoes and a Tahitian type, the *tipairua*, that the latter, rather than voyaging canoes (*pahi*), carried the colonists to New Zealand. Polynesian seamen being also canoe builders, the crew of a *pahi* would include craftsmen skilled in constructing every kind of canoe (including specialised coastal and fishing craft) known on the home island. The *pahi* in which the voyagers probably arrived would be too clumsy for routine work round the Hawaiian and New Zealand shores. Other Tahitian types, the *tipairua* and *va'a motu* among them, would be far more suitable, and the evidence we have about the canoes of these lands suggests that they were, indeed, derived from such models.

which are known from the Tahiti-Tuamotus region in Eastern Polynesia and the Tonga-Samoa area in Western Polynesia, were all planked, vee-sectioned and high sided. They were primarily sailing vessels, whose auxiliary power was usually provided by sculling, except in the Marquesas where platforms for the paddlers were rigged outside the hulls when necessary (Mathias G[rarcia], 1843: 233).

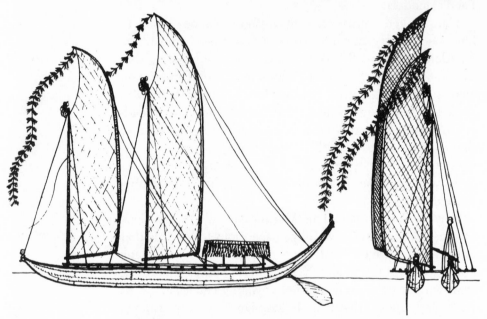

Fig. 50   A Tahitian pahi *(from Neyret, 1967)*

THE MAIN VARIETIES OF VOYAGING CANOE

We will refer in the discussion below to the following types of canoe:

Pahi. This was the ocean-going vessel of the Tahitian and Tuamotuan archipelagos. It was a twin-hulled two-masted sailing vessel some 50-70 feet long. Caulking between the planks was with fine coconut fibre, adhesive breadfruit sap being used as pitch (Banks, 1962: 320n.; Haddon and Hornell, 1936: 139). There were substantial differences in *pahi* design between the two areas (above water cross-section, shape of ends, rig) but performance would seem to have been similar (Haddon and Hornell, 1936: 79-92, 137-40). *Pahi,* like *tongiaki* in Western Polynesia (see below), were specialised deep sea ships, good for long distance work but

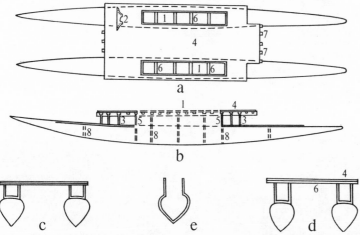

Fig. 51 A Tongan tongiaki *(after Cook, 1777).*
a. plan; b. longitudinal section through one hull, vertical dotted lines indicate position of inserted ribs; c. cross-section through fore end of vessel under fore part of platform; d. corresponding section at after end of platform; e. cross-section of one hull amidships; 1. hatchway; 2. mast shoe; 3. supporting pillars; 4. deck; 5. breakwater; 6. cross-beams supporting deck; 7. fore-and-aft beams under deck.

'very unwieldy' (Beaglehole, 1955: 131) and 'rather too clumsy for fishing' (Banks, 1962: 364) (see fig. 50).

Tongiaki. This classical type of Tongan double canoe was analogous to contemporary craft in Samoa and Rotuma. Like the *pahi* it had hulls of equal length. It was similar in cross-section though different in profile and carried a sizable platform. It seems to have differed very little from the *pahi* in size and performance (see figs. 51 and 52).

Ndrua. The Fijian double canoe differed substantially from the ones we have been considering in having hulls of un-

Fig. 52 A Fijian ndrua, *prototype of late eighteenth-century Tongan* kalia *(from Williams, 1858)*

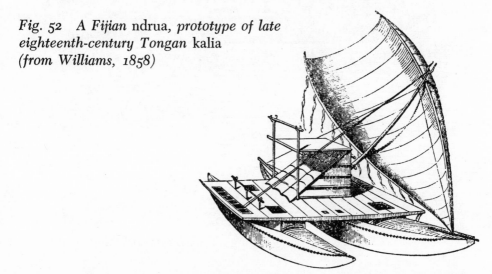

Fig. 53 *A Tongan* tongiaki *with bonito fishing canoe* (tafa'ang

foreground; seen by Tasman, 1643 (after Dalrymple. 1770-1)

equal length, the smaller of which functioned rather like
an outrigger. It was an adaptation of a Micronesian design,
and being much more manoeuvrable than the *tongiaki* and
its ilk, it replaced the older twin-hulled canoes in Western
Polynesia (Tonga, Samoa, etc.) about 200 years ago. The
Tongan version of the *ndrua* was called the *kalia* (see fig.
53).

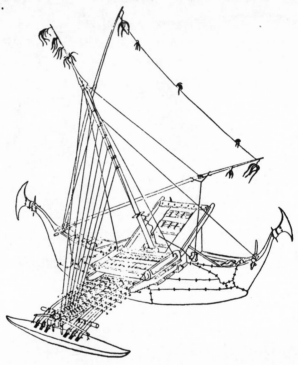

Fig. 54   A Marshallese canoe (from Alexander, 1902)

MICRONESIAN OUTRIGGER VOYAGING CANOES

These craft all shared the principles of design and operation that will be discussed in the next section. The Gilbertese *baurua* (canoe for voyaging) differed from other
Micronesian types mainly in its extreme lightness and flexibility (see pl. IX, X, XI). Carolinian, Marshallese, and
Marianas models resembled each other very closely (see
fig. 54 and pl. III). Ninigo, and to a lesser extent Santa
Cruz canoes (*te puke*), had less in common, though they exhibited so many Micronesian features (see p. 7n.) that they
may be considered 'para Micronesian' (pl. XII, XIII, II).

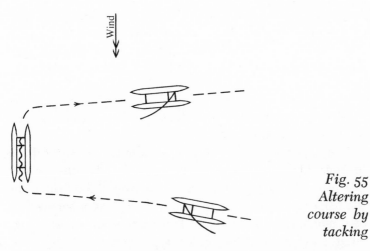

*Fig. 55
Altering
course by
tacking*

It is all too easy to forget that every one of the deep sea craft we have been discussing, vessels that Cook considered to be 'fit for distant navigation' (1777: 215), was constructed entirely with the tools and technology of the stone age.

THE TWO CONTRASTING DESIGN PRINCIPLES

The great functional division of the sailing canoes of Oceania is between those that come about by tacking in the European manner and those that alter direction by changing ends (Haddon and Hornell, 1936: 441, 445).

Tacking canoes, which have distinctive and permanent bows and sterns like Western craft, included all the classical Eastern and Western Polynesian twin-hulled canoes as well as those of Hawaii and New Zealand. The only exceptions were the Tuamotuan variety of *pahi* and the Manihikian vessels. The sailing outrigger canoes of Tahiti, Samoa, and Tonga, but not Pukapuka, also came into the tacking category (see fig. 55).

All Micronesian, Outlier Polynesian, and Melanesian (except Shortland Islands) canoes had, and have, identical ends. The bow and stern are, therefore, interchangeable and they can sail either end foremost. The outrigger float is always kept to windward, where it acts largely as a balance weight. In order to go onto the opposite tack, the mast is raked towards the new bow, the sail is swung round behind the mast and the steering paddle moved to

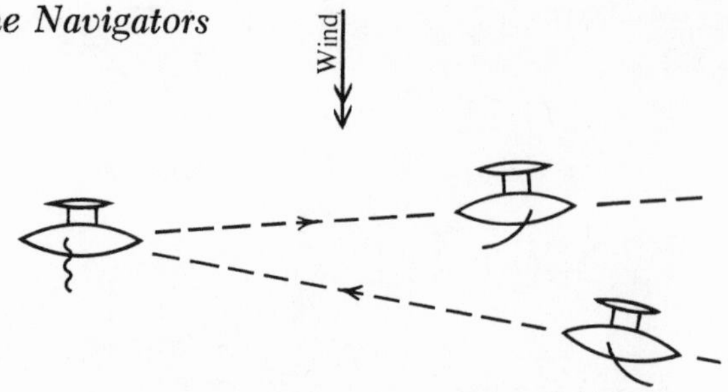

Wind

Fig. 56 Altering course by changing ends

what will become the stern, whereupon the canoe shoots off in a nearly reciprocal direction (see fig. 56).[7]

The changing ends system was adopted by the Fijians in their double canoes (*ndrua*), in which the smaller hull was always kept up-wind, exactly as was the outrigger of the Micronesian canoes, to which the *ndrua* is believed to owe much of its inspiration.[8] During the latter part of the eighteenth century this Fijian type came to replace the more sluggish classical Polynesian double canoes in Tonga, Samoa, Tokelau, Rotuma, the Ellice Islands, and probably New Caledonia, though not Tahiti, nor anywhere else apparently in Eastern Polynesia (Haddon and Hornell, 1936: 265, 241, 282; 1938: 41, 42). Thus, in Tonga, the traditionally clumsy *tongiaki* gave way to the more easily handled *kalia*.[9]

TODAY'S VOYAGING CANOES

We have been speaking so far in the past tense. But ocean-going canoes, albeit only 25-27 feet long, are still freely ranging the Carolinian seaways and, as we saw earlier, one from Satawal this year reopened communication with the distant Marianas after a lapse of about seventy years (see plate III).

---

[7] In Ninigo, Pukapuka, and Aitutaki the mast is re-stepped instead of being raked.

[8] The fact that it was the Fijians, rather than the Tongans, who adopted Micronesian ideas, suggests extensive Fijian voyaging prior to the eighteenth century (see p. 15n.). Some confirmation of this comes from the Polynesian-speaking island of Nukuoro in the southern Carolines. Eilers (1934: 179) cites traditions of canoes from 'Hiti' (Fiji) visiting or being driven to the island on several occasions. It lies more than 1800 miles north-west of Fiji and neither winds nor currents would favour drift.

[9] Haddon and Hornell (1936: 272) quote Thomson (1908: 295) as saying that the *tongiaki's* rig was so unmanageable that 'if the wind changed there was nothing for it but to change the course', implying that the vessel could only sail on one tack. This is absurd and is directly contradicted by Anderson's description of a *tongiaki's* sail being shifted to the opposite side in tacking, a manoeuvre that was 'done very quickly' (Beaglehole, 1967: 937-8).

Plate IX   Gilbertese 100-foot baurua, *photographed under construction at Tabiteuea in 1939 by H. E. Maude*

Villagers on Aranuka in the Gilberts are currently constructing a large voyaging canoe (*baurua*) of traditional design and out of local materials. The half-inch planks are being hand sawn from *tetai* wood and the gum and fibre for caulking is also from the island. The lashings securing the planks to each other every few inches and to the frames are of sennit. This graceful long-ended vessel was three-quarters planked up when I visited the island in 1969. Its measurements are 58 feet length overall, 4 feet 6 inches beam, 4 feet depth of hull and the outrigger float is 22 feet 9 inches long. There will be two masts. Its purpose is to carry big parties to communal occasions at other villages on the atoll and the islands of Kuria and Abemama. (See photographs of this *baurua* under construction and an earlier one from Tabiteuea, plates IX to XI).

Itilon of Ninigo has built a narrow easily driven 52-foot outrigger canoe. It is two-masted with oblong pandanus mat sails. In a moderate breeze, with the wind free, it covered the 14 miles from Ami in Ninigo to Pelleluhu atoll over long easy swells at an average speed of 10 knots and probably touched about 15 in gusts (pl. XIII, VII, XII).

But in most places traditional sailing vessels are being rapidly eclipsed. The 30-foot double canoes of the Papuan Mailu still trade to the Trobriands under sail. Elsewhere, apart from the Central Carolines, the fleets have vanished into memory. Tevake's claw-sailed *te puke* was wrecked in the early 1960s. The last Fijian *ndrua* was built on the island of Ongea in 1943 to carry copra. It was 48 feet long and its deck, which supported a small hut, measured 25 feet 6 inches by 12 feet 6 inches. The sail was pandanus

Plate X   Interior of 58-foot Gilbertese baurua *under construction at Aranuka. Note vee-shaped ribs.*

Plate XI   Exterior of 58-foot Gilbertese baurua *under construction at Aranuka. Note coir plank lashings.*

and the rigging made from plaited wild hibiscus bark
(Reid, pers. comm., 1946). Today, however, even this
lone *waga ni tagane*, 'ship fit for men', has disintegrated
as completely as did the last voyaging *pahi* on the fore-
shores of Tahiti 150 years ago. Vessels that the Fijians
term *waga ni yalewa*, 'ships fit for women' or European
ships have, with few exceptions, taken over the Pacific
seaways.[10]

SPEED

We are here concerned with the average progress that
could be maintained by a voyaging canoe day after day
through the choppy seas of the Pacific. The maximum
speeds attainable in sheltered waters have little bearing on
long distance open sea performance.

Cook (Beaglehole, 1967: 164) trailed a patent log behind
what appears to have been a *tongiaki* and recorded a
mean speed of 7 knots close-hauled, which he thought
would be a reasonable average for 'such breezes as generally blow in their sea'. The sailing time given him from
Tongatapu to the 'high but very fruitful island' of 'Fidgee'
was three days with the wind fair (p. 163). The distance
would be nearly 400 miles if Viti Levu, the main Fijian
island, were meant. Samoa was said to be two days' sail
north-east from Vava'u, a distance of 300 miles on a close
reach. The passage times quoted for both these voyages
are in accord with Cook's speed estimate.[11]

Cook stated that Tahitian 'Paheas' (*pahi*) could sail
much faster than his ship and gave it as his opinion that
they could 'with ease sail 40 Leagues [120 miles] a day or
more' (Beaglehole, 1955: 157).

---

[10] Rivers (1912: 598) makes some interesting observations about the
disappearance of useful arts like canoe building, and, by analogy, their
persistence in some areas.

'It is often impossible to find adequate motives for this loss in such
obvious factors as lack of raw materials or unsuitability to a new environment. Social factors not at once obvious, and even magical beliefs and
practices, have to be brought in to explain the loss.'

[11] We must note, however, that chief Finau, whose *tongiaki* sailed
'about three miles to our two' and 'rund us nearly out of sight before the
evening' (Beaglehole, 1967: 121) told Cook that he needed two days to
cover the 70 miles between Ha'apai and Vava'u (Cook and King, 1784:
259). The explanation of the discrepancy may have been the need to
anchor at night, for this passage lies among a maze of reefs and islands.

Plate XII
Small
mat-sailed
canoe, Ninigo
Lagoon

Plate XIII
Itilon's 52-foot
canoe at
Ninigo

Pahi and *tongiaki* were equivalent in length, the middling sized *pahi*, that Banks affirmed were best esteemed for voyaging, being upwards of 50 feet long. The underwater cross-section of the hulls was almost identical. Their speed would seem to have been of much the same order. To sum up, then, on speed. Twin-hulled Polynesian voyaging canoes could be expected to cover between 100 and 150 miles a day on any point of sailing where they could lay a direct course to their objective without having to tack. The speed of the large Micronesian outriggers, when fully loaded, would probably have differed very little from that of the *pahi* and the *tongiaki*.

WINDWARD ABILITY

Speed with a free wind is but one facet of a sailing ship's performance. Weatherliness, or the ability to stand to windward, is at least as important. Micronesian outriggers very possibly (though not certainly) scored over the Polynesian double canoes in this respect. The *tongiaki* and *pahi* seem to have pointed quite high and their vee-shaped hulls would effectively reduce leeway, though the vee of the major Micronesian designs was deeper still. Be that as it may, the undoubted asset of the Micronesian canoes and their Fijian and Tongan derivatives lay in their superior manoeuvrability.

No canoes in Oceania were fitted with deep sailing keels (neither were European workboats), though the enormous steering oars used on some types would have helped subserve the same purpose.

The theoretical windward ability of sailing canoes is, however, a largely academic question if it is divorced from the actual method of handling. Every kind that I know is invariably sailed a good full and bye, that is, not very close to the wind, though often the hull form and rig would have allowed it to be kept much closer to the wind. This apparently universal handling technique tends to mask differences in potential weatherliness, so that the efficient sailing machines of the Carolines and Gilberts are sailed in such a manner that they make good no better than 75°-80° off the true wind, which is about the same as Papuan and Rarotongan outriggers and a recently tested replica of a Hawaiian round-bottomed paddling-sailing double canoe.[12] There seems no reason to suppose that the larger craft of yesterday were handled any differently.

The Gilbertese, and after them the Carolinian canoes are probably the best performers for their size in the western Pacific, so some discussion of their windward showing and how they are handled on this point of sailing may not come amiss.[13]

The rig, which is identical in both regions, concentrates the sail area near the bow (see fig. 57). They are steered to windward by the sheet, not by the steering paddle. When the sheet is hauled in the wind pressure on the sail towards the front of the canoe is increased, so that the bow is forced down-wind. Now a sail is setting at the correct

---

[12] See Gladwin (1970: 103) for the Carolines; Finney (pers. comm., 1969) for Hawaii. My own observations in the Carolines, Gilberts, Ninigo, Papua, and Rarotonga gave substantially the same results.

[13] I timed a fully loaded 25-foot Carolinian (Puluwat) canoe on a 48-mile two-way open sea passage in bad weather. An average speed of 4.5 knots was maintained with a free wind on the outward journey and 4 knots on the return when we were close-hauled, but did not need to tack. Gladwin (1970: 124) reports Puluwat canoe builders as saying that modern canoes are much faster (and hence more weatherly) than earlier ones because of the smooth hull surface obtainable with metal tools. This could well be a rationalisation on the Carolinians' part, for Drake in 1579 saw canoes in the archipelago that were 'very smooth within and without and bearing a glass [gloss?] as if it were a horn daintily burnished' (Alexander, 1916: 114).

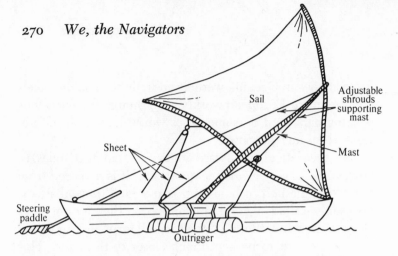

Fig. 57 Gilbertese canoe under way, mast raked towards bow and sail area concentrated forward

angle for windward work only when the sheet is hardened in, but immediately this is done the Micronesian canoe pivots down-wind. Conversely, wind is spilled from the sail when the sheet is slacked away, so that the boat then turns up into the wind. The sheet has to be slackened, thereby allowing the sail to flap and impairing its driving power, before the canoe can point higher again. It therefore proceeds to windward in a series of curves, between a direction about 50° off the true wind and one of 70°, mostly rather nearer the latter. Leeway being something like 15°, the course made good to windward will average out at about 80° from the wind.

Fig. 58 Plan of Gilbertese/Carolinian canoe showing asymmetric hull form (degree of convexity of side A-A-A greatly exaggerated)

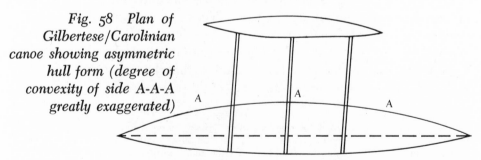

This remarkably inefficient technique makes no use whatever of a peculiarity of Micronesian hull design that should theoretically reduce leeway and improve windward performance. The feature in question is a slight asymmetry whereby the side towards the outrigger, which is always kept to windward, is more convex than the other (see fig. 58).

Canoe builders in Ninigo, the Carolines, and the Gilberts
are unanimous in asserting that the reason for this asymmetry is to balance the pull of the outrigger, so that the
craft will run straight. They add that this is particularly
important when going to windward, for in its absence, the
drag of the outrigger float would tend to spin the canoe
up into the wind, when it would be likely to be caught
aback. This term implies the wind catching the wrong side
of the sail, resulting, in any appreciable breeze, in a dis-
masting or a capsize.[14]

Actual figures for the windward performance of really
large voyaging canoes are, not unnaturally, hard to come
by, but we do have approximate ones for the 48-foot Ongea
ndrua. It will be recalled that the Fijian *ndrua*, unlike
other ocean-going designs, was round rather than vee-
sectioned, and so would be less efficient on the wind. This
is confirmed by Diaper (1928: 115), who drew attention
to the great amount of leeway they made. The modern
one took five hours with a fair wind for the first 40 miles
of a passage from Vatoa towards Ongea. After this the
wind became contrary and eight hours were required to
tack the remaining 17 or so miles—something like 2 knots
made good on course (Reid, pers. comm., 1946). This would,
in fact, be better than one would expect from such a craft
in open water.

Lest we view Pacific Ocean sailing vessels out of proportion, however, we should keep in mind that their mediocre windward ability was by no means exceptional in the
days of sail. In 1653, for instance, the *Swallow* and the
Revenge beat against the trades from Mayo to Sal in the
Cape Verdes. This 70-mile voyage took them a week (Anderson, 1935: 82)—10 miles a day made good, compared
with over 40 for the Ongea *ndrua*.

---

14 When canoe builders explain that the asymmetry of their craft is for
windward sailing, they generally omit to point out the danger of being
caught aback, regarding it as self evident. Thus Hipour gave the full
explanation only when asked in what way was this feature important
for windward work. An unjustified analogy with the 'lift' of an aircraft's
wing has sometimes been drawn and the asymmetric hull form taken to
be a device to draw a canoe up-wind (Gladwin, 1970: 95, 119). If any
proof be needed, apart from the canoe-men's own clear statements, that
it is nothing of the sort, it is the fact that these canoes are *never* sailed
anything like close enough to the wind for such an effect to come into
play.

Indeed, it is worth reminding ourselves that the modern ocean racing fleets of the post-war era are the first sailing vessels ever to embark regularly and deliberately on upwind passages and to break with the time-hallowed practice of awaiting a favourable slant before setting out.

STRENGTH AND FLEXIBILITY

Canoes 'tied together with vegetable fibres' have been said to be more vulnerable to the stresses of beating to windward than craft 'fastened together with bolts or nails' (Sharp, 1963: 56). This ignores the importance attached to flexibility by canoe builders in Oceania and modern multihull designers alike. Voyaging canoes are invariably constructed so as to be flexible and are no more (perhaps less) likely to break up under stress of weather than are present day catamarans and trimarans.[15] Sennit lashings will, of course, ultimately fray and loosen. According to Hipour and other Carolinian navigators, if the canoe is rarely or never used they need renewing in two or three years. They should be replaced, however, after three months continuous seagoing.[16] Since not even the longest hypothetical voyage in the distant past could have occupied three months without landing, the traditional methods and materials used in lashing or sewing a well-found vessel would provide an ample margin of safety. We know that the former big voyaging canoes did leak at the seams and required bailing, as indeed all sea-going canoes do today. But this fact reflects the difficulty in obtaining water-tight joints between planks of flexible vessels and is not related to structural strength.

Having made this point, we must at once qualify it. Certain types were particularly liable to strain, like the Tuamotuan double canoes (*pahi*), which being of necessity, through shortage of suitable timber, constructed of

[15] Mason (1966) states that 'nails and spikes are just *not* the things the Marshallese canoe-builder needs to strengthen his craft' (author's italics). Marshallese had repeatedly assured him 'that the demands of the sea upon a canoe, both hull and outrigger, are such that lashing with sennit is the only practical way to hold the craft together'. Diaper (1928: 113) says virtually the same.

[16] Hipour was discussing voyages involving a good deal of windward work with stops only long enough to replenish supplies and was not speaking of the conditions of contemporary Carolinian voyaging.

inferior wood, leaked excessively in a seaway. Because Ninigo canoes, for the same reason, are built out of worm-eaten and immersion-softened drift logs, their active life outside the lagoon is reckoned to be as short as three years (Itilon, Papi). The 40-foot Santa Cruz *te puke* had a high superstructure supported by a pontoon-like hull. When this was repeatedly immersed in steep seas severe wracking strains were produced, so much so that the *te puke* has been abandoned in recent years in favour of a Central Solomon Islands model (Dawea, pers. comm., 1969).

CARRYING CAPACITY

The ability of voyaging canoes, even the outriggers, to carry weight and bulk was considerable.

The largest Marquesan (Polynesian) outriggers seen by Grarcia carried 40-50 people on fishing and war expeditions (Mathias G[rarcia], 1843: 233). The Polynesians of Puka-puka gave shortage of timber as the reason why few double canoes were ever constructed on their island (Beaglehole, E. and P., 1938: 180), but their outrigger craft were still formidable vessels. A 60-footer that was in existence in 1938 could carry 3 tons of copra (Haddon and Hornell, 1936: 251-3). This particular vessel was for lagoon use, open sea canoes of similar dimensions being built up higher and almost completely decked-in (Beaglehole, E. and P., 1938: 171).

Turning to Micronesia, we find reports of Marshallese outriggers carrying 40-50 people (Alexander, 1902: 806; Winkler, 1901: 504), though Winkler drew attention to the prevalence of gross overloading. Indications that former Carolinian craft could carry three times as many people as they can now are that two canoes which were storm-driven to the Philippines in 1696 started out with a total complement of 35 (Burney, 1967: 7), and that a canoe which came to Guam from Faraulep in 1721 contained 24 men and women (Cantova, 1728: 192). The contemporary 26-foot Carolinian canoes comfortably carry crews of five or six, with provisions and trade goods, and sometimes even a 250 lb turtle, on voyages of up to a week, though we shall see in the next section that they were capable of remaining out much longer. This gives an idea of the probable capacity of the Carolinian 65-footers seen by Lutké in the Carolinian Mortlocks in 1828 (Nozikov, ?1946: 139).

Polynesian twin-hulled voyaging canoes, with their literally doubled buoyancy and enhanced stability, were obviously even better load carriers that the outriggers we have been discussing. Thus Samwell saw Tongan double canoes (*tongiaki*) carrying 80-100 men and capable, in his opinion, of keeping the sea for a very long time (Beaglehole, 1967: 1038). Anderson says that these vessels always carried at least four times more people than were necessary to handle them (Beaglehole, 1967: 939). The 48-foot Ongea *ndrua*, a pygmy compared with those of the past, could carry a ton of copra, or on short trips, 50 people (Reid, pers. comm., 1946).

PROVISIONING FOR VOYAGING

The carrying capacity of big voyaging canoes was enormous, so that the availability of relatively non-perishable provisions and storage facilities clear of salt water would be important in determining the possible duration of voyages. We cannot give exact figures but there are certain pointers.

In bad weather the voyage from Pikelot to Saipan (450 miles) took as long as 20 days (Hipour), yet the canoes involved in this traffic last century were no larger than contemporary ones (26 feet long) and storage space safe from spoilage would have been strictly limited. The staple long-term diet of Carolinian voyagers includes pre-cooked fermented breadfruit, pounded taro (Repunglug and his four companions took 60 lb on their 1970 canoe voyage to Saipan), drinking and eating coconuts, and baked fish. Fish caught at sea are either eaten raw or cooked over a fire of coconut husks that is built in a bowl carried for the purpose.

The Santa Cruz sea-going diet, upon which we also lived, included a variety of thick pastes or puddings of banana or taro in coconut oil, dried breadfruit chips and *nyali* nuts. All these are said to keep indefinitely. They were supplemented by baked sweet potato and breadfruit and a plentiful supply of drinking coconuts.

Pandanus, raw and prepared in various ways, is the basic ingredient of the canoe fare of the Gilbertese. We found that one such preparation, a paste the consistency of cream cheese called *tuae*, kept perfectly for over two months.

Banks (1962: 366) took a rather pessimistic view of Tahitian provisioning when he wrote: 'They cannot . . . remain at sea above a fortnight or 20 days . . . for want of proper provisions and places to put them in safe, as well as water of which however they carry a tolerable stock in hollow Bamboes'. Cook (Beaglehole, 1955: 157), however, seems to be implying unbroken passages of '30 or more' days' duration, when he quotes from Tupaia on the subject of returning from the far western islands.

The experiences of involuntary drifters may have some relevance to this discussion. We have seen how Sernous and his crew were at sea for four weeks and caught on the average a fish each day, and how Iotiebata was storm driven for five weeks. A more recent accidental voyage was that of Robati Teinamati of Onotoa in the Gilberts. He neglected to take with him the customary coconuts and water when he went fishing in his 8-foot canoe. Gales drove him westward so he sun dried such fish as he had already caught and supplemented them with flying fish that fell into the canoe and rainwater. He landed at an island off New Guinea 1300 miles from his home after 42 days at sea (Colony Information Notes, July 1970).

The conclusions that we can draw from this collection of rather disparate data must be tentative. I think it would be safe to assume that there would be no real difficulty in adequately provisioning a large voyaging canoe for a month and that this period could be extended, without undue hardship, for another fortnight. Given the average speeds of Polynesian and Micronesian ocean-going vessels (100-150 miles a day), this would give a range, in winds that were not contrary, of 3000-4500 miles, thus bringing even the furthest outposts of Polynesia within scope of the voyager.

CHAPTER ELEVEN

Reasons for voyaging

We will now tentatively approach the problem of defining the role played by conscious navigation in inter-island contact—remembering how complex and variable must have been the social history of the centuries before written records begin. Impossible as it is to re-create the world of a prehistoric voyager, failure to attempt a partial appreciation of his motives may lead to the assumption by default that they equated with our own—and the one certainty is that they did not. In suggesting certain attitudes on the part of the voyagers and dividing the voyages themselves into categories, I want to stress that both motives and categories were mixed and overlapping and, moreover, did not exactly correspond to the European terms we have perforce used to describe them. The maintenance of clan and kinship relations and obligations do not, for instance, fit into a European social mould.[1] We will concentrate, then, on illustrative examples, considered in the light of the efficacy of indigenous navigation.

ADVENTURE[2]

All over Oceania a wandering spirit persists to this day. The approach to voyaging of Rafe and other present-day Tikopians, of Tevake, Hipour, and Iotiebata, shows that confidence at sea has in no way abated. There is no element of 'conquering' the ocean in their attitude. Untold generations have studied the sea's moods, so that the navigators' knowledge, even when residual, has made it for them a familiar and friendly place. They are as much at ease and at home with the aquatic environment as the Australian Aboriginal is with his inland ecosystem.

---

[1] As motivation for voyaging can hardly be considered in isolation from the sea lanes traversed, a number of the contact areas and islands indicated on map 2 and the endpaper map will be referred to in this chapter.

[2] This section could equally well have been entitled 'curiosity', 'wandering', or 'exploring' and cannot be strictly separated from trading ventures, assertion of traditional authority, or even raiding.

Firth (1936: 32), in an evocative passage, writes of the Tikopians:

Fired by the lust for adventure and the desire to see new lands canoe after canoe set out and ranged the seas . . . Fear of storms and shipwreck leaves them undeterred, and the reference in an ancient song to the loss of a man at sea as a 'sweet burial' expresses very well the attitude of the Tikopia.

Examples abound from earlier times of this restless urge. There were the Raiateans (from the Tahiti group) who, according to Banks (1962: 366), went on 'very long voyages, often remaining out from home several months, visiting in that time many different islands of which they repeated to us the names of near a hundred'. In the twenties of the following century the missionary John Williams (1846: 48) was told of the Raiatean chief Iouri, an 'enterprising spirit, he determined to go in search of other countries'; and had navigated his *pahi* to Rarotonga, 600 miles away, and when he came home again, it 'became an object of ambition with every adventurous chief to discover other lands'. At very nearly the same time Fr Mathias Grarcia (1843: 235n.) was speaking in Hawaii to 'several adventurers', who had run 'the greatest dangers in an attempt at a voyage of discovery', and having found nothing, had returned home.

Similarly in the Fiji-Tonga-Samoa area we find mid-nineteenth-century Islanders making voyages of '600 or 800 or even 1,000 miles—being not infrequently absent a year or two from home, wandering and gadding about from island to island, . . . Samoa, Fiji, and all the Friendly Islands [Tonga] . . . Wallis, Fortuna, Nieuafou, Nieuatobutabu' (Diaper, 1928: 111-12).

They were proud and arrogant, these Polynesians of an earlier day, and they stood much less in awe of Europeans than many accounts would lead us to believe. Vancouver (1801: vol. III, 146) mentions a young seaman who was so upset by the Marquesans jeering at him and pulling his hair that, hardly in accord with Royal Navy traditions, he burst into tears. Equally contemptuous were the 80 returned voyagers who tramped uninvited through Diaper's trade store in Vava'u (Tonga) appropriating trinkets for their fair companion. These youths and one 'physically, perfect;

morally, very imperfect' young woman had been away in a large *kalia* on a year's cruise to outlying islands, mostly Samoa (Diaper, 1928: 218, 219).

THE PRIDE OF NAVIGATORS

A proud self-respect permeates Carolinian voyaging to this day. Thus there are three sets of circumstances, according to Beiong, in which visitors to an island will feel shamed and in honour bound to put to sea at once regardless of storms or even certainty of disaster. These are:

Any suggestion that they are becoming a burden to feed.

Any injury to one of their number in a fight with no apology offered.

A decision by the captain that the weather is too bad for voyaging, followed by a local canoe putting out even to fish a little way offshore.

It would be more in keeping with the dignity of a Puluwat captain to beat 150 miles to windward for five days to Moen Island in Truk lagoon to obtain cigarettes than to wait a short time for the administration's motor vessel (Hipour).

The return voyage of the respected navigator brothers Repunglug and Repunglap and their three companions between Satawal in the Carolines and Saipan in the Marianas in April/May 1970 has been referred to (p. 274). One important motive for the enterprise seems to have been that they felt shamed by Hipour's exploit the previous year and a revival of voyaging between the archipelagos would both renew their prestige and enhance their skill. The star courses and auxiliary sailing directions had been given the Repung brothers over thirty years previously by their father, who had not himself been to Saipan. Neither brother had any acquaintance with Western seamanship or navigation. There was no memory on Satawal of the voyage having been made in the present century.

There were no charts aboard the 26-foot canoe, though in accordance with modern Carolinian custom, a boat compass was used for secondary orientation in the daytime. A 'walkie-talkie' set with a range of 40 miles was carried.

The first stage was to uninhabited West Fayu, 52 miles from Satawal, where favourable winds were awaited. The remaining 422 miles to Saipan were covered in under four days. On the return journey the canoe was set to leeward by a storm so the brothers decided to proceed direct to Satawal, omitting the call at West Fayu (this would have been more than 470 miles non stop). However, they first contacted by radio a party of Islanders who were on West Fayu, and these requested assistance in transporting the eight turtles they had caught.[3] The travellers were guided to Fayu by a cloud that stood over it and they rested there two days before completing their journey to Satawal. (Highlights, May 1970, supplemented and corrected by McCoy, pers. comm., 1970).

The following story was recounted as a specific illustration of the pride of navigators.[4] A Woleai canoe, driven south by contrary winds, decided to try for Kapingamarangi atoll, which lies in total isolation midway between the Carolines proper and the Solomons, 465 miles south-east of Pulusuk. None of the crew had been there but they knew the star course and were fortunate enough to arrive safely. Now the Kapingamarangi language is a Polynesian one quite unlike the Micronesian tongues spoken in the rest of the Carolines, so the inhabitants' speech was incomprehensible. This tended to confirm the identity of the landfall but the voyagers were uncertain, and being trained navigators, they were too proud to inquire. Instead they kept their ears open, and after about a week, overheard children at play (fishermen in another version) mention the island's name. They thereupon set off home, their dignity unimpaired.

All the examples here given have been from the Carolines, because there voyaging attitudes persist almost in their entirety. Traditions from other parts of Oceania, however, while less detailed, leave little doubt that exactly the same attitude was held throughout Polynesia in former times (see Lewis, 1967: 270-2).

---

[3] These turtles each weigh 200-250 lb, according to sex.

[4] Told by the oldest Pulusuk navigator Asarto (Lykke, pers. comm., 1969). Another informant gave the same account to Riesenberg (pers. comm., 1969).

RAIDING AND CONQUEST

Tongan Raids. There is no absolute division, of course, between raiding and exacting tribute or maintaining hegemony, especially since spheres of influence seem to have been even more tenuous and transitory in the Pacific than in land-based empires. The Tongans raided well beyond their normal contact sphere, especially to the Polynesian Outliers fringing Melanesia away to the north-west.[5] The nearest Outliers to the mis-named 'Friendly Islands' (Tonga) are Tikopia and its neighbour Anuta, 960 miles from Tongatapu and 550 from Fiji.

'It appears from the accounts of the Tucopians and Anutoans', wrote Dillon (1829: vol. II, 112), 'that in the days of their ancestors these islands were invaded by five large double canoes from Tongataboo, the crews of which committed dreadful outrages'. Firth (1930: 117) puts this (or a similar invasion) at eight generations ago—at 25 years to a generation, about 200 years.

Further to the westward still, on Nukapu, one of the Santa Cruz Reef Islands, traditions of Tongan raids are well remembered (Davenport, 1964: 137; traditions related by Tevake).

West-north-west another 200 miles, the story was repeated on the Outlier, Sikaiana. Towards the close of the seventeenth century, or nine generations before the publication of the account (Woodford, 1906: 166-7), a large Samoan double canoe came to Sikaiana. Typically the Samoans were peaceful, but a big Tongan party who arrived in the time of the same ruling chief (Alima) were the reverse. Having ravaged the island, they left for Taumako, 240 miles on their way towards home. They were not destined to see Tonga again, however, for they had taken with them Semalu, Alima's son, who revealed their depre-

---

[5] For Tongan relations with Rotuma and the Ellice Islands, see especially Dillon (1829: vol. I, 294-5, vol. II, 103-4). For early Tongan-Samoan relations and contacts with the Gilberts, see Grimble (1922: 101), Maude (1963: 7), and Gifford (1929: 14, 15).

The Tongan raids of the Outliers took place against established populations. The original settlement of the Polynesian Outliers was by Samoic rather than Tongic speaking peoples (Green, 1966: 7-38; Pawley, 1967: 259-96). Ward's computer analysis of model drift voyages has shown that drifters could have reached all the Outliers from Samoa (pers. comm., 1969).

dations on Sikaiana. The Taumakoans thereupon exterminated the Tongans with bows and arrows. The kidnapped chief's son eventually returned home.

There are several points of interest about this tradition. 'Tonga' is a word denoting some southerly direction in most Polynesian dialects, but this and similar accounts invariably draw such a definite distinction between Tongans and Samoans, that the geographical Tonga is clearly meant. Then Taumako, unlike most of Polynesia, is an island where bows and arrows were used in warfare. An elderly Sikaianan, Teai, who is most unlikely to have had access to Woodford's article in *Oceania*, told me the same story in 1968, except that he said the events had occurred not nine but eleven generations ago, a discrepancy accounted for by the 62 years that had passed since the original recording of the tradition.

In common with others I have been puzzled by the fact that, in Tonga itself, neither Mariner, Gifford, nor Collocott seems to have come across any traditions of these far western sallies of the Tongan warriors. This contradicts the apparent tendency for Tongan traditions to have been elaborated to bolster the prestige of aristocratic rulers (Groube, pers. comm., 1970) and is in marked contrast to the many detailed stories retailed by the victims. It is also out of keeping with Tongan memory of distant thrusts in other directions.[6] We are left to search for possible explanations.

The first possibility to spring to mind is that the Tongan seamen were incapable of returning across the 500-mile-wide 'Melanesian trench' between the Anuta-Tikopia-New Hebrides region in the west and Fiji-Rotuma in the east. However, this crossing does not present particularly formidable navigational problems. The target presented by Fiji is very extensive; to find favourable winds it would only be necessary to wait for the westerlies that interrupt the

---

[6] Suggestions of sporadic links with Rarotonga, 850 miles to the eastward, directly or via Samoa, come from Gill (1876: 166, 167), Stair (1895: 99-131) and traditions related by Kaho and Ve'ehala. We saw on p. 248 how the Tongans told Cook of a Gilbertese island 1170 miles to the north. Emory (1934: 15) has reported Tongan-type ruins on Fanning Island, one of the Line Islands north of Tahiti, 1600 miles to north-eastward of Vava'u.

trades in this region at frequent intervals during the November-March season.

In any case we have one specific tradition of a two-way voyage. Two canoe loads of Tongans, who had stayed some time on Anuta, 'returned to Tonga bearing with them news of the settlement [Anuta]. They warned their Anuta hosts before leaving that future Tongan raids might eventuate', a prediction that was borne out by events (Firth, 1954: 123).

The suggestion has been put forward by Reid (pers. comm., 1969) that these raiders began and ended their voyages in overseas Tongan communities in the Fijian Lau group, where subsequent Fijian traditions would have ultimately overlain their memory. The matter is still open, however, for Groube (pers. comm., 1970) questions the antiquity of Tongan footholds in Fiji, citing particularly the absence of the Fijian dog from Tongan archaeological sites. There are also suggestions that the Fijians were once the chief voyagers (see Wilkes, 1845: vol. III, 347; Eilers, 1934: 179, and the fact that it was the Fijians, rather than the Tongans, who introduced the Micronesian modification of the classic double canoe).

New Guinea Raids on the Carolines. The people of Sonsorol, Kodgube (Tobi), and Merir, Hipour told me, were in former times afraid of the west wind lest it bring down raiders from New Guinea upon them. These westernmost of the Carolines are well over 1000 miles from Hipour's home island of Puluwat, yet he was substantially correct in his assertion. The westerners had indeed had ample occasion for apprehension, for numerous savage raids did take place over a period of many generations (Eilers, 1935: 208-10, 349). It had, however, been southerly rather than westerly winds that had filled the sails of the raiders, who seem to have mostly come from the Jobi-Sarmi, Tarkur-Saar region of West Irian (Riesenberg, 1965: 136). The same authority points out that these are the only New Guineans to use the loom, which is characteristic of Micronesia.

These raids force us to reconsider the generally accepted opinion of Melanesians and New Guinea Papuans as essentially coastal sailors. For from Jobi-Sarmi in New Guinea to Sonsorol and Tobi in the Carolines is 600 miles. There is a possible staging point at Mepia Island (Pegun), but even this leaves an unbroken stretch of 360 miles culminating in a difficult landfall.

DEEP SEA FISHING

A drawing of a Tongan bonito fishing canoe (*tafa'anga*) made during Tasman's visit in 1643 is identical with present-day craft and shows the bonito rod in position behind the steersman (Haddon and Hornell, 1936: 260) (see fig. 53), demonstrating the relative antiquity of this type of deep-sea fishing. There is evidence from Samoa of similar boats being carried aboard large double canoes. Stair, who saw the last surviving *va'a tele* (analogue of the *tongiaki*) in 1838, wrote of them making long fishing expeditions carrying on deck two *va'a alo*, which were 25-30-foot bonito canoes equivalent to the Tongan *tafa'anga* (Haddon and Hornell, 1936: 231-8). On reaching the destination reef these were used for fishing, 'the large canoe being reserved for crew and cargo' (Stair, 1895b: 617).

There are similar Tongan stories of long-range ventures like that to a distant fishing ground near Niue called Aka, 250 miles from the Ha'apai group (Ve'ehala). Now the Samoan *va'a tele* and its Tongan counterpart, the *tongiaki*, were notorious for their clumsiness in bad weather. It seems likely that some of these seaworthy but unhandy vessels would be driven far afield by storms. Should they accidentally come upon unknown or forgotten islands, such ships with their trained navigator-captains would be more capable than most of returning home with accurate information as to the position of their discovery.

TRADING VOYAGES

We have touched already upon a special example of indigenous trade in Kau Moala's ill-fated load of sandalwood. The tribute voyages to Yap, considered below, were another. The long voyages from isolated Pukapuka to Samoa and other islands have also been mentioned. There is only soft rock on Pukapuka and the island's legends make it apparent that the procurement of stone from which adzes could be made was an important motive for voyaging and, in confirmation, a basaltic adze found in a grave was similar to Samoan types (Beaglehole, E. and P., 1938: 164-5). This is a reminder of how imperative it was to supplement the resources of the stark atoll environment even at the cost of lengthy and hazardous journeys. Naturally other reasons for putting to sea operated on Pukapuka. Among them Beaglehole, E. and P. (1938: 400) list the search for adventure, desire to see lands known of old, prestige, and the exiling of men who might disrupt the community.

There is no space for further examples. We can only mention the existence of the complex trading cycles that were, and still are, typical of Melanesia.

TRIBUTE AND EMPIRE: THE SPHERE OF YAP (see fig. 46)

Tongan and Tahitian spheres could well have been considered under this heading, but since Tongan control and raids overlap and the Tahitian world is discussed in the next chapter, we will confine ourselves here to this single example from Micronesia. The Gagil district of the Carolinian island of Yap once exercised political and religious hegemony as far to the eastward as Puluwat (Lessa, 1950: 47, 48; 1956: 67-71; Goodenough, 1953: 1). That is, its power extended more than 700 miles with gaps of as long as 290 miles between individual atolls. As well as regular tribute-bearing fleets from the eastward, west Carolinian canoes transported the great wheel-sized discs known as 'stone money' from the south-west. These objects were quarried on Palau and taken across 230 miles of open sea to Yap. The navigational problems involved in some of these voyages, and how a proportion of the traffic missed its destination, are discussed elsewhere.

DELIBERATE RETURNS AFTER FORCED DRIFTS (see fig. 46)

There are a number of reports of such episodes which are deserving of notice. In the first place they reveal how blurred is the line that really divides the somewhat Euro-centric categories of purposeful and accidental voyages. In the second, they emphasise the extent and complexity of inter-island contact made possible by the widely known and extremely efficacious land-finding techniques. We will give two examples.

Returns after drifting from Carolines to Philippines. Not a few of the canoes that were storm-drifted to the Philippines from the Yap region (see pp. 227-8) made successful return voyages. As late as 1910 the *Deutsches Kolonial-blatt* (cited by Riesenberg, 1965: 164) wrote of canoes being cast away to the Philippines from the Carolines and returning. There were old people who had 'been five times to the Philippines and made their own way back home, against the prevailing east wind, despite strict German regulations to the contrary'.

It might be supposed that such recent return voyagers owed their success to European geographical knowledge were it not for the fact that similar episodes were recorded by Spanish missionaries in the Philippines at a time when the Carolines were virtually a closed book to Westerners.[7] In the early 1690s the Jesuit Fr Paul Clain was told by a Carolinian castaway named Olit that 'six natives from Eap [Yap] island had been stranded in the Philippines and then returned to Eap, and that the voyage had lasted 10 days' (Krämer, 1919: 27-32). The distance is 700 miles. Since the episode occurred some time in the 1680s no European could have directed them; the sailing directions they used must have been exclusively their own.

A little later, in 1696, two canoes were driven to the Philippines. The survivors eventually set off for home again, though the outcome of their voyage is uncertain (Burney, 1967: 4, 5, 9). What is significant is that it was these Carolinians who were eagerly questioned about their islands by the Spaniards and not the other way round. They listed

---

[7] European contact with the Carolines amounted by 1700 to a number of sixteenth-century sightings and two sojourns ashore in the Yap area. Both the latter were by Portuguese, so would have been unknown to their Spanish rivals in the Philippines (Lessa, 1962: 313-403). There followed a century of quiescence when the prescribed track for ships from New Spain (Mexico) was drawn well clear of the unknown dangers of the archipelago, so that the earlier ill-documented sightings were forgotten (Burney, 1967: 3). In 1686 Lazeano happened upon an island that he named 'La Carolina' and a decade later Rodriguez discovered Faraulep before himself being wrecked (pp. 4, 5).

thirty-two islands including 'Saypen' (Saipan) in the Marianas, and a map was drawn from their statements that depicted even more islands (pp. 8, 10). It is not surprising that many of the positions shown are inaccurate, since Carolinian star courses and geographical data are, as we saw, expressed in terms very different from static maps. What is abundantly clear is that the castaways' range, extending as it did 2000 miles east of the Philippines and embracing Saipan 500 miles to the north, far surpassed the sketchy knowledge of the Europeans.

Even more striking is the fact that the oldest of the party had once before been cast on the Philippines, on Mindanao, 'where he had seen only infidels', and whence he had sailed back to his own islands (p. 9). In this instance also no 'borrowing' of Western information can possibly have occurred since the old man encountered no Europeans. His accomplishment was formidable in that his probable landfall targets would have been either Palau, 450 miles from Mindanao, or Yap a full 700.

Returning Tuamotuan drifters. When Captain Beechey landed on the Tuamotuan atoll of Ahunui in 1826 he encountered thirty-one Polynesians who were busy repairing a double canoe 'upwards of thirty feet long' (Beechey, 1831: 212-53). They had been bound from Anaa in the Tuamotus towards Tahiti 200 miles to the westward, the craft perilously overloaded with forty-eight souls and three weeks' provisions. Near Mehetia, 145 miles along the route, they encountered a series of westerly gales. Only after seventeen had died did they fetch up on Vanavana, an uninhabited Tuamotuan island, 420 miles east-south-east of Anaa and about 520 from the spot near Mehetia whence they had been drifted.[8] After recouping their strength they set out for home and had reached Ahanui 100 miles along the way when Beechey encountered them. The manner in which the Anaa navigator retained his orientation, enabling the castaways successfully to complete the first quarter of their homeward voyage, is typical enough. The

---

[8] This incident is very unusual in being a long west-to-east drift, the great majority of accidental voyages in the trade wind Pacific having been in the reverse direction (Golson, 1963: 'Table of Voyages').

unusual feature was their meeting with someone who could record the episode.

VOYAGES BY ONE-WAY EXILES

This type of exodus, a journey of no return deliberately undertaken towards some mythical or very ill-defined destination, is well documented. For instance in 1813 Captain Porter was told of big parties of such voluntary exiles being encouraged by the priests to leave the Marquesas for legendary 'lands', and of hundreds of people having so departed over the years (Porter, 1822: 51). There are examples of like nature from other parts of Oceania, although less institutionalised than the Marquesan custom appears to have been.

A late eighteenth-century chief's son on the Polynesian island of Uvea, west of Samoa, was accidentally hurt during the construction of a canoe. Fearing the father's wrath, his companions decided to 'leave for lands unknown'. Rather surprisingly in the circumstances, the injured man elected to join them. The fugitives eventually came to an island in the Loyalty group off New Caledonia 1000 miles to the south-west, which was named 'Uvea' after their homeland, a designation it bears to this day. Practically the same story is told on the Loyalty Islands Uvea as on the Polynesian one (Burrows, E. G., 1937: 50-2; Guiart, 1963: 615).

A modern commentator has chosen to ignore long deliberate voyaging of any other character than these virtually unnavigated one-way enterprises (Sharp, 1963: chap. IV), a selectivity that would seem to stem in large part from a failure to appreciate the practical value of indigenous navigational techniques. There is no reason, incidentally, why a proportion of even these emigrations should not have been consciously navigated towards known objectives, that had either been reported by castaways or remembered from previous two-way contact. The latter would appear to have been the case when Marianas refugees fled across the ocean to the Carolines to escape massacre by the seventeenth-century Spaniards (Burney, 1967: 4).

ACCIDENTAL DRIFTS

The picture of inter-island contact in Oceania as having been made up of a complex pattern of deliberate and accidental voyages (and ones that defy such easy classification) has been discussed earlier. However, since 'pure' drifts shed little light on navigational questions, we have perforce concentrated on the more planned varieties of voyaging, and if a sense of proportion is to be maintained, we must recognise this lack of balance. Other works give more detailed information about drifts.[9] We will restrict ourselves here to two general comments. Ward's computer analysis of ideal drifts (pers. comm., 1969) showed that, contrary to the author's expectations, such fortuitous episodes could only in part account for known population distribution. And even when a particular voyage is on record as having been made accidentally, and we have seen the selective 'news value' of drifts, it does not follow that it was only, or usually, made in that manner. A place that can be reached accidentally by drifting can generally be arrived at much more easily by the application of conscious maritime skills.

If this necessarily incomplete examination of voyaging motivation has illuminated the subject at all, it will have shown the plurality of the travellers' aims, the only common factor in their attitudes being self-confidence at sea. Extant Carolinian practice shows that this is the reverse of recklessness, caution and conservatism being stressed (see pp. 27, 123-4, and Gladwin, 1970: 203). What we know of other archipelagos suggests that this applied generally. However, stone age seamen totally lacked present day facilities for assessing risks, so their terms of reference must of necessity have been very different from our own —in some circumstances hidebound within the restrictive limits of traditional systems of thinking, in others, placing a reliance on their techniques to (what would seem to us) a foolhardy extent.

POSSIBLE VARIATIONS IN THE SCOPE OF ANCIENT VOYAGING

Much of our data about voyaging spheres come from relatively late periods when the Islanders had for some time been in touch with Europeans. Evidence about pre-

---

[9] See Golson (1963) and Sharp (1963) for Polynesia, Davenport (1964a) for Santa Cruz, and Riesenberg (1965) for Micronesia.

historic fluctuations in range is naturally hard to come by, it is generally indirect and is often ambiguous.

The advent of Western technology not uncommonly facilitated wars of dynastic succession and conquest through the introduction of firearms. The effect on voyaging patterns seems to have been generally disruptive of traditional relations. On the other hand there are instances of European-imposed peace removing tribal barriers of hostility that had previously limited voyaging. A case in point is the trade conducted by the Mailu of south-eastern Papua. Formerly this was confined to friendly parts of the mainland coast, but nowadays the lateen-rigged Mailu double canoes carry their cargoes of shell armbands with impunity as far afield as the Trobriand archipelago (Saville, 1926: 130-95; Lauer, pers. comm., 1970).

But these examples are directly related to European impact. What of pre-contact times? George Forster in the late eighteenth century was convinced 'that the natives of the Society Isles [Tahiti group] have sometimes extended their navigation further than its present limits, by the knowledge they have of several adjacent countries' (Forster, G., 1777: vol. I, 398). We saw on pp. 28, 31 how Santa Cruz voyaging last century, though continuing to be carried out in traditional craft and by the use of purely indigenous navigational techniques, had markedly declined since the time of Quiros's 1606 visit. Similarly Krämer gave details of extensive voyaging networks in the Central Carolines, which had later been abandoned or at best become sporadic (1935: 103, 272).

There is a probability that something of the opposite has also occurred, namely a tendency to 'update' certain Carolinian star courses in the far west from the observations of a Carolinian navigator travelling aboard a European ship (Gladwin, 1970: 202). We have to judge whether such importations would more than balance the general decline and whether the navigator would be obtaining new data or revitalising old. From what we know of the knowledge of their archipelago possessed by the seventeenth-century Carolinians, the later alternative would appear to be the most likely. Considering the precision required of Carolinian navigational techniques, it seems very doubtful if any new input by such means could anything like balance the steady shrinkage of navigational lore that has undoubtedly accompanied contraction of the voyaging sphere. In all other parts of Oceania this decline and contraction has proceeded very much further than in the Carolines.

A common metaphor in Oceania when old relationships have been severed is to say that the islands have 'drifted apart' or that the 'bridge' between them has sunk. The two examples that follow are from the Tahitian and Tongan areas respectively.

The island of Rarotonga was discovered by Fletcher Christian in 1789 after the *Bounty* mutiny (Maude, 1968: 22). It was sighted again in 1813 and visited by a schooner in search of sandalwood the following year (pp. 344, 348). Its existence and position remained, however, still generally unknown to Europeans when the missionary John Williams heard tell of it a decade later on Raiatea, 550 miles to the north-east (Williams, 1846: 47, 48). An old priest informed him that in times gone by some Rarotongan priests, bringing tribute to the Raiatean high altar at Opoa, had been murdered. Up to that time Rarotonga had been united to the southern end of Raiatea, but following this sacrilege, the gods had carried Rarotonga away. The priest did not know where they had taken it but he believed to the south.

Williams drew conclusions about the position of Rarotonga from this and other stories and eventually succeeded, not without difficulty, in finding the island. A question asked of a Raiatean member of his party when they arrived in Rarotonga was 'why did you Raiateans kill those men, whose death induced the gods to remove our island to its present situation?' (1846: 88).

The Western Polynesian tradition comes from Niue and is reported by Loeb (1926: 12). The Niueans, he says, have a very strong tradition that Niue and Tonga were once connected by a land bridge, long since sunk, and that friendly relations existed between the two islands in early days. Loeb adds that it is clear from a number of stories that there was fairly constant intercourse with Tonga in prehistoric times, although this was, more recently, of a hostile nature. The metaphorical 250-miles-long land bridge is obviously analogous to the Raiatea/Rarotonga separation legend.

Leaving aside altogether any hypothetical 'golden age' of sea wandering, the available evidence does seem to indicate that there were temporal fluctuations in ranges of contact, though whether such variations were Pacific-wide or confined to particular regions is less easy to determine. We can only speculate at present why the peripheral contacts of so many important island centres seem to have been lost. Perhaps the process was correlated with improvements in agricultural technique permitting inland settlement and a generally more land-based economy. Possibly political developments were the major determinants. Whatever the underlying reasons, it is not surprising that in such times the ever perilous trans-oceanic connections of the community should become tenuous and the more arduous distant voyages become sporadic or cease altogether.

---

[1] Cook (Beaglehole, 1955: vol. I, Portfolio Chart XI) and Forster, J. R. (1778: 512) both print versions of the chart. Hale (1846: 123) has an amended one and drew attention to a confusion over orientation. Sharp (1957: 25, 26; 1963: 75-6, 80-2), White (1961: 471-3), Dening (1963: 132-6), and Lewthwaite (1966: 41-3; 1967: 81-6; 1970a: 1-19) have made important contributions towards the identification of Tupaia's islands.

CHAPTER TWELVE

The long seaways
of Eastern Polynesia

The object of this final chapter is to apply navigational criteria to certain ancient routes, that we know were once traversed either accidentally or with intent, as a contribution
to the investigation of the possibilities of contact between
the more isolated parts of Oceania. We begin with Tahitian
geographical knowledge in the late eighteenth century, the
time of the first European explorers, and discuss in this
light the likelihood of there having once been communication between Eastern and Western Polynesia. Then,
entering a field where facts are sparser still, we go on to
consider the settlement of the Marquesas and the practica-
bility of voyaging between Eastern Polynesia and Hawaii,
New Zealand, and Easter Island. What follows, unlike
the content of any of the previous chapters, is speculative
—but the speculation is, we hope, navigationally informed.

THE TAHITIAN WORLD: CONTACTS WITH
WESTERN POLYNESIA

It will be recalled that the Tahitians were aware of the
existence and approximate bearing of every major group
in Polynesia (and Fiji) with the exception of Hawaii and
New Zealand (Hale, 1846: 122), though Easter Island
certainly, and Mangareva probably, should be added to
these lacunae. Their world was comparable in extent with
the Carolinian and overshadowed the Tongan, but whereas the Carolinians sailed over virtually the whole of their
known seaways, and the Tongans a substantial portion, the
Tahitians, at any rate in immediate pre-contact times,
appear to have voyaged over only a relatively small part
of theirs.

Our basic documents on Tahitian geography are the
several versions of a chart showing seventy-four islands
that was drawn for Cook under Tupaia's direction.[1] There
are also lists of the names and bearings of a number of islands that were collected by Cook on his first visit in 1769

---

[1] Footnote on facing page.

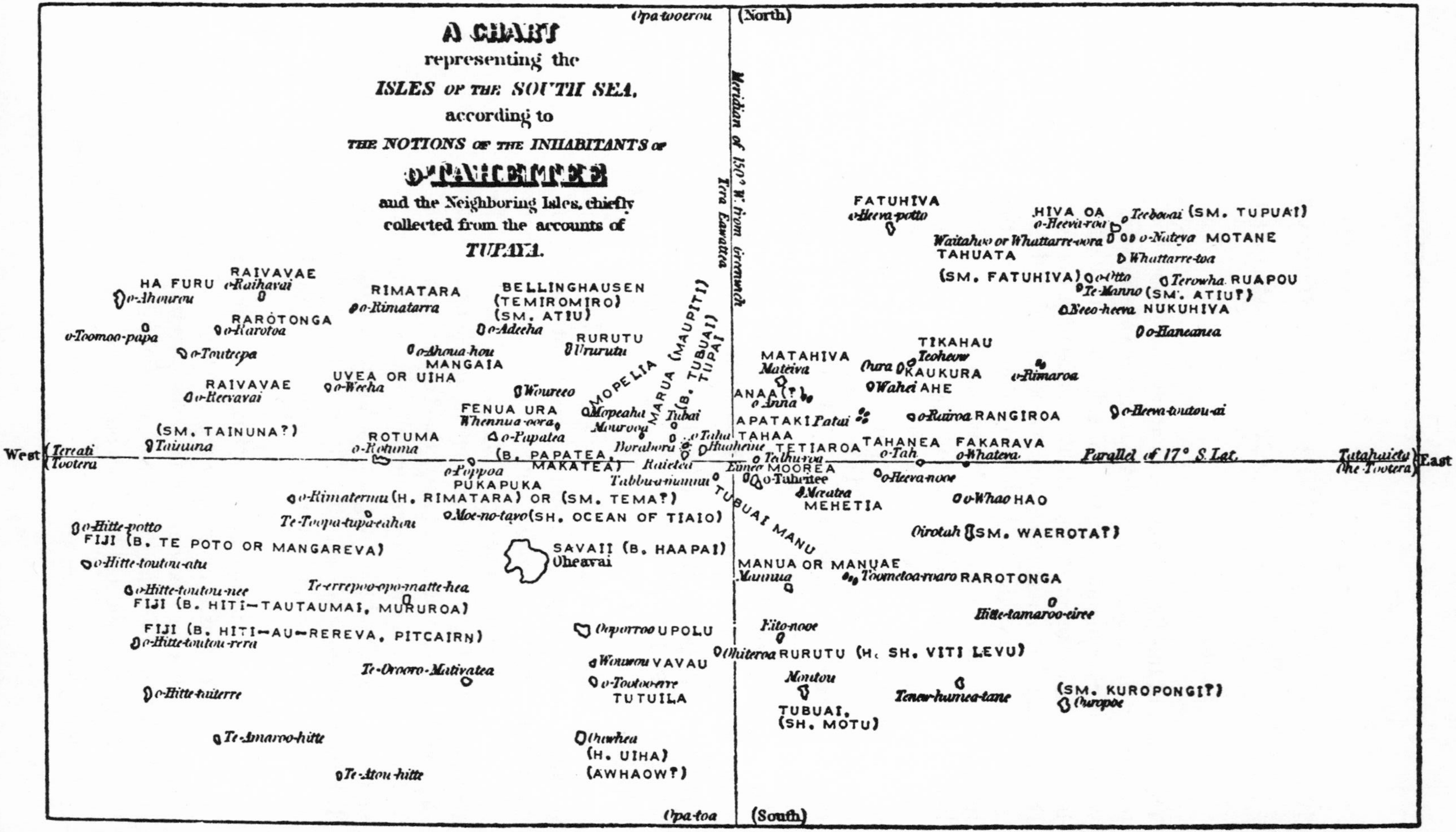

Map 6 Tupaia's islands. Contemporary names imposed on Hale's edition of Forster's version of the map. (After Lewthwaite, 1966.)

(1955: vol. I, 291-4), the Forsters, who were with him in the *Resolution* in 1772-3 (Forster, J. R., 1778: 513-24; Forster, G., 1777: 397) and the Spaniards in 1774-5 (Corney, 1914: vol. I, 305, 306; vol. II, 190-4, 300).[2]

It is impossible now to disentangle the Raiatean navigator's exact original meaning, due to the phonetic spelling

Fig. 59   Diagram of some of Tupaia's islands. Transposed islands marked with an asterisk.

---

[2] The data supplied to the explorers by different Tahitians overlap but are not identical, a reminder that the share in the totality of oral lore held by individuals varies. Such oral traditions as have been retained (see p. 144n.) are subject to embellishment or to losses with time, the passing away of a single generation being potentially able to extinguish them for ever. There would be less incentive to tamper with island names and bearings than with the tales of heroic exploits, the main danger in this instance being the incorporation of European knowledge (see p. 298n.). We are fortunate in that most of the data in this work concern techniques subject to verification.

of the explorers, island name changes, and a partial trans-
position caused by confusion between the Tahitian words
meaning north and south whereby, as Hale (1846: 123)
pointed out, islands with which the English were not acquainted were laid down incorrectly and those they knew
(the Marquesas and Tuamotus) in their proper positions.
Nevertheless, the information that can be deduced from
the chart and lists of islands is invaluable.

Tupaia guided Cook in the *Endeavour* to the hitherto
undiscovered (by Europeans) island of Rurutu, 300 miles
south of Tahiti. He seems to have once voyaged to this or
a neighbouring island in his *pahi*. He himself had no knowledge of lands further southward, but added significantly
that, 'his father once told him that there were islands to
the south of it' (Beaglehole, 1955: 157). Tupaia's other
voyages had been confined to the Society Islands in the
periphery of Tahiti and to a mysterious 'Manua', which
cannot with certainty be identified—the only indisputable
fact being that it was not where Tupaia said it was.

This brings us to speculate on the extent of the Tahitians'
contacts with the distant lands to the westward that Tupaia's chart shows were within their ken. The most likely
'Manuas' to have been suggested have been Manuae in the
Cooks and Manua, the easternmost of the Samoas (see
Dening, 1963: 127; Lewthwaite, 1970: 17).[3] How well
were the Tahitians acquainted with these two places?

They knew the Cook Islands well enough, as evidenced
by the names of at least four of the group appearing in the
correct (when transposed) quadrant of Tupaia's chart or
in the Spanish lists.[4] Even more to the point, the Spanish

---

[3] Uninhabited Scilly atoll, westernmost of the Society Islands, was
known as Fenua Manua or Land of Birds (Varady, 1958: 80; Jourdain,
1970: 363). But Tupaia's Manua was explicitly stated to have been a
high island (Forster, J. R., 1778: 515), though the Spaniards recorded
an ambiguous description (Corney, 1915: vol. II, 192). Moreover
Tupaia's sailing times to the west would be grossly excessive unless he
was referring to small local canoes. I have discarded Scilly atoll, therefore, as a reasonable identification of Manua.

[4] O-Rarotoa (Rarotonga)
   O-Ahou-Hou (Mangaia—an old name)
   Oorio or Oaurio (possibly Aitutaki, whose old name was Arauaa.
             Not transposed)
   Atiu   }
   Matea (Makatea) } From the Spanish lists.

captain Boenechea was given the bearing of and a sailing time to the Cook island of Atiu (Corney, 1914: vol. I, 306).

As to Samoa, the evidence is more tenuous. Tupaia referred to islands to the westward, '10 or 12 days in going thither and 30 or more in coming back' (Beaglehole, 1955: 157), though there is nothing to show whether his 'Manua' was among them. He could hardly have been referring to anywhere else, however, than the Cooks or the Samoas. The former do not lie west but south-west, 400 miles from Raiatea, the latter (Manua Island, Eastern Samoa), 1000 miles down-wind of the high islands of the Tahitian cluster or 900 from its outliers, on a bearing only a little north of west.

The logical step is to convert Tupaia's sailing days into distance. We may assume, I think, that he was referring to voyaging *pahi*, for it is in the same paragraph that Cook (Beaglehole, 1955: 157) estimated that a *pahi* could easily cover 120 miles a day or more. Tupaia's 10 or 12 days running before the trade wind would clearly be ample time in which to reach Samoa. This is what Cook himself thought (p. 157), for he considered these far western islands to be, not indeed Samoa, but the Boscawen and Kepple Islands (Tafahi and Niuatoputapu) discovered by Wallis in the same Western Polynesian region, but even further from Tahiti.

The return passage would almost certainly be seasonal. Tupaia asserted that his countrymen knew 'very well how to make the proper use of' the westerly winds that he said prevailed from November to January (Beaglehole, 1955: 154 n.2). To cover the 1000 miles from the Samoan Manua back to the Tahiti group in 30 days would mean averaging 33 miles a day. This is not an unreasonable figure, considering that a *pahi* could complete the passage given only nine days of favourable westerlies.[5] An alternative to the

---

[5] West winds hardly predominate, as Tupaia seems to imply, even in the summer season. Near Tahiti at this time the Trades are interrupted by the wind backing into a westerly quadrant for a day or so at something like weekly intervals. Westerlies are more common than this near Samoa. In the opposite direction north-east towards the Marquesas, the trades are steady and virtually continuous (Routeing Charts South Pacific, 5128 (1-12); *Pacific Islands Pilot*: vols. III, 35-7, II, 19, 20, 22).

direct route would be via the Cook Islands, which we have
seen were within the Tahitian orbit, and could have provided a convenient first stage landfall 630 miles east-south-
east of Manua in Samoa—a little over five days sailing
with west winds. The expanded targets presented by either
the Cooks or Tahiti and its neighbours would be quite adequate, both being around 14°.

The next question is whether there is any evidence of
prehistoric contact between Tahiti and the Cooks on the
one hand and the Samoa-Tonga area on the other. The
data are suggestive rather than conclusive.[6] Tupaia referred
to 'O-heavai' which is most likely to have been Savai'i in
Samoa, the alternative being Ha'apai in Tonga, as 'the
father of all islands' (Forster, J. R., 1778: 524), and linguistic and archaeological evidence has confirmed Samoa as
the place of origin of the Eastern Polynesians (Green, 1966:
7-38; Emory, 1928, 1963; Pawley, 1966; Elbert, 1953; Suggs,
1961 a and b). Western Polynesian stories of one-time
sporadic links with the east have been mentioned in n.6
in the previous chapter, and Elliott (pers. comm., 1969)
quotes a specific tradition told him by High Chief Tufele
Fau'oga, former district governor of Manua, of there
having been voyaging contact between the Samoan Manua
and Tahiti.

On grounds, then, of maritime technology and rather less
reliable tradition, the most likely identification of Tupaia's
'Manua' would appear to be in Samoa.[7]

Two important questions arise out of the wide range of
Tahitian geography. How did they learn so much? Secondly, had their voyaging sphere contracted since earlier times?

On the first point, the issue is, of course, whether it was
accidental or deliberate contacts that played the major (not
the sole) part in supplying the Tahitians with their information. The great majority of accidental drifts have been
in an east to west direction, that is *from* Tahiti *towards*

---

[6] One should be wary of interpreting geographical contact traditions
too literally because of the readiness with which Polynesians took passage
on European ships (see Sharp, 1963: 86; Dening, 1963: 136n. 2). There
were even two Tahitians who served (in the British ranks) at Waterloo
(Tagart, 1832: 284-92).

[7] Lewthwaite (1970a: 17, 18), after thoroughly reviewing the evidence, also inclines towards this view.

Tonga, and only two have been reported from Western to Eastern Polynesia (Dening, 1963: 129, 130). Because of the overwhelmingly westward movement of involuntary voyagers, the Tongans stood to profit more in terms of data about other lands than did the Tahitians (Dening, 1963: 103). Yet though the Tongans were the more active seafarers in Cook's time, their horizons were restricted by comparison with their Eastern Polynesian contemporaries, of whom they seem to have been relatively ignorant, whereas the Tahitians undoubtedly knew a good deal about the Tongans' sphere. Should accidental voyagers have contributed the greater part of what the two sections of Polynesia knew of each other, we should have expected the situation to have been the reverse of what it actually was, and for the Tongans to have had the greater geographical awareness.

A rather more general consideration is that it is no easy matter to maintain a sense of location during a thousand miles of drifting, and one hesitates to postulate the plethora of expertly orientated accidents that would be required to account for Tupaia's very comprehensive knowledge. Nor would there be any motive for keeping such haphazard data in memory if it did not serve, in some measure, the purposes of voyaging. All available evidence would seem to point, therefore, towards Tupaia's data mainly reflecting information gained by earlier seafarers whose wanderings came into the many categories discussed in the previous chapter.

This brings us to the second question, the possibility of Tahitian voyaging having formerly been more extensive. Among suggestive pointers are the Rarotonga-Raiatea separation myth, and Tupaia's statement that his father had known more islands to the southward than he did. It is hard to conclude otherwise than in the affirmative.[8]

---

[8] The absence (or loss) of Tahitian traditions of contact with Hawaii and New Zealand helps neither to confirm nor to refute this conclusion, for it can equally be interpreted to mean that these lands were colonised by one-way voyagers who never returned or that such long-abandoned distant voyages had been forgotten.

Neither are language differences any indication of physical isolation. For instance, the language of Fenualoa in the Santa Cruz Reef Islands is a non-Austronesian one (Davenport, 1964a; Laycock, pers. comm., 1971), while on Nufilole, which is joined to it by a drying reef and

WESTERN POLYNESIAN SETTLEMENT OF THE MARQUESAS

Archaeological excavation at Nuku Hiva in the Marquesas has shown that the island was settled by Western Polynesians very early in the Christian era (Suggs, 1961a and b), well before the colonisation of Tahiti, which, of course, is very much nearer Samoa. This unexpected finding lends support to the previously neglected tradition of the Marquesans that their homeland was Vava'u (Porter, 1822: 134). Linguistic evidence confirms the Western Polynesian origin of the Marquesans, though it was from Samoic, rather than Tongic, that their language developed (Green, 1966: 7-38; Pawley, 1966: 39-64). This raises the puzzling problem of how Tahiti, 1000 miles east of Samoa, could have been missed by voyagers who succeeded in reaching Nuku Hiva, which is 2000 miles east, and to windward of, the Samoan island of Upolu. Even supposing 25 miles a day to have been made good against the strong trades and the contrary current of this part of the Pacific (an over optimistic assumption), the voyage would still have taken 80 days, so would have been impossible without staging.[9]

A contrary (west-south-west going) current of 5-15 miles per day is fairly uniform over the whole seaway. In summer prolonged calms and occasional westerlies may be encountered as far east as Manihiki, but thereafter in this latitude, for 1200 miles, the south-east trades blow continuously all the year round, unbroken by any west winds at all, and only altering direction between south-east and north-east (see Routeing Charts, 5128 (1-12)). The probability would be that, beyond Manihiki, an eastbound canoe, close-hauled on the starboard tack, would be forced north-eastward towards the Line Islands.

Assuming the wind pattern to have been the same in the distant past as it is today, an accidental drift from Samoa or one of the atolls to the eastward to the Marquesas

---

shares intimate trade and family connections, a Polynesian language is spoken. It is equally clear that the languages of Europe have developed primarily in response to cultural and historical factors, rather than geographical isolation.

[9] We are referring to the shortest route, which runs north of Tahiti. To bypass Tahiti on the south would entail a very much longer voyage.

would be well nigh impossible. The alternative is that the settlers pressed stubbornly to windward, moving from atoll to atoll. Such persistence seems most improbable in the absence of a known geographical objective, the one-way migrations to ill-defined goals of which we have record being all down-wind. The only conceivable motive that would be strong enough would be if Tahiti, Raiatea, or Borabora had earlier been sighted by some sea rover, for it would then be known with absolute certainty that a high fertile island did exist somewhere in the direction whence the trade wind blew. Barren atolls would be necessary stepping stones but obviously not the sought-for goal. The south-east prevailing wind would tend to push a canoe northward so that it might all too readily bypass Tahiti and continue eastward on its quest for a new Vava'u. Naturally, any such sequence could well have involved numerous canoes and taken place over a period of many years or even generations.

Some indirect support for our surmise comes from the discovery of stonework of Tongan type on Fanning Island, one of the Line Islands (Emory, 1934: 14, 15, 16). These, it is true, were sixteenth-century structures, 1300 years later than the initial Marquesan colonisation, but they bear eloquent witness to exceedingly deep Western Polynesian penetration in this most unfavourable direction—which has not, incidentally, been preserved in Tongan story.

The computer analyses of Levison *et al.* have been noted in chapter 1 (Levison, Ward and Webb, 1971; Ward, G., pers. comm., 1971). As well as drifts they simulated purposeful voyages. Starting out from Samoa and sailing a preferred course due east, even assuming the canoe to be capable of laying no nearer than 90° off the wind, 31 per cent of voyagers reached the Northern Cooks, 12 per cent the southern Line Islands and nearly 7 per cent the Marquesas. No drifts at all reached the Marquesas and a negligible number the Cooks.

Finally there is a legend told by Ve'eto to his grandson Ve'ehala, which may have originated in an attempt to explain the name of the Marquesan island Nuku Hiva, or alternatively, could represent a genuine memory of events long past. According to this story some people of Vava'u set off in search of a new home. In the course of their quest they stopped at eight islands before coming eventually to Nuku Hiva, which means the 'Ninth Island'. The return voyage, which would have been necessary if tidings of the settlement ever got back to Tonga, would have been relatively easy, whether by intent or under stress of weather.

This speculative reconstruction has been advanced as an exercise in the application of navigational data. It shows how, within the limitations imposed by indigenous marine technology and wind and sea conditions, the settlement of the Marquesas *could have* occurred. Further evidence gleaned from other disciplines, notably archaeology, would be needed to change this possibility into either probability or refutation.

TAHITI-HAWAII VOYAGE

The 2220-mile route lies across the ocean currents and across the wind, so that it is hardly possible that any combination of circumstances could arise to drift a canoe either way between the archipelagos. We are left with the alternatives of a random one-way voyage or of some far-ranging wanderer happening upon Hawaii and returning home with the information on courses and conditions required to initiate planned contact. In favour of the latter hypothesis is the circumstance that it is in precisely this cross-wind direction that an explorer would choose to sail, so as to penetrate far into the unknown while, at the same time, being sure of a fair beam wind to speed his return.

Finney (1967: 152-61) has analysed the sailing conditions for the voyage in the context of the prevailing winds and currents and his own experiments with a replica of a Hawaiian double canoe. He concludes that two-way voyaging would be practicable enough.

There is no need to recapitulate Finney's detailed analysis here. Suffice it to say that the wind and current zones involved are exactly the same as those extending some 840 miles from south to north through the, until recently, well travelled Carolinian voyaging sphere, between Kapingamarangi and the Marianas, with additional much longer stretches across the steady trades with their relatively uniform and predictable currents. The equatorial counter current, the only major Pacific stream whose general direction cannot be deduced from the prevailing wind (pp. 101-4), would be crossed, just as it is in the Marshalls' and Carolines' seaways. Its only effect in practice, however, would be to give a welcome boost to windward, so rendering landfall more certain on either extensive archipelago— incomparably better targets, incidentally, than anything the Carolines, Marshalls, or Marianas have to offer.

The arc of sight landfall on the high Hawaiian islands east of Kauai is itself 10°, and a conservative 'expansion' would take in the line of islands, reefs, shoals, bird zones, and wave phenomena that extends at least to Lisianski Island and provides an expanded arc of 20°. The sight ranges and the bird zones of the Tahitian and Tuamotuan archipelagos very nearly overlap when approached from the direction of Hawaii. Their combined expanded arc is 17°.

The courses in both directions are roughly north-south, though since Tahiti is a little east of Hawaii, a southbound vessel would have to sail a little closer to the wind than one heading northward. But in neither case would it be necessary to point closer to the wind than is customary in sailing sea-going canoes in Oceania. Finney (1967: 158), basing his conclusions on the performance of his Hawaiian double canoe, opines that return voyages 'would appear to be within the capabilities of the Polynesian double canoe'. Yet his was a round-bottomed specialised coastal craft, much less efficient to windward than the classical Polynesian voyaging types.

The expanse between Hawaii and Tahiti is not unbroken. The uninhabited Line Islands, some of which bear traces of former Polynesian occupation (Emory: 1934), lie along or to leeward of the track. Zenith (latitude) stars seem to have been remembered in a navigational context in Hawaii (see pp. 238-9) and we saw on pp. 239-40 that certain zenith stars, which would be particularly useful for estimating progress along this lengthy route, and as guides to islands of refuge lying conveniently down-wind, had a significant place in Tahitian cosmogony. Three of the Line Islands have their corresponding 'star pillars'.[10]

A north-bound canoe will pass between Flint, Caroline, and Vostok Islands, 400-450 miles, and near Filippo Reef, about 700, from Tahiti. Some 800 miles from the start first Starbuck then Malden Island will be left to leeward.[11] After 1200 miles the vessel will begin to come abreast of the chain of Christmas, Fanning, Washington, and Palmyra Islands and Kingman Reef, which are between 200 and 300 miles down-wind.

As voyages go in Oceania, especially long ones, the Tahiti-Hawaii passage, in either direction, is clearly not very difficult navigationally, being easier, for example, than that between the Carolines and Saipan. A Tahitian *pahi* would be more than equal to the voyage in terms of speed, windward ability, strength, and food storage capacity. Even allowing for gale force exacerbations in the north-east trades and for equatorial calms, it should average at least 80-100 miles a day, and so complete the journey in three to four weeks.

The next question is, naturally, whether there is any evidence to suggest that voyages in both directions ever did take place. Finney (1967: 152) refers to 'archeological, linguistic and traditional evidence indicating a prolonged relationship between these two areas occurring between the 12th and 14th centuries A.D.'. Fornander (1880: 6-58) and Buck (1959: 260, 262) give a number of Hawaiian legends of two-way contact with Tahiti.[12] The existence of such a substantial volume of tradition,

---

[10] The Tahitian 'star pillars' whose declinations correspond to the latitudes of the Line Islands are:

Star	Dec. 1000 A.D.	Island	Latitude
Spica	5°46′S.	Starbuck	5°40′S.
Alphard	4°41′S.	Malden	4°20′S.
Procyon	7°15′N.	North of Kingman Reef	6°30′N.
Betelgeuse	6°38′N.	Kingman Reef	6°30′N.

[11] Eastern Polynesian ruins similar to those on Raivavae, south of Tahiti, have been found on Malden (Emory, 1934: 1-4, 37-40).

[12] Fornander (1880: 30) points out that the Hawaiian word *Kahiki* means any island outside the home archipelago. However, since it is very unlikely that the Hawaiians could have visited any other island than Tahiti (save for the Line atolls), *Kahiki*, in pre-contact times, seems likely to have referred to the geographical Tahiti.

coupled with Finney's demonstration of the feasibility of the route, provides strong support for the supposition that Tahiti and Hawaii were, in fact, for some time in communication with each other.

The original settlement of Hawaii is now known to have come from the Marquesas (Emory, 1963; Emory and Sinoto, 1965; Green, 1966; Sinoto, 1962). The Tahitians arrived only several centuries later. When we consider the conditions of Marquesan-Hawaiian voyaging, we find them to be very different from those of the Tahitian-Hawaiian seaway. Colonisation from the Marquesas must, as Finney (1967: 155, 156, 161) points out, have of necessity been a one-way venture, because direct return to the Marquesas against strong steady winds and current would have been virtually impossible for any type of Polynesian voyaging vessel. The only practicable way of reaching the Marquesas from Hawaii would have been to head south to Tahiti-Tuamotus and then north-eastward towards the Marquesas—a laborious undertaking, which one would hesitate to postulate without some confirmatory evidence.

EASTERN POLYNESIA-NEW ZEALAND

The south-east Trades prevail over the tropical portion of the route, where they are interrupted every week or so by westerlies of brief duration. The remainder of the course, which passes close east of the uninhabited Kermadec Islands, lies through a zone of variables wherein easterlies usually predominate in summer. The current sets west-south-westward in the Trades; further south it is weak and variable (see p. 101 and Lewis, 1967: 274-85). Tradition has it that canoes bound south-west for New Zealand staged at Rarotonga in the Cook Islands, which has cultural affinities with it, and would provide a convenient stepping stone (Buck, 1952: 37, 38). As we have seen, Rarotonga was formerly within the Tahitian sphere. Its distance from New Zealand is some 1600 miles. The sight landfall arc is 15°, so that navigationally this voyage, despite its length, would be very much easier than Hipour's to the Marianas. Moreover, the sea conditions would be much more kindly.

The return passage to Eastern Polynesia would be a

much more difficult proposition.[13] The north-east course would present no difficulties through the variables, though calms and fickle winds would be likely to cause delays. But a canoe would have to sail very hard on the wind when it reached the trade wind belt in order to make further easting. The Cooks offer only a 7° landfall arc (about the same as Kapingamarangi from Pulusuk) with the individual Tubuai islands lying further east. The distance to the Cooks is 1600-1700 miles depending upon which part of the group landfall is made.

Should the Cooks be missed, the distance is substantially increased to 2100 miles or more, but the completely overlapping Tahitian and Tuamotuan 'screens' that lie behind form an expanded arc of 16°. Assuming only 80 miles a day to be the average distance made good (on account of variables and head winds), a *pahi* should be in the neighbourhood of the Tahiti group four weeks after leaving New Zealand. The landfall being an 'expanded' one on the scattered islands of one of the target archipelagos, several days would most likely be occupied in casting about in search of land. There would be no difficulty, however, in provisioning such a planned enterprise for forty days (see pp. 274-5).

A reasonable conclusion would be, I think, that this return voyage would be difficult navigationally and subject to the mischance of unseasonably prolonged head winds. It would be risky but far from impracticable.[14] This seems a

---

[13] As mentioned on p. 4 voyages to New Zealand cannot have been consciously navigated unless someone had returned after discovering New Zealand to give the necessary sailing directions to the Tahitians (or Rarotongans).

[14] There is one item of archaeological evidence suggestive of early New Zealand Maoris having made voyages to the Cook Islands.

Duff (1956), writing of the original New Zealand Maoris (Moa-Hunters), describes the rich diversity of Moa-Hunter adze forms that were excavated mainly from a site in Wairau in the northern South Island. These included numerous late Moa-Hunter adzes labelled Type 1A with lugs. A few examples of this very characteristic late Moa-Hunter adze were also found in the Southern and Northern Cook Islands.

It was assumed by Duff at the time that these assorted adze types had been developed in some as yet unidentified site in East Central Polynesia (1956: fig. 32, 146-70). However, despite fifteen years intensive archaeological search, the anticipated site evidence in tropical Eastern Polynesia has not come to light. Groube, therefore (pers. comm., 1971), points to the distinct possibility on present evidence that the Type 1A adzes with lugs were developed in New Zealand and carried thence to the Cook Islands in the late Moa-Hunter period.

case where the information obtainable by a non-instrumental voyage in a *pahi* replica would pay handsome dividends.

EASTER ISLAND

This isolated target could theoretically be reached by sailing east from the Tuamotus or Mangareva beneath the appropriate zenith (latitude) star. However, there is no evidence at all that the Polynesians ever did indulge in long-distance latitude sailing in this manner. Unless facts to the contrary should come to light, therefore, deliberate navigation to Easter Island would seem highly improbable and settlement must needs have been fortuitous. One-way voyages *from* Easter Island to the Tuamotus and Tahiti, on the contrary, are practicable, and several have been made without charts or instruments in recent times (Lewis, 1967: 226, 227). But these were one-way voyages. Prehistoric counterparts of such adventurers would have been precluded by the limitations of their navigational technology from returning home to Easter Island, so no two-way intercourse could have developed.

THE ANCIENT ART IN PERSPECTIVE

Highly organised systems of complex navigational lore existed throughout Oceania in pre-European times. The degree of magico-religious significance and associated secrecy varied, but all embodied precise lists of star courses, concepts of orientation, and voluminous information on land signs and seaway conditions. They were 'closed' mental concepts but their application demanded not only memorisation, but also patient and discriminating observation of natural signs. Training was rigorous and prolonged over many years and it involved instruction both ashore and afloat.

Particular ideas or techniques were favoured in different archipelagos in accordance with local geographical and social factors, but as far as can be determined by haphazardly recorded items of information and what is still remembered, methods were surprisingly homogeneous. So much was this the case that we would overstep the evidence by speaking of separate or typical Polynesian and Micronesian 'systems'. Navigation seems to have been equally efficient in both areas and the techniques were very often identical.

The advent of Europeans seems to have led very quickly to the falling into disuse and virtual disappearance of the bulk of the more sophisticated and esoteric concepts —and of the great deep-sea canoes. The Western ships that were beginning to criss-cross the Pacific soon brought knowledge of the existence and location of new or forgotten islands and the eventual advent of peace in some instances stimulated voyaging. The general tendency, however, was for long-distance voyaging rapidly to decline and for later generations to be increasingly ill-informed by either Western or indigenous standards. Systematic instruction and the oral transmission of exact information broke down with the adoption of alien religion and technology, the old navigational concepts tending to be replaced rather than modified.

Nevertheless, some fragments of the old lore did persist, largely unsuspected by the European, for want of anyone asking the appropriate questions. Preservation seems to have depended in the main on the following factors: retention of a social structure in which voyaging remained an integral part, as in the Central Carolines; remoteness and isolation, of which Tikopia, Ninigo, and the Santa Cruz Reef Islands are examples; incompatability between concepts like charts and 'moving' reference (*etak*) islands; navigational utilisation of phenomena such as deep phosphorescence and land loom, that have no place among Western maritime arts.

When the methods of indigenous navigation come to be tested at sea they are seen to be remarkably efficient and practical. The results attainable by the techniques we have been considering demonstrate how it was possible to accomplish formidable journeys. They explain equally the confidence of storm-driven islanders in retaining their bearings and locating land. It follows that the barriers which so often inhibited intercourse between navigationally accessible islands must have been essentially of a cultural nature.

It is all too easy to underestimate Polynesian and Micronesian methods, perhaps because the Western scientifically conditioned mind finds difficulty in grasping the concepts involved and in appreciating the degree of precision attainable. It is hoped that this study will go some way towards demonstrating the navigational feasibility of fairly intensive inter-island contact over considerable stretches of ocean.

A letter dictated by Tevake came to me early in 1970. It concluded with these words: 'Now I am still alive. But you will meet me one day or not? Because I am getting old'. Then in November the Santa Cruz District Officer wrote:

You will be sorry to hear that Tevake was lost at sea over three months ago while on a lone voyage from the Reefs to Santa Cruz. News did not reach me until he had been missing for two weeks and by that time it was too late for a search to be of much use. Shipping and all outlying islands were alerted but no trace was ever found.

Subsequent inquiries have shown that Tevake made something in the nature of a formal farewell before his departure from Nufilole and it would seem that either he had a premonition of disaster or, more likely, that he simply paddled out to sea in the manner of the Tikopians and did not intend to arrive. A voyage from the Reefs to Santa Cruz would be nothing to a seaman of his calibre.

An era of Polynesian voyaging has closed with his passing.

Variations of star bearings with latitude

V. Radhakrishnan

The formula relating to the declination, azimuth, and latitude for rising and setting objects (i.e. for zero altitude) is a simple one:

$$\cos Rz = \sin d / \cos L$$

where Rz is the azimuth at rising, d is the declination of the object and L is the latitude of the observer. Setting azimuths (Sz) are given simply by $Sz = (360° - Rz)$.

This simple equation takes care of both positive and negative declinations and north and south latitudes. Inspection of the equation shows at once that:

1. If the declination is zero the azimuth is always 90° (rises due east) for observers at all latitudes.

2. If the observer is on the equator (L = 0) the azimuth is given by (Rz = 90 — d); e.g. a star with north declination 37° will rise at an azimuth of (90° — 37°) = 53°.

3. Changing the sign of the declination from positive to negative changes the azimuth to (180° — Rz): e.g. if a star of declination +5° rises at an azimuth of 83° for an observer at a certain latitude, then a star with declination —5° will rise at (180° — 83°) = 97° for the same observer.

These three facts are more or less obvious. What to me was an astonishing discovery from the equation was the fact that the sign of the latitude did *not* matter. The cosine of an angle is independent of the sign of the angle. In other words, if a given star rises at a certain azimuth from say north latitude 31°, then it will rise at exactly the same azimuth as seen from south latitude 31°. Of course, the declination of the star must be such that it can be seen rising and setting from a latitude of 31°. In the above example this means that the declination must be less than (90° — 31° = 59°). A limiting case is for a declination of +59° when the star will be seen from north lati-

---

Dr V. Radhakrishnan is a radio astronomer who, until May 1971, was a principal research scientist at the CSIRO Radiophysics Division in Sydney. He is also an extremely competent ocean-going yachtmaster and practical small ship navigator. We first met in 1965 in Tahiti, where *Rehu Moana* crossed the track of Dr Radhakrishnan's trimaran *Cygnus A*, in which, with two companions, he was *en route* from England to Australia. It is a tribute to his seamanship and ability as a navigator that, despite periods of more than usually adverse weather, he accomplished this major voyage without mishap.

tude 31° to set momentarily at 0° azimuth only to rise again immediately at the same point on the horizon. From south latitude 31° it will be seen to rise momentarily at 0° azimuth only to set again immediately where it rose. Vice versa for the other limiting case of declination —59°.

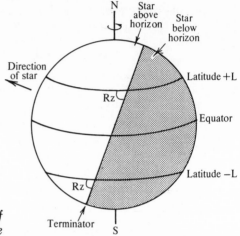

Fig. 60   Variation of azimuth with latitude

A simple pictorial proof of the remarkable fact that the rising (or setting) azimuths of a given star are independent of the sign of the observer's latitude is given in fig. 60. For a star of arbitrary declination one can at any given instant of time draw an imaginary line around the earth called a terminator separating the halves of the earth from where the star is either visible above the horizon or not visible because it is below. As the earth rotates about its north-south axis the terminator continually slides around its surface. Points which lie on this terminator therefore represent places where at that instant of time the star is either rising or setting. The azimuth of the star at that instant is the angle between the direction of north and that of the star. Since the parallel of latitude at that place is perpendicular to the direction of north and the terminator is perpendicular to the direction of the star, the azimuth is equal to the angle between the parallel of latitude and the terminator. The angles made by the terminator with two parallels of latitude equally spaced north and south of the equator are indicated in fig. 60. Since the terminator must be a great circle it is obvious from the figure that the two angles in question must be equal by symmetry.

The significance of the equivalence of north and south latitudes from the point of view of this discussion is that the azimuth (at rising or setting) of a given star changes with latitude in the following way. As you move towards the equator from wherever you are the rate of change of azimuth with latitude decreases as you approach the equator; the rate of change vanishes as you cross the equator after which it changes sign and builds up again as you move away from the equator on the other side. The same value of azimuth is reached when you are as far on the other side of the equator as you

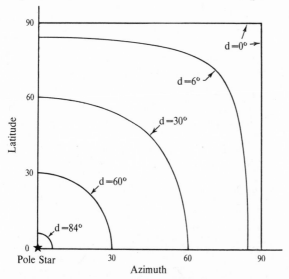

Fig. 61   *The dependence of the azimuth at rising of a celestial object as a function of the latitude of the observer. Each curve corresponds to an object of declination indicated on the figure and shows the azimuth at rising of the object at different latitudes. Note that as the declination d increases from 0° to 90° the range of latitudes over which the object will cut the horizon decreases from 90° to 0°. In the limiting case when d = 90° (Pole Star), it can be seen on the horizon from only one latitude namely 0° (equator) and its azimuth will always be 0° (due north); the other limiting case is for an object of declination 0°; such an object can be seen rising due east (90°) from all latitudes except for an observer at the pole who will see it grazing the horizon and having all possible azimuths.*

were on the one side when you started. By the same token, if you had started from the equator and moved away from it, the rate of change of azimuth with latitude would have increased with every mile you travelled, getting out of hand as you approached the latitude past which the star either never rises or never sets (latitude = ±90°—absolute value of declination). Figure 61 shows how the azimuth (rising) varies with latitude of observer for stars of declination 0°, 6°, 30°, 60°, and 90°. The shape of the curves shows how favourably situated the Polynesians were for practising their system.

The latitude of an observer who sees an object of given declination rising at a given azimuth

Azimuth	Declination = 6	12	18	24	30	36	42	48	54	60	66	72	78	84	90
0	84.0	78.0	72.0	66.0	60.0	54.0	48.0	42.0	36.0	30.0	24.0	18.0	12.0	6.0	0
3	84.0	78.0	72.0	66.0	60.0	53.9	47.9	41.9	35.9	29.9	23.8	17.8	11.6	5.2	
6	84.0	77.9	71.9	65.9	59.8	53.8	47.7	41.6	35.6	29.4	23.3	17.0	10.4	0.0	
9	83.9	77.8	71.8	65.7	59.6	53.5	47.4	41.2	35.0	28.7	22.3	15.7	8.0		
12	83.9	77.7	71.6	65.4	59.3	53.1	46.8	40.6	34.2	27.7	20.9	13.5	0.0		
15	83.8	77.6	71.3	65.1	58.8	52.5	46.2	39.7	33.1	26.3	19.0	10.1			
18	83.7	77.4	71.0	64.7	58.3	51.8	45.3	38.6	31.7	24.4	16.1	0.0			
21	83.6	77.1	70.7	64.2	57.6	51.0	44.2	37.2	29.9	21.9	11.9				
24	83.4	76.8	70.2	63.6	56.8	50.0	42.9	35.6	27.7	18.6	0.0				
27	83.3	76.5	69.7	62.8	55.9	48.7	41.3	33.5	24.8	13.6					
30	83.1	76.1	69.1	62.0	54.7	47.3	39.4	30.9	20.9	0.0					
33	82.8	75.6	68.4	61.0	53.4	45.5	37.1	27.6	15.3						
36	82.6	75.1	67.5	59.8	51.8	43.4	34.2	23.3	0.0						
39	82.3	74.5	66.6	58.4	50.0	40.9	30.6	17.0							
42	81.9	73.8	65.4	56.8	47.7	37.7	25.8	0.0							
45	81.5	72.9	64.1	54.9	45.0	33.8	18.9								
48	81.0	71.9	62.5	52.6	41.6	28.5	0.0								
51	80.4	70.7	60.6	49.7	37.4	20.9									
54	79.8	69.3	58.3	46.2	31.7	0.0									
57	78.9	67.6	55.4	41.7	23.4										
60	77.9	65.4	51.8	35.6	0.0										
63	76.7	62.7	47.1	26.4											
66	75.1	59.3	40.6	0.0											
69	73.0	54.5	30.4												
72	70.2	47.7	0.0												
75	66.2	36.6													
78	59.8	0.0													
81	48.1														
84	0.0														
87															
90															

The table of figures gives the same information in a different manner. A computer program was used to calculate the latitude at which a star of given declination will have a given azimuth at rising. I have chosen the steps of azimuth values to be 3° to accord with the criterion of steering accuracy for Islanders' craft. The difference between any two successive numbers in a column indicates the distance (in latitude) one may travel before exceeding the 3° error margin when using a steering star of declination given at the head of the column; e.g., if one started at latitude 30° (north or south) and if one were steering by a star of declination 18°, then one could go 600 nautical miles to latitude 40° or 1800 nautical miles to the equator before the azimuth of the star changed by 3° from 69° to 66° or 72° respectively. In fact, one could go 4200 miles to a latitude of 40° on the other side of the equator before the 3° margin was exceeded. The zeros at the bottom of all the columns refer to the equator (latitude = 0) and the numbers immediately above the zeros are the latitudes where the azimuth at rising has changed by 3° from the equatorial value.

ON USING THE ZENITH STAR OF AN ISLAND TO STEER TOWARDS IT

Let O be an observer trying to reach an island I by steering towards S, the known zenith star for the island. When the star is at its highest point in the sky as seen by O it must by definition be on the N-S meridian for O. The error in steering for the island will be ø degrees where ø is the bearing of the island for the observer O. The error is therefore O° if the observer is due north or south of the island, 90° if due east or west and in between for other angles. (See fig. 62.)

Fig. 62
Steering by zenith star

Directional marks ashore

Sighting stones seem to have been used to align canoes on taking departure in the same manner as natural landmarks, and probably also for recording and teaching star courses.

The ones so far reported have been on Niuafo'ou in Tonga and on Arorae and Butaritari, respectively the southernmost and almost the northernmost of the Gilberts.

THE STONES OF ARORAE, GILBERT ISLANDS

Te Atibu ni Borau, 'The Stones for Voyaging', stand near the north-western point of Arorae. They are mostly grouped in threes in the manner shown to indicate the bearings of islands in the Southern Gilberts and Banaba (Ocean Island) with which the Gilbertese were once in contact (Maude, 1932: 265, 267). Sighting along the stones was possible in either direction but generally appears to have been towards the single marker.

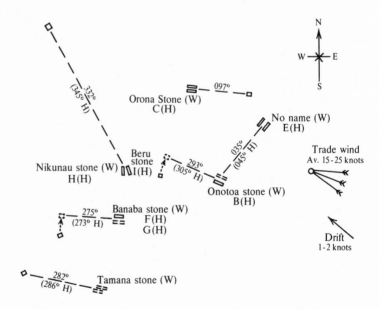

Fig. 63 Te Atibu ni Borau *(the navigation stones), Arorae Island. (After V. Ward, pers. comm., 1969). Names of stones from Ward = W, letter of identification from Hilder = H. Bearings as given by Ward, Hilder's bearings in parentheses. All bearings true. Distances: Tamana, 50 miles; Banaba, 448 miles; Nikunau, 75 miles; Beru, 87 miles; Onotoa, 85 miles.*

H. E. Maude, later Resident Commissioner, sketched the stones in 1933, but the first full description of them was made in 1946 by Captain E. V. Ward, author of the Sailing Directions for the Gilbert and Ellice Islands (Ward, E. V., 1967). Unfortunately his paper on Arorae was never published, but he has been generous enough to supply me with the scale plan that he plotted with prismatic compass and tape together with his observations (referred to as Ward, pers. comm., 1969). 'There were 13 stones (not counting the entrance stone), 11 of which were in their original place. The old positions of two of the Onotoa stones and one of the Banaba stones could still be seen', he writes. The main published accounts are by Captain Brett Hilder, who visited Arorae in 1957, by which time there were only eight stones left—again excluding the entrance stone (Hilder: 1959, 1963a and b).

The atoll of Arorae is elevated no more than 15 feet above sea level though its palms rise to 75 feet. Ward describes the stones as 'flat slabs of coral about five feet by four feet and about six inches thick. They are set on edge and secured about the base by paving. They are untrimmed and in the natural shape and texture.'

Besides having the advantage of more nearly intact material, Ward was able to converse with his informants in Gilbertese, whereas Hilder's guide 'spoke about ten words of English', equivalent, Hilder adds, to his own command of Gilbertese (1963a; 86). In places where the two accounts differ I have therefore taken Ward's to be the more definitive. To supplement these sources we have a commentary by Captain Douglas, Marine Superintendent, Honiara, who was fifteen years in the Gilberts and is another Gilbertese speaker (pers. comm., 1968), and data contributed by the navigators Teeta and Abera and by three elders of Nikunau.

One set of stones whose name cannot be accepted is that named by Ward 'Orana'. Orana or Hull Island is in the formerly uninhabited Phoenix group, of whose very existence the pre-contact Gilbertese were ignorant (Maude, pers. comm., 1970). Furthermore the name 'Orana' was bestowed only in 1938 by a party of which Maude himself was a member. How this name came to be applied then is a mystery for it obviously can be no older than that date. The stones do point in the general direction of the Phoenix group, but when sighted in the opposite direction they indicate a bearing of 277°True, or exactly towards Tamana 50 miles away. It is possible therefore that they comprised a second set of marks for Tamana, and perhaps it is significant that the navigator Teeta did tell me that there were two sets for that island.

Hilder remarks on the bearings being 'all about five degrees out' in a windward direction (1963a: 87). This, however, can be accepted only with reservations. For instance Hilder gives a bearing of 345° for stones 'H' and 'I' (1963a: fig. 1, 85) which he regards as both being Nikunau ones. On his fig. 2 (1963a: 87) this bearing is shown as east of Nikunau, whereas in fact it points directly towards the island's western shore as measured in Admiralty Chart 731. In Ward's plan, on the other hand, stone 'I' is identified as the Beru stone and the bearing is given as 332°, not 345°. This does lead about 5° up-wind (east) of Beru. With Onotoa the position is reversed, Hilder's 305° line leading to the east of the island and Ward's 293° to the south-west. The Tamana bearings as recorded by both observers (282° Ward, 286° Hilder) point north-east of the island.

When we come to consider the origin and purpose of the stones we find only too many traditions—most of them incompatible. In spite of this plethora there are none which shed any light on the origin of the stones (Hilder, 1963a: 84). Nevertheless extant tradition is not without interest.

Ward's informant, who was an old man in 1946, said that his father had known how to use the stones, which gave courses that allowed for set and drift. We have seen above that this proposition is suspect, some of the courses being geographically direct if anything. He also claimed his grandfather as the *tia borau* who had laid them (pers. comm., 1970).

Teitema, Douglas's informant, who was aged about 72 when questioned in 1961, stated that 'the stones were set up in his father's lifetime by a man named Tamake from Tamana, who married a Tamana woman and settled in Arorae. Tamake used the stones for frequent voyages to Tamana'. Teitema makes the surprising statement that the stones labelled 'E' by Hilder and 'No Name' by Ward, which puzzled both commentators by not pointing anywhere, had been 'set up in Teitema's own lifetime by the master of the *John Williams*' (Douglas, pers. comm., 1969).

The navigator Teeta, who comes from Kuria much further north, told me that the Arorae stones pointed towards Tamana (two sets) and to Nikunau, and had been put up 'long before the Europeans came'. Yet another tradition was given by Abera. The stones had been erected, he said, by Tabukirake, a great Nikunau fisherman, who had lived a very long time ago, and who had so detested working on land that he preferred to sail all the way to Arorae to steal *babai* (a root vegetable).

An item added by three Nikunau elders is in line with ancient Gilbertese sailing directions that stress the existence of *betia* or 'sea marks' (Grimble, n.d.(a)). The alternative name for the Nikunau stone on Arorae (which incidentally they said had been erected long ago by one Marikina) was *Teatibunikamamate* or the 'Dead Stone'. It was so named because the direct course it showed was barred by a turbulent meeting of currents called *Rin Teaira* which would swamp any canoe that attempted to pass. It was therefore necessary, they said, to sail west of this unusually lethal *betia*, and only when safely past it to turn eastward.

Can anything of value be gleaned from these patently contradictory stories that obviously cannot be accepted at their face value? I think they may indirectly indicate certain probabilities. In the first place their very variety and incompatibility suggests that the stones were actually erected a long time ago, though it seems likely that some might have been re-erected and re-positioned at different periods since, to suit the needs of particular seafarers. Secondly, the use of some of them as marks for current voyaging is mentioned. Lastly the tale of the 'Dead Stone' may echo some more remote geographical/astronomical function than that of immediate departure marks.

As objects by which to take back bearings, the stones suffer the disadvantage of being visible from at best 4 miles out at sea. Hilder suggests that temporary beacons might have been erected above them (1963a: 86) and also points out that the coastline has advanced seaward (1963a: 87). If one adds the possibility of each voyager selecting palms in line with particular stones, the difficulty in using them for this purpose disappears.

There is no reason to doubt their function as 'transits of the azimuths of certain fixed stars during the Aumaiki or good sailing season' (Ward). Ward goes on to point out that in August Regulus would be in line of transit, low down on the western horizon, of the Tamana stones, that at midnight Arcturus would be almost on the same bearing and that there are similar star correlations with other stones.

But were the stones more than this? Did they record star courses in so permanent a form solely for the use of a single generation of mariners? It seems more likely that, as Hilder says, 'The stones may have been erected to preserve that knowledge [of orally taught star courses] and to help in teaching it. This suggests the existence of a school of navigation at the site' (1963a: 88). There is one piece of data that, while proving nothing, does tend to support Hilder's view. This is the significance of the Banaba stones. Should the name be authentic (and in the case of Orana we have seen one that is not), it implies an astro-geographical bearing rather than a course to be actually sailed, for neither tradition nor navigational feasibility supports the possibility of direct Arorae-Banaba contact.

A migration from Beru in the Gilberts to Banaba is said to have taken place about eleven generations ago (from 1932), and intercourse was kept up with the Gilberts and especially with the island of Beru, apparently during two separate periods (Maude, H. C. and H. E., 1932: 266, 267). Grimble lists among the Gilbertese 'sea marks' one called *Kaibābā*, 'half a day's sail from Banaba (Ocean Island)', where 'the waves are seen to sweep from north to south across the prevailing swell' (Grimble, n.d.(a)).

En route from Beru to Banaba either Nonouti or Tabiteuea would be sighted but from there onwards 274 miles of open sea in the first case, 300 in the second, separate the traveller from his solitary target. Banaba is indeed 280 feet high and two miles across, which means that it would top the horizon 24 miles off when seen from a canoe. The range at which terns and noddies can be relied on to indicate land is only 20 miles, so they would be of little help here. However, brown boobies still breed on Banaba despite the phosphate working (King, 1967: 112) and these birds are quite a different proposition since they are accepted in the Gilberts and Carolines as nearly certain guides up to 30 miles and often much further still (see chap. 8). The voyage from Beru to Banaba, despite favourable wind and current, was obviously a dangerous one (the return was navigationally much easier, being towards an archipelago rather than a single speck of land), so it is no wonder that regular contact came to be abandoned. How much less possible then would have been a far longer hypothetical route from Arorae!

So the Banaba stones on Arorae can only, if genuine, be indicators of a bearing (it is only approximate) that had been worked out from a knowledge of the relative positions of the two islands obtained through voyages from Arorae to Beru and Beru to Banaba. As we saw in chap. 5, this is in accordance with the known capabilities of at least one indigenous orientation system.

We must leave the uncertainties of *te Atibu ni Borau* in this rather unsatisfactory state, with the probabilities being in favour of them having been mnemonic and teaching devices of some antiquity, that were also made use of in various ways and perhaps adapted by later generations of voyagers. The other two sets of directional stones require less detailed discussion.

The Stones of Butaritari   These were seen by Ward, who describes them as 'a group of similar stones [to Arorae] at the northern tip of Namoka islet, Butaritari Atoll' (pers. comm., 1969). Now Namoka lies on the north-east part of the rim of the big atoll, and in plain view 5 miles away to the north is Makin, the last of the Gilberts. Why were the stones set up? Not as guides to Makin certainly, and the rest of the Gilberts are beyond the opposite (southern) segment of Butaritari. The evidence strongly favours Mili, only 165 miles away in the Marshalls.

Butaritari tradition tells of a chief called Rairaueana going to 'Bukiroro' in the Marshall Islands. In the next generation his nephew Kakiaba, also ruling chief of Butaritari, went to the Marshalls (Nakiroro) in his turn (Grimble n.d.(b)). Maude identifies the Marshall island concerned as probably Mili and states that there are further traditions of not infrequent two-way contacts and of chiefs from Butaritari going to rule over Mili (pers. comm., 1969).

There was also a 'sea mark' called *Te maabubu* far to the northward of Butaritari, where 'the voyager runs into a belt of low visibility which indicates he is in the latitude of Taaruti—i.e. Jaluit Island, East Marshalls, about 250 miles north-west of Little Makin—and must run west for two or three days before he can make land' (Grimble, n.d.(c)).[1]

It may be significant that in 1841 Wilkes saw canoes on Butaritari, longer and better built than any in the southern Gilberts, some being nearly 60 feet in length (pp. 74-94). Such large *baurua* (voyaging canoes) would be formidable vessels, seaworthy and very fast, in which the navigationally far from difficult 165 mile voyage from Butaritari to Mili and its neighbours would present few problems.

The fact that I was given a geographically correct star course for the Marshalls by Teeta can be no more than suggestive at such a late date as this (1969). Nevertheless I do not believe that a statement like his should be dismissed out of hand as post-European knowledge. It is very possible that there has been far less contact between the groups recently than there was a century and a half ago, not unduly long for a star course tradition to survive in a simple form. When I questioned Teeta suspiciously about the source of his information, he replied. 'This I had from my grandfather in the *maneaba*', and in answer to a further query, 'Even if I see a chart I wouldn't know what it was all about'.

Fortunately we need not speculate about the direction indicated by this stone 'pointer', for its name means 'Facing Uvea' (Rogers, pers. comm., 1969).[2]

Unlike the sighting stones in Micronesia that we have been considering this Polynesian marker is single. It stands 'in the centre of one old village of Niuafo'ou, about one mile from the northern coast', and is 'a very large basalt stone on edge. . . . Approximate compass bearings along the five foot length of this stone indicate an imaginary course which would take

Hanga'i'Uvea, on Niuafo'ou, Tonga

---

[1] Tradition collected on Butaritari.
[2] This stone was examined in 1968 by the New Zealand anthropologist and ocean yachtsman Garth Rogers, who was then residing on the island. I am indebted to him for the following description contained in a letter to Maude in February 1969 and amplified later when we met on Tongatapu.

a voyager some ten or so miles east [i.e. upwind in the trades]
of 'Uvea some 132 miles distant'. Rogers goes on to say that
the bush is too dense to reveal if there was a second stone on
the coast, but that a pole or a fire would be sufficient to give
an accurate back-sighting. He also mentions that several
Niuafo'ou genealogies record evidence of connections with
Uvea.

Niuafo'ou is the most isolated of the Tongas, lying some
200 miles north-west of the main northern island of Vava'u.
Uvea 130 miles further north was part of what A. C. Reid
(pers. comm., 1969) has aptly referred to as 'Greater Tonga'.
It was the island where the Lomibeau canoe, famous in Tongan
legend, was built at the behest of a young Tui Tonga (Ve'ehala).
It is included as 'Oowaia' in the list of Tongan islands and
others in that neighbourhood given to Cook (Cook and King,
1784: vol. I, 368-9).

There seems no reason to doubt that *Hanga 'i 'Uvea* was
situated on one of the links of the Tongan close-contact voyaging sphere, or that it served a purpose analogous to its
Micronesian counterparts.

Fires Ashore   These very practical night guides to landfall should be
mentioned for the sake of completeness. Akerblom (1968:
50) cites Woodford (1888: 352) on their use to facilitate
passages between Nukufetau and Vaitupu in the Ellice
Islands. These are low atolls some 35 miles apart. Fires
were lit by the Nukufetauans when they wished to visit
their neighbours. When they saw the glow of answering fires
on Vaitupu they made ready and set out the following morning. The Vaitupu beacons were kept burning until the last
canoe had arrived. Although these fires were used as signals,
there is no reason to doubt that guiding belated canoes
towards their destination was one of their purposes.

That the fires had this dual function is suggested by a
report from another pair of islands. Nanumanga and Nanumea
in the Ellice Islands are also 35 miles apart. 'Both islands
being very low, the one is not visible from the other, but the
natives signal across by means of fires at night. . . The journey
is always begun at dusk, so as to avoid paddling in the heat
of the day.' (Becke, 1909: 87.) Setting out at such an hour
the canoes would certainly arrive in darkness, when guide fires
would be welcome.

The practice is also reported from Mauke in the Cook
Islands (Mills, pers. comm., 1965). It is standard procedure on
Puluwat when a canoe is expected from another island after
dark. We ourselves, arriving from Pulusuk in Hipour's canoe,
found the blaze lighted on shore to guide us to be a most convenient landmark.

References

Note: All references cited are included in the list with the addition of some important ones relevant to the subject.

Aea, H., 1948. *The History of Ebon* (*1862*), Hawaiian Historical Society 56th Annual Report, 1947.

Akerblom, K., 1968. *Astronomy and Navigation in Polynesia and Micronesia*, Stockholm Ethnographical Museum, Monograph no. 14.

Alexander, A. B., 1902. *Notes on the Boats, Apparatus and Fishing Methods Employed by the Natives of the South Sea Islands*, U.S. Commission of Fish and Fisheries Report for 1901, pp. 741-829, pls. 30-7. Washington.

Alexander, P. F., 1916. *The Earliest Voyages round the World* (*1519-1617*), Cambridge: Cambridge University Press.

Alkire, W. H., 1965. *Lamotrek Atoll and Inter-island Socio-economic Ties*, Illinois Studies in Anthropology no. 5, Urbana: University of Illinois Press.

——, 1970. 'Systems of Measurement on Woleai Atoll, Caroline Islands', *Anthropos*, vol. 65, 1-73.

Anderson, R. C., 1935. 'The Royalists at Sea, 1651-1653', *Mariner's Mirror*, vol. 21, 61-90.

Baddeley, A. D., 1966. 'Time Estimation at Reduced Body Temperature', *American Journal of Psychology*, vol. 79, 475-9.

Banks, J., 1962. *Endeavour Journal Vol. I, 1768-1771*, J. C. Beaglehole (ed.), Sydney: Angus and Robertson.

Banks, R., and Cappon, D., 1962. *Perceptual and Motor Skills*, London: Penn.

Barton, E. R., 1910. 'The Annual Trading Expedition to the Papuan Gulf', in Seligman, C. G. (ed.), *The Melanesians of British New Guinea*, Cambridge: Cambridge University Press, pp. 96-170.

Beaglehole, E. and Beaglehole, P., 1938. *Ethnology of Pukapuka*, Honolulu: Bishop Museum Bulletin no. 150.

Beaglehole, J. C. (ed.), 1967. *The Journals of Captain James Cook, Third Voyage 1776-1780*, Cambridge: Cambridge University Press, for the Hakluyt Society, vol. III.

——, 1955. *The Journals of Captain James Cook on his Voyages of Discovery*, vol. I, Cambridge: Cambridge University Press, for the Hakluyt Society. Addenda and Corrigenda 1968.

Beattie, H., 1918. 'Traditions and Legends of Southland', *Journal of the Polynesian Society*, vol. 27, no. 107, 137-61.

Becke, L., 1909. *'Neath Austral Skies*, London: John Milne.

Beechey, F. W., 1831. *Narrative of Voyage to Pacific . . . H.M.S. Blossom . . . in the Years 1825-28*, London: Colburn and Bentley, vol. I.

Best, E., 1922. *The Astronomical Knowledge of the Maori*, Wellington: Dominion Museum Monograph no. 3.

Brum, Raymond de (as told to Cynthia R. Olson), 1962. 'Marshallese Navigation', *Micronesian Reporter*, vol. 10, no. 3, 1-10.

Bryan, E. H. Jr, 1964. 'Stick Charts from the Marshall Islands', Honolulu: Pacific Science Information Centre, Bishop Museum, mimeographed.

Buck, P. (Te Rangi Hiroa), 1932. *Ethnology of Manihiki and Rakahanga*, Honolulu: Bishop Museum Bulletin no. 99.

——, 1938a. *Ethnology of Mangareva*, Honolulu: Bishop Museum Bulletin no. 157.

——, 1938b. *Vikings of the Sunrise*, Christchurch: Whitcombe and Tombs.

——, 1952. *The Coming of the Maori*, Wellington: Maori Purposes Fund Board, Whitcombe and Tombs.

Bunton, G. W. and Valier, L. A., 1963. 'Stars Over Paradise', *Pacific Discovery*, vol. 16, no. 6, 2-9.

Burney, J., 1967. *A Chronological History of the Discoveries in the South Seas or Pacific Ocean . . .*, Amsterdam: N. Israel, facs. of the 1803-17 ed. (5 vols.), vol. 5.

Burnett, F., 1910. *Through Tropic Seas*, London: Francis Griffiths.

Burrows, E. G., 1937. *An Ethnology of Uvea (Wallis Is.)*, Honolulu: Bishop Museum Bulletin no. 145.

——, and Spiro, M. E., 1957. *An Atoll Culture: Ethnography of Ifaluk in the Central Carolines*, New Haven, Conn.: Behavior Science Monographs.

Burrows, W., 1923. 'Some Notes and Legends of a South Sea Island (Faka'ofo of the Tokelau or Union Group)', *Journal of the Polynesian Society*, vol. 32, no. 127, 143-73.

Cantova, J. A., 1728. *Edifying and Curious Letters Written about the Foreign Missions*, Collection 18, Paris, Cantova's letter dated March 1722. (Translation Micronesian Seminar, Woodstock College. Reprinted by the Jesuit Bureau, Buffalo.)

Chamisso, A. von, 1907. *Reise um die Welt mit der Romanzoffischen Entdeckungs Expedition in den Jahren 1815-1818 auf der Brig Rurik, Capitän Otto von Kotzebue*, H. Tardel (ed.), vol. 3, pt I: Tagebuch, pt II: Anhang, Leipzig and Vienna.

Child, P., 1960. *The Birds of the Gilbert and Ellice Islands Colony*, Washington: Pacific Science Board, Atoll Research Bulletin no. 74.

Collocott, E. E. V., 1922. 'Tongan Astronomy and Calendar', Honolulu: Bishop Museum Press, *Occasional Papers of the Bishop Museum*, vol. 8, no. 4.

Colony Information Notes, 1970, '42 days on an Open Canoe from the Gilberts to Papua/New Guinea', Tarawa, Gilbert and Ellice Islands Colony, July 1970, p. 3.

Cook, J., 1777. *A Voyage Towards the South Pole and Round the World . . . in the years 1772-5*, London: Strahan and Cadell, vols. I and II.

——, 1893. *Captain Cook's Journal during his First Voyage Round the World (1768-71)*, W. J. L. Wharton (ed.), London: Elliot Stock.

—— and King, J., 1784. *A Voyage to the Pacific Ocean . . . in the years 1776-80*, London: Nicol and Cadell, vols. I and II by Cook, vol. III by King.

Coote, W., 1882. *Wanderings, South and East*, London: Sampson Low.

Corney, B. G. (ed.), 1913-19. *The Quest and Occupation of Tahiti by Emissaries of Spain during the Years 1772-6* (3 vols.), London: Hakluyt Society.

Couper, A. D., 1968. 'Marine Casualties in the Pacific Islands and the Economic Consequences', *Journal of the Institute of Navigation* (London), vol. 21, no. 1.

Dalrymple, A., 1770-1. *An Historical Collection of Seven Voyages and Discoveries in the South Pacific Ocean* (2 vols.), London: Nourse.

Damm, H. and Sarfert, E., 1935. 'Inseln um Truk', *Ergebnisse der Südsee-Expedition 1908-1910*, G. Thilenius (ed.), II, B, pt 2, Hamburg: Friedrichsen, de Gruyter and Co.

De la Costa, H., 1961. *The Jesuits in the Philippines 1581-1768*, Cambridge, Mass.: Harvard University Press.

Davenport, W., 1953, 'Marshallese Folklore Types', *Journal of American Folklore*, vol. 66, 236-7.

——, 1960. 'Marshallese Islands Navigational Charts', *Imago Mundi*, vol. 15, 19-26 (s'Gravenhage). Reprinted. Indianapolis: Bobbs-Merrill.

——, 1964a. 'Notes on Santa Cruz Voyaging', *Journal of the Polynesian Society*, vol. 73, no. 2, 134-42.

——, 1964b. 'Marshall Islands Cartography', *Exposition, the Bulletin of the University Museum of the University of Pennsylvania*, Philadelphia: vol. 6, pp. 10-13.

Dening, G., 1963. 'The Geographical Knowledge of the Polynesians', in *Polynesian Navigation*, J. Golson (ed.), Wellington: Polynesian Society Memoir no. 34, pp. 102-31, table 1, pp. 132-6.

Deutsches Kolonialblatt, 1910, cited by Riesenberg, S., 1965, p. 164.

Diaper (or Diapea), W., 1928. *Cannibal Jack*, London: Faber and Gwyer.

Dillon, P., 1829. *Narrative of a Voyage in the South Seas . . . to ascertain the actual fate of La Perouse's Expedition*, London: Hurst and Chance, vols. I and II.

Duff, R., 1956. *The Moa-Hunter Period of Maori Culture*, Wellington: Govt Printer.

Duperrey, L. I., 1827. *Voyage autour du monde* ("La Coquille"), Paris: Atlas.

East Coast of United States Pilot, 1960. London: Hydrographic Dept Admiralty, 6th ed., vol. I.

Eilers, A., 1934. 'Inselm um Ponape', *Ergebnisse der Südsee-Expedition 1908-1910*, G. Thilenius (ed.), II, B, 8, pt 2, Hamburg: Friederichsen, de Gruyter and Co.

——, 1935. 'Westkarolinen', *Ergebnisse der Südsee-Expedition 1908-1910*, G. Thilenius (ed.), II, B, 9, pt 1, Hamburg: Friederichsen, de Gruyter and Co.

——, 1936. 'Westkarolinen', *Ergebnisse der Südsee-Expedition 1908-1910*, G. Thilenius (ed.), II, B, 9, pt 2, Hamburg: Friederichsen, de Gruyter and Co.

Elbert, S. H., 1953. 'Internal Relationship of Polynesian Languages and Dialects'. *Southwestern Journal of Anthropology*, vol. 9, 147-73.

Ellis, A. F., 1935. *Ocean Island and Nauru*, Sydney: Angus and Robertson.

Ellis, W., 1831. *Polynesian Researches, during a Residence of Nearly Eight Years in the Society and Sandwich Islands* (2nd ed., 4 vols.), London: Fisher, Son and Jackson.

Emory, K. P., 1928. *Archaeology of Nihoa and Necker Islands*, Honolulu: Bishop Museum Bulletin no. 53.

——, 1934. *Archaeology of the Pacific Equatorial Islands*, Honolulu: Bishop Museum Bulletin no. 123.

——, 1943. *South Sea Lore*, Honolulu: Bishop Museum Special Publication no. 36.

——, 1963. 'East Polynesian Relationships: Settlement pattern and time involved as indicated by vocabulary agreements', *Journal of the Polynesian Society*, vol. 72, no. 2, 78-100.

——, 1965. *Kapingamarangi*, Honolulu: Bishop Museum Bulletin no. 228.

—— and Sinoto, Y. H., 1965. 'Preliminary Report on the Archaeological Investigations in Polynesia', Honolulu: Bishop Museum, mimeographed.

Erdland, P. A., 1914. 'Die Marshallinsulaner', *Anthropos Ethnologische Bibliothek*, Münster: Bd 2, Heft 1.

Finney, B. R., 1967. 'New Perspectives on Polynesian Voyaging', in *Polynesian Culture History*, Essays in Honor of Kenneth Emory (ed. A. Highland *et al.*), Bishop Museum Special Publication no. 56, pp. 141-66.

Firth, R., 1930. 'Report on Research in Tikopia', *Oceania*, vol. 1, no. 1, 105-17.

——, 1931. 'A Native Voyage to Rennell', *Oceania*, vol. 2, no. 2, 179-90.

——, 1936. *We, the Tikopia*, London: George Allen and Unwin.

——, 1954. 'Anuta and Tikopia: Symbiotic elements in social organization', *Journal of the Polynesian Society*, vol. 63, no. 2, 87-131.

——, 1961. *History and Traditions of Tikopia*, Wellington: Polynesian Society Memoir no. 32.

Fornander, A., 1878. *An Account of the Polynesian Race*, London: Trübner, vol. 1.

——, 1880. *An Account of the Polynesian Race*, London: Trübner, vol. 2.

Forster, G., 1777. *Voyage Round the World . . . in the Resolution 1772-5* (2 vols.), London: White and Robinson.

Forster, J. R., 1778. *Observations made during a Voyage round the World* (*in the Resolution 1771-5*), London: G. Robinson.

Frankel, J. P., 1962. 'Polynesian Navigation', *Navigation* (Journal of the Institute of Navigation, Washington), vol. 9, 35-47.

Frisbie, R., 1938. pp. 351-3, in Beaglehole, E. & P., *Ethnology of Pukapuka*, Honolulu: Bishop Museum Bulletin no. 150.

Fritz, G., 1907. 'Eine Reise nach Palau, Sonsol und Tolsi', *Deutsches Kolonialblatt*, vol. 18, 659-68.

G[rarcia], Le Père Mathias, 1843. *Lettres sur les isles Marquises*, Paris: Gaume Libraires.

Gatty, H., 1943. *The Raft Book*, New York: George Grady Press.

——, 1958. *Nature is Your Guide*, London: Collins.

Gill, W. W., 1876a. *Life in the Southern Isles*, London: Religious Tract Society.

——, 1876b. *Myths and Songs*, London: King.

Gladwin, T., 1970. *East is a Big Bird*, Cambridge, Mass.: Harvard University Press.

Golson, J. (ed.), 1963. *Polynesian Navigation. A symposium on Andrew Sharp's theory of accidental voyages*, Wellington: Polynesian Society Memoir no. 34.

Goodenough, W. H., 1951. 'Native Astronomy in Micronesia: a rudimentary science', *Scientific Monthly*, vol. 73, no. 2, 105-10.

——, 1953. *Native Astronomy in the Central Carolines*, Philadelphia: University Museum, University of Pennsylvania.

Green, R., 1966. 'Linguistic Subgrouping within Polynesia: The implications for prehistoric settlement', *Journal of the Polynesian Society*, vol. 75, no. 1, 7-38.

Grimble, A., 1924. 'Canoes of the Gilbert Islands', *Journal of the Royal Anthropological Institute*, vol. 54, 101-39.

——, 1931. 'Gilbertese Astronomy and Astronomical Observances', *Journal of the Polynesian Society*, vol. 40, no. 160, 197-224.

——, 1943. 'War Finds its Way to the Gilbert Islands', *National Geographic Magazine*, vol. 83, no. 1, 7-92.

——, n.d. a. MS. notes on navigation (by courtesy of H. E. Maude).

——, n.d. b. MS. notes, 'Kings of Butaritari and Makin' as narrated by informant 1938 (by courtesy of H. E. Maude).

——, n.d. c. M.S. notes on navigation (by courtesy of R. Grimble).

Guiart, J., 1963. *Structure de la Chefferie en Mélanésie du Sud*, Paris: Société d' Ethnologie.

Gulick, L. H., 1862. 'Micronesia of the Pacific Ocean', *National Magazine* (London), vol. 31, 168-308.

Haddon, A. C., and Hornell, J., 1936-8. *Canoes of Oceania*, vol. I 'The Canoes of Polynesia, Fiji and Micronesia', by James Hornell, Honolulu: Bishop Museum Special Publication no. 27; vol. II 'The Canoes of Melanesia, Queensland and New Guinea', by A. C. Haddon, Bishop Museum Special Publication no. 28; vol. III 'Definitions and Conclusions', A. C. Haddon and James Hornell, Bishop Museum Special Publication no. 29.

Hale, H., 1846. *Ethnography and Philology of the Wilkes Exploring Expedition*, Philadelphia: Lea and Blanchard.

Hambruch, P. and Sarfert, E., 1935. 'Inseln um Truk', *Ergebnisse der Südsee-Expedition 1908-1910*, G. Thilenius (ed.), II, B, 6, pt 2. Hamburg: Friedrichsen, de Gruyter and Co.

Hawkesworth, J., 1785. *An Account of Voyages . . . performed by Commodore Byron, Captain Carteret, Captain Wallis and Captain Cook*, 3rd ed., London: Strahan and Cadell, vol. 1.

Henry, T., 1894. 'The Birth of New Lands', *Journal of the Polynesian Society*, vol. 3, 136-9.

——, 1907. 'Tahitian Astronomy', *Journal of the Polynesian Society*, vol. 16, no. 62, 101-4.

Heyen, G. H., 1963. 'Primitive Navigation in the Pacific', in Golson, J. (ed.), *Polynesian Navigation*, Wellington: Polynesian Society Memoir no. 34.

——, 1966. 'Gilbertese Astronomy and Navigation', written for the Journal of the Company of Master Mariners of Australia, MS. in possession of H. E. Maude.

Heyerdahl, T., 1951. *The Kon-Tiki Expedition*, London: Allen and Unwin.

——, 1961. *Easter Island and the East Pacific*, vol. I, 'Archaelogy of Easter Island', Santa Fé, Monographs of the School of American Research and the Museum of New Mexico, no. 24, pt I.

Highlights, 1970. 'Carolinians Sail on Old Route to Saipan', Saipan: Office of High Commissioner, Trust Territory of the Pacific Islands.

Hilder, B., 1959. 'Polynesian Navigational Stones', *Journal of the Institute of Navigation* (London), vol. 12, no. 1, 90-7.

——, 1963a. 'Primitive Navigation in the Pacific' in Golson, J. (ed.) *Polynesian Navigation*, Polynesian Society Memoir no. 34.

——, 1963b. 'Polynesian Navigation', *Navigation* (Journal of the Institute of Navigation, Washington), vol. 10, 188-91.

Hollyman, K. J., 1959. 'Polynesian Influence in New Caledonia', *Journal of the Polynesian Society*, vol. 68, no. 4, 357-89.

Hops, A., 1956. 'Die polynesische und mikronesische Seefahrt'. *Der Seewart*, vol. 17, no. 3, 86-93; no. 4, 125-34; no. 5, 172-83.

Hornell, J., 1932. 'Was the Double Outrigger Known in Polynesia and Micronesia?', *Journal of the Polynesian Society*, vol. 41, no. 162, 131-43.

——, 1935. 'Constructional Parallels in Scandinavian and Oceanic Boat Construction', *Mariner's Mirror*, vol. 21.

——, 1946. 'The Role of Birds in Early Navigation', *Antiquity*, vol. 20, no. 77, 142-9.

Jourdain, P., 1970. 'Découverts et Toponomynie des Îles de la Polynésie Française', *Bulletin de la Société des Études Océaniennes*, vol. 14, no. 171.

Kamakau, S. M., 1891. 'Instructions in Ancient Hawaiian Astronomy as Taught by Kaneakahoowaha . . .' (translated from the *Nupepa Kuokoa* of 5 Aug. 1865, for the *Maile Wreath* by W. D. Alexander), Honolulu: Thrum's Hawaiian Annual.

Kennedy, D. G., 1931. *Culture of Vaitupu, Ellice Islands*, New Plymouth: Polynesian Society Memoir no. 9.

Kepelino, 1932. *Traditions of Hawaii*, Martha Warren Beckwith (ed.), Honolulu: Bishop Museum Bulletin no. 95.

King, W. B., 1967. *Seabirds of the Tropical Pacific Ocean*, Washington: Smithsonian Institution.

Kotzebue, O. von, 1821. *Voyage of Discovery in the South Sea . . . undertaken in the years 1815, 16, 17, 18 in the ship Rurik*, 3 vols., London: Richard Phillips, vol. I.

Krämer, A., 1902. *Die Samoa-Inseln*, Stuttgart: E. Schweizerbartsche Verlags-buchhandlung, vol. 2.

——, 1906. *Hawaii, Ostmikronesien und Samoa*, Stuttgart: Strecker and Schröder.

——, 1919. 'Palau', *Ergebnisse der Südsee-Expedition 1908-1910*, G. Thilenius (ed.) II, B, 3. Hamburg: Friederichsen, de Gruyter and Co.

——, 1935. 'Inseln um Truk', *Ergebnisse der Südsee-Expedi-*

tion 1908-1910, G. Thilenius (ed.), II, B, 6. Hamburg: Friederichsen, de Gruyter and Co.

——, 1937. 'Zentral Karolinen (Lamotrek Gruppe, Oleai, Feis)', *Ergebnisse der Südsee-Expedition 1908-1910*, G. Thilenius (ed.), II, B, 10, pt I, Hamburg: Friederichsen, de Gruyter and Co.

Laubenfels, M. W. de, 1950a. 'Ocean Currents in the Marshall Islands', *Geographical Review*, vol. 40, no. 2, 254-9.

——, 1950b. 'Native Navigators', *Research Reviews* (June 1950), Office of Naval Research, pp. 7-12.

Laval, H., 1938. *Mangareva, L'histoire ancienne d'un peuple polynésien*, Brain-le-Comte: Maison des Pères des Sacré Coeurs de Picpus.

Lemaître, Y., 1970. 'Les relations inter-insulaires traditionelles en Océanie: Tonga', *Journal de la Société des Océanistes*, vol. 26, no. 27, 93-105.

Lessa, W. A., 1950. 'Ulithi and the Outer Native World', *American Anthropologist*, vol. 52, 27-52.

——, 1956, 'Myth and Blackmail in the Western Carolines', *Journal of the Polynesian Society*, vol. 65, no. 1, 67-74.

——, 1962. 'An Evaluation of Early Descriptions of Carolinian Culture', *Ethnohistory*, vol. 9, 313-403.

Levison, M., Ward, R. G., and Webb, J. W., 1972. *The Settlement of Polynesia: A computer simulation*, Minneapolis: University of Minnesota Press.

Lewis, D. H., 1964a. 'Ara Moana, Stars of the Sea Road', *Journal of the Institute of Navigation* (London), vol. 17.

——, 1964b. 'Polynesian Navigational Methods', *Journal of the Polynesian Society*, vol. 73, no. 4, 364-74.

——, 1966a. 'Stars of the Sea Road', *Journal of the Polynesian Society*, vol. 75, no. 1, 84-94.

——, 1966b. 'An Experiment in Polynesian Navigation', *Journal of the Institute of Navigation* (London), vol. 19, no. 2, 154-68.

——, 1967, *Daughters of the Wind*, London: Gollancz; Wellington: Reed.

——, 1969a. *Children of Three Oceans*, London: Collins.

——, 1969b. 'Voyages of the Boundless Place', *Hemisphere*, vol. 13, no. 10, 14-18.

——, 1969c. 'Navigational Techniques of the Early Polynesians and Micronesians', *Navigation* (Journal of the Australian Institute of Navigation), vol. 3, no. 2, 184-99.

——, 1970. 'Polynesian and Micronesian Navigation Techniques', *Journal of the Institute of Navigation* (London), vol. 23, no. 2, 432-47.

Lewthwaite, G. R., 1966. 'Tupaia's Map', *Association of Pacific Coast Geographers Yearbook*, vol. 28, 41-53.

——, 1967. 'The Geographical Knowledge of the Pacific

Peoples', in H. R. Friis (ed.), *The Pacific Basin*, New York: American Geographical Society, pp. 57-86.

——, 1968. 'The Geographical Knowledge of the Pacific Peoples', *Journal of the Polynesian Society*, vol. 77, no. 3, 300-4.

——, 1970. 'The Puzzle of Tupaia's Map', *New Zealand Geographer*, vol. 26, no. 1, 1-19.

Loeb, E., 1926. *History and Traditions of Niue*, Honolulu: Bishop Museum Bulletin no. 32.

[Lucett, E.,] 1851. *Rovings in the Pacific from 1837 to 1849: by a merchant long resident at Tahiti* (2 vols.), London: Longmans.

Macgregor, G., 1937. *Ethnology of Tokelau Islands*, Honolulu: Bishop Museum Bulletin no. 146.

McKee, A., 1968. *History Under the Sea*. London: Hutchinson.

Macleod, R. and Roff, M. 'An Experiment in Temporal Disorientation', *Acta Physiologica*, Hague, vol. 1, 381-423.

Makemson, M., 1938. 'Hawaiian Astronomical Concepts', *American Anthropologist*, vol. 40, 370-83; vol. 41, 589-95.

——, 1939. 'South Sea Sailors Steer by the Stars', *The Sky*, The American Museum of Natural History, vol. 3.

——, 1941. *The Morning Star Rises*, New Haven, Conn.: Yale University Press.

Malinowski, B., 1915. 'The Natives of Mailu', *Royal Society South Aust. Trans. Proc.*, vol. 39, 494-706.

——, 1922. *Argonauts of the Western Pacific*, London: G. Routledge & Sons (Studies in Economic and Political Science No. 65).

Marcus, G. J., 1953. 'The Navigation of the Norsemen', *Mariner's Mirror*, vol. 39, 112-31.

Mariner, W., 1817. *An Account of the Natives of the Tonga Islands . . .* J. Martin (ed.), London: John Murray, vol. I.

Markham, C. (ed.), 1904. *The Voyages of Pedro Fernandez de Quiros* (2 vols.), London: Hakluyt Society.

Mason, L., 1966. 'Early Micronesian Voyaging: A comment', *Oceania*, vol. 37, no. 2, 155.

Mathews, G., 1968. *Bird Navigation* (2nd ed.), Cambridge: Cambridge University Press.

Maude, H. E., 1963. *The Evolution of the Gilbertese Boti*, Wellington: Polynesian Society Memoir no. 35.

——, 1968. *Of Islands and Men*, Melbourne: Oxford University Press.

——, and Maude, H. C., 1932. 'The Social Organisation of Banaba or Ocean Island', *Journal of the Polynesian Society*, vol. 41, no. 164, 262-301.

Meinicke, C. E., 1875-6. *Die Inseln des Stillen Oceans: eine geographische Monographie*, Zweiter Theil. (2) *Polynesien und Mikronesien*, Leipzig: Frohberg.

Micronesian Reporter, 1964. Vol. 12, no. 2 (cited by Riesenberg, S. H., 1965).

Nevermann, H., 1923. Die Schiffahrt in Ozeanien—Ph.D. dissertation, Hamburg.

Neyret, J. M., 1950. 'Notes sur la navigation indigène aux îles Fidji', *Journal de la Société des Océanistes*, vol. 6, 5-31.

——, 1962-3. 'Pirogues Océaniennes', *Triton*, vols. 52-60, 63, 65.

——, 1965-7. 'Pirogues Océaniennes', *Neptunia*, nos. 80, 81-3, 85.

——, 1969. 'Pirogues Océaniennes', *Neptunia*, no. 95.

Nozokov, N., ?1946. *Russian Voyages Round the World*, Sergeyev (ed.), London: Hutchinson.

O'Ferral, W. C., 1903. *Santa Cruz and the Reef Islands*, London: The Melanesian Mission.

'The Orkneyingers Saga', 1894. In *The Icelandic Sagas*, vol. 3, London: H.M.S.O.

Pacific Islands, 1943-5: R. Firth, J. W. Davidson and M. Davies (eds.), Naval Intelligence Division, London, Admiralty. BR 5193 (Restricted) Geographical Handbook Series, 4 vols.: vol. II, 1943, vol. III, 1944, vols. I and IV, 1945.

Pacific Islands Pilot (8th ed.), 1956-7. Taunton, Ministry of Defence, vols. I-III.

Parsonson, G. S., 1963. 'The Settlement of Oceania: an examination of the accidental voyage theory', in *Polynesian Navigation*, J. Golson (ed.), Wellington: Polynesian Society Memoir no. 34.

Pawley, A., 1966. 'Polynesian Languages: a subgrouping based on shared innovations in morphology', *Journal of the Polynesian Society*, vol. 75, no. 1, 39-64.

——, 1967. 'The Relationships of Polynesian Outlier Languages', *Journal of the Polynesian Society*, vol. 76, no. 3, 259-96.

Playdon, G. W., 1967. 'The Significance of Marshallese Stick Charts', *Journal of the Institute of Navigation* (London), vol. 20, no. 2, 155-66.

Pollock, I. W., Ochberg, F. M., and Meyer, E., 1969. *Archives of General Psychiatry*, vol. 21, p. 1.

Porter, D., 1822. *Journal of a Cruise made to the Pacific Ocean* . . . (3 vols., 2nd ed.), New York: Wiley and Halsted.

Pukui, M. K. and Elbert, S., 1957. *Hawaiian-English Dictionary*, Honolulu: University of Hawaii Press.

Reche, A. D., 1927. 'Die Dreisternavigation der Polynesier', *Marine-Rundschau*, vol. 32, 214-19, 266-71.

Reid, A., 1946-7. 'Double Canoe: Vatoa Island, Lau, Fiji', MSS.

Ricard, M., 1969. *The Mystery of Animal Migration* (English ed.), London: Constable.

Riesenberg, S. H., 1965. 'Table of Voyages Affecting Micronesian Islands', supplement to Simmons, R. *et al.*, 'Blood Group Genetic Variations . . . Micronesia', *Oceania*, vol. 36, no. 2, 155-68.

Rivers, W. H. R., 1912. 'The Disappearance of Useful Arts', Report of the British Association for the Advancement of Science, pp. 598, 599.

Routeing Charts 1969—North Pacific Ocean, Jan.-Dec. Nos. 5127(1)-(12).

——, —South Pacific Ocean, Jan.-Dec., Nos. 5128(1)-(12). Taunton, Ministry of Defence.

Ruhen, O., 1963. *Minerva Reef*, Sydney: Angus and Robertson.

Sabatier, E., 1939. *Sous l'équateur du Pacifique. Les Îles Gilbert et la Mission Catholique 1888-1938*, Paris: Sacré-Coeur, edn. Dillen.

——, 1954. *Dictionnaire Gilbertin-Français*. Tarawa: Sacred Heart Mission.

Sanchez y Zayas, E., 1866. 'The Marianas Islands', *Nautical Magazine*, vol. 35, 263.

Sarfert, E., 1911. 'Zur Kenntnis der Schiffahrtskunde der Karoliner', *Korrespondenz-Blatt der deutschen Gesellschaft für Anthropologie, Ethnologie und Urgeschichte*, vol. 42, Brunswick.

Saville, W., 1926. *In Unknown New Guinea*, London: Seeley Service.

Schott, G., 1935. *Geographie des indischen und Stillen Ozeans*, Tafel 29-30, Hamburg.

——, 1943. 'Nachtrag zu dem Aufsatz die Grundlagen eine Weltkarte der Meerströmungen', *Annalen de Hydrographie und Maritimen Meteorologie*, Berlin.

Seligman, C. G., 1910. *The Melanesians of British New Guinea*, Cambridge: Cambridge University Press.

Shapiro, H. L. and Suggs, R. C., 1959. 'New Dates for Polynesian Prehistory', *Man*, vol. 59, no. 3, 12-13.

Sharp, A., 1957. *Ancient Voyagers in the Pacific*, Harmondsworth, Middlesex: Penguin Books.

——, 1960. *The Discovery of the Pacific Islands*, Oxford: Clarendon Press.

——, 1963. *Ancient Voyagers in Polynesia*, Auckland and Hamilton: Paul's Book Arcade; Sydney: Angus and Robertson.

——, 1966. 'David Lewis's Experimental Voyage', *Journal of the Polynesian Society*, vol. 75, no. 2, 231-3.

——, 1968. Correspondence in reply to Lewthwaite on Sharp's review of 'The Geographical Knowledge of the Pacific Peoples', *Journal of the Polynesian Society*, vol. 77, no. 3, 305-6.

——, 1969. 'Prehistoric Voyages and Modern Experimenters', *Oceania*, vol. 39, no. 3, 231-3.

Sinoto, Y. H., 1962. 'Chronology of Hawaiian Fishhooks', *Journal of the Polynesian Society*, vol. 71, no. 2, 162-6.

Slocum, J., 1963. *Sailing Alone Around the World*, London: Rupert Hart-Davis.

Smith, P., 1915. *The Lore of the Whare-Wananga*, part II, *Things Terrestrial*, Polynesian Society Memoir no. 4.

——, 1921. *Hawaiki—the original home of the Maori* (4th ed.), Christchurch: Whitcombe and Tombs.

Stair, J. B., 1895a. 'Flotsam & Jetsam . . . early Samoan voyages', *Journal of the Polynesian Society*, vol. 4, 99-131.

——, 1895b. 'Early Samoan Voyages and Settlements', *Australian Association for the Advancement of Science*, vol. 6, 612-19.

Stimson, J. F., 1932. 'Songs of the Polynesian Voyagers', *Journal of the Polynesian Society*, vol. 41, no. 163, 181-201.

——, 1957. *Songs and Tales of the Sea Kings*, Salem, Mass.: Peabody Museum.

Suggs, R. C., 1961a. 'The Derivation of Marquesan Culture', *Journal of the Royal Anthropological Institute*, vol. 91, 1-10.

——, 1961b. 'The Archaeology of Nuku Hiva, Marquesas Islands, French Polynesia', *Anthropological Papers of the American Museum of Natural History*, vol. 49, pt 1.

Tagart, E., 1832. *A Memoir of the late Captain Peter Heywood, R.N.* London: Effingham Wilson.

Thompson, L., 1949. *Native Culture of the Marianas*, Honolulu: Bishop Museum Bulletin no. 185.

Thomson, B., 1908. *The Fijians: a study of the decay of custom*, London: Heinemann.

Threlkeld, L. E., 1853-5. 'Reminiscences', Sydney. Typescript from newspaper articles in possession of Dr W. N. Gunson.

Turner, G., 1876. Journal, L.M.S. Archives, abstracts and excerpts from material relating to the Ellice Islands. Compiled by J. D. Freeman, MSS. by courtesy of H. E. Maude.

Tyerman, D. and Bennet, G., 1841. *Voyages and Travels Round the World*, London: John Snow (2nd ed.).

Ullman, J. R., 1964. *Where the Bong Tree Grows*, London: Collins.

Vancouver, G., 1801. *A Voyage of Discovery to the North Pacific Ocean Round the World 1790-1795* (6 vols.), vol. III. London: John Stockdale.

Varady, R., 1958. *Many Lagoons*, London: Gollancz.

Vernon, J. A., and McGill, T. E., 1963. *Journal of General Psychology*, vol. 69, no. 11.

Voitov, V. I. and Tumarkin, D. D., 1969. 'Navigational Conditions of Sea Routes to Polynesia', *Asian Perspectives*, vol. 10.

Waldman, R. H., 1969. 'Commercial Navigation Systems for

Long-range Subsonic Transports in the 1970s', *Journal of the Institute of Navigation* (London), vol. 22, no. 4.

Ward, E. V., 1967. *Sailing Directions, the Gilbert and Ellice Islands Colony,* Tarawa: Secretariat, Gilbert and Ellice Islands Colony.

White, P., 1961. 'Tupaia's Voyages: a note on the MSS', *Journal of the Polynesian Society,* vol. 70, no. 4, 471-3.

Whitney, H. P., 1955. 'An Analysis of the Design of the Major Sea-going Craft of Oceania', M.A. thesis, University of Pennsylvania. Copy in Department of Pacific History, A.N.U. (MF 183).

Williams, J., 1846. *A Narrative of Missionary Enterprises in the South Seas.* London: Snow.

Williams, T., 1858. *Fiji and the Fijians,* G. S. Rowe (ed.) (2 vols.), vol. I, London: Heylin.

Wilkes, C., 1845. *Narrative of the United States Exploring Expedition during the Years 1838-42* (5 vols.), Philadelphia: Lea and Blanchard.

Winkler, Capt., 1901. 'On Sea charts formerly used in the Marshall Islands, with Notices on the Navigation of these Islanders in General', *Annual Report of the Smithsonian Institution, 1899,* Washington, pp. 487-509.

Woodford, C. M., 1888. 'Exploration of the Solomon Islands', *Proceedings of the Royal Geographical Society,* vol. 10.

——, 1906. 'Some Account of Sikaiana', *Man,* vol. 6, 164-9.

Index

Abera: 38; clouds, 174-6; deep phosphorescence *(te mata)*, 210; drift objects, 212; loom, 180; swells, 182-4

Accuracy attainable: Banaba, 228-9; Carolines-Saipan, 223; Kapingamarangi, 231; not a function of length of voyage, 104, 223; Nurotu, 230-1; Pasco Bank, 231; Pukapuka, 58-9, 224-7; Puluwat-Satawal, 231; Tonga, 229-30; Yap, 227-8

Akerblom, K.: current allowance in star courses, 59; identifying star, 58; Marshallese stick charts, 203-5; Pole Star, 242; sun bearings, 83; zenith stars, 235n.2, 239, 242, 243

Alkire, W. H.: *etak* in Woleai, 133, 135-8 *passim*

America: theory of origins from, 16; contacts with, 25

Andia, Y. Varela, 47, 87, 93-4

Astronomy in Pacific: Carolines and Marshalls, 73-4; decline, 60, 77, 82; *Ha'amonga a Maui*, Tonga, 7n. 5, 79n.; similarity Micronesian and Polynesian, 80-3 *passim*; subservience to navigation, 80; sun observations, 79n., 83; stars and currents, 113-14; stars and weather, 114, 214n., 247n.

Ata, Iotiebata, *see* Iotiebata

Atiu, 19, 96

Attitude towards ocean, 1, 25, 124, 232, 277, 289

Bakapu, 31

Banaba (Ocean Island): bird messengers, 166; indicated by directional stones, 319-20; voyages to, 228-9

Banks Islands, *see* New Hebrides

Baurua canoe, *see* Gilberts

Beiong, Chief, 37; *etak* and drift, 140-2; grasps chart/*etak* concepts, 143

Beniata, Abera, *see* Abera

Birds indicating land: bird landfall on Marianas and Carolines, 167, 217-22 *passim;* Carolines, 166-8; Gilberts, 164-6; morning and evening flight paths, 163-4; Santa Cruz, 168; tame birds, 165-6, 169, 173n.; Tikopia, 168-9; Tonga, 169; uninhabited islands, 167n.; useful species, 163-72 *passim*, (flight ranges) 169-72

Birds, migrating, 4; a Melanesian tradition, 178; a Tuamotuan tradition, 173; speculative, 172; Vikings, 173n.

Bongi, 36, 132; demonstrates deep phosphorescence *(te lapa)*, 208-10 *passim*

Brum, Raymond de, 198-200 *passim*

Canoes, voyaging: construction, 254-5; diffusion theories, 255; distinct from inshore craft, 253; flexibility and lashings, 253, 255, 272; Micronesian asymmetric hull, 270-1; performance, 266-72; preferred size, 254, 273-4; range, 272; tacking and changing ends systems, 261-2; varieties, *see* separate archipelagos

Carolines: birds, 166-8; canoes, 260, 268-74 *passim*; contacts Marianas (antiquity) 32-5 *passim*, (Guam and Saipan) 32n.12, 287, (recent) *see* Carolines-Saipan voyages, Hipour and Repunglug; currents, 104, 106, 107-9; deep reefs, 51, 158-9; dignity of navigators, 279-80; drift objects, 212; initiated navigators *ppalu*, 16n., 37; land swells, 193; latitude (zenith stars) 242, (Pole Star) 144, 242-3; orientation after 400 miles, 147-8; *see also Etak*, Compass, magnetic; sea life, 215, 249; screens, 157-9, 217-22; sorcery, 213; sphere, 33, 62, 109, 227-8, 285, 286-7, 293; swell orientation, 90-3; traffic/losses, 27, 123-4; voyages, *see* Kapingamarangi, New Guinea, Philippines, Ponape, Pulusuk, Puluwat, Satawal, Truk, Yap

Carolines-Saipan voyages, Hipour and Repunglug: Hipour, 32; birds *en route*, 167; dead reckoning (current) 107-9, (leeway) 116-17, (speed) 119, 217; land- 337

ting birds, 173; navigators, 38; reconsideration maritime ability needed, 283-4; Siassi wind compass, 78; voyaging, 15n., (Motu *hiri*) 95, (trade cycles) 285; zenith star, 243; *see also* Fiji, New Guinea

Mendaña, 19, 28n.

Micronesia: bounds, 14; navigation equivalent to Polynesian, 11; persistence navigation and voyaging, 127; voyaging canoes (outrigger) 253, (adopted by Fiji) 254; *see also* Carolines, Gilberts, Marshalls

Mortlocks, Carolinian, 59

Motu *hiri*, 38, 95

Nautical miles, 21n.

Navigational training: Carolines, 137; Gilberts (*Maneaba*) 37, 57, (stone canoe) 38, 186-7; Marshalls, 198n., 200-1

Navigators, characteristics of, 10-11, 232, 277-80, 289; acuity of observation, 172, 217-22 *passim*; contrast unskilled Islanders, 96; correspondence between descriptions, 176; prudence, 170, 209, 217, 231

Ndrua canoe, *see* Fiji

New Guinea: Mailu (double canoes) 263, (voyages longer European times) 290; Motu (*hiri*) 38, 95, (*kino kino* used) 95; raids on Carolines, 15n., 283-4; Siassi wind compass, 78

New Hebrides, 28; Tevake's voyage to, 36; Rafe's voyage to, 56

New Zealand: canoes, 255, 261; drift objects, 211-12; isolation, 21; land swells, 193; late Moa-Hunter adzes and Cooks, 306n. 14; Tahiti and Cook Islands seaway, 101, 305-6

Ninigo Islands: canoes, 7n. 6, 260, 262n.7, 263, 271, 273; canoe passages, 27; current lore, 113, 115; essentially Micronesian, 7n. 6; high star techniques, 247; navigators, 38; speed estimates, 119; star courses, 46

Niue, 291

Oral lore: absence, 28n., 299n., 301; conservative and stereotyped, 10-11; incorporation European knowledge, 18, 298n. 6; individuality, 89, 295n.; selectivity of re-

tention, 28n.; subject to interruption, 295n.; survival of incompatible concepts, 2, 70-1, 143-4, 207-8, 307

Orientation: Carolinian *etak*, 128, 129, 133-45; *see also* Etak; home centre, mixed, and self centre systems, 128-30 *passim*, (used in visualising position) 130; Polynesian concepts (effectiveness) 132, 149, (Kau Moala) 148-9, (Santa Cruz boys) 132, (Tevake) 131-2, (Tupaia) 128, (unknown) 130, 149

Orientation ability: Hipour (positions of islands) 147-8; Iotiebata gale-driven, 124; Kau Moala, 148-9; Philippines to Carolines, 286-7; Sernous gale-driven, 146; Tevake (positions of islands) 131-2, (accurate angled course) 147; Tuamotuans begin return, 287

Outer Reef Islands, *see* Santa Cruz Islands

Overcast frequency, 56, 82, 95-6

Pahi canoe, *see* Tahiti, Tuamotus

Pahulu, Ve'etutu, *see* Ve'etutu

Papi, 38

Papuan voyaging, *see* Melanesia, New Guinea

Pedro: geographical information, 17; prisoner from Sikaiana on Taumako, 16-17

Philippines: drifts from Carolines, 228; navigated returns, 286-7

Phosphorescence, deep: distant land sign, 208-11; distinct from surface luminescence, 208, 209, 210, 211; nature uncertain, 208n. 7, 209, 211; no European counterpart, 211; *te lapa* of Santa Cruz, 208-10, (its demonstration) 209; *te mata* of Gilberts, 210; *ulo detahi* of Tonga, 210-11

Pikelot, 32, 51; landfall from Saipan, 147-8, 220-2; star course from Puluwat, 50; star course to Saipan, 52

Pole Star: Carolines, 144, 242-3; Gilberts, 72; Tahiti, 73, 240; Tonga, 72-3

Polynesia-Micronesia, virtual identity concepts, 11, 80-1, 88, 149, 161-2, 168, 307; *see also* individual techniques

Polynesia: bounds, 14; double voyaging canoes typical, 253; early

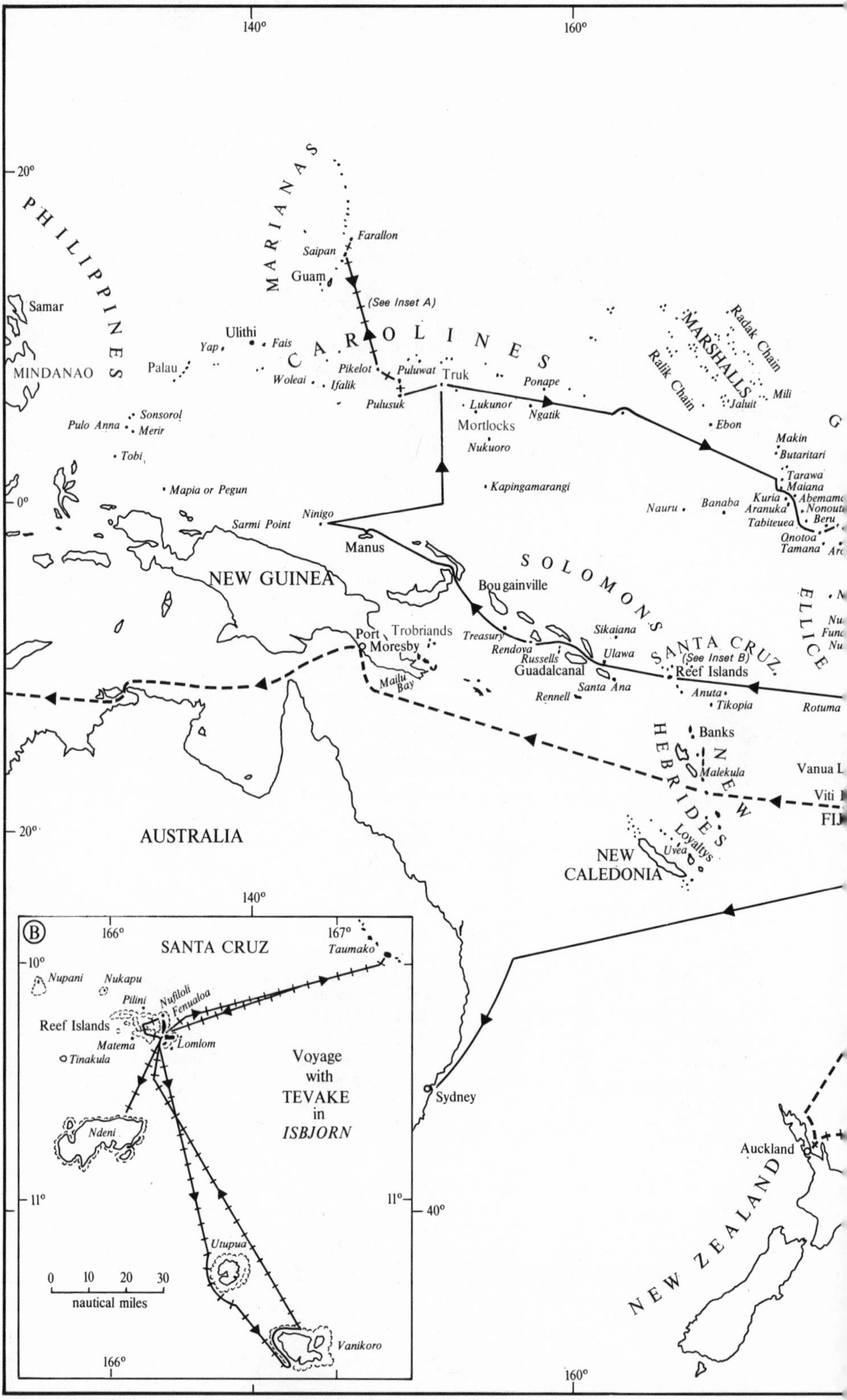

140°
160°
20°
0°
20°
40°
PHILIPPINES
MARIANAS
Farallon
Saipan
Guam
(See Inset A)
Samar
MINDANAO
Ulithi
Yap
Fais
Palau
CAROLINES
Pikelot
Puluwat
Truk
Woleai
Ifalik
Pulusuk
Ponape
Lukunor
Ngatik
Mortlocks
Nukuoro
Kapingamarangi
Sonsorol
Pulo Anna
Merir
Tobi
Mapia or Pegun
MARSHALLS
Radak Chain
Ralik Chain
Jaluit
Mili
Ebon
Makin
Butaritari
Tarawa
Maiana
Kuria
Aranuka
Tabiteuea
Onotoa
Tamana
Nauru
Banaba
Ninigo
Sarmi Point
Manus
NEW GUINEA
SOLOMONS
Bougainville
Port Moresby
Trobriands
Treasury
Rendova
Russells
Guadalcanal
Sikaiana
Ulawa
Santa Ana
Rennell
Mailu Bay
SANTA CRUZ
(See Inset B)
Reef Islands
Anuta
Tikopia
Rotuma
ELLICE
Banks
NEW HEBRIDES
Malekula
Vanua L
Viti
FIJ
AUSTRALIA
NEW CALEDONIA
Loyaltys
Uvea
Sydney
Auckland
NEW ZEALAND
B
SANTA CRUZ
166°
167°
10°
11°
Taumako
Nupani
Nukapu
Pilini
Nufiloli
Fenualoa
Reef Islands
Matema
Lomlom
Tinakula
Voyage with TEVAKE in ISBJORN
Ndeni
Utupua
Vanikoro
0 10 20 30
nautical miles

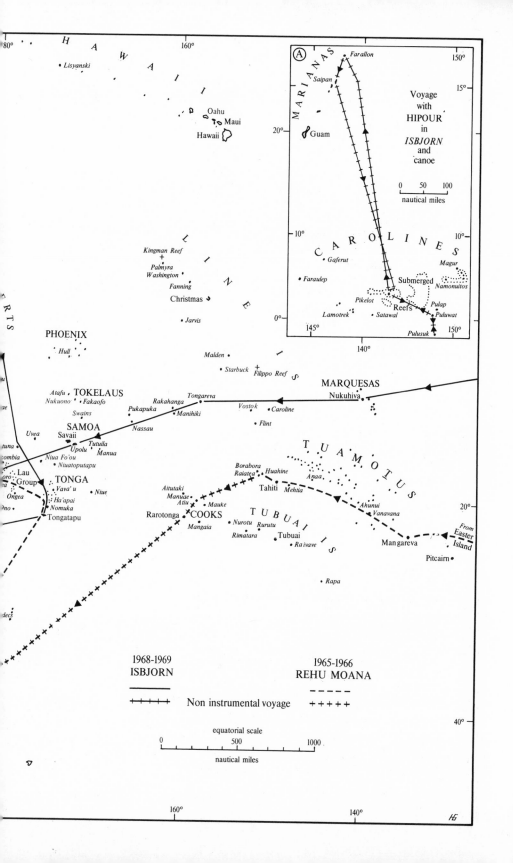

A Voyage
with
HIPOUR
in
ISBJORN
and
canoe

0   50   100
nautical miles

MARIANAS
Farallon
Saipan
Guam

CAROLINES
Gaferut   Magur
Faraulep   Submerged
                            Reefs   Namonuitos
              Pikelot   Pulap
     Lamotrek   Puluwat
              Satawal
                            Pulusuk

HAWAII
Lisyanski
Oahu
Maui
Hawaii

LINE ISLANDS
Kingman Reef
Palmyra
Washington
Fanning
Christmas
Jarvis
Malden
Starbuck
Filippo Reef

PHOENIX
Hull

TOKELAUS
Atafu
Nukuono Fakaofo
Swains
Nassau

SAMOA
Savaii
Uvea
Tutuila
Upolu Manua
Niua Fo'ou
Niuatoputapu

Rakahanga   Tongareva
Pukapuka
Manihiki
Vostok   Caroline
Flint

MARQUESAS
Nukuhiva

TUAMOTUS
Borabora   Anaa
Raiatea Huahine
Tahiti Mehtia
Ahunui
Vanavana

Aitutaki
Manuae
Atiu Mauke
Rarotonga COOKS
Mangaia

TUBUAI IS
Nurotu Rururu
Rimatara Tubuai
Raivave

From
Easter
Mangareva   Island
Pitcairn

Rapa

Lau
Group
Ongea
Ono

TONGA
Vava'u Niue
Ha'apai
Nomuka
Tongatapu

1968-1969
ISBJORN

1965-1966
REHU MOANA

+ + + + Non instrumental voyage + + + + +

equatorial scale

0   500   1000

nautical miles

David Lewis was educated in New Zealand and in a native school on Rarotonga. He graduated in medicine at Leeds University in 1942 and was Medical Officer with a parachute battalion and other units from 1943 to 1946. Though he practised medicine until 1964, his love has always been the sea and small-boat sailing. He has made three single-handed crossings of the Atlantic and in 1964-7 he sailed from England in a 40-foot catamaran with his wife and two small daughters, across the Atlantic, through the Straits of Magellan, and across the Pacific back to England. During this voyage he made an experiment in using ancient Polynesian non-instrumental navigation techniques.

In 1968 Dr Lewis was granted a research fellowship at the Australian National University to visit and sail with surviving indigenous navigators in the Pacific. This journey covered 13,000 miles of the western Pacific, 1,680 of them of open sea sailing without instruments under the instruction of the Island navigators. The data obtained in this way form the major part of this book.